Imprints of History, Religions & Revolutions on Law – Perspectives from Prominent Jurisdictions

 Edited by **Vivek Jain**

Imprints of History, Religions & Revolutions on Law – Perspectives from Prominent Jurisdictions

Foreword

I thank Dr. Vivek Jain for his invitation for my organisation, *Jain Education Institute Support,* to write a Chapter based on our expertise in *Jain Jurisprudence.* He initially requested that we write a Chapter on the topic of how Jain Jurisprudence has left imprints on law and policy in India for thousands of years. It was a unique topic, and I was delighted to allocate a scholar with expertise in Jain jurisprudence to contribute, and later came to know Dr. Jain himself actively participated in writing that Chapter alongside our scholar, based on his own knowledge of Jainism.

My organisation was also delighted to support the cause of connecting historical links with religion and history on the current laws of various countries. I realised that this was in harmony with the philosophy of Jainism, in particular its important ideological viewpoint of *Anekāntavāda. Anekāntavāda* relates to the doctrine of a multiplicity of viewpoints, and accordingly accommodates the views and perspectives of all religions and philosophies, as the main objective in Jainism is to gain wisdom from multiple axes in the universe.

The above principle can be instrumental in bringing about harmony in the world. Laws emerging from the shadows of culture and history are the best possible fit within their countries and for us this is, therefore, another step towards attaining wisdom (ultimate truth) and is in harmony with the Pluralistic *(Anekāntika)* view, as prescribed by Jainism.

Anekāntavāda is also in accordance with Einstein's theory of relativity and can be understood as such by way of an example. Suppose a part of planet or star several billion light-years away from us disintegrates, causing lightning, thunder and so on. Observers on earth will only recognise this event years later, due to the speed of light and sound. Therefore, there is a big difference in what is experienced by the observed (disintegrated planet) and the observer (us) and subsequently, the views expressed by us. Accordingly, our stage of knowledge is dependent on our state of knowledge, place and time and other factors.

In view of the above inadequacies, ordinary mortals cannot rise above the limitations of their senses, intentions and knowledge level as present within finite dimensions. Accordingly, our appreciation of reality is partial, and only valid from a particular point of view known as *Naya;* the same concept can be extended to 'truth' in our lives.

The three pillars of *Anekānta* are namely:

- Relativity, i.e. our knowledge is relative to our own capability, objectives, time, place, knowledge of others, etc.
- Co-existence of opposites, i.e. existence such as we just mentioned - universal and particular, being and non-being etc.

- Reconciliation/collaboration, i.e. since opposites co-exist and our knowledge itself is relative, we have to reconcile to move forward.

Anekāntavāda had a significant effect on the Father of the Indian nation, Mohandas Gandhi's, activism and non-violent philosophy, since different viewpoints are easily accepted. *Anekāntavāda* itself led to the principle of Jainism, *ahiṁsā*, or non-harming others (including their intellectual perspectives).

My organisation, *Jain Education Institutes Support* (a not-for-profit trust, a division of the Amar Prerana Trust of the Firodia family based at Pune, and formerly called the International School for Jain Studies) decided to support the editor in relation to some of the costs associated with the publication, as through this scholarly exercise this project attempts to bring harmony to the world. Our organisation aims to promote the global principles of Jainism by encouraging academic studies of the philosophy of Jain jurisprudence through teaching in universities around the world, teaching young students across the world and by supporting worthwhile projects, such as this book.

Dr. Shugan C Jain,

Chairman
Jain Education Institutes Support

President
International School for Jain Studies
(www.isjs.in)

22 Feb 2022

PREFACE

Dr., Capt. Vivek Jain

Most countries are witnessing protests in one form or another, and one can easily observe in many societies that there is a noticeable loss of credibility in both law and the systems responsible for implementing the law. In the last two years, the COVID-19 pandemic has amplified this phenomenon. In those countries with the most advanced economies, the population is resisting governments on various issues; for example refusing to wear masks, rejecting Stay Home Notices, or openly having parties without caring about the consequences, not just for themselves but for the world as, particularly in poorer countries, viruses are mutating in the absence of large-scale vaccination programmes. The irony is that most of these protesters are from relatively wealthy economies that have all the amenities provided by their governments, including advanced legal systems, yet this populace is extremely unhappy and has been protesting against unfair laws and governance during the pandemic. There are echoes of the hippie movement of the 1960s and 1970s in the United States in these protests. Even the World Wars that broke out during the last century were not fought between deprived countries, but among countries and peoples who were, in fact, at the zenith of prosperity and power at time of these devastating wars, genocide and holocaust. What went wrong and what is going wrong? The same phenomenon is no longer limited to wealthy and powerful countries, but is in fact fast expanding across the globe in the form of protests on many topics.

I have been searching for answers to the above issues since my teenage years as a member of "world is a family'. For the last few decades, I have been observing an inclination amongst scholars and lawyers in most jurisdictions to detach current law, both in its contents and practice of law from – (a) past historical events, (b) prevailing religious jurisprudence, and (3) past reboots due to major historical events or revolutions. Adding to the above mix are the twin concepts of '*secularism*' and '*political correctness*' that preclude, and at times also make it a taboo, to discuss any impact of history and religious jurisprudence on the content and practice of law. Arguments supporting this perspective by adherents of liberal jurisprudence are that the current constitutional principles should be the lone piloting factor and any discussion on prevailing religious jurisprudence or history can affect harmony and peace in society. At another level, it is argued that any kind of emotion should be removed from the practice of law and it must be seen as a very logical arrangement of processes within a society made for people.

I submit, as a result of the above phenomenon that the soul has been taken out of the thought processes of the population, and adherents of liberal jurisprudence in most jurisdictions have coerced societies to artificially detach *imprints of history, religion and revolutions on law* and thus are immensely impeding the natural evolution of those societies. Hence, this phenomenon is leading to a loss of credibility in systems of law and governance as a whole.

In a jurisdiction, laws are made for people in that society. My question is – can any society function in the context of law-making or practice of law in a vacuum that does not take into account its *history, culture, traditions, norms, customs, customary law, religions and so forth* (invisible factors and contexts)? In jurisdictions that do not acknowledge the imprints on law of such invisible factors and contexts, it is impossible for the system to function properly and I submit dissatisfaction among the population and artificial harmony will be the norm in those jurisdictions.

Additionally, I observed that even if scholars, lawyers and judges do sub-consciously acknowledge that there are impacts of the above mentioned invisible factors and contexts on law, they are very reluctant to openly acknowledge the fact, as it has the possibility to offend one group or another or the people who have set the liberal benchmarks for societies. In some cases, adherents of radical liberal jurisprudence do not allow scholars, lawyers and judges to acknowledge the impacts of the above mentioned invisible factors and contexts, let alone use them as customary laws to fill the gaps in law. As a result, over the years, in many jurisdictions, the populace has started to believe that law is detached from all impacts from the above invisible factors and contexts, and anything to the contrary would be too radical for them.

Accordingly, to build on the preceding paragraph, in many jurisdictions this state of affairs results in judges not having enough tools as there could be – (1) lacunas in available law, (2) dissatisfied groups, (3) a lack of social tools available in law to counter the challenges facing society and sub-groups within the population, (4) laws and a system of justice that lacks credibility within the population or groups or sub-groups of population and so forth. I submit this is not an ideal state of affairs.

It must be appreciated from the start that even in most democracies, laws are made by legislators/politicians, who have won on the basis of the first past the post system; this effectively means though the legislators are winners in elections, there are still a lot of people who do not agree with those legislators' views or their ideologies. Then how can the laws they make be credible to all the people, including those who did not vote for them? It is easy to say that is how a political system works, and people just have to accept it. However, can the same system be improved? I can explain this issue with an example from my teenage years – when I was 12 years old, my parents warned me to take care of the communal park's boundary wall, where I use to play badminton and warned me that I would be fined by the local authority, if I were not to follow this rule. My first reaction was why I should be warned and fined about this and what proof would the housing society have against me when so many kids play there? My mother realised there was an issue of understanding and approached it in a different way. She explained to me that we all live in a society, and it is our *'Dharma',* a concept from the prevailing *Hindu* jurisprudence in the area where I lived, meaning a *duty*, whereby we need to take care of our surroundings for our everyone's benefit. The same issue was now couched differently, and I could accept the message much more easily, as compared to the earlier message that had been embedded in terms of sanctions and fines.

In any jurisdiction, law evolves over a period of time among constantly changing demographics within its boundaries due to – *(a) immigration, (b) emigration, (c) slavery, (d) international trade, (e) invasion, (f) colonisation, (g) the export & import of religions, (h) the export & import of ideas, (i) the influence of external laws due to - treaties, alliances, coercion or just pure legal transplants, (j) revolutions, (k) the displacement of indigenous people and their customary beliefs and so forth.* This means that, in any jurisdiction, there are multiple sources contributing to law-making or the practice of law.

Because of this, there are many questions that come to my mind:

- ✓ Do the imprints of an *ancient value system* in any society evaporate gradually or do they themselves evolve by assimilating newer influences and impacts over time?
- ✓ Do written laws erase *customary laws or the laws of indigenous peoples/natives* that were prevalent for thousands of years?
- ✓ *Revolutions* can reboot the whole governance model by abolishing previous laws, for example, in the Russian Revolution of 1917 or the Communist Revolution of 1949 in China. Do such reboots ever manage to erase the historical customs, norms, and customary laws prevalent in a society?
- ✓ Are *colonisation* or *invasion* capable of not just conquering lands but can they erase any *traces of customs, norms, existing traditions, and customary law* from the minds of the conquered, to the extent that only new ideas introduced by the victors will remain in those countries, such as in India, Brazil, Ukraine, Indonesia or Nigeria?
- ✓ What has been the role of *Christian Jurisprudence* in colonised lands?
- ✓ Does the fall of *empires such as the enormous Ottoman Empire of Turkey or the centuries-long banishment of Jewish people* from historical Jewish lands lead to erasure of their jurisprudence from the territories or from the minds of Turkish and Jewish people respectively?
- ✓ Will the dominant *Islamic jurisprudence,* that replaced the previously-existing Hindu Jurisprudence that had lasted for thousands of years, erase all traces of *Hindu jurisprudence* in Indonesia or will later colonial Dutch jurisprudence be the dominant jurisprudence?
- ✓ Can a pacifist *Jain Jurisprudence* really impact the law of Bharat (India), as countries need defence forces and the concept of non-violence is not compatible with sanctions and fines or able to prevent violent sub-groups, dictators or monarchies?
- ✓ Are *legal transplants/ external laws* necessary or is a mix of ideas from legal transplants along with the local value system the ideal in a jurisdiction?
- ✓ Religion is artificially separated from laws, but the swearing of oaths is still carried out in courtrooms pursuant to the adherence to religions? Why?

All the above are stimulating questions. In addition, due to history there are a *plurality of sources* of law that can emerge in any jurisdiction. This aspect of plurality of sources cannot be swept under the carpet in society. As a result of multiple sources, in many jurisdictions, there are *unwritten laws* that are applied in spite of the availability of written laws, the acceptance of *customary laws* or even *religious laws* which are used by judges in some cases in a few jurisdictions.

In order to find answers to the above-mentioned questions, I have selected key jurisdictions from around the globe. These **nine prominent jurisdictions** are – (a) Russia (Chapter 2), (b) China (Chapter 3), (c) Ukraine (Chapter 4), (d) India (Chapters 5 & 6), (e) Israel (Chapter 7), (f) Turkey (Chapter 8), (g) Indonesia (Chapter 9), (h) Brazil (Chapter 10), and (i) Nigeria (Chapter 11). There are hardly any books that have explored the evolution of law historically, taking into account the imprints of history, religions and revolutions on law within different jurisdictions in our world. These selected jurisdictions together occupy approximately 28.65% of the world's land, approximately 48% of the world's population in 2020, 52.77% of GDP in Purchasing power parity terms ('PPP') terms (in 2021), will have 65-70% of the world's GDP (PPP terms) by 2050, and practice many religions such as Christianity, Judaism, Islam, Hinduism, Jainism, State atheism to give just a few insights. Interestingly, before 1800 CE, that is before violent colonisation and invasions, these territories/countries together used to account for 60-70% of the world's GDP in PPP terms.

Therefore, I decided that if I need to find answers for humanity, I need to find the answers from these *prominent jurisdictions*. I have attempted to go as far back in history as possible to evaluate the historical evolution of laws in these selected jurisdictions, with the assistance of scholars/experts from these countries. I could not have found these answers for so many jurisdictions spanning thousands of years alone. I feel fortunate to have discovered learned scholars and lawyers from all the selected jurisdictions and am eternally grateful to them for having trusted in the common theme and structure of this book for their authored chapters. I cannot thank these authors enough for allowing me to – (1) ask questions about their jurisdiction's history and law, and (2) to amend the content of their authored chapters, with their approval, in order to maintain consistency between chapters. I must admit I learned a lot from thought-provoking explorations with these scholars/experts and without doubt humanity needs such collaborative projects to study the evolution of societies and law and possibly find solutions for the above raised issues and obtain different perspectives – global, regional, local, cultural etc.

Within its few pages, this book covers – (1) a brief history of all the selected jurisdictions, (2) legal history, (3) legal history along with evolution of civilisation in the selected jurisdictions, (4) the relationship between society and law, (5) customs, practices, customary law, norms, unwritten laws, cultural aspects behind the law in any jurisdiction, (6) religious jurisprudence and its impact on law (7) the influence of external laws and legal transplants, (8) the status of current laws and their practice and much more. A snap shot of all these issues for every jurisdiction is available in the Tables shown in Chapter 1, and this can be used as background when reading subsequent chapters.

It is an appropriate time to emphasise that the readers should not try to explore the issues in different jurisdictions solely from the perspective of the concepts and terminologies of their own jurisdiction.

I am grateful to *Dr. Shugan C Jain* and his organisation for their partial sponsorship, which definitely assisted the editor to cover a portion of costs leading to the publication of the book. The organisation admired my efforts for taking into account the multiplicity of views from various jurisdictions. I am also grateful to *Ms. Pauline Swarbrick* who, in spite of her demanding professional career as a management consultant, agreed to cast her eyes as an objective reader of the book to detect any inconsistencies in formatting, language and by providing other useful inputs over the last two months on this major project.

This book is a major project, and all my free time was taken over by this project during the last 18 months of the pandemic, and therefore, I am grateful to my family and friends for their extreme patience. Many of my friends and professional colleagues were expecting a book from me on Maritime Law, but I had to explain to them that I am also a member of the global family, and I feel duty-bound to write on such topics as cut across history, sociology, legal history, legal ethnology, comparative law and so forth, especially during the ongoing pandemic. In addition, this is my second book in the Comparative law series. The first book in the series is '*Common Law v Chinese Law*'. I must acknowledge that I managed to remain sane during these times by focusing on this project rather than on human suffering, which was making me feel rather miserable. In a way, the additional time I had available due to the pandemic assisted me, as did travelling less on business for my employers and saving commuting time by not going to my workplace. Accordingly, I managed to find an additional 1-1.5 hours per day that I used productively to contribute to this project, and I always function with a principle "*drop-drop makes an ocean*", consequently the book is ready after 16-18 months of sustained focus.

This is a non–political book and as a disclaimer, is not meant to offend any religion(s), philosophies or any country's history. In times of political correctness or secularism, I must therefore issue clarification and apologise in advance if this book were to offend anyone even inadvertently. This book is an honest scholarly attempt to find solutions. I wish readers pleasant reading, and I hope they will actively assist in finding solutions to the various problems facing humanity.

Dr., Capt. Vivek Jain
28 Feb 2022

CONTENTS

CHAPTER 1

IMPRINTS OF HISTORY, RELIGION & REVOLUTION ON LAWS IN THE JURISDICTIONS OF RUSSIA, CHINA, UKRAINE, INDIA, ISRAEL, TURKEY, INDONESIA, BRAZIL & NIGERIA

Dr., Capt. Vivek Jain

CHAPTER 2

RUSSIAN HISTORY & REVOLUTIONS – IMPACT ON GENESIS, EVOLUTION OF RUSSIAN COURT SYSTEM AND JURISPRUDENCE

Dr. Svetlana Chugunova

CHAPTER 3

THE HISTORICAL DEVELOPMENTS OF CHINESE CIVIL LAW OVER THE CENTURIES, AND A NEW CIVIL CODE 2021

Prof. Xiaojuan Shi

CHAPTER 4

UKRAINIAN NATIONAL LEGAL SYSTEM – THE IMPACT OF HISTORY AND, RECENTLY, OF ENGLISH LAW ON ITS DEVELOPMENT

Attorney Svitlana Sergeyeva

CHAPTER 5

JAIN JURISPRUDENCE & ITS IMPACTS ON THE PRACTICE OF LAW

IN INDIA

Dr. Malay R. Patel

CHAPTER 6

IMPACT OF HINDU JURISPRUDENCE ON LAWS OF INDIA

Assist. Prof. Shrut S. Brahmbhatt & Mr. Nilang Soni

CHAPTER 7

THE YIN-YANG OF ISRAEL AS THE NATION-STATE OF THE JEWISH PEOPLE

Dr. Hadas Peled and Mr. Roy Katz

CHAPTER 10

THE IMPACT OF HISTORY, COLONISATION, SLAVERY, RELIGION, IMMIGRATION & EXTERNAL LAW ON THE EVOLUTION OF BRAZILIAN LAW

Attorney Flavio Bermudes Damaceno

CHAPTER 11

IMPACT OF INDIGENOUS LAW ON LAWS IN NIGERIA

Dr. Olugbenga Oke-Samuel

LIST OF TABLES

LIST OF FIGURES

ABOUT THE EDITOR

Dr, Capt. Vivek Jain is currently a Director (Marine Services) of a renowned firm in Singapore, where he handles and pursues commercial and maritime international arbitrations in various international forums. He has also been appointed as arbitrator on various commercial and maritime disputes and has been a committee member of arbitration institutions for a number of years. He would like to be called a *"problem solver"* by his clients.

As a result of the nature of his work, which involves cross-border litigation/arbitration work, he has developed expertise in comparative law backed by pursuing a PhD from the top-3 ranked law school, CUPL, Beijing, in the topic of Comparative Analysis of Interim Measures. He has worked for many years in London, Shanghai, Hong Kong and Singapore in law firms and insurance companies as a lawyer. He has also worked for a few years as a Senior Lecturer at a University in the UK teaching law to graduate and postgraduate students.

Over the years, he has pursued an LLB (Hons.) and LLM (Maritime Law) with merit from the University of London, BVC (Very Competent) (London), MBA (Norway), PGC in Compliance (Singapore), PGCE (Singapore) and BSc (N Sc) (India) by way of First Class with Distinction from the very selective and prestigious T.S. Rajendra College of Nautical Science, Mumbai. He has recently authored a book, *Common Law v Chinese Law* (Notion Press, 2019) and co-authored a book, *Comparative Interim Measures* (Routledge, 2022).

He sailed on merchant vessels for number of years and completed his Master Mariner Certificate of Competency (unlimited) from the UK with an award. His experience of travelling to several nations and proficiency in transparently and candidly sharing ideas with scholars from these nations is exhibited in this book. He feels that global problems are fashioned through the acts and omissions of mankind and accordingly solutions that can alleviate some of these problems will come through collaborative projects.

Authors' Biographies

Chapter 2 (Russia)
Dr. Svetlana Chugunova, Ph.D., is an international legal practitioner and attorney-at-law admitted to the Bar Association of the *Russian Federation*. She is an associated partner within Jurinflot International Law Firm, with a more than 15 years of aggregate experience in legal practice. She holds an academic degree Juris Doctor in International Law and EU Law. She graduated magna cum laude from Moscow State Institute of International Relations of the Ministry of Foreign Affairs of Russia (MGIMO). She has a dual LLM granted by MGIMO and the College of Europe (Bruges, Belgium) and a post-graduate degree obtained at the Autonomous University of Barcelona (UAB). In addition to legal practice, she actively pursues scientific research, in the capacity of an editorial board member for a number of reputed international periodicals, such as the International Journal of Law and Society, Beijing Law Review of SCIRP Global Scientific Research and Academic Publishing community, and the International Law Journal of India. She has authored numerous articles and legal surveys in both Russian and foreign languages, including contributions to law journals accredited by the Ministry of Science of the Russian Federation and periodicals of the Oxford University Press.

Chapter 3 (China)
Prof. Xiaojuan Shi is a law professor at the College of Humanities and Law, Hebei University of Technology, *China*. Her main areas of Research are contract law, WTO, and international arbitration. She is also a part-time lawyer at Beijing DHH (Tianjin) Law Firm and a part-time arbitrator of CIETAC. She is President of Hebei Tourism Law Research Association, and Vice President of Tianjin International Economic Law Research Association. From 2005 to 2017, she participated in 25 legislative works of national laws and Tianjin local regulations in China and has participated in revision work related to the draft of *"the Foreign Investment Law of the People's Republic of China"* and *"the UNCITRAL Technical Guidelines on Online Dispute Resolution."* She is the author of many publications such as Economic Criminology, Typical Case Analysis of International Trade Disputes and Guide to Claims, International Economic Law, and Research on New Issues in Foreign Economic Law. Her research interests are Maritime Law, International Trade, International Human Rights, WTO, the Legal Profession amongst others.

Chapter 4 (Ukraine)
Attorney Svitlana Sergeyeva is an Attorney-at-law, Mediator DAA (Deutsche Anwalt Akademie), Vice-president of the Ukrainian Academy of Mediation, and Head of the Odesa Regional Branch of the *Ukrainian Bar Association*. She is Partner and Head of the Attorneys' Partnership "Sergeyevs' Law Office", and also an expert in the Project EU "Pravo-Justice".

Chapter 5 (India)
Dr. Malay R. Patel is an Associate Professor in Management and currently serving as Joint Director with the International School for Jain Studies, *India.* He is presently pursuing his second Ph.D. from the University of Warsaw, Poland; his thesis topic is "*Modern reformation in Jainism in Gujarat in 19th Century*". He holds his first doctorate degree in Business Studies from Sardar Patel University, Gujarat. He also had a short stint of 3 years working as Associate Dean in a Law college. Dr. Patel is armed with two master degrees: an M.Sc. in Paints & Polymer Sciences and an M.B.A. with specialisation in Marketing and Human Resource Management. In addition to his regular qualifications, his research interests are ancient Indian philosophy, jurisprudence, entrepreneurship, and innovation. He has a knack for management case-writing and teaching. Many of his management cases and research have been published in national and international journals.

Chapter 6 (India)
Assist. Prof. Shrut S. Brahmbhatt is currently working as Assistant Professor of Law and Director of the Centre for Corporate Governance and Corporate Training (CCGCT) at the United World School of Law, Karnavati University, Gandhinagar, *India*. He has almost seven years' experience in academics; his previous employment includes working at Gujarat National Law University, Gandhinagar, India and Oakbrook International Education & Research Pvt. Ltd., Ahmedabad, India. He is a keen researcher and an author and editor of "*Advancement of Human Rights in India*", book chapters, journal articles, and empirical research reports on legal as well as interdisciplinary subjects published with renowned publishers including SAGE publications, US, Academia Press etc.

Mr. Nilang Soni is currently an undergraduate student for the course of B.B.A. & LL.B. in Intellectual Property Law from the United World School of Law, Karnavati University, Gandhinagar, *India*. He holds key positions in various student organisations and is an avid student of law as well as an international mooter and researcher. He was the first Convenor of the Centre for Advanced Research in Law and Philosophy at the United World School of Law. He has also had key publications on the Nanotechnology Regulatory Framework in India published with the Bar Council of Gujarat, India.

Chapter 7 (Israel)
Dr. Hadas Peled, Dr. Adv., is an experienced university lecturer and legal practitioner based in Israel. She holds an LL.B. from the Hebrew University of Jerusalem, and LL.M. and Ph.D. in legal sciences from Tsinghua University, Beijing, China. Currently, she is a research associate at the dangoor centre for universal monotheism in Bar Ilan University, and lecturer at the multidisciplinary studies program, faculty of humanities, Bar Ilan University, Israel. Her research aims are to advance the multi-cultural rule of law.

Mr. Roy Katz is an experienced journalist, lecturer, manager in media outlets and an award-winning interviewer in Iisrael. Currently part of the Swiss Center for Conflict Research at the Hebrew University of Jerusalem, as well as VP content and new media at Radio Tel Aviv, he lectures on digital media and serves as chair of the digit conference for digital media at Reichman University.

Chapter 8 (Turkey)

Attorney Tuğçe Ergüden graduated from Bahçeşehir University's Faculty of Law in *Turkey*. She completed her master's degree in International Energy Law and Regulation at City University, London. She won The City Law School Prize in Energy, Sustainability and Security and The City Law School Prize in Low Carbon Energy. She wrote her master's thesis on the extent to which the *Energy Charter Agreement provides the investor states with environmental protection* and graduated with distinction. At the same time, she published her articles on environmental and energy law in Turkish, English and French in various magazines. In addition, she is Vice Secretary General at the Energy Disputes Arbitration Center and an arbitrator at the Chambers of Arbitrators-Minsk. She is a lawyer focusing on energy and environmental law. Finally, she was on the organising committee of the Turkey Arbitration Week.

Chapter 9 (Indonesia)

Attorney Yuliannova Lestari is from Banda Aceh, Indonesia. She was conferred with an LL.B. degree in International Law from Syiah Kuala University, Banda Aceh, Indonesia. She has been working as an Associate in the reputed law firm, Beni Murdani, in Aceh since 2016 after obtaining her licence as an *Advocate*. In order to advance her practice in International Law, she also successfully pursued an LL.M. degree in International Relations from the Central China Normal University in Wuhan, China. She is now pursuing her PhD degree from the same University, while continuing her legal practice. Her main practice areas include Intellectual Property Rights, Environment & Forestry law, Law of the Sea, Foreign Direct Investment, Arbitration law, and Family law. She was delighted to write a chapter for the book under the guidance and recommendations of Dr. Vivek Jain, as she found the theme presented around which to write the chapter very novel and interesting.

Chapter 10 (Brazil)

Attorney Flavio Bermudes Damaceno was born in Vitória, State of Espírito Santo, *Brazil*. He graduated in law from the Faculdades de Vitória in 2005 and is registered at the Brazilian bar, State of Rio de Janeiro Section. During his graduation period he was an intern in the Civil Courts, where he was able to learn the nuances of jurisdictional activity. After graduating and passing the Bar exams, he went on to undertake further studies in 2006 at the University of Southampton, UK. After concluding a master's degree in Maritime law, he moved to London in 2007 to handle marine casualties on behalf of worldwide cargo underwriters and subsequently joined an International Group P&I Club. After years of living in the cold weather, he decided in 2013 to move back to the warm tropics, making the beautiful city of Rio de Janeiro his place of residence. Since then, he has been acting as a lawyer and marine broker, handling a book of over one thousand insured vessels.

Chapter11

Dr. Olugbenga Oke-Samuel is an Associate Professor of law and current Dean of the Faculty of Law, Adekunle Ajasin University, Akungba – Akoko, *Nigeria*. He was born in Idanre, Western part of Nigeria and attended Lagos State University, Lagos, Nigeria for his first and second degrees in Law. He attended Nigerian Law School, Victoria Island and was admitted to the Nigerian Bar in February 1995. He obtained a Doctorate Degree in Law from the University of Zululand, South Africa (2014). He has been the prolific author of *Legislation and Control of Gas emission in Nigeria and South Africa* (Lambert Academic publishing, 2017), *Outline of Nigerian Legal System* (OGI Publishers, 2008). He co-authored *Freedom of Information Handbook for Law Clinics* (NULAI, Nigeria, 2015), *Street Law Freedom of Information Manual* (NULAI, Nigeria, 2016), and *Comparative Analysis of Customary and Islamic Laws As sources of Nigerian Legal System* (Createspace Independent Publisher, 2017). He has also been the editor of *Trends in Nigerian Law* (Constellation publishers, Nigeria 2007).

CHAPTER 1

IMPRINTS OF HISTORY, RELIGION & REVOLUTION ON LAWS IN THE JURISDICTIONS OF RUSSIA, CHINA, UKRAINE, INDIA, ISRAEL, TURKEY, INDONESIA, BRAZIL & NIGERIA

Dr., Capt. Vivek Jain

1 INTRODUCTION

This Chapter needs to be read together with *Preface* of this Book. Law evolves over a period of time within geographical borderlines, as can be clearly observed in any contemporary legal jurisdiction. Even these geographical borderlines keep shifting over the centuries, enhancing or shrinking the extent of legal jurisdictions. The demography of people who live within those geographical boundaries also transforms/alters/modifies/adjusts over time due to invasion and colonisation, [1] immigration, [2] emigration, [3] slavery, [4] legal treaties, [5] alliances/membership[6] and other factors.

As discussed earlier, *the plurality of sources* of law within any jurisdiction will emerge as a result of changing demography, while at the same this will also contribute to law-making by providing different perspectives to legislative bodies in that jurisdiction. Thereafter, even the application of these laws within any jurisdiction would be impacted by plurality of sources, history, customs, norms, historical laws, unwritten customary laws and precedents and so forth. For example, in any jurisdiction, as a result of an influx of immigrants, invasion by an occupying force or colonisation, new ideas will be conveyed within that jurisdiction

---

[1] Refer to Chapter 9 **(Indonesia)** for an analysis of the impact of colonisation by the Dutch on Indonesian laws; Chapter 10 **(Brazil)** for the impact on Brazilian laws due to its colonisation by the Portuguese; example analysis of the impact on law due to the *colonisation* of India by the British and Islamic empires from Central Asia in chapters 5 & 6 **(India)**; Chapter 11 **(Nigeria)** for the effects of colonisation of Nigeria on Nigerian laws; or Chapter 4 **(Ukraine)** for analysis of the impact on Ukrainian law due to *invasions* from various empires that ruled Ukraine from 1800 CE until 1990. Refer to Chapter 8 **(Turkey)** for analysis of the impact on laws in the Ottoman Empire due to the impact of conquered land, or similarly refer to Chapter 2 **(Russia)** for the influence of laws from various lands within the Russian empire on Russian law.

[2] Refer to analysis of the infusion of ideas due to *immigration* in **Brazil** in Chapter 10 over many centuries, first from Portuguese & Africans, later other Europeans, Japanese and Middle Easterners. Refer also to previous footnote 1, where immigration could result from invasion, colonisation and slavery and how this can impact the philosophy and laws in any jurisdiction over a period of time.

[3] Refer to Chapters 2 & 3 on **Russia** and **China** respectively, where many *revolutions* led to *emigration* and, at times, brain drain. Refer also to Chapter 8 on **Turkey** where, due to military coups and the recent crisis under the new legal governance model, there is widespread emigration from the country. Emigration can also result from professionals' needs to obtain financial security and that too can impact the development of law in a jurisdiction. Refer also, to Chapter 4 **(Israel)**, where over history, Jewish people have been exiled numerous times and suffered immensely over 2000 years, and how these experiences have shaped current laws in Israel. Refer to Chapter 11 **(Nigeria)**, where emigration from its territories occurred as a result of slavery.

[4] Refer to Chapter 2 **(Russia)**, 10 **(Brazil)** & 11 **(Nigeria)** on issues arising from the abolishment of *serfdom and slavery* and their impact on laws in those jurisdiction, for better or worse. These chapters also discuss the need to modernise laws and how such issues affect them, even in periods of a change of governance model or revolution.

[5] Refer to Chapter 4 **(Ukraine)** and Chapter 8 **(Turkey)** and their desire to harmonise their laws with *external* European Union Laws in order to seek membership of the European Union. Refer also to Chapter 3 **(China)**, for how coercion by western powers in the 19th century prompted the Qing Dynasty to attempt refashioning and adapting their laws to satisfy the needs of trade with western powers and bring subtle social change. Also, recently, after accession to the WTO, China brought in various legal reforms.

[6] Refer to Chapter 3 **(China)**, where membership of the WTO led them to make drastic changes in their civil laws, which could be one of the catalysts for the new civil code in 2021 (the first civil code in the history of China).

through new customs, new religions and new perspectives, due to the intermixing of populations.

In theory, which the editor discusses very briefly in this chapter, the issues discussed in the preceding paragraphs also raise the question of the very nature of laws in any jurisdiction, that is – (1) whether the law is a *state centred law,* which is fully focussing on controls and functions, or (2) the law should be seen in the context of a *social function,* where different groups and their values and norms are assimilated in an organised fashion within a jurisdiction.[7] Even if law needs to be seen from the perspective of *state centralism,* then in that context too, the law that emerges will largely have imprints of perspectives of a dominant group or sub-group within the demographics of that jurisdiction.[8] In any event, in any jurisdiction, law-making is accomplished within a legislative body, and dominant groups are obviously influential and compelling in that body.

Therefore, in any jurisdiction with regard to existing law, it is important to consider the impact of the above discussed issues over a period of time, in particular, the transformation of demography within a boundary and, as a result, the transfer of ideas, philosophies, ideology, customs, culture, norms, and so forth.

---

[7] See John Griffiths, "What is Legal Pluralism?," *The Journal of Legal Pluralism and Unofficial Law,* vol. 18, no. 24, (January 1986): 1–55, 3, 8, 38, doi:10.1080/07329113.1986.10756387, for debate about *legal centralism,* which he refers to as either a top-down approach through sovereign commands or bottom upwards, deriving legal validity through the use of norms at various levels until one reaches the top level called ultimate norms. He viewed the development of law from a social perspective (theory of *legal pluralism*) and dissected law on the basis of *'state of affairs in a society'.* Law provides a social control and assists in the organisation of society through legal ways; See also, Baudouin Dupert, "Legal Pluralism, Plurality of Laws, and Legal Practices," *European Journal of Legal Studies,* vol. 1, no. 1, (2007): 1-26, 1-5, halshs00178422, where the author of this article discusses an interesting debate about the two concepts of *legal centralism* and *legal pluralism* and discusses the views of John Griffiths; See also, B. Tamamaha, *Realistic Socio-Legal Theory: Pragmatism and A Social Theory Of Law* (Oxford: Clarendon Press, 1997) for further exploration on socio–legal theories of law, in particular, the functional theory of law; See also, S. F. Moore, *Law as Process: An Anthropological Approach* (London: Boston, Routledge & Kegan Paul, 1978); See also, Roger Cotterrell, The Sociology of Law: An Introduction, 2nd ed. (London: Butterworths,1992); See also, Roman Tomasic, The Sociology of Law (London: SAGE, 1985).

[8] See Baudouin Dupert, "Legal Pluralism, Plurality of Laws, and Legal Practices," *European Journal of Legal Studies,* vol. 1, no. 1, (2007): 1-26, halshs00178422, where he discussed the views of George Gurvitch that *state centralism* could be the result of history and political context; See also, G. Gurvitch, *l'idée dy droit social* (Paris, 1932); See also, G. Gurvitch *L'expérience juridique et la philosophie du droit* (Paris:1935) and his views on *state centralism* and *legal pluralism* were extensively discussed in the article.

There are also additional influences on the growth and expansion of law within these geographical boundaries – (*1*) the influences of foreign laws,[9] (2) the influence of religions from various sub-groups within a jurisdiction.[10] (3) the development of philosophies and political thoughts over a period of time, (4) the growth of commercial trade, (5) commercial and social constraints developed over time (6) the advent of new technology amongst others.

At times, revolutions within geographical borderlines can halt the organic development and evolution of law and may obligate a powerful body to reboot the law and legal system in jurisdictions, as happened in Russia and China after their revolutions.[11]

---

[9] Refer to various chapters describing how different philosophies/jurisprudences and external laws influenced legal development over time in a jurisdiction. For example, Chapter 3 **(China)**, where, over many decades, laws from Germany, France and so forth influenced the development of its *Civil Code*. Refer also to Chapter 9 **(Indonesia),** where their laws were influenced by laws from the Netherlands and other European jurisprudence. In all other chapters, development has been influenced by foreign laws to some extent. Similarly, Chapter 11 **(Nigeria)** adopted common law principles from England.

[10] Refer to Chapters 5 & 6 **(India),** where the impact of *Jain and Hindu jurisprudence* on the evolution of law in India is analysed, Chapter 4 **(Israel)**, where the impact of *Judaism* is analysed on its law, Chapters 2 **(Russia),** 4 **(Ukraine)** & 10 **(Brazil)**, where the impact of *Christian jurisprudence* is analysed on their laws, or Chapter 8 **(Turkey)**, Chapter 9 **(Indonesia)** and Chapter 11 (in some parts of **Nigeria**), where the impact of *Islamic jurisprudence* on their laws is analysed. In particular, Indonesia presents a unique case where 1500 years of Hindu/Buddhist dominant philosophy/jurisprudence was replaced, to some extent, by another dominant Islamic jurisprudence around the 13th century. However, all their philosophies/jurisprudences, irrespective of which jurisprudence is dominant or accepted by the majority, have retained relevance in current Indonesian written and unwritten laws. A few of the old jurisprudence survive as *customary law*. In most jurisdictions, in the author's view, in particular advanced economies, the crusade to *secularise* laws has snuffed out the soul from laws and limited the ability of society to find solutions for various problems. It also affects the acceptance of laws, due to various factors such as a distrust of politicians in general. After analysis, it is submitted by the editor that, in spite of *secularisation/political correctness* for everything under the sun in various jurisdictions, the religious jurisprudences available within a society cannot be wished away and will remain a compelling perspective in most jurisdictions, whether through content of laws, interpretation of laws or when such perspectives are used as customary law/unwritten laws in these jurisdictions. The editor has observed and reached the conclusion that this acceptance of religious jurisprudence in many jurisdictions has ensured that laws continue to retain mass appeal among the population in a jurisdiction and provide legitimacy to laws imposed upon the populace through the compelling power of influential groups within a society.

[11] Refer to Chapters 2 **(Russia)** & 3 **(China)** for further analysis. Refer also to Chapter 10 **(Brazil)**, where the sudden abolition of slavery resulted in the abolition of the monarchy and, as a result, there was a new development in laws, accompanied by economic progress.

The editor considers the above factors as *invisible factors and contexts* that leave their imprints within law,[12] and accordingly law within any jurisdiction will evolve without negating these imprints either in substantive law and/or in its application within the jurisdiction. Therefore, the ensuing law and its practice within any jurisdiction will always have imprints of past events in history or imprints of religion(s), revolution(s), immigration or slavery, or influences of foreign/external laws (intentional and/or unintentional) and so forth.

In any jurisdiction, according to the system of governance, there are devices developed over time, which are used to promulgate laws. Laws will come into effect within any jurisdiction soon after the notification of promulgation of new laws. These laws are applicable to all within a jurisdiction. Sanctions for behaviour, law for commerce, family law and so on will be governed pursuant to these laws promulgated by nation/state legislatures.

The editor has discussed earlier the issue of nature of law and debates surrounding it.[13] Again, to briefly discuss the theory of legal pluralism, and on this occasion, the exploration looks from another perspective of the context of concept of legal pluralism - that is, from the eyes of a non-western scholar. This perspective will be particularly relevant to most jurisdictions that have been

---

[12] For further details on the role that invisible factors and contexts play in any jurisdiction, in particular for horizontal comparative analysis between two jurisdictions, see Vivek Jain, *Insight into China through Comparative Analysis of Invisible Factors and Contexts – Common Law v. Chinese Law*, (India, Singapore, Malaysia: Notion Press 2019), where the comparison of two jurisdictions was carried out on these invisible factors and contexts; See also, Hein Kotz, "Comparative Law in Germany Today," *Revue Internationale de Droit Compare* 51, no. 4 (1999): 756, where the author quoted Ernest Rable, who said:

> [T]he student of the problem must encompass the law of the whole world, past and present, and everything that affects the law, such as geography, climate and race, developments and events shaping the course of country's history - war, revolution, colonisation, subjugation - religion and ethics, the ambition and creativity of individuals, the needs of production and consumption, the interests of groups, parties and classes. Ideas of every kind have their effect, for it is not just feudalism, liberalism and socialism, which produce different types of law; legal institutions once adopted may have logical consequences; and not least important is the striving for a political or legal ideal. Everything in the social, economic and legal fields interacts. The <u>law of every developed person is in constant motion</u> [emphasis added], and the whole kaleidoscopic picture is one which no one has ever clearly seen.

[13] Refer to footnotes 7 & 8 of this Chapter.

selected in this book. The potential of non-official law, which is not written or legislated, can be quite useful in many jurisdictions, as discussed in this book and was particularly analysed by a Japanese scholar, Chiba.[14]

In this book, many experts from local jurisdictions referred to this as customs or customary law, which operate in tandem with written laws in those jurisdictions. Can there be a limit on such unofficial laws or how a legal practice within any jurisdiction will consider such unofficial laws as a pivotal factor? This is precisely the interesting perspective that has been dealt with in the book. Can such customary laws be trumped or banned by any written law or ideology, as experienced in the aftermath of Communist & Marxist revolutions in Russia and China?

Generally, judges apply the relevant laws that are promulgated for society and at times exercise their discretionary power [15] to fill in the gaps – (1) using customs/customary law, based on religion(s) or morality, or (2) using rules of sub-

---

[14] M. Chiba, "Three Dichotomies of Law in Pluralism: An Analytical Scheme of Legal Culture," *Tokai Law Review*, (1987): 173-183,173 & 177-79, where Chiba also discussed three levels of law – *official law, unofficial law, legal postulates* comprising of values and ideals influencing both official state law and unofficial law operating within the populace; See also, Baudouin Dupert, "Legal Pluralism, Plurality of Laws, and Legal Practices," *European Journal of Legal Studies*, vol. 1, no. 1, (2007): 1-26, halshs00178422, where the author of the article discussed the views of Chiba, in particular his discussion on Chiba's three dichotomies – (1) official law v. unofficial law, (2) legal rules v. legal postulates, and (3) indigenous law v. transplanted law; See also, M. Chiba, *Sociology of Law in Non-Western Countries* (Oñati: Oñati International Institute for the Sociology of Law, 1993); See also, Baudouin Dupert, "Legal Pluralism, Plurality of Laws, and Legal Practices," *European Journal of Legal Studies*, vol. 1, no. 1, (2007): 1-26, halshs00178422, where Dupert was of the view that focus on *customary law* or *indigenous law* or concepts similar to this are imagined by scholars and has criticised an over-emphasis on such concepts within the scheme of things in any jurisdiction.

[15] Jurisprudents such as Positivists like H. L. A. Hart in England & Wales agreed with the concept of the exercising of 'discretionary power' by judges. According to Hart, the employment of discretionary power is based on the 'court's principles'. These principles are even considered as a part of law in many jurisdictions and are therefore argued by a few jurisprudents as not the equivalent of judges' exercise of discretionary power; See also, J. Raz, "Legal Principles and the Limits of Law," *Yale L.J.* 81, no. 5 (1972): 838–47 for discussion on the principles of law and discretionary power of judges; See also, for further exploration of this topic, Ronald Dworkin, *Taking Rights Seriously* (London: Duckworth, 1977), 29–36; See also, Vivek Jain, *Insight into China through Comparative Analysis of Invisible Factors and Contexts – Common Law v. Chinese Law*, (India, Singapore, Malaysia: Notion Press 2019),160-183, for discussion on the comparison of discretionary power in two very different legal jurisdictions and for thorough discussion on the exercising of discretionary power by judges.

groups, in particular in the practice of family law, or (3) arguing on the basis of intention behind the drafting of a law in the legislature, or (4) arguing on the basis of constitutional principles and so forth. It is trite that the promulgated laws cannot always solve societal problems, or that answers are not available in the promulgated laws for a few of the problems that emerge in a society, or the new laws could lead to dissatisfaction in society as the promulgated laws can subtly shift the norms or customs developed over centuries in any jurisdiction,[16] for example.

The book is not about whether promulgated laws will acknowledge the influences of aforesaid invisible factors and contexts within society; rather the focus of the book is on how those laws and legal systems evolved with influences and imprints of the aforesaid *invisible factors such as history, religion, revolution, invasion, colonisation, immigration, emigration, slavery* and so forth in these jurisdictions. In addition, these imprints are hard to ignore in both issues – (1) pertaining to contents within laws, and (2) pertaining to their application in cases or their role in governing the social norms applicable to groups within a society. In addition, in any jurisdiction, even when Constitution mandates particular rules to solve issues facing society, these rules can at times be insufficient to deal with the issues.[17] It may be that the laws, customs or norms available to judges cannot lead to solution(s) for the problem(s) that they may encounter in their courtrooms. How then can judges be expected to resolve societal issues?

---

[16] Some examples of the norms that are shifted by new laws may relate to providing more power to women in certain jurisdictions, or more rights to oppressed groups within a society or create new rights altogether in light of technological advancement within a society. In many chapters, such issues of new norms or altered norms due to influence of external laws are explored as well.

[17] Refer to Chapters 5 & 6 **(India),** where concepts from *Jainism and Hinduism* jurisprudence and their impact on law are analysed, Chapter 4 **(Israel),** where the impact of *Judaism* is analysed within the legal system, Chapters 2 **(Russia),** 4 **(Ukraine)** & 10 **(Brazil),** where the impact of *Christian jurisprudence* is analysed on their laws, or Chapter 8 **(Turkey)** & Chapter 9 **(Indonesia),** where the impact of *Islamic jurisprudence* is analysed for resolving societal issues in these countries. Similarly, in Chapter 10, the customs and value of indigenous people in Brazil have been utilised for the protection of the environment and so forth and accordingly their impact is discussed on the current laws of Brazil.

In any jurisdiction, in that scenario, where judges are facing lacuna in written laws, in order to find solutions – (1) can judges rely on customary laws based on the religions or laws of indigenous peoples, or the laws of a foreign country (external laws) that have the most influence on laws within their jurisdiction, or (2) can judges rely on some other norms to fill in the gap(s) in available law by utilising historical jurisprudence, which includes historical laws or norms or customs?

Can those historical laws or norms or customs even be borrowed from another historical dynasty or another form of government within the same jurisdiction?[18] It is the right time to discuss; in theory, historical law can connote many ideas – (1) the influence of historical events or norms which have evolved in a particular kind of scenario and direct stakeholders towards a particular interpretation of law, or (2) applying historical laws that are still valid currently in a jurisdiction and available to judges, or (3) the issue of applying old concepts (even though the law was promulgated based on norms of society that were relevant at that time),[19] or norms or even historical law that is still valid and applying these within the matrix of modern society and technological development before a judge. In fact, in any jurisdiction, the importance of history and past laws will always be very important in order to limit excesses of officials and judges and to affirm the power of sitting legislatures.[20]

---

[18] Refer to Chapters 2-11, where these issues are dealt with – (1) principles established historically or obtained from imprints of religions, or (2) by discussing how even revolutions have not been able to cease the influence of these imprints of history, religion, customs, norms and so forth. Often judges fill in the gaps in laws by utilising the concept of "**Customary Law**" that is even allowed by constitutions in some countries such as Indonesia, Turkey, India, Nigeria.

[19] William Baude and Stephen E. Sachs, "Originalism and the Law of the Past," *Law and History Review*, vol. 37, no. 3 (2019): 809-820, Duke Law School Public Law & Legal Theory Series No. 2019-46, Available at SSRN: <https://ssrn.com/abstract=3400463>, where the authors of this article have discussed the implications of the role of history in law and in particular, the context of past laws (that might still be valid) when applied in modern times.

[20] See Frank H. Easterbrook, "Textualism and the Dead Hand," *George Washington Law Review* 66 (1998): 1119-26, 1120, where Judge Frank Easterbook succinctly said, "*affirming the force of old laws is essential if sitting legislatures are to enjoy the power to make new ones.*"; See Also, William Baude and Stephen E. Sachs, "Originalism and the Law of the Past," *Law and History Review*, vol. 37, no. 3 (2019): 809-820, 812, Duke Law School Public Law & Legal Theory Series No. 2019-46, Available at SSRN: <https://ssrn.com/abstract=3400463>, where Judge Easterbrook's views were discussed in context of legal concept of *originalism*; See also, H.L.A. Hart, *The Concept of Law* (Oxford: Oxford University Press, 3d ed. 2012), 55.

The editor submits that even in the countries, which have professed secularism,[21] or strictly follow Jefferson's famous principle – *"wall of separation of church and state"*[22], they also cannot avoid the imprints or influence of religions on written

---

[21] Refer to footnote 10 of this Chapter regarding the issue of secularisation of laws and even directing the thought process of the populace in the jurisdictions. In addition, in many jurisdictions, political debates revolve around *secularism*, where politicians try to accuse each other of vote bank politics. These discussions are commonplace in most countries with a culture of debate. However, with customs and religion being an important part and parcel of people's lives – (1) can it be avoided by judges and can laws be kept immune from the influences of religion or historical events? For many centuries, there have been debates amongst philosophers and jurisprudents about the relationship between the concepts of '*law*', '*morality*' *and* '*religion*'. The theory of *Natural law* has gradually been taken over by the theory of *positive law,* whereby divine law or concepts that could not be tested or verified are superceded by laws made by people through a legislative process. A few jurisprudents have no compulsions to follow religious or moral principles. However, the editor of the book submits that the imprints of norms or customs or morals in religions or the practices of the local population have deep imprints even on positive law and, of course in unofficial law, in a jurisdiction; See also, for further exploration into the role of religion, morality and law in general, Stephen M. Feldman, ed., *Law and Religion: A Critical Anthology* (New York: NYU Press, 2000); See also, Lon Fuller, *The Morality of Law* (Conn., New Haven: Yale University Press, 1969); See also, H. L. A. Hart, "Positivism and Separation of Law and Morals," *Harvard L. Rev.* 71, no. 4 (1958): 607; See also, Richards Nobles and David Schiff, "The Evolution of Natural Law," in *Introduction to Jurisprudence and Legal Theory: Commentary and Materials*, by Anne Barron, et al. (London: Butterworths, 2002), 39; See also, Lon L. Fuller, *The Law in Quest of Itself* (Boston, Mass.: Beacon Press, 1940), 33–42; See also, Richard Nobles and David Schiff, "Debating with Natural Law; the Emergence of the Legal Positivism," in *Introduction to Jurisprudence and Legal Theory: Commentary and Materials*, Anne Barron, et al. (London: Butterworths, 2002), 92; See also, David Schiff, "Modern Positivism: Kelsen's Pure Theory of Law," in *Introduction to Jurisprudence and Legal Theory: Commentary and Materials*, Anne Barron, et al. (London: Butterworths, 2002), 191; See also, Xianyi Zeng and Xiaohong Ma, "A Dialectic Study of the Structure and Basic Concept of Traditional Chinese Law and an Analysis of the Relationship between Li (Ceremony) and Fa (Law)," *Frontiers of Law in China* 1, no. 1 (2006): 35, where the debate amongst Chinese jurisprudents was not much different on these issues as compared to debate amongst the western jurisprudents; See also, Harold J. Berman, *The interaction of Law and Religion* (Nashville: Abingdon Press, 1974), where he emphasised that focusing on separating law from religion has threatened the integrity of western society, where he succinctly commented, "*Subject is radically separated from object, person from act, spirit from matter, emotion from intellect, ideology from power, the individual from society. The overcoming of these dualisms is the key to the future.*" He further stated in the book that thinking of law in terms of efficiency only is self–defeating as without religion there is nothing to provide that efficiency to promulgated laws; See also, Huston Smith, *The Religions of Man* (Ishi Press: Tokyo, 2013 (first published in New York in 1958)), where he said that concepts of ritual tradition are shared between law and religion, and according to the author, it is very difficult to separate law from religion; See also, Harold J. Breman, *Justice in the U.S.S.R.: An Interpretation of Soviet Law* (Cambridge: Harvard University Press, 1963), 46-65, where he considered belief in socialist law led to a system where law is considered as temporary. He also compared it with a scenario where divorcing morality created another kind of danger that is anarchy, which is distinct from the concept of tyranny due to laws made by dominant groups.

[22] Thomas Jefferson was third President and author of *Declaration of Independence of the United States* and was of the view that the United States' *Constitution* prohibits establishing a particular state's faith or restraining the personal faith of citizens of the United States. In 1802 CE, he also made it clear in his letter to the Baptist's Association of Connecticut that the state has no role in religious matters of the population; See also, <https://time.com/5103677/church-state-separation-religious-freedom/>, accessed on 2 November 2021, for further details on interesting aspects of Thomas Jefferson.

laws.[23] In many jurisdictions, religions play a big part in the day to day life of citizens and therefore, in spite of secular constitutions, they are bound to have imprints of religions in the development of principles of law and their application in courtrooms.[24] In any jurisdiction, religions will also affect jurisprudence and can be used to fill the gaps in written laws. In many cases, religious codes, norms and even customs provide legitimacy to written laws as well. Why would something that is written by a group of people, even if they are legislators, be believed by the population at large? In any event, in most democracies following a 'first past the post' system of election, not everyone would have voted for those elected legislators. So those who have not voted would need a reason other than their belief in democratic norms for believing in law.

In order for laws to remain credible and acceptable to a populace, the philosophy/jurisprudence presented in moral or religious codes are useful in many jurisdictions.[25] In addition, religious jurisprudence that is integrated within law has assisted many of these jurisdictions to retain the credibility of their citizens in their legal systems.

The effectiveness of integration of religion with laws is due to – (1) the sanctity that integration of religion with law provided, and (2) credibility and trust in the

---

[23] Harold J. Berman, *The Interaction of Law and Religion* (Nashville: Abingdon Press, 1974), where in the context of western society's interaction with law, he wrote succinctly in "Introduction," *"Law without (what I call) religion degenerates into a mechanical legalism. Religion (what I call) law loses is social effectiveness)."* He gave the example of numerous mini-revolutions by a rebellious American society in the late 1960's, where strict separation of written laws from religion led to chaos, and he was of the view the missing anchor was religion; See also, Thomas M. Frank, *The Structure of Impartiality: Examining the Riddle of One Law in a Fragmented World* (New York: Macmillan, 1968), 62, where the author examined the legal process as a completely human process that is separated from religion and as a result can affect – (1) the sanctity of laws, and (2) the mass following of those laws by people: See Jean Piagnet, *The Moral Judgment of the Child* (London: Kegan Paul, Trench, Trübner & Co.,1932), where more than the coercive power of law, facets such as fairness, credibility, trust and affiliation have proved successful.

[24] Refer to the analysis in Chapters about the role of religions such as Christianity on the development of laws in Russia (Chapter 2), Ukraine (Chapter 4) & Brazil (Chapter 10), the role of Hinduism and Jainism on the development of laws in India (Chapters 5 & 6), the role of Judaism on the development of laws in Israel (Chapter 7), the role of Islam on the development of laws in Indonesia and Turkey (Chapters 8 & 9 respectively) and the role of a *Maliki school of Islam* in Nigeria (Chapter 11).

[25] Ibid.

system. [26] The principles of fairness, justice and morality through religious jurisprudence (at times many religions concurrently impacting the laws, for example, Hinduism, Jainism, Islam, Christianity, Sikhism all having an effect on Indian laws at the same time due to diversity) [27] has, in fact, assisted many jurisdictions to develop and evolve laws for society.

The editor submits that this phenomenon of religious jurisprudence being allowed to interact with law can be contrasted with jurisdictions that have relied completely on logic that is devoid of emotions, as can be observed in many western societies that have been hugely successful in economics and trade, but are found deficient for not having sufficient tools to deal with other societal issues.

It is important to appreciate the connection of religion to laws in these jurisdictions is not limited to the thought process, but extends to customs, etiquettes, norms, rituals and so forth, as well as gently persuading its populace over the centuries to believe in the system of governance, albeit through the assistance of religions. For example, in ancient India, it was difficult to distinguish religion from law through the concept of *Dharma* (see chapter 6 for further discussion). The obligations of the population in ancient Bharat (now known as India) were put across in terms of duty (in the Hindu religion) toward the environment and other stakeholders, which were also duties in law in its jurisdiction, if one were to analyse it deeply.

In many jurisdictions, there are different laws applicable to different groups of people based on their religions, and that too can influence the development of customs and norms within the country. This will also leave its imprints on the

---

[26] Refer footnote 10 of this chapter; See, Jean Piagnet, *The Moral Judgment of the Child* (London: Kegan Paul, Trench, Trübner & Co.,1932), where the author discussed that more than the coercive power of law, principles such as fairness, credibility, trust and affiliation have proven successful in societies. These conclusions were reached in a different context, but are not far from the school of thought that emerged in many jurisdictions selected in this book; See also, Harold J. Berman, *The Interaction of Law and Religion* (Nashville: Abingdon Press, 1974), where in the context of western society's interaction with law, he wrote in the first chapter "Religious Dimensions of Law" that even Stalin in communist Russia had to rely on a few sacred elements to increase mass appeal, along with propagating socialist principles.

[27] Refer to Chapters 5 & 6 **(India)**, 8 **(Turkey)**, 9 **(Indonesia)**, 10 **(Brazil)**, 11 **(Nigeria)** of this book.

norms and customs of other sub-groups.[28] In a scenario where parallel law is applicable within a jurisdiction, this is a classic case of *legal pluralism*, where different rules interact with the main constitutional principles. Legal pluralism also exists where indigenous people's customs and values are taken into account by judges along with written laws.[29]

At times, imprints of legal pluralism can be seen in laws in spite of distinct written laws to deal with problems facing societies. In practice, at times, laws can incorporate local elements of culture and beliefs.[30] This is also important for maintaining and enhancing the legitimacy of a legal system as a whole within a jurisdiction. Do the imprints of previous laws, norms, customs and so forth evaporate with a reboot of the system within any jurisdiction as a result of revolutions,[31] a change of regime as a result of colonisation or invasion or occupation or even a reverse influence on colonisers from occupied subjects,[32] a change of religion in society,[33] an influx of immigrants,[34] the influence of foreign

---

[28] Refer to Chapters 5, 6, 7, 8 & 9 for parallel impacts of *Judaism, Jainism, Hinduism, and Islam* along with another written law in Israel, India, Turkey and Indonesia respectively.

[29] Refer, Chapters 9 & 10, where the customs and practices of indigenous peoples are taken into account by judges, and accordingly separate constitutional principles are created. In some cases, judges have even created precedents in their courtrooms by adopting them.

[30] See Sally Merry, "Everyday Understandings of the Law in Working-class America," *American Ethnologist*, vol. 13, no. 2 (May 1986): 253–270, doi:10.1525/ae.1986.13.2.02a00040; See also, John Griffiths, "What is Legal Pluralism?," *The Journal of Legal Pluralism and Unofficial Law*, vol. 18, no. 24, (January 1986): 1–55, doi:10.1080/07329113.1986.10756387.

[31] Refer to Chapter 2, for an analysis of the impact of the *Communist revolution 1917* on then existing laws in Russia; Refer also to Chapter 4, regarding the impact of the *Communist revolution of 1949* on then-existing Chinese laws and future laws; in particular, on the advent of the new *Civil Code 2021*; Refer also to Chapter 10, for the influence of *Portuguese explorers/colonisers* on laws of *indigenous people* in Brazil; See also, Harold J. Berman, *The Interaction of Law and Religion* (Nashville: Abingdon Press, 1974), where in "Introduction," he was of the view that revolutions in the context of western society presented a 'religious or quasi religious' view that had helped shaped a new legal system in these societies. He also presented a legal dimension of religion – (1) that is concerned with maintaining social order and (2) that is focused on tolerance, forgiveness and so forth.

[32] Refer to Chapter 8 for the influence of values of the *Ottoman Empire* in Turkey on laws; refer also to Chapter 9, on the influence of *Dutch colonisation* in Indonesia on laws; refer also to Chapters 5 & 6 on the impact of *British colonisation* on laws in India; refer also to Chapter 10, for the impact of *Portuguese and Spanish rulers* on law in Brazil; refer also to Chapter 4, on the influence of *Russian empires* that ruled Ukraine, *Magdeburg Law (German), Polish–Lithuanian laws, Cossack Hetmanate laws, Austrian-Hungarian laws* on laws in modern Ukraine.

[33] Refer to Chapter 5, where the impact of *Jainism* is discussed on modern laws in India; refer also to Chapter 6, where the impact of *Hinduism* is discussed on modern laws in India; refer also to Chapter 7, where the impact of *Judaism* is discussed on modern laws in Israel; refer also to Chapter 8, for the impact of *Islam* on laws in Turkey and the resultant importance of customary laws; refer

laws due to treaties,[35] or the impact of laws of indigenous peoples/ancient laws?[36] Do the imprints of an ancient value system in any society evaporate gradually or do they themselves evolve by assimilating newer influences and impacts over time? Are these new influences and impacts on law really in conflict with earlier laws, values, customs, norms and so forth?[37] All such issues are analysed in the selected jurisdictions in the book.

Evolving social structure over the centuries affects laws and norms within a society,[38] although it is a different matter that sometimes a promulgated law may also affect social structures in the very same society. For example, giving more rights to minorities and women by promulgated law may change social norms within those societies.[39] Similarly, in any jurisdiction, impactful historical events may have changed the norms within a society and as a result could have affected the evolution of the legal system and laws. For example:

---

also to the impact of *Islam* along with the ancient predominant religions of Hinduism and Buddhism in Indonesia in Chapter 9 on laws in Indonesia and the resultant importance of customary laws; refer also to Chapters 2, 4 & 10 regarding the influence of *Christianity* on laws in Russia, Ukraine and Brazil respectively.

[34] Refer to Chapter 10, the *influx of slaves and later years' immigrants from Portugal, Japan and other European countries* in Brazil on its laws; refer also to Chapter 2, the impact on the laws of Russia due to various cultures assimilated in the Soviet Union (predecessor of Russia); refer also to Chapter 8, on the reverse influence of cultures assimilated into the *Ottoman Empire*.

[35] Refer to Chapter 3, for the influence of *western, Japanese and civil laws from Germany and France* on the development of laws in China; refer also to Chapter 4, where a deliberate attempt to reconcile Ukrainian Law with *European Law and assimilate the principles of English law* in modern Ukrainian law is discussed in the context of the evolution of laws.

[36] Refer to Chapter 9 for the influence of the *customary laws of indigenous peoples* on laws in Indonesia, or Chapter 10 for the impact of the *laws of indigenous peoples* or ancient laws on laws in Brazil or Chapter 7 for the impact of *Torah Law*, written by Moses, on the laws of modern-day Israel.

[37] Refer Chapters 2-11 for further analysis on these aspects.

[38] Iris I. Varner & Katrin Varner, "The Relationship Between Culture and Legal Systems and the Impact on Intercultural Business Communication," *Global Advances in Business and Communication Conference and Journal* vol. 3 no. 1: 1-14, where it was said, *"... culture does not act in isolation. It is closely connected to law. Culture influences law, and law influences culture. For example, an egalitarian culture may establish laws that respect the rights of individuals and guarantee that these rights are not violated. By the same token, laws that enforce equal rights for men and women may foster a change in cultural values of the position of men and women in society."*

[39] Refer to footnote 16 of this Chapter, where examples of change in norms within societies have been discussed.

- the invasion of the Indian sub-continent by colonising invaders from the Middle East/Central Asia from 900 CE until it was colonised by Great Britain from Europe in 18th-19th century;

- the communist revolutions in Russia and China in the 20th century incorporating socialist, communist and Marxist ideologies;

- the colonisation of Indonesia by the Dutch around the 18th century;

- the subjugation of natives by the Dutch in Indonesia in the 16th century or the displacement of indigenous peoples in Brazil by explorers who later became invaders in the 16th century; and

- the rapid expansion (as compared to present day Turkey) of the Ottoman Empire in Europe and Asia in the 13th century CE, with the result that the Empire experienced reverse influences from these invaded lands that started to affect Ottoman laws. All such examples are analysed in subsequent chapters in the book.

Accordingly, in this book, the editor selected key jurisdictions around the globe. Thereafter, the aim was to try to find answers to the mystery of '*Imprints of History, Religion and Revolution on Law*' in these selected jurisdictions with the assistance of local expert lawyers/researchers/professors, who are the authors of subsequent chapters. These imprints have been analysed in particular in the context of their influence on – (1) the development of promulgated laws and (2) the application of written and unofficial law (influenced by these imprints) by judges in their courtrooms.

2 METHODOLOGIES OF STUDYING IMPRINTS IN THE EVOLUTION OF LAW IN VARIOUS JURISDICTIONS

2.1 IS THERE A NEED TO STUDY THE IMPRINTS OF HISTORY, RELIGION AND REVOLUTION ON LAWS IN VARIOUS JURISDICTIONS?

No lawyer or jurisprudent can say with certainty that there is a law that is common to all civilisations or all nations, and accordingly law cannot then be aptly called a *common law of mankind.*[40] If there is no one law that is common to all civilisations/jurisdictions in the world, the only way is to analyse the evolution of laws along with their application in other jurisdictions that have most influenced human history, or to study laws in the nations that have the greatest potential to change the course of human evolution in the near future.

Accordingly, the editor submits that through the intellectual exercise pursued in the book, both laymen and scholars alike can appreciate the analysis of the evolution of laws in various jurisdictions. Readers may also find evidence in the historical evolution of societies for events that are transpiring in the modern world and, as a result, possibly find solutions for future. After all, the world is a family.[41]

There are hardly any books that have analysed the evolution of law historically, taking into account the imprints of history, religions and revolutions on law within different jurisdictions in our world. In order to appreciate the inter-connectivity between the histories of selected jurisdictions, and solutions that are available in law within these jurisdictions for various problems, the editor of this book, with the assistance of various authors, has pursued an analysis of the evolution of law in these jurisdictions. The analysis of the evolution of law is pursued with regard to present configurations of the jurisdictions' laws, in respect of both substantive and procedural law.

---

[40] Lambert ideally wished for the law of humanity as *"droit, commun de l'humanite"* in "Conception Generale et Definition de la Science Due Droit Compare, Proces-Verbaux Des Seances et Documents, Congress International de Droit Compare I," *Congress International de Droit Compare I* (1905): 26.

[41] It is adopted from a Sanskrit phrase *'Vasudhaiva Kutumbakam'* found in Hindu jurisprudence and ancient texts such as the *Maha Upanishad*, when translated into English it means "the world is one family".

This book is also an attempt to bring together learned scholars & experts from different jurisdictions, using common research methodologies to carefully dissect the evolution of law and analyse the various influences on legal jurisprudence and laws over thousands of years.

Readers can then analyse and compare the process of evolution of laws in different jurisdictions, while considering the influences of history, religion, immigration, colonisation, slavery, external law and so forth. This exercise in itself is intended to further enrich the evolution of human society, as it advances the understanding of societies in a comparative context. The editor hopes that this intellectual exercise will assist readers in finding answers, or even help them define the problems facing their societies or the world in general.

2.2 SELECTION OF JURISDICTIONS

The editor has selected nine jurisdictions, based on percentage land area compared to the total area of the world (see *Table 1*), percentage of population as compared to the total population of the world (see *Table 2*), percentage of GDP (both nominal, Purchasing Power Parity ("PPP") terms in 2021, and future GDP in Purchasing Power Parity ("PPP") terms in 2050) of the world (see *Table 3*), and the prevalence of religions in these nine jurisdictions (see *Table 4*). The figures in these tables are just an estimate and compiled by analysing various sources, in particular, figures from various atlases, IMF and World Bank data. However, even though the figures are estimated, they do provide a broader overview regarding the relevance of the selected jurisdictions.

Jurisdictions were also selected on the basis of soft power and relevance to possible future discourse within humanity. The historical significance of these lands and their peoples was an important factor in the selection of these jurisdictions.

These nine jurisdictions are – (a) Russia (Chapter 2), (b) China (Chapter 3), (c) Ukraine (Chapter 4), (d) India (Chapters 5 & 6), (e) Israel (Chapter 7), (f) Turkey (Chapter 8), (g) Indonesia (Chapter 9), (h) Brazil (Chapter 10), and (i) Nigeria (Chapter 11). These are all non-western jurisdictions and a few statistical analyses for the selected jurisdictions that the readers will find startling are as follows:

♦ these selected jurisdictions together occupy approximately 28.65% of the world's land mass; and

♦ these selected jurisdictions together comprised approximately 48% of the world's population in 2020. This percentage is set to increase in a few decades; and

♦ these selected jurisdictions together comprise approximately 52.77% of GDP in Purchasing power parity terms ("PPP") terms (in 2021); and

♦ these selected jurisdictions combined are projected to have approximately 65-70% of world GDP (PPP terms) in 2050.[42] They are galloping as far as economic progress is concerned. In fact, reviewing the imprints of history, religion and revolutions in the period of rapid transition that is taking place in these jurisdictions is even more exciting to observe and analyse.[43]

♦ in all these jurisdictions, historically, GDP in PPP terms was very high, for example, Indian GDP (PPP) in the 17th century accounted for around 35% of world GDP and was at around this figure from the 1st century CE

---

[42] See, <https://www.pwc.com/gx/en/research-insights/economy/the-world-in-2050.html>, accessed 28 November 2021; See also, <https://www.theceomagazine.com/business/competition/pwc-world-2050>, where countries with the highest projected share of world GDP at PPPs by 2050 are – i) *China*, ii) *India*, iii) US, iv) *Indonesia*, v) *Brazil*, vi) *Russia*, vii) Mexico, viii) Japan, ix) Germany, x) UK. The editor has selected 5 of these jurisdictions in this book.

[43] While reading chapters, readers will note that economic progress and trade are responsible for much evolution of law in history and this factor cannot be ignored.

onwards. Similarly, China's GDP (PPP) was hovering at around 29% of world GDP, being at its highest around 1820 CE.

By comparison, the Roman Empire's highest GDP (PPP) was around 24% in 14 CE, and that reduced to around 7% in 1000 CE. Similarly, other selected jurisdictions such as Russia also had glorious economic achievements, and that should not be ignored by the global population.[44]

♦ In fact, carefully observed, the recent economic progress in the selected jurisdictions is not new, they are merely reverting to the previous state of affairs that existed before colonisation and the industrial revolution.

♦ By 2050, the countries with the highest projected share of world GDP by PPPs are – i) *China*, ii) *India*, iii) US, iv) *Indonesia*, v) *Brazil*, vi) *Russia*, vii) Mexico, viii) Japan, ix) Germany, x) UK. The editor has selected 5 of these jurisdictions in this book.[45] The two other selected jurisdictions in this book, *Nigeria* and *Turkey* will see rapid economic expansion also.

♦ in all these selected jurisdictions, many religions are practised.

The selected jurisdictions also have colourful histories in the form of many tumultuous events that took place over thousands of years, significant immigration & emigration, invasions & colonisation that have shaped the destiny of the peoples living in them. The populations in these jurisdictions follow many religions (*see Table 4*). As a result, an imprint of religious jurisprudences can be readily observed in these jurisdictions' laws and/or practice of laws.

---

[44] Angus Maddison, *HS-8: The World Economy 1-2001 AD* (Oxford: OUP, Illustrated edition, 20 Sept. 2007); See also, <HS-8_2003.pdf (theatlantic.com)>, accessed on 10 December 2021; See also, <https://en.wikipedia.org/wiki/List_of_regions_by_past_GDP_(PPP)#Indian_empires_(1%E2%80%9931947_CE)>, accessed on 11 December, 2021; See also, http://www.ggdc.net/maddison/maddison.htm, accessed on 11 December, 2021.
[45] See, <https://www.theceomagazine.com/business/competition/pwc-world-2050>, accessed on 13 December 2021.

S. No.	Country	Area Km² (approximately)	% of Overall Area in world
1	Russia	17,098,242	11.50%
2	China	9,596,960	6.40%
3	Ukraine	603,500	0.40%
4	India	3,287,263	2.20%
5	Israel	20,770	0.01%
6	Indonesia	1,904,569	1.30%
7	Turkey	783,562	0.52%
8	Brazil	8,515,770	5.70%
9	Nigeria	923,768	0.62%
TOTAL			**28.65%**

Table 1: <u>Land Area of the selected jurisdictions</u>[46]

S. No.	Country	Population (estimated 2020 and approx.)	% of Overall Population in world (approx.)
1	Russia	146,171,015	1.85%
2	China	1,411,778,724	17.80%
3	Ukraine	41,319,838	0.52%
4	India	1,385,779,401	17.50%
5	Israel	9,446,780	0.12%
6	Indonesia	271,350,000	3.43%
7	Turkey	83,614,362	1.06%
8	Brazil	214,103,664	2.70%
9	Nigeria	211,401,000	2.67%
TOTAL			**47.65%**

Table 2: <u>Population of the selected jurisdictions</u>[47]

---

[46] The figures are estimated after examining many sources. The main purpose was to get approximate percentage areas in the world.

S. N o.	Country	GDP (nominal) (US million) (est. 2021) (approx.)	% of Overall GDP of world (approx.)	GDP (PPP) (US million) (est. 2021) (approx.)	% of Overall GDP in PPP terms (appro x.)	GDP (PPP Terms) world rank in 2016	GDP (in PPP terms) world Rank in 2050[48]
1	Russia	1,710,734	1.74%	4,328,122	4.32%	6	6
2	China	16,642,318	17.80%	26,656,766	26.65%	1	1
3	Ukraine	164,593	0.18%	576,106	0.58%		Not available
4	India	3,049,704	3.10%	10,181,166	10.18%	3	2
5	Israel	446,708	0.45%	399,488	0.39%		Not available
6	Indonesia	1,158,783	1.21%	3,507,239	3.50%	8	4
7	Turkey	794,530	0.84%	2,749,570	2.72%	14	11
8	Brazil	1,491,772	1.73%	3,328,459	3.32%	7	5
9	Nigeria	514,049	0.51%	1,116,255	1.11%	22	14
TOTAL			27.55%		52.77%		(around 65-70% of the world's GDP in PPP terms)

Table 3: <u>Nominal GDP & GDP (PPP) of the selected jurisdictions</u>

---

[47] The figures are estimated after reviewing many sources. The main purpose was to get approximate percentage population in the global population. See also, <https://www.pwc.com/gx/en/research-insights/economy/the-world-in-2050.html>, accessed 28 November 2021.

[48] See, <https://www.theceomagazine.com/business/competition/pwc-world-2050>, accessed on 13 December 2021.

S. No.	Country	Religion[49]
1	Russia	**Russian Orthodox**, Islam, Protestant ,Catholicism
2	China	**State atheism**, Buddhism, Confucianism, Daoism, Islam, Catholicism
3	Ukraine	**Orthodox Christianity**, Protestant, Catholicism, Islam, Judaism, Hinduism, Buddhism
4	India	**Hinduism, Jainism**, Islam, Catholicism, Protestant, Sikhism, Judaism, Syrian Christians
5	Israel	**Judaism**, Islam, Christianity
6	Indonesia	**Islam, Hinduism**, Buddhism, Catholicism
7	Turkey	**Sunni Islam**, Shia Islam, Christianity, Judaism, Tengrism, Yazidism
8	Brazil	**Catholicism**, Protestant, Evangelical, Spiritualism, Umbanda, Candomblé
9	Nigeria	**Christianity, Islam**, Indigenous beliefs

Table 4: <u>Religions in the selected jurisdictions</u>

2.3 METHODOLOGY ADOPTED IN THE BOOK

The editor aims to provide a detailed methodology for other researchers to work on similar projects. For the purposes of this book, important jurisdictions from around the globe were selected, as discussed in preceding §2.1 and key points in history were noted for these jurisdictions. Thereafter, the next step was to identify learned scholars and experts from these jurisdictions, who were willing to think from a particular perspective - that is, as per the theme of this book. This was the most important and difficult step, to convince these scholars/experts to provide expertise about their own jurisdictions from a specific perspective. Although the

---

[49] The religions in bold are the most prevalent religion within that jurisdiction.

editor of this book has researched the history and evolution of law in these selected jurisdictions, nevertheless this knowledge pales in comparison to the invited scholars'/experts' knowledge in the context of the local and specialised knowledge that these contributors possess about their home jurisdictions.

In addition, there was a need for these scholars/experts to research issues from a specific perspective; in particular to analyse the evolution of law in their jurisdictions taking into account history, religions, revolutions etc., and how these elements connect with current law in that jurisdiction. The connections between history, religion, revolutions and current law, and how law has evolved are the central subject matters of this book. The editor maintained regular communication with these experts/scholars, and accordingly answered queries or clarified the perspectives for research they needed to pursue in order to write chapters regarding their home jurisdictions. At times, the editor was audacious enough to present some historical facts regarding their jurisdictions to a few of these scholars/experts, to help them think from a particular perspective, or provide further food for thought in their research.

In order for readers to carry out a comparison of the process of evolution of law in multiple jurisdictions, it was important that the editor received input in a similar structure from all contributors. Where this was not feasible, the format was subsequently adjusted by the editor with the permission and approval of scholars/experts who wrote the chapters 2-11. It must be emphasised that the majority of content in the subsequent chapters is as received from the learned scholars/experts, although the editor at times suggested some amendments to content and structure, or motivated the scholars/experts to pursue further research in a particular area in some jurisdictions.

In a few of the chapters, due to the editor's own expertise, slightly more involvement in filtering or developing content was undertaken by the editor. However, this exercise was carried out with the utmost respect to the individual authors of chapters 2-11, keeping in mind cultural sensitivity or local nuances that the editor himself might miss or be unable to appreciate. However, in the end, all amendments or changes in structure/contents were approved by the learned scholars/experts. In the editor's view, this step was sheer hard work and readers should appreciate that there were no short cuts. However, it was an intellectual exercise and definitely tested the editor's soft skills.

The editor was involved from the beginning answering queries from scholars/experts, and later clarifying chapter structure to them. The editor submits that he was heavily enriched in this intellectual journey. In the editor's view, this journey proved to be very sweet, and in fact, the final product, that is the book, is just the icing on the cake. In every intellectual discussion, the learned scholars/experts influenced the editor's thinking as well, and that was subsequently indirectly transmitted to the authors of other chapters during further discussion on their own research. So, such collaborative research is an amazing exercise, and the resultant benefits are multiplied by the number of experts/scholars involved in the project.

The purpose of the book is to provide positive value to humanity, and the editor feels that this purpose is already achieved through the intellectual process itself, as so many researchers from different countries have been involved in the project. For the editor or any researcher, it can be an enriching experience, and the process could have practical value for human society and for researchers pursuing projects in comparative law or for experts involved in collaborative projects.[50]

---

[50] Konrad Zweigert, Hein Kotz, and Tony Weir, trans., *An Introduction to Comparative Law: Volume I: The Framework*, 2nd Revised ed. (Oxford: Clarendon Press, 1987), 53, where they described the main purpose of Comparative law as, "...*practical, namely reform and improvement of the law* [emphasis added] *at home, rather than theoretical, philosophical, or speculative; but a part was played also by natural curiosity about other peoples' law and by the impartial feeling that perhaps those others had something to offer - a contrast with the haughty concentration of legal scholars on their own newly codified systems.*"

In their own jurisdictions, most of these scholars/experts pursue their day-to-day work in their native languages; therefore, it was essential to ensure that communication between the editor and scholars always remained crystal clear. A huge effort was put in to ensure that nothing could be lost in such communications, and there was a need for the editor to be precise as to what scholars/experts were stating in their write-ups. In many cases, after obtaining the scholar's approval, clarification of the written material was provided by the editor to maintain consistency in the book.

However, there was always an ongoing fear in the mind of the editor of the possibility of an error in his understanding,[51] and this fear lasted until approval was received from the scholars/experts for even minor proposed changes to a draft. Furthermore, there was always another lingering fear that the editor would inadvertently offend scholars/experts when seeking clarification, as can easily happen due to an ignorance of understanding history or merely cultural sensitivity. This stage of the project was important, difficult, and undoubtedly the most delicate step for such a collaborative project.

The final stage of the project incorporated many iterations of proof reading/copy editing to maintain consistency throughout all chapters, in particular, consistency in citations and bibliography. As the very last phase of this final stage, the editor

---

[51] Janet E. Ainsworth, "Categories and Culture: On the 'Rectification of Names' in Comparative Law," *Cornell L. Rev.* 82, no. 1 (1996): 19–42, <http://scholarship.law.cornell.edu/clr/vol82/iss1/3>. Understanding needs to be based on the *sub-context* behind the law, and ensure that factors such as culture, language, socio-cultural contexts are clearly understood by the author as conveyed by the scholars. Also, it was important that editor should not be limited by lack of his own knowledge having studied in his own jurisdiction only; See also, V.V. Palmer, "From Lerotholi to Lando: Some Examples of Comparative Law Methodology," *Global Jurist Frontiers* 4, no. 2 (2004): 1-29, 15, where he cited Gordley; *See also*, James Gordley, "Comparative Legal Research: Its Function in the Development of Harmonized Law," *Am. J. Comp. L.* 43, no. 4 (1995): 555–68, where he stressed that scholars should free themselves from *'limitations and distortions of their legal culture'*; See also, Janet E. Ainsworth, "Categories and Culture: On the 'Rectification of Names' in Comparative Law," *Cornell L. Rev.* 82, no. 1 (1996): 19–42, 17, n 53, where Ainsworth, "the very concepts and categories with which the scholar organizes this purportedly universal legal framework are freighted with culturally contingent normative baggage."; See also, V.V. Palmer, "From Lerotholi to Lando: Some Examples of Comparative Law Methodology," *Global Jurist Frontiers* 4, no. 2 (2004): 1-29, 7, where it was clarified that every important element of law or doctrine must be looked at through the prism of culture in detail to capture *'its essence as a unique manifestation of the community.'*

also requested an experienced third party, not involved in content of the project, to carefully review the chapters as an objective reader and obtained advice regarding inconsistencies in formatting and language, along with other relevant advice. This last phase was important, as there had been numerous drafts and re-drafts between the editor and authors of the chapters, as most authors are non-native speakers. It also helped avoid any slip ups with regard to consistency of language and format used in the book and the possibility of inadvertent errors that could have been missed by the editor.

The above steps were carefully followed, in order that readers would be able to pursue the comparison of the evolution of law in the selected jurisdictions with ease. The editor submits that any attempt by him to leapfrog the above-mentioned steps would have invited disaster for any researcher. It is important to highlight that this study could only be accomplished when the focus on input from scholars/experts was not based on perception, bias or perspective from the editor's own jurisdiction.[52] Rather, it came from the experts'/ scholars' own views on the evolution of law and the richness of different kinds of philosophies - in particular, the influence of history, religion and revolution on the development of law in their jurisdictions. From the process, it is hoped that scholars and readers will be enriched after reviewing the analyses and conclusions obtained by this research, along with studying timelines prepared for the various jurisdictions.

2.4 TIMELINES IN VARIOUS JURISDICTIONS

Even though detailed analysis of the imprints of history, religion and revolution on laws is carried out in chapters 2-11, nevertheless, the editor has endeavoured to give a detailed snapshot in **Tables 5-14**. The editor alone prepared these Tables and takes full responsibility for the content.

---

[52] Konrad Zweigert, Hein Kotz, and Tony Weir, trans., *An Introduction to Comparative Law: Volume I: The Framework*, 2nd Revised ed. (Oxford: Clarendon Press, 1987), 4, where they mentioned that *"legal studies only become scientific when they rise above the actual rules of any national system, as it happens in legal philosophy, legal history, the sociology of law, and comparative law."*

The editor has included some additional historical context in these tables to provide a relevant backdrop to history, legal history and important personalities in order to deliver more value to readers. These tables should be useful when reading subsequent chapters. In addition, this background will provide the necessary framework to analyse the evolution of law in various selected jurisdictions.

The tables will also provide a snapshot to readers of key important events in the evolution of the human race.The editor has attempted to go as far back in the historical evolution of laws as possible in the selected jurisdictions, with the assistance of local scholars/experts.

In many cases, the evolution of law has been discussed from many thousands of years ago [many *years BCE*]. For example, if the content says something happened in the year 2000 BCE, and we are analysing the issues in the year 2022, then those readers who are not well-versed as to how chronology is used in history, should appreciate that the discussion is about an event in chronology (2000 + 2022 = 4022), that is, that event happened 4022 years ago.

Table 5: Timeline for the Evolution of Law in Russia (Chapter 2)

200 BCE-1000 CE	1000-1200 CE	1200-1800 CE	1800-1917 CE	1917- Present
Migration and Ancient 'Rus'	**Christian jurisprudence**	**Dramatic turn of events in history**	**Expansion, Tsar's absolute power, Revolution**	**Bolshevik Revolution, Soviet Union and its break up in 1991**
Migration of Slavic tribes. 0900 CE, formation of Ancient 'Rus'. Focus on *customs* of *the Rus'*, even mentioned in treaty with the Byzantine Empire in the early 10th century CE. Focus on *community* ('*obschina'*) in laws and concepts such as community responsibility or guilt '*krugovaya poruka'*.	Official recognition of Russian Orthodox Church and arrival of Greek and Byzantine monks. Influence of *Roman Law/Cannon Law.* In the 10th-11th century CE, the first *Statutes of Clerical Courts* bring about judicial procedure. Late 11th century, *Rus justice*, with secular principles.	Powers of '*vetche'*, the power of community meetings decreased. Rus justice further evolved. 13th and 14th century CE, *Legal Codes of Novgorod and Pskov* were adopted. 14th century CE, various Russian principalities conquered by Genghis Khan's clans and *Islamic jurisprudence* was brought into Russia. Polish and Lithuanian influence in the vacuum brought about further *Christian jurisprudence.* 15th century, gained independence and victory of *Grand Duchy of Moscow. 1497 and 1550 CE,* large-scale codifications. Ivan the Great multiplied Russian territories by 1505 CE. *Time of Troubles (a.k.a. 'Smutnoe vremya')* in the 17th century and Russian ended victors.	Victory of Russia over Sweden and empire grew at an astronomical pace. Tsar Peter I became the first Emperor of the Russian Empire in 1721. Official Emancipation of serfs in second half of 19th century, and influence of German law was enhanced in Empire's laws. *Imperial absolutism* along with aristocracy increased in Russian empire. Court system evolved that distinguished people by their social class and estates. It ended with the *First Russian Constitution 1906.* In 1917, the Russian Empire fell after the *Communist Revolution* combined with effects of World War 1 and loss to Japan in Far East, and was replaced by the Soviet Union. Civil War broke out in 1917 and set the stage for next revolution.	*Bolshevik Revolution* until 1923. Large scale casualties and emigration. Jurisprudence of *Marxism and Lenin's socialism* introduced in laws. All previous laws abolished. World War II and attack by Nazi Germany. Russia came out victorious and liberated China. *Gorbachev's perestroika 1991* caused the break-up of Soviet Union. Russia takes over the responsibility of previous Soviet Union. *Constitution 1993, as amended in 2020* acknowledges an uninterrupted existence and legal continuity of the Russian statehood for thousands of years. *Russian ethnos* is officially acknowledged as the 'ethnos constituting the State'. *Jus gentium* and international treaties made over centuries contributed to current jurisprudence and law.

Table 6: Timeline for Evolution of Civil Law Code in China (Chapter 3)

2100 BCE-1644 CE	1644 -1911 CE	1912-1949 CE	1949-2021 CE	2021- Present
Ancient phase	**Qin Dynasty**	**Republic of China**	**Communist & Cultural Revolution**	**Civil Code 2021**
2100 BCE some form of legal system took shape in ancient China. Western Zhou Dynasty was from 1046-771 BCE, where further development of legal system took place. BCE 400, Zhanguo Period, Li Kui's "Fa Jing," however, focus only on criminal law. Tang Dynasty (681-981 CE) Yonghui Law, the code of the Song Dynasty (960-1279 CE) Song Xingtong, and the code of the Ming Dynasty (1368-1644 CE) Daming Law all embodied the criminal legal system whereas a portion of the civil legal system was mixed together with criminal law in one. Role of etiquettes as part of legal code and use of morals to provide legitimacy to dynasties. Accompanied by concepts of *Ling, Geshi, Li,* and *Shu.*	Influence from *western jurisprudence* and pressures in the late 19th century after the opium war of 1840 was seen in laws of China. Trade with European powers also created a need for modern laws. Scholars started to bring in *western and Japanese legal concepts* in 1904 in an attempt to modernize and thwart foreign pressure. *1911, the "Draft Civil Code of the Qing,"* the first Civil Code of China in thousands of years of history. Western concepts plus feudal concepts were married in this Code. Civil Code was not implemented due to fall of last imperial Qing dynasty.	1912, First Republic in history of China. Beiyang Government of the Republic of China from 1913 to 1928. Draft Civil Code 1925 was attempted. Nanjing Government of the Republic of China from 1928 to 1949. *Civil Law of the Republic of China 1931* influenced by *German Civil Code 1896.* First law was planned to be implemented in China.	All laws were abolished after ***Communist Revolution in 1949.*** Influence of *Soviet laws* began. Individual laws promulgated that were influenced by Soviet laws. Influx of *communist, socialist and Marxist jurisprudence* on laws. Adopted *Civil Law System.* 1956-1976, **Great Leap Forward** and *Cultural* **Revolution.** It led to very high economic distress and deaths. The development of *The Draft Civil Code 1956* was interrupted. Influence of *Soviet Russian Civil Code 1922 on laws. The Second Draft Civil Law 1964* was also not implemented. *General Principles of Civil Law 1987* and many separate laws were enacted.	China achieved unprecedented prosperity due to reforms including in the legal system and laws after joining **WTO** in 2001. Substantial legal reforms from 2001 and still ongoing. 2021 - First *Civil code* in history of China implemented with future in mind for Chinese society.

Table 7: Timeline for Evolution of Laws in Ukraine (Chapter 4)

800 CE-1200 CE	1200-1600 CE	1600-1800 CE	1800-1990 CE	1990-Present
Ancient Phase	**Impact of Lithuanian, Magdeburg and Christian Jurisprudence**	**Independence and Rapid Legal Development**	**External Influences on law after Invasions**	**Independence and Influence of English law**
Agreement *Kievan Rus* and Byzantium dated 907 CE, 911 CE, 944 CE and 971 CE are considered to be one of the first written sources of law. Role of *Rus' Jusitice* 1072 in legal development in the region. *Rus' Justice* Code was supplemented by *Princes' Statutes*, as well as statutes from the Church, following *Christian jurisprudence* in 11th and 12th centuries.	14th-16th century Impact of Grand Duchy of Lithuania (namely the Statutes of Lithuania. Impact of *Statutes of Lithuania* (1529, 1566 and 1588), especially the 1588 Statute on individual's rights. Infusion of *Christian jurisprudence*. 13th-18th century, Impact of *Magdeburg Law* from Germany in particular on commercial laws.	The *Cossack Hetmanate* (the Zaporizhian Host) (16th-18th century CE) was founded, after **independence** from Poland. It created its own jurisprudence. In 1649 CE, the *Treaty of Zboriv* that granted autonomy and *Treaty of Korsun* with Sweden in 1657 CE. These had a major impact on legal development. 1710 CE, the Constitution of *Pylyp Orlyk* that clearly laid down rules for separation of power within the governance of land.	Ukrainian territory came under the *Russian Empire, the Austria-Hungarian Empire, Poland, Czechoslovakia* and so forth and accordingly influenced by External Laws. As part of *Soviet Union* for 70 years, influence of *socialism on laws.*	*Declaration of State Sovereignty of Ukraine* dated 16 July 1990 and the Act of *Declaration of Independence* of Ukraine dated 24 August 1991. The *Affiliation of Ukraine to the Council of Europe* on 9 November 1995. EU laws began to influence Ukrainian laws. *Constitution of Ukraine* in 1996. The *Ratification of the European Convention on Human Rights* on 17 July 1997. Attempt to bring common law principles of *English Law* into Ukrainian law.

Table 8: Timeline for Impact of Jainism on Evolution of Laws in Bharat (India) (Chapter 5)

>5000 BCE-500 BCE	500 BCE-152 BCE	152 BCE-1200 CE	1200 CE-1955	1955-Present
Origin of Jain Jurisprudence	**Significant Jain Rulers in India**	**Jain Kingdoms applying Jain law**	**Influence of Jainism on Independence**	**Jain law subsumed in Hindu law**
>5000 BCE in the current human cycle, **Rishabdev** was the First Trithankara of Jainism. 599-527 BCE, last Trithankara of Jainism, **Mahavira**. **Main Principles of Jain Jurisprudence & Law:** • Time is eternal and begininglesss. • *Ahimsa* (**Non-violence**) • *Satya* (Truth) • *Achorya* (Non-stealing) • *Bramhacharya* (Celibacy) • *Aparigrapha* (Non-possessivenes-s) • *Anekantvada* (Multiplicity of views) • Attaining	Around 500 BCE–King Chetaka of Vaisali spread the tenants of non-violence and Jainism. 543 BCE-491 BCE, King Srenika (known as Bimbasara) and his descendants of powerful Kingdom of Magadh. 321 BCE-298 BCE, *Emperor Chandragupta Maurya* became a Jain monk. He is famous for completely removing Greek remnants from the periphery of Bharat (old name of India) and uniting various parts of Bharat under the tutelage of Jain teacher and strategist **Chanakya**. 273-232 BCE, **Emperor Ashoka**, grandson of Chandragupta Maurya whose symbols are currently adopted in the current	350-550 CE, Ganga Dynasty in South India. 550-625 CE, Kalacuri dynasty around present day Nagpur. 650-950 CE, King Sivakoti of Kanchi. 746-780 CE, Vanaraja Chavada and King Chalukya of present day Gujarat. 749-753 CE, King Ama of Gwalior. 800-878 CE, Rastrakuta Dynasty and Amoghhavarsa. 940-989 CE, Chamundraya, chief minister of powerful province of present day Karnataka province	Wide-spread destruction of culture and extreme violence against adherents of Jainism from (1150-1800 CE) by invaders from Turkey/Central Asia/Middle East. The nation state of India was established in 1947 after nearly 850 years of remaining as a **colony** of Central Asian Republics/Islam ic Empires (hence ruled by *Islamic jurisprudence*) and British (hence ruled by western and *Christian jurisprudence* from 1800 CE). **Mahatma Gandhi** was influenced by a Jain scholar Raychandbhai who influenced	*Jain law* subsumed within *Hindu Law* after Independence of India. Foreign policy of India largely influenced by the principle of Jainism and India became a founding member of **Non-aligned movement** advocating freedom of countries in Asia and Africa from extreme colonisation in spite of suffering apathy in its own economic development from rich countries as a result of supporting non-aligned movement. Domestic Laws were accordingly affected by such principles. Principles of the foundations of India were based on non-violence and Mahatma

moksha, that is ultimate knowledge. • *No belief in God*, but a believer in great individuals who attained Moksha (ultimate knowledge).	Indian constitution, although adopted Buddhism but was influenced by Jainism principles of non-violence. He spread Buddhism, a relatively new philosophy/religion as compared to Jainism to China/Far East/Sri Lanka. Buddhism again is based on principles of non-violence. 232 BCE-152 BCE, Emperors such as Sampranti of Magadha and Kharvela of Kalinga, in present-day province of Orissa.	oversaw the construction of renowned statue of Bahubali. 1116-1343 CE, Hoyasala dynasty in the present day Karnatka province. 1092-1142 CE, Siddharaja Jayasimha, who motivated a Jain scholar Hemachadra. 1142-1173 CE, King Kumarapala of present day Gujarat.	him on principles of **non-violence.** Case *Gateppa v. Eramma 1927 and others* reported in AIR 19, Madras 228, identified Jainism as an ancient religion. Case *Hirachand Gangji v. Rowji Sojpal* reported in AIR 1939 Bombay 377, identified it as a religion before Brahminism in India. *Harijan Temple Entry Act, 1947* (C.A. 91 of 1951), Jainism as distinct from Hinduism. *Madras v. Sri Lakshmindra Thirtha Swamiar of Sri Shirur Mutt* reported in AIR 1954 SC 282, Jainism was a separate faith, and customs should be taken into account.	Gandhi was proclaimed as Father of Nation. Peace. Harmony, non-interference in other states remains the bedrock of principles of Indian foreign policy and laws and is influenced by the ***jurisprudence of Jainism***. *Appeal (Civil) 4730 of 1999 - Bal Patil & Anr v. Union of India & Ors*, Date Of Judgment: 08/08/2005, Jainism and its customs are part of Hinduism ethos. Attempts by Jain scholars for *Jainification of Indian Laws & Jurisprudence* by incorporating principles of Jainism such as *Ahimsa, Aparigraha, and Anekant* in legal jurisprudence. Principles of non-violence from India/Jainism impacted great leaders like **Martin Luther King** (US), **Nelson Mandela** (South Africa).

Table 9: <u>Timeline for Impact of Hinduism (Sanatan Dharma) on Evolution of Laws in Bharat/Aryavrat (India) (Chapter 6)</u>

>5000 BCE-1500 BCE	1500 BCE-200	300 CE-1200 CE	1200 CE-1950	1950-Present
Sources of Hindu Jurisprudence	Hindu Rulers	Hindu Rulers applying Hindu	Colonisation/Slavery/Violence/Upheaval	Post-Independence and new name of Bharat
Sources of Hindu (actually called 'Sanatana Dharma' and Hindu name was given by invaders) ***Jurisprudence:*** *Vedas, Smritis, Upnishads and Arthasastra, Shrimad Bhagwad Gita and commentaries over millennia.* *Originator –* ***Manu,*** during each cycle of human life. Each cycle lasts 306,720,000 years. **Naturally secular in character as there is no concept of attaining salvation through one route or one God** *and based on principles of Dharma (Natural Justice).* Accordingly all religions are accepted naturally. *Multiple views are encouraged including criticism.* It means righteousness, duty and law. **Law and religion cannot be**	*A few exampl es (dates are approx imate)* Pundhr avan Empire (1280 – 300 BCE). Kuru Empire (1200 - 525 BCE). Anga Empire (100 - 500 BCE). Chola Dynast y (300 BCE- 1200 CE). Maham eghava hana Dynast y (100BC E- 400 CE).	*A few examples (dates are approximat e)* Gupta dynasty (240-550 CE). Chera Dynasty (300 BCE-1345CE). Pandyan Empire (300 BCE- 1345 CE). Kingdom of Champa (192- 1832 CE). ***Foreign Hindu empires'*** *influence on* ***Hindu Jurispruden ce:*** - Malla Dynasty in present day Nepal (1200-1768 CE). - Sriviya Empire ruling	<u>Time of great upheaval,</u> foreign invasions, mass conversions by forcing people to accept religions other than (Hinduism/Sikhism/Jainism /Buddhism), subjugation of population by brutal violence, colonisation in territories from present day Afghanistan to Myanmar **from 1200 CE onwards until 1947.** GDP shrank from 30% of world's GDP in 1800s to less than 3% of world's GDP in 1947 (at independence) due to British Colonisation causing widespread poverty and suffering. ***In just 150 years! Indian sub-continent became a poster child for poverty and suffering*** after consistently being called a Golden bird due to highest GDP in the world over 2000 years. With less commerce, developments of laws were affected. It resulted in the influence of foreign laws and jurisprudence with attempts made by colonial powers to completely wipe out traditional jurisprudence spanning	*1947 Independence of Bharat after 850 years of colonialism from Islamic Empires & British Empire. It adopted a new name given by colonial power for the sake of continuity.* 1947 Indian sub-continent was divided based on religions into two parts – India and Pakistan. Pakistan was divided later into Pakistan and Bangladesh in 1971 on ethnic grounds. *1950 First Constitution of India.* - Concept of duty from Hindu jurisprudence is reflected in concept of Fundamental rights. - Secular by character due to Hindu jurisprudence, but still 'secular' word added by constitutional amendment to mollify doubters. Hindu Jurisprudence continues to

distinguished. *'Vasudhaiva Kutumbakam'* (***'world is a family'***) *concept.* *Dharmasastra or* holy principles based on 'righteousness'. Kings and Emperors were never above Dharma. >5000 BCE Vedic Civilisation with emphasis on Hindu Jurisprudence based on Sanatana Dharma. *Indus Saraswati* civilization before 5000 BCE and its decline due to the lost Saraswati river. Later *Indus Valley Civilisation / Harappan Civilisation* from 2300 BCE, though it is argued, these were parts of ancient Indus-Saraswati civilisation. <u>The debates on theories on Indian civilsation are controversial.</u> >500 BCE Suryavamsha and Chandravamsha Dynasties still existing from ancient ages, Epic Ramayana highlighting epic that happened >5000 BCE written for masses.	Gandhara Kingdom 800 - 535 BCE. Surasena Kingdom 700-300 BCE. Paurva Dynasty (400-301 BCE). Mauryan (322-184 BCE). Satvayahn (100 BCE-200 CE). Hindu Jurisprudence evolved from interaction and implementation of Dharma in all these kingdoms without having any central authority except literature/scriptures.	in present day Indonesia (650- 1377 CE). - Shailendra Dynasty in present day Indonesia 650-1025 CE. Bali Kingdom (900-1900 CE) in present day Indonesia. - Haripunjaya Kingdom in present day Thailand (750-1250 CE). - Khmer Empire present day in Myanmar, Laos, Cambodia, Vietnam (802-1431 CE). **Hindu Juris.** evolved from interaction and implementation of *Dharma* in all these kingdoms without having any central authority and approving multiple views as a common thread.	thousands of years. The nation state of India was established ***in 1947*** after nearly 850 years of remaining as a **colony** of Central Asian Republics/Islamic Empires (hence ruled by *Islamic jurisprudence*) and British (hence ruled by *western and Christian jurisprudence* from 1800 CE). The name given to Bharat as 'India' by colonial power **adopted** by post-independence regime following socialist principles. *Common* Law concepts from England influenced the legal system from 1857 onwards. Wide spread destruction of culture and extreme violence against adherents of Hinduism from (1150-1800 CE). Resistance to Foreign invaders and attempt to salvage local pride continued by following Hindu empires applying Hindu Laws and Jurisprudence – - Great Maratha empire under ***Shivaji Maharaj*** from (1674-1818 CE); - Sikh Empire – (1700-1849 CE). . Renaissance of Hindu Jurisprudence commenced after 800 years of extreme colonisation and violence, approximate date is around 1880CE.	influence laws in India through customary law, family laws and so forth. However, courts can modify the principles of Hindu Jurisprudence, if required. Adopted common law principles, in particular, of case precedents in the legal system. ***2014*** – A new non-socialist government with full majority after 1947 *promising revival of ancient Hindu Jurisprudence,* that is naturally secular and its implementation has commenced in full swing with a revival of respect for ancient customs and laws. It is naturally secular. This revival exercise is carried out taking into account: ***colonisation and subjugation by extreme violence*** of Indian sub-continent from 1000 CE. It is accompanied by accepting influence of external laws for reviving economy and restoring trading with other countries with appropriate commercial laws to retrieve lost economic space due to colonisation.

Table 10: Timeline for Evolution of Laws in Israel (Chapter 7)

2000 BCE-1000 BCE	1000 BCE-600 BCE	600 BCE-60 BCE	60 BCE-1948	1948-Present
Ancient Phase	**King David & the Influence of Babylonia**	**Exile of Jewish People**	**Third period of Colonial Phase**	**Post-Independence**
2000 BCE, **Abraham** founded principles for Jewish people. Beginning of jurisprudence of *Judaism*. Subjugation of Jewish people by Egyptians and migration back to Jewish lands. 1450 BCE, Moses wrote *Torah Law*, a critical source of jurisprudence and led the people to ancestral lands.	King **David** started his rule in the land of Jewish people around 1000 BCE. 586 BCE, First Jewish temple in Jerusalem. 600 BCE, Jewish land is captured by Babylonia and Jewish people exiled from their ancestral lands.	470 BCE, Persian ruler allowed Jewish people to return to their ancestral lands. 60 BCE, Romans deported Jewish people from their land. Jewish people moved to different lands around the world.	Persecution of Jews in Europe, in particular, in Spain in 1492, Russia in 1880 and **Holocaust** of Jews by Nazi Germany in early 1940s in Europe. 1897, First Zionist Congress. *Balfour Declaration* of the 2nd November, 1917 confirming the right of Jewish People to have their own land.	Israel *Declaration of Independence 1948*. Fine balance between *Jewish philosophy and jurisprudence and secularism* and other rights of groups. **2018** – *13th Basic law: Israel as the Nation State of the Jewish People*. Supreme Court decision *HCJ 5555/18* on petitions on *Basic Law 2018* confirms the influence of Judaism, history of Jewish nation without diluting rights of minorities, women and equality of race, religions and so forth. Law affected by history, external influences due to experiences over the centuries.

Table 11: Timeline for Evolution of Laws in Turkey (Chapter 8)

220 BCE-900 CE	900 CE-1838 CE	1839 CE-1920 CE	1920-2002	2002- Present
Ancient Phase	**Influence of Islam & Ottoman Empire (Classical Period)**	**Ottoman Empire (Tanzimat Era)**	**World War I and Modern Turkey**	**Impact of AKP Party's Jurisprudence**
220 BCE, Turk Empire founded and laws in various states obtain legitimacy, for example, from the authority of *Tanrikurt*. 800 CE *Göktürk* Inscriptions with various laws. Laws based on *traditions and customs –Töre*.	Adoption of law followed by adoption of *Islamic Law & Jurisprudence*. Islamic law adopted customs considered as *kanunname* tradition. **Ottoman Empire** established in 1299 CE and Sultans' edicts plus customary law *Örfi hukuk* (however within limits of Islamic Law). Role of *customary rules* decreased from 1700 CE.	1839-1876 *Gulhane Restrict-* modernised Turkey, reduced external pressure and revived trade with European powers. It was a proto-constitutional document. Influence of *western jurisprudence* on laws. *Kanun-i - Esasi 1876* introduced concept of separation of powers. Drafting of many new Codes during this era. Prepared Turkish society for modern reforms and rule of law. *Mecelle 1876*, the first civil code of Islamic world.	*First World War, Armistice of Mudros 1918* and the *Treaty of Sevres 1920*. Ottoman Empire ended. The *Constitution of 1921*. *Judicature Reform Act 1924*, judicial reforms, and abolition of the religious courts. **Secularisation of laws** to make a modern Turkey. Great influence towards this objective from founding leader **Mustafa Kemal Atatürk**. Military coups in 1961 and 1980. *Constitution 1982*. EU harmonisation process commenced in 1982. Influence of *EU laws* on Turkish Law.	AKP Party in power. Harmonisation of law with EU continued in hope to achieve EU membership. **2017** Presidential system introduced in Turkey that replaced Parliamentary system in use since 1876. *2017 amendments to Constitution* seem to have displaced the concept of separation of power with a huge impact on the legal system. Legal dilemma among scholars whether *Constitution 1982* is still in place? Major currency and debt crisis since 2018.

Table 12: Timeline for Evolution of Laws in Indonesia (Chapter 9)

>500 BCE- 1500 CE	1500-1800 CE	1800 CE-1865 CE	1865-1945 CE	1945-Present
First Phase	**2nd Phase-First Period of Colonial Phase**	**2nd Phase- Second period of Colonial Phase**	**3rd Phase-Third period of Colonial Phase**	**Independence & Post- Independence**
Influence of Hindu & Buddhist Dynasties and *Hindu-Buddhist Jurisprudence* until 15th Century. From 13th century, the influence of *Islamic Jurisprudence* commenced in the Archipelago. Old name of Indonesia was **Nusantara**, a name commonly for powerful Hindu/Buddhist kingdom in SE Asia and first used by Hindu Prime Minister, national icon and Indonesian nationalist **Gajah Mada** in 1332 CE.	*Portuguese Jurisprudence* in the early 16th century. Impact of *Dutch colonial rule Jurisprudence* on Indonesian laws and prevalence of customary rule. 1814-1824, Malaya and Indonesia separated.	Influence of *western jurisprudence* as a result of Dutch (**'VOC'**) rule. Roots of *the civil law system* in Indonesia established in its legal system. *Islamic law and jurisprudence* were allowed in a few scenarios in spite of an emphasis on *Dutch Law* and the growing role and development of *customary law.*	Development of *customary law* continued and challenged *Islamic laws and jurisprudence increased.* 1942 – Dutch surrendered to Japan and Japanese occupational force followed *Japanese military regulations*, while taking away the privileges of Dutch and other westerners living in the Archipelago.	Independence of Indonesia, 1945. Acceptance of **Islamic law** and jurisprudence and with the advent of local autonomy, many provinces adopted *Sharia law.* Old order – until 1965 coup. Focus on plurality of sources within the legal system and role of customary law retained. 1965-1998, called the *New order*, where a judiciary was placed under executive and there was a focus on investments. 1998 - present, *Reformation period*, social reforms, acceptance of *unwritten customary law.*

Table 13: Timeline for Evolution of Laws in Brazil (Chapter 10)

>1000 BCE-1500 CE	1500 CE-1822 CE	1822-1889 CE	1889-1988 CE	1988-Present
Ancient Phase	**Colonial Period**	**Imperial Period**	**Republic of Brazil**	**Modern Brazil**
Indigenous Peoples migrated from Asia during the ice age, around twelve thousand years ago, using the Bering Strait to cross to the Americas. **Indigenous Peoples** occupy the region. *Community law* of Indigenous Peoples in force.	1500 CE, **Portuguese explorers** & colonisers conquered the region. Influence of *Portuguese law.* Impact of *Roman law, Canon law and German Law.* Influence of *Christian Jurisprudence.* *1821 Spanish Constitution* imposed. **Migration** of Africans and new ideas/philosophies brought in by them. Impact of **Slavery**.	1822, D. Pedro I declared an independent Brazil and became a monarch. *First Constitution of Brazil 1824.* *Royal Ordinations* replaced earlier Portuguese ordinations. **Migration** of other than Portuguese commenced to Brazil. The *Brazilian Commercial Code 1850* based on then existing *French, Spanish and Portuguese Codes.* Influence of *United States of America Constitution 1787.*	Abolishment of slavery led to overthrow of monarchy in 1889. Brazil became a Republic. Rapid development in commerce and urban areas. Japanese immigrants started to arrive in 1908 CE. Wave of immigration after World Wars I and II. *Military dictatorship* for nearly two decades.	*Brazilian Constitution 1988 (seventh since 1824)* after two decades of military dictatorship. 25 religions in Brazil influence law-making. *Catholicism* the largest but *evangelism* is growing in strength in last few decades. Impact of religions can be seen, in particular, on Family laws. *Civil Code 2002* and drafting of many specialised laws.

Table 14: Timeline for Evolution of Laws in Nigeria (Chapter 11)

>1500 BCE-1000CE	1000 CE-1800 CE	1800-1960 CE	1960-1999 CE	1999-Present
Ancient Phase	**Rise of Islamic Dynasties, local dynasties, slavery, contact with European traders**	**Colonisation**	**Independence**	**Modern Nigeria**
Nok Civilisation around 1500 BCE-200 CE, a powerful civilisation emerged in and around territories now known as Nigeria. *Indigenous Peoples* of various ethnicities, languages, such as Hausa, Yoruba, Igbo, Fulani, Kanuri, Ibibio, Ijaw and others. Evidence of trade between different people in territories. Population was not homogeneous. Evidence of *Customary law* present to resolve day to day issues.	Spread of Islam from 7th century CE in many cities associated with Hausa. Kanem–Bornu Empire (700-1380 CE) rose as major Islamic civilisation in these territories. 1100-1780 CE – Rise of Yourub Kingdom, Oyo Empire. Rise of Sokoto Caliphate (1804-1903) and spread of *Islamic Jurisprudence* in areas and war with Oyo. *Sharia law* was applied. Kingdom of Nri remained an independent entity until 1911 CE. Evidence of central power and vassal states. Local governance structure developed – *Palace courts and native courts.* Portuguese explorers started trading around Lagos approx. 1600 CE (*influence of Christian jurisprudence*). 1754-1814 many wars, areas affected by **slavery**, whereby many were taken to Southern America & Caribbean.	Geographical area which is Nigeria today is colonised by British Empire in 1800 CE. 1807 **Slavery outlawed** in southern territories. Britain consolidated power by 1861. *Berlin Conference 1885* divided West Africa between European Powers. Northern Protectorate Southern Protectorate formed by British in 1886. Northern and Southern Protectorate merged in **1914** by British. **Nigeria as an entity is founded.** *Common law* principles introduced in territories. British expanded territories in North in early 20th century. *The Clifford Constitution of 1922, the Richard Constitution of 1946, Macpherson Constitution of 1951, and the Lyttleton Constitution of 1954.*	*Declaration of Independence 1960* Republic and initial Constitution with role for Queen of UK. *Constitution 1963,* and role of Privy Council (UK) done away with and Nigeria declared itself as a full sovereign nation. Two *Military coups* 1966 and civil war. Oil Boom from 1970. **Military coups** of 1975 and 1976. *Constitution of 1979,* did away with Parliamenta-ry system.	*Constitution of 1999.* Military rule ended and civilian rule commenced after 33 years. *Common law* principles retained. Role of *Customary law* or *indigenous law* retained. Subject to validity of customs Role of Islamic law (*Maliki school of Islam*) retained in personal laws in some territories. Islamic law is not considered as customary law.

3 THEORETICAL UNDERPINNINGS FOR EXAMINING VARIOUS IMPRINTS

In order to fully appreciate the analysis in the forthcoming chapters and to carry out comparative analysis, it is important to again briefly discuss the theoretical underpinnings.

In any jurisdiction, imprints from history and ancient civilisations within written law, as well as the manner in which law is practised, can shed light on important facets of current law in that jurisdiction. These imprints can also provide unique insights that can enable scholars, and even laypeople, to have a better understanding of the workings of law within their own jurisdictions.[53] To observe and analyse imprints will invariably involve the evaluation of history, society, culture, norms, philosophy, society, external influence, legal transplants and so forth, as discussed previously in this chapter.

The exercise of analysing imprints will also involve an exercise in comparison,[54] which is attempted in this book. In that case, a comparative study will become part of the process to compare laws, as one can only analyse something foreign from the perspective of one's own laws, customs, norms etc.[55] How then can one tell –

---

[53] Edward J. Eberle, "The Method and Role of Comparative Law," *Wash. U. Global Stud. L. Rev.* 8, no. 3 (2009): 454–55, where he articulated, "*Evaluation of <u>older cultures</u>* [emphasis added] *in place before the rise of legal systems can yield important information about the basic elements and structure of modern societies. Looking at ourselves through these mirrors could reveal important ideas, norms, rules or principles, forcing a reevaluation that may improve the social order or, alternatively, lead us to confirm the tenets of our own legal system.*"

[54] See, Mathias Reimann, "Comparative Law and Neighbouring Disciplines," in *The Cambridge Companion to Comparative Law*, ed. Mauro Bussani and Ugo Mattei, Cambridge Companions to Law (Cambridge; New York: Cambridge University Press, 2012), 13-34, where the study of comparative law involves various disciplines, for example, analysing foreign law and then comparing with ones' own laws, philosophy & legal jurisprudence when evaluating the evolution of law, legal history, the sociology of law and so forth. In this book, readers will make an attempt to reach these objectives, not just for just one jurisdiction, but for many important selected jurisdictions.

[55] G. Swanson, "Framework for Comparative Research: Anthropology and the Theory of Action," in *Comparative Methods in Sociology: Essays on Trends and Applications*, ed. Vallier Ivan and Aptter. David E. (Berkeley: University of California Press, 1971), 141-202, where he propounded that any study devoid of comparison cannot be classed as scientific. Therefore, the editor of this book requests that, when reading the various chapters, readers should keep comparing explorations in

(1) what can be considered as a foreign/external influence on laws, or (2) whether that external influence could be the result of the evolution of laws over time in that jurisdiction. In order to be successful in pursuing such comparative studies for any jurisdiction, one has to look not just at national laws or their evolution, but also to consider 'non-state'[56] norms that are very different in origin from state laws, or the evolution of laws with current law as a focal point.

In this book, the editor, with the assistance of foreign experts/scholars, has attempted to analyse foreign ideas and the influence of external laws in a jurisdiction - legal transplants, religious philosophy, political ideology, political events, history and so forth - on the development of laws. Along with this analysis, an attempt has been made to seamlessly connect this analysis with that of the evolution of society and changing demographies in a jurisdiction. Accordingly, the issues of legal sociology, legal history, legal jurisprudence, legal ethnology, political ideology, legal philosophy, types of legal system and so on are discussed and analysed in each of the selected jurisdictions.

An element of theory again needs to be discussed to highlight the various theoretical underpinnings behind the chapters; for example, it is important for readers to appreciate how comparative law and legal history are connected.[57] In this book, in various jurisdictions, analysis over time of the evolution of law, legal process, governance and political structure is pursued, along with an analysis of the historical dimensions peculiar to geography and demography in that jurisdiction. *Legal ethnology* is the term that combines the study of legal history

---

various jurisdictions; See also, Konrad Zweigert, Hein Kotz, and Tony Weir, trans., *An Introduction to Comparative Law: Volume I: The Framework*, 2nd Revised ed. (Oxford: Clarendon Press, 1987), 2, where according to the author, comparison of law when combined with Internationalism can be considered as an exercise in Comparative law. For example, readers when analyzing the contents in various chapters in a book, then that exercise in itself could be considered as Comparative Law and this itself can provide a unique window regarding evolution of human society.

[56] G. Teubner (ed.), *Global Law without a state* (Aldershot: Dartmouth, 1997).

[57] See, Mathias Reimann, "Comparative Law and Neighbouring Disciplines," in *The Cambridge Companion to Comparative Law*, ed. Mauro Bussani and Ugo Mattei, Cambridge Companions to Law (Cambridge; New York: Cambridge University Press, 2012), 13-34.

with the evolution of civilisation in a particular geographical area.[58] The subject of legal ethnology focuses on the historical development of culture, norms and so forth.[59] In most chapters, analysis is pursued in relation to norms, customs, customary law and their relevance in current law in that jurisdiction.

Legal historians tend to compare the evolution of law over a particular period of time within a geographical area. On the other hand, legal ethnologists lean towards the study of the history of law in order to understand the civilisation itself.[60] Accordingly, legal ethnologists guide lawyers and jurisprudents on the evolution of modern societies.

Similarly in *legal sociology*, whenever there is a relationship between society and law, it becomes a matter of study, for example – (1) the impact of religions on law, (2) various modes that have historically combined with law to control societies, (3) the way law operates in courts.[61] This exploration will involve a study of the evolution of laws in countries impacted by the philosophies of socialism and Marxism, such as China and Russia as outlined in this book.[62] Similarly, the

---

[58] Konrad Zweigert and K. Kotz, trans., Tony Weir, *An Introduction to Comparative Law*, 3rd Revised ed. (Oxford: Clarendon Press, 1998), 8-9; See also, a discussion on the topic of legal ethnology in Mathias Reimann, "Comparative Law and Neighbouring Disciplines," in *The Cambridge Companion to Comparative Law*, ed. Mauro Bussani and Ugo Mattei, Cambridge Companions to Law (Cambridge; New York: Cambridge University Press, 2012), 13-34, 23.

[59] H.P. Glenn, *Legal Traditions of the World*, 3rd edn. (New York: Oxford University Press, 2007).

[60] Zweigert, Kotz, and Weir, *Introduction to Comparative Law*, 9, where they quoted Genzmer, where he said, *"...no longer believe that legal history unrolls independently, but see law and history as fully interfused [emphasis added] and try to illuminate the extra-legal context and hidden stimuli of legal development. Legal history is therefore, not simply self-serving, but contributes to a critical evaluation of the policy of law, which is, after all, the principal aim of pure comparative law.";* See also, Genzmer E., "Verhaltnis von Rechtsgeschichte und Rechtvergleichung," *ARSP 41* (1954/55): 334.

[61] David Nelken, "Comparative Sociology of Law," in Reza Banakar and Max Travers (eds), *An Introduction to Law and Social Theory* (Oxford: Hart 2002), 329. See also, Annelise Riles, "Comparative law and Socio-legal Studies," in *The Oxford Handbook of Comparative Law*, ed. Mathias Reimann and Reinhard Zimmermann (Oxford: Oxford University Press, 2008); See also, Max Rheinstein, *Collected Works: Jurisprudence and Sociology, Comparative Law and Common Law,* vol. 1 (Tübingen: J.C.B. Mohr, 1979).

[62] Refer to Chapters 2 **(Russia)** and 3 **(China)** respectively for the impact of socialism on current law over the last few decades.

impact of religions and philosophy in the jurisdictions of Russia, India, Israel, Indonesia, Turkey, Brazil & Ukraine is discussed in subsequent chapters.[63]

Concepts from *legal anthropology* such as customs, practices, customary law, norms, unwritten laws, cultural aspects behind the law and their effects are discussed when analysing imprints on law in all selected jurisdictions.[64] In any event, the selection of non-western jurisdictions makes it essential that all tools are applied to analyse the imprints and evolution of laws in these locations. It is pertinent to note that, even though there is an attempt in most countries to secularise laws, the imprints of religions developed over the centuries will not just disappear from written/unwritten laws/customary laws or even the practice of law in these jurisdictions.[65] In a few jurisdictions, even the issue of legitimacy of promulgated laws may be affected by extreme secularisation/political correctness, due to a prevalence of extreme liberal jurisprudence.

Factors that ultimately mold history and accordingly influence the evolution of law, including its practice at any point of time in a jurisdiction, have been discussed earlier in §1 of this chapter. Over thousands of years, societies have evolved absorbing both positive and negative influences. Nevertheless, in many societies, there are certainly influences that have affected the development of law, for example – (1) the spread of religion to another area, thus affecting norms/customs/expectations within that society,[66] (2) immigration bringing different norms and customs that become infused within the new geography,[67] (3)

---

[63] Refer to Chapter 2 **(Russia)**, Chapters 5 & 6 **(India)**, Chapter 7 **(Israel)**, and Chapter 8 **(Turkey)**, Chapter 9 **(Indonesia)** & Chapter 11 **(Nigeria)** for the impact of religions on the evolution of written and unwritten law. See also, W. Ewald, "What Was It Like to Try a Rat?," *Pensylvania Law Review* (1995):1889 for an exploration of issues in the context of the need to appreciate the legal philosophy behind the laws.

[64] See, L. Nader, *The Life of the Law* (Berkeley: University of California Press, 2002); See also, W. Fikentscher, *Law and Anthropology* (Munich: Bayrische Akademie der Wissenschaften, 2009).

[65] See footnote 10 of this chapter.

[66] Refer Chapters 5 & 6 **(India)**, Chapter 8 **(Turkey)**, Chapter 9 **(Indonesia)**.

[67] Refer Chapter 10 **(Brazil)** about the evolution of law due to immigration at various stages and immigration policies. Furthermore, it was suggested that the current immigration policy in Brazil could be considered as one of the most flexible in the world, as it takes into the account the development of the law of human rights, due to its unique history.

the practice of slavery, (4) the imposition of ideas on invaded societies. All such issues are explored in subsequent chapters, along with chronological timelines.

Another issue of the imprint of *revolutions* on law in jurisdictions has been discussed, as it has a tendency to change the course of organic development of law and practice. However, older imprints from before the revolution will no doubt exist even afterward, no matter how much revolutionary leaders tried to erase earlier history and law from society. For example, after the *1917 Russian revolution*, the new leaders who came to power at first did their best to erase all traces of past laws, however, in later years, new leaders reverted back to Russian legal heritage and aligned them to Soviet realities.[68] A similar case was the *Chinese revolution* of 1949;[69] the "Six Laws"[70] of the Nanjing National Government were abolished immediately, and the Civil Law of the Republic of China was consequently not made applicable in Chinese jurisdiction. However, the imprint of ethos and civilisation values going back many centuries can be seen in the law and the way laws are practised in modern China,[71] even after the Communist revolution,

---

[68] Refer § 2.1 of Chapter 2 on *Russian History & Revolutions – Impact on Genesis, Evolution of Russian Court System and Jurisprudence.*

[69] Refer § 4 of Chapter 3 on *the historical developments of Chinese Civil law over the centuries, and a new Civil Code 2021.*

[70] The "six laws" refer to the constitution, civil law, criminal law, civil procedure law, criminal procedure law, and administrative law promulgated and formulated during the time of the Nanjing Nationalist Government.

[71] Geoffrey MacCormack, *The Spirit of Traditional Chinese Law*, The Spirit of the Laws (Athens; London: University of Georgia Press, 1996), 32 for discussion on the key elements of *conservatism*, in particular, the effect of *conservatism* in the context of the symbolic spirit of law in China; See also, Ching-I Tu, "Conservatism in a Constructive Forum: The Case of Wang Kuowei (1877–1927)," *Monumenta Serica 28* (1969): 188, as quoted in Geoffrey MacCormack, *The Spirit of Traditional Chinese Law*, The Spirit of the Laws (Athens; London: University of Georgia Press, 1996), 32, where scholars from the Qing Dynasty of China (1644-1911 CE), Wang Kuo-Wei and Ching-I Tu, discussed the concept of *conservatism* – " *The essence of conservatism is "preservation of the ancient moral traditions of humanity." A conservative has a great respect for the wisdom of his ancestors and is somehow dubious of sweeping change. He regards society as "a spiritual reality, possessing an eternal life, but a delicate constitution: it cannot be scrapped and recast as if it were a machine." Most important is the conservative's belief that a civilized society "requires order" and the "tradition and sound prejudice can provide checks upon man's anarchic impulse," especially in a revolutionary age.";* See also, Vivek Jain, *Insight into China through Comparative Analysis of Invisible Factors and Contexts – Common Law v. Chinese Law*, (India, Singapore: Notion Press 2019), 57.

Similarly, *legal transplants, or influences of External Law* such as – (1) the impact of western jurisprudence in China due to treaties agreed under duress, (2) the impact of English jurisprudence in India due to colonisation, (3) the impact of Dutch law in Indonesia due to colonisation, (4) the impact of Portuguese law and the import of concepts from immigrants/slaves in Brazil, (5) the impact of foreign laws due to history and the desire to copy in common law principles in Ukraine, (6) the impact of foreign laws due to coercion and commercial trade in history from western powers. These issues are explored in detail in subsequent chapters.

3.1 A WARNING FOR READERS

In their own jurisdiction, lawyers/scholars/philosophers make assumptions about issues or how things may evolve from certain unique circumstances, however they should not assume the same when reading about other jurisdictions.[72]

It is an appropriate time to emphasise that readers should not try to analyse issues in different jurisdictions whilst wearing the lenses of their own jurisdiction. Each jurisdiction has evolved due to its own history, the influence of religions on its laws, and its share of revolutions that have contributed to the evolution of its unique features such as – (1) legal philosophy, (2) jurisprudence, (3) substantive and procedural laws, (4) legal culture, (5) norms, (6) traditions, (7) customs, (8) political philosophy, (9) the influence of religions embedded in the conscience of the populace, (10) nuances in languages, and so forth.

---

[72] See also, Vivek Jain, *Insight into China through Comparative Analysis of Invisible Factors and Contexts – Common Law v. Chinese Law* (Singapore, India: Notion Press, 2019), where the author has discussed how lawyers cannot assume the same about other jurisdictions while relying on translations of other jurisdictions' statutes and laws.

4. FINAL COMMENTS

Readers can utilise within this chapter – (1) the tables containing history and legal development devised for various jurisdictions, (2) theoretical underpinning for the analysis of imprints in various chapters, and (3) a few concepts of comparative law, to compare the evolution of law in different jurisdictions in order to decipher the evolution of human society.

Finally, the editor submits that even though past history, religions and revolutions leave imprints in present laws either in content or their application within a jurisdiction; it is important to note that practising lawyers and scholars should focus on the role of past doctrines in the present legal system and how the current law and systems give legitimacy to those past doctrines. However, practising lawyers and scholars should not over-concentrate on these past doctrines' roles in previous societies.[73] In any jurisdiction, these comments are for lawyers practising law and are not for scholars who are involved in exploring the evolution of laws.

For the sake of completeness, it is present jurisprudence and substantive law that should be the background for any analysis by practising lawyers and scholars, and notes on history, though useful, cannot be the sole guide in courts.[74] However, scholars/lawyers should be mindful that this issue may itself vary from jurisdiction to jurisdiction. On the other hand, the analysis pursued in the book for different

---

[73] William Baude and Stephen E. Sachs, "Originalism and the Law of the Past" *Law and History Review*, vol. 37, no. 3 (2019): 809-820, 813Duke Law School Public Law & Legal Theory Series No. 2019-46, Available at SSRN: <https://ssrn.com/abstract=3400463>, where the authors of this article warned the practising lawyers not to focus on 'external' account of operation of law within the population in the past, but the lawyers should instead focus on 'internal' aspects such as treatise, case laws, court commentaries, scholar's commentaries on cases and so forth; See also, Helen Irving, "Outsourcing the Law: History and the Disciplinary Limits of Constitutional Reasoning," Fordham Law Review 84 (2015): 957-67, 960, where she warned judges that their role is to interpret law and not history.

[74] William Baude and Stephen E. Sachs, "Originalism and the Law of the Past" *Law and History Review*, vol. 37, no. 3 (2019): 809-820, 820, Duke Law School Public Law & Legal Theory Series No. 2019-46, Available at SSRN: <https://ssrn.com/abstract=3400463>, where the authors wrote, *"What was thought and said in the past are questions of history; which of the answers supply legal rules today is a matter for jurisprudence and substantive law."*

jurisdictions will be useful to help explore the process of the development of law and its practice.

Lastly, the editor submits that many solutions to current-day problems can be found by appreciating the relevance of history, religious jurisprudence, and even the impact of revolutions on the natural development and practice of laws in any of the selected jurisdictions. It will be seen in subsequent chapters that even intense revolutions cannot erase history or the natural course of society in the context of the development of law in any given jurisdiction.

In light of the above, in any society, attempts by adherents of extreme *liberal jurisprudence* to push forward an agenda of political correctness can bring disaster, through their ideas of 'secularism' or 'modernity' or by banning any discussion – (1) on customs and customary law, and/or (2) on religious jurisprudence, and/or (3) on the relevance of history, and/or (5) by curtailing free speech amongst others. In fact, the results achieved will be just the opposite of what adherents of liberal jurisprudence intended in the first place; that is to have a liberal society. In fact, as seen in the following chapters, there will always be imprints of history, religions and revolutions on law in any jurisdiction. Is it then difficult to comprehend why such attempts are made to go against the tide?

The editor suggests the coercive actions of such adherents of extreme liberal jurisprudence will leave deep scars in society, and in the longer run will affect even the legitimacy of laws in the eyes of the populace that are pushed to remove from their thought process any elements of history or religious jurisprudence. Basically, such adherents of liberal jurisprudence are asking the populace to snuff out the soul from their thought process and subsequent debates. These issues can further create superficial harmony within the society, and the probability of achieving actual harmony may take a knock for decades to come.

In addition, the editor proposes that the best course of action is for laws to develop organically, taking into account different kinds of customary jurisprudence, the relevance of history and religions, or even liberal jurisprudence, and none should be discounted unless there is a need to change the norms that are very much against the concept of modern human rights - for example, the rights of women or minorities in a few jurisdictions. However, counter-arguments against any change of norms, even on the basis of conservative religious jurisprudence (any religion) should be allowed freely, and should not be repressed on the pretext of political correctness or secularism. The societies in jurisdictions must provide space for free debate and only then can we have a truly liberal society. As can be seen from the chapters on all selected jurisdictions, none of the imprints of history, religion or revolution can be wished away from law, including the practice of law-making by legislators or judges who were selected for analysis.

BIBLIOGRAPHY

- Angus Maddison, *HS-8: The World Economy 1-2001 AD* (Oxford: OUP, Illustrated edition, 20 Sept. 2007); See also, <HS-8_2003.pdf (theatlantic.com)>, accessed on 10 December 2021.

- Annelise Riles, "Comparative law and Socio-legal Studies," in *The Oxford Handbook of Comparative Law*, ed. Mathias Reimann and Reinhard Zimmermann (Oxford: Oxford University Press, 2008).

- Baudouin Dupert, "Legal Pluralism, Plurality of Laws, and Legal Practices," *European Journal of Legal Studies*, vol. 1, no. 1, (2007): 1-26, halshs00178422.

- B. Tamamaha, *Realistic Socio-Legal Theory: Pragmatism and A Social Theory Of Law* (Oxford: Clarendon Press, 1997).

- Ching-I Tu, "Conservatism in a Constructive Forum: The Case of Wang Kuowei (1877–1927)," *Monumenta Serica 28* (1969): 188.

- David Nelken, "Comparaitve Sociology of Law," in Reza Banakar and Max Travers (eds), *An Introduction to Law and Social Theory* (Oxford: Hart 2002).

- David Schiff, "Modern Positivism: Kelsen's Pure Theory of Law," in *Introduction to Jurisprudence and Legal Theory: Commentary and Materials*, Anne Barron, et al. (London: Butterworths, 2002).

- Edward J. Eberle, "The Method and Role of Comparative Law," *Wash. U. Global Stud. L. Rev.* 8, no. 3 (2009): 454–55.

- Frank H. Easterbrook, "Textualism and the Dead Hand," *George Washington Law Review* 66 (1998): 1119-26.

- Geoffrey MacCormack, *The Spirit of Traditional Chinese Law*, The Spirit of the Laws (Athens; London: University of Georgia Press, 1996).

- Genzmer E., "Verhaltnis von Rechtsgeschichte und Rechtvergleichung," *ARSP 41* (1954/55): 334.

- G. Gurvitch, *l'idée dy droit social* (Paris, 1932).

- G. Teubner (ed.), *Global Law without as state* (Aldershot: Dartmouth, 1997).

- G. Swanson, "Framework for Comparative Research: Anthropology and the Theory of Action," in *Comparative Methods in Sociology: Essays on Trends and Applications*, ed. Vallier Ivan and Aptter. David E. (Berkeley: University of California Press, 1971), 141-202.

- Harold J. Berman, *The interaction of Law and Religion* (Nashville: Abingdon Press, 1974).

- Harold J. Berman, "Introduction" in *The Interaction of Law and Religion* (Nashville: Abingdon Press, 1974).

- Harold J. Berman, "Religious Dimensions of Law" in *The interaction of Law and Religion* (Nashville: Abingdon Press, 1974).

- Harold J. Breman, *Justice in the U.S.S.R.: An Interpretation of Soviet Law* (Cambridge: Harvard University Press, 1963).

- Hein Kotz, "Comparative Law in Germany Today," *Revue Internationale de Droit Compare* 51, no. 4 (1999): 756.

- Helen Irving, "Outsourcing the Law: History and the Disciplinary Limits of Constitutional Reasoning," Fordham Law Review 84 (2015): 957-67.

- <https://en.wikipedia.org/wiki/List_of_regions_by_past_GDP_(PPP)#Indian_empir es_(1%E2%80%931947_CE)>, accessed on 11 December, 2021.

- <https://time.com/5103677/church-state-separation-religious-freedom/>, accessed on 2 November 2021.

- <https://www.theceomagazine.com/business/competition/pwc-world-2050>, accessed on 13 December 2021.

- <https://www.pwc.com/gx/en/research-insights/economy/the-world-in-2050.html>, accessed 28 November 2021.

- H.L.A. Hart, *The Concept of Law* (Oxford: Oxford University Press, 3d ed. 2012).

- H. L. A. Hart, "Positivism and Separation of Law and Morals," *Harvard L. Rev.* 71, no. 4 (1958): 607.

- H.P. Glenn, *Legal Traditions of the World*, 3rd edn (New York: Oxford University Press, 2007).

- Huston Smith, *The Religions of Man* (Ishi Press: Tokyo, 2013 (first published in New York in 1958)).

- Iris I. Varner & Katrin Varner, "The Relationship between Culture and Legal Systems and the Impact on Intercultural Business Communication," *Global Advances in Business and Communication Conference and Journal* vol. 3 no. 1: 1-14.

- J. Raz, "Legal Principles and the Limits of Law," *Yale L.J.* 81, no. 5 (1972): 838–47.

- James Gordley, "Comparative Legal Research: Its Function in the Development of Harmonized Law," *Am. J. Comp. L.* 43, no. 4 (1995): 555–68.

- Janet E. Ainsworth, "Categories and Culture: On the 'Rectification of Names' in Comparative Law," *Cornell L. Rev.* 82, no. 1 (1996): 19–42.

- Jean Piagnet, *The Moral Judgment of the Child* (London: Kegan Paul, Trench, Trübner & Co.,1932).

- John Griffiths, "What is Legal Pluralism?," *The Journal of Legal Pluralism and Unofficial Law*, vol. 18, no. 24, (January 1986): 1–55, doi:10.1080/07329113.1986.10756387.

- Konrad Zweigert, Hein Kotz, and Tony Weir, trans., *An Introduction to Comparative Law: Volume I: The Framework*, 2nd Revised ed. (Oxford: Clarendon Press, 1987).

- Konrad Zweigert and K. Kotz, trans., Tony Weir, *An Introduction to Comparative Law*, 3rd Revised ed. (Oxford: Clarendon Press, 1998).

- Lambert, "Conception Generale et Definition de la Science Due Droit Compare, Proces-Verbaux Des Seances et Documents, Congress International de Droit Compare I," *Congress International de Droit Compare I* (1905): 26.

- L. Nader, *The Life of the Law* (Berkeley: University of California Press, 2002).

- Lon Fuller, *The Morality of Law* (Conn., New Haven: Yale University Press, 1969).

- Lon L. Fuller, *The Law in Quest of Itself* (Boston, Mass.: Beacon Press, 1940).

- Max Rheinstein, *Collected Works: Jurisprudence and Sociology, Comparative Law and Common Law,* vol. 1 (Tübingen: J.C.B. Mohr, 1979).

o   M. Chiba, "Three Dichotomies of Law in Pluralism: An Analytical Scheme of Legal Culture", *Tokai Law Review*, (1987): 173-183.

o   M. Chiba, *Sociology of Law in Non-Western Countries* (Oñati: Oñati International Institute for the Sociology of Law, 1993).

o   Mathias Reimann, "Comparative Law and Neighbouring Disciplines," in *The Cambridge Companion to Comparative Law*, ed. Mauro Bussani and Ugo Mattei, Cambridge Companions to Law (Cambridge; New York: Cambridge University Press, 2012).

o   Richards Nobles and David Schiff, "The Evolution of Natural Law," in *Introduction to Jurisprudence and Legal Theory: Commentary and Materials*, by Anne Barron, et al. (London: Butterworths, 2002).

o   Roger Cotterrell, *The sociology of law: An introduction*, 2nd ed. (London: Butterworths, 1992).

o   Roman Tomasic, *The sociology of law* (London: SAGE, 1985).

o   Sally Merry, "Everyday Understandings of the Law in Working-class America," *American Ethnologist*, vol. 13, no. 2 (May 1986): 253–270.

o   S. F. Moore, *Law as Process: An Anthropological Approach* (London: Boston, Routledge & Kegan Paul, 1978).

o   Stephen M. Feldman, ed., *Law and Religion: A Critical Anthology* (New York: NYU Press, 2000).

o   Thomas M. Frank, *The Structure of Impartiality: Examining the Riddle of One Law in a Fragmented World* (New York: Macmillan, 1968).

o   Vivek Jain, *Insight into China through Comparative Analysis of Invisible Factors and Contexts – Common Law v. Chinese Law*, (India, Singapore, Malaysia: Notion Press, 2019).

o   V.V. Palmer, "From Lerotholi to Lando: Some Examples of Comparative Law Methodology," *Global Jurist Frontiers* 4, no. 2 (2004): 1-29.
o   W. Ewald, "What Was It Like to Try a Rat?," *Pensylvania Law Review* (1995):1889.

o   W. Fikentscher, *Law and Anthropology* (Munich: Bayrische Akademie der Wissenschaften, 2009).

o   William Baude and Stephen E. Sachs, "Originalism and the Law of the Past," *Law and History Review*, vol. 37, no. 3 (2019): 809-820, Duke Law School Public Law & Legal Theory Series No. 2019-46, Available at SSRN: <https://ssrn.com/abstract=3400463>.

o   Xianyi Zeng and Xiaohong Ma, "A Dialectic Study of the Structure and Basic Concept of Traditional Chinese Law and an Analysis of the Relationship between Li (Ceremony) and Fa (Law)," *Frontiers of Law in China* 1, no. 1 (2006): 35.

CHAPTER 2

RUSSIAN HISTORY & REVOLUTIONS – IMPACT ON GENESIS, EVOLUTION OF RUSSIAN COURT SYSTEM AND JURISPRUDENCE

Dr. Svetlana Chugunova

1 INTRODUCTION

This chapter is aimed to give a general overview on the evolution and development of Russian legal philosophy and Russian law from the very beginning of Russia's statehood, which originated more than one thousand years ago, up to the present day.

1.1 INTRODUCTION TO RUSSIA

Nowadays, Russia is the largest single country in the world by geographical area, spreading over two continents – Europe and Asia. It has a huge territory equal to nearly one sixth of the whole land surface of our planet, extending around 17 million square metres and crossing eleven time zones.

Russian history goes back more than one thousand years and over that period of time Russia has managed to contribute immensely to the overall evolution of mankind in areas such as art, culture, philosophy, science and so forth. In the mid-20th century, Russia initiated the space era, launching the world's first satellite and putting the first human into space. What is even more impressive is that Russia managed to demonstrate resilience and determination by achieving this outstanding level of scientific and technological development only few years after the end of the World War II, in which nearly one third of the Russian territory was devastated and some 28 million of its people perished.

It may come as a surprise to some readers that, according to the Human Development Index (HDI)[1] calculated and published by the United Nations Organization in its annual reports as a part of UN Development Program, Russia now ranks among the most developed countries of the world. Russia's population benefits from a universal healthcare system, free university education and a strong economy.

At present Russia is structured in the form of a federation and consists of 85 integral parts, literally '*federal subjects*'. Its federal composition includes *inter alia* various republics, regions, areas, districts, autonomies and three cities of federal importance, each having their own governments, parliaments and top public officials. This whole territorial and institutional kaleidoscope is enshrined within one single Sovereign State, namely the Russian Federation. One of the most important ties which hold this impressive diversity together is the Russian court system and its jurisprudence.

---

[1] <http://hdr.undp.org/en/content/human-development-index-hdi>, accessed on November 18, 2021.

2 HISTORICAL BACKGROUND AND TIME LINES IN HISTORY

2.1 OVERVIEW OF RUSSIAN HISTORY

As mentioned in preceding paragraphs, Russia has a fascinating history of statehood which goes back more than one thousand years. Its history has experienced twists and turns – sometimes real drama, sometimes a genuine thriller, but at any point of time in history, it can be described as anything but dull or simple.

Russia's historical background is of course much more detailed and complex than the periodisation below. However, for the sake of convenience, the optimal way is to structure the timeline as follows.

We omit the period starting from 2nd century BCE, which in some doctrinal sources is highlighted as a period of widespread migration of various Slavic tribes. This was also the time when the original proto-states of the Slavs were believed to have come into being.[2] These issues are, however, debatable among the most prominent scholars and any further discussion is beyond the scope of this book.

The first indisputably recognisable Russian state, the so called Ancient 'Rus', dated back to the 9th century CE,[3] and lasted almost until the 12th century CE.

During the next period, 12th-14th century CE, Russia was represented by a mixture of self-standing, competing or allied feudal principalities or duchies. These small states (*knyazhestva*) not only often fought among themselves, but also had to

---

[2] A. N. Sakharov, History of Russia from ancient times till present (Russia, Moscow: Prospect, 2021), 18-19.

[3] The name "Russia" or Ρωσία (in Greek) with the reference to Ancient Rus' as an existing independent state was already present in some works on the Byzantine Emperor Constantine VII Porphyrogenitus, those works are mostly known under their Latin titles, in particular *De Ceremoniis* and *De administrando imperio*.

defend themselves from many external invaders. Such scenarios sometimes led these knyazhestva to build up quite extraordinary and creative political alliances.

By the 15th century CE, the feudal principality of Moscow, also known as the Grand Duchy of Moscow or *Muscovy,* had mostly won over its closest neighbours, successfully expelled invaders and conquered their territories, including some of those initially occupied by the Great States of nomads of the Golden Horde, Livonian and Teutonic Orders, and others. The Muscovy Prince became Tsar of the united Russian principalities and added the newly conquered areas to his sovereign throne.

In the early 18th century CE, Russia finally defeated one of its long-standing historical rivals – the Swedes – and thus mitigated the Northern Threat which had persisted for nearly five hundred years. The Russian Tsardom officially became the Russian Empire.

The period of 18th-mid 19th century CE was a period of imperial absolutism in Russia. It finished with a series of large-scale reforms, the emancipation of serfs, and adoption of the *First Russian Constitution 1906,* whereby the monarch agreed to share power. The Constitution came about after revision of the *Manifesto of the enactment of the Code of Laws of the Russian Empire 1833-36*. The Russian Empire, governed by the *Code of laws, grew* significantly during the period of the second half of the 19th century until the early 20th century CE.

In 1917, the Russian Empire fell, following the *Communist Revolution*, and was replaced by the Soviet Union. The Soviet period of the Russian history lasted until 1991 when the Soviet Union was dissolved.

Following dissolution, Russia took over all liabilities of the Soviet Union and those of the former Soviet Republics, including all their external debts and other outstanding international liabilities. By doing that Russia also accepted all the rights of the Soviet Union, thus sustaining continuity of the Russian state and its uninterrupted presence in the realm of international law. Since 1991 Russia has officially been known as the Russian Federation.

Throughout the whole period the Russian state has existed, in whatever form, its evolution has always been marked with a certain 'time linkage' and concept of legal continuity. In other words, all elements of the Russian State and its law experienced continuing transformation. As a result, older forms of law, even when they had run their course, been outlived or abandoned, still served as a basis for building new legal forms or concepts, and thus sustained one single ongoing historical perspective of continuing development of Russian law and jurisprudence. This in spite of the fact that, after the 1917 *Russian revolution*, the new leaders who came to power initially did their best to erase all traces of past law, but in the end had to revert to using Russian legal heritage and adapt it for the new Soviet realities. After the Soviet Union was dissolved in 1991, acceptance of former Russian/Soviet law continued.

2.2 ANCIENT RUS' (900- 1200 CE)

The origins of ancient Russian law and case law (jurisprudence) are found in the traditions of local tribes, mystical (during the pagan period) and later on religious rules, rites and ceremonies, and various customs. All these formed a phenomenon called juridical habits that initially regulated nearly all aspects of daily life at that time.

Being customary rules of common use, repeatedly applicable in a particular territory for a long period of time, abided and recognised by people living there, such juridical habits formed the law of the Ancient Rus' and were inscribed as such in a series of international treaties made by the ancient Russian State with some of its neighbours. Thus, references to '*Russian law*' or the '*customs of the Rus*' with particular wordings of the relevant legal provisions were already present

in the treaties made by Rus' with the Byzantine Empire in the early 10th century
CE (e.g. those made in years 911 CE, 945 CE and 971 CE) and cover a broad
scope of matters including *inter alia* civil law, family law, commercial law, penal
law, levies, taxes, penalties, rules on dispute resolution and rules on the conflict of
laws.[4]

The concept of community was one of the milestones in ancient Russian legal
philosophy. Basically, it had the power to generate customs and at the same time
it was regulated by customs. Hence, the community would decide on the
distribution of land slots between its members, and would regulate the way in
which people should use and dispose of available natural resources including
forests, water, and so forth. The community (*'obschina'*) would distribute the share
of levies and contributions between its members and ensure community decisions
were correctly observed and implemented by all its members.

In addition, the community had some functions of policing society. A few of the
functions were that it could – (1) trigger and convey investigations, (2) search for
criminals, and (3) impose punishment and control over enforcement thereof. The
community was also tasked with resolving various financial and economic
disputes or crimes in society. In some cases, the community could accept joint
liability for a breach of obligations or a crime committed by one of its members.
Such a concept of collective responsibility or collective guilt (when it dealt with
crimes) was called *'krugovaya poruka'*, which can be literally translated as
'roundup guarantee'.

Decisions by the community would be made in the course of community meetings
(*'skhod'*). Skhod was also in charge of building up a common strategy of
interaction with the neighbours and/or the lord (*'knyaz'*). It is important to note that
there were no professional judges, prosecutors or lawyers among the community
members at the time. Likewise, no set of rules had yet been put in writing. The

---

[4] M.V. Bibikov, "Russo-Byzantine treaties" in *Big Russian Encyclopaedia, Vol. 29,* ed. Yu. S. Osipov
and S. L. Kravetz (Russia, Moscow: BRE, 2015), 75-76.

community was governed through a collective memory of rites, customs, and ceremonies which together formed certain juridical habits, acceptable by all as binding rules.[5]

In order to let this collective memory endure and pass from one generation to another, it was a matter of routine to let children and youngsters be present when the community tried various cases, resolve on disputes or crimes or evidence transactions. In other words, case law was formed and contained in the memory of community members of all ages. *Customs* were hence the basis of ancient Russian jurisprudence.

Social development eventually led to urbanisation. In addition to rural settlements, towns and cities gradually appeared on the Russian landscape. Each Russian town usually had a dedicated ruler. The gender of the ruler was not crucial, thus the town could be ruled by the lord (*'knyaz'*) or the lady (*'knyaghinya'*). Some towns of that time period were exceptions, such as Novgorod. Basically this was a self-governed city state, led by a group of people (*"vetche"*) elected by the town population from the most reputed and respected inhabitants.[6]

However, in most Russian towns, the common people (commoners) would still have to deal with the lord or lady of the town and their respective courtiers and officials. Taking into account that people who came to a town had a rural background, it is quite logical that they would opt for the most familiar and habitual way in order to organise themselves. Thus, urban communities also emerged in towns. It should be noted that a community of a town was much more complex in terms of its structure and its functioning compared to rural communities. Thus, an urban community would normally have a group of elected 'officials' (*"startsi gradiskie"* or literally *'elders of the town'*). The elders did not necessarily have to

---

[5] V.V. Chernih, G.A. Tsykunov, "Legal Customs of Ancient Russia as source of law," *Journal of the East-Siberian Institute of the MIA of the Russian Federation*, 84, no. 4 (2017): 178.
[6] Prof. R.L. Hachaturov, Common law in the history of old Russian law, *Report to the Togliatti State University* vol. 1 (Russia, Togliatti: TSU Department of history and theory of law, 2010).

be the oldest people in the town. Their gender or marital status was irrelevant. The main criterion was their reputation and high esteem among all members of the town's community. The community would meet on a regular basis or for some extraordinary reasons. The agenda would be prepared by the elders for each meeting. Smaller communities, called guilds or "*tsekha*", developed into professional bodies and accordingly started having their own set of rules and customs.

Since controversies between the lord or lady of the town and its population were quite frequent, urban communities started to make treaties ("*ryady*") with the towns' rulers. These domestic treaties are one of the few ancient sources of Russian law available in writing. According to these treaties, urban communities were usually competent to resolve fiscal and economic issues, form a home guard and provide volunteer corps in case of war, and handle certain disputes unless the judicial power was retained by the town ruler in full.

According to the rules of the Byzantine Eastern Orthodox Church, the transition from pagan beliefs and rites to Christianity happened in the 10th century CE. It brought into focus the need to review the existing set of rules, customs and juridical traditions of that period. Due to the arrival of many Greek and Byzantine monks and scholars and official recognition of the Russian Orthodox Church as a self-standing clerical power in conjunction with the power of the secular ruler (a male *knyaz* or a female *knyaghinya*), the legal philosophy of Orthodox Russia experienced the influence of Byzantine legal traditions, including the core of Byzantine law originating from the period of the Roman Empire. However, a simple copy-paste of foreign law was not acceptable for Russian society. As a result, a synthesised corpus of Russian law was formed where ancient customs of old Rus' were intertwined with Roman and Byzantine legal culture.[7]

---

[7] Yu. V. Ruzmanov, M. A. Eldin, "The influence of the Byzantine legal culture on Russia and the Russian political and legal space," *Eurasian Union of Scientists*, 76, no. 7 (2020): 76.

In the 10th-11th century CE, the first *Statutes of Clerical Courts* were adopted, in particular, the Statute enacted by Knyaz Vladimir the Saint and that enacted by Knyaz Yaroslav the Wise.[8] These statutes basically became the first official codes of juridical procedure in Russia of the time, although their legal technics and structure were far from perfect. The competence of clerical courts was not limited to purely religious matters and jurisdiction over the clergy. In fact, clerical courts tried all family law disputes, from divorce to the separation of property of ex-spouses. Clerical courts were also competent to resolve matters of morality (insults, sexual crimes and sexual perversions, false accusation, blasphemy, infanticide), small crimes (such as home violence, fights using pagan methods, and traditional medicine treatment which caused injury or accidental death of the patient, among others). Due to the fact that monasteries were entitled to own and possess land, clerical courts were also entitled to exercise their powers in any matters involving people living within the land territory owned by monasteries[9].

Evolution of secular jurisprudence went hand in hand with that of clerical courts. During the rule of Knyaz Yaroslav the Wise in the late eleventh century, the first edition of *Rus' Justice* was publishedThe Rus' Justice (or *Russkaya Pravda*) was a set of codified rules formed on the basis of existing old Russian customary practices of resolving various sorts of disputes and crimes. The Rus' Justice was further amended and supplemented many times. Today, scholars are able to study more than one hundred editions of said document.[10] It became the manual for secular judges, although they still retained the autonomy to resolve some cases on the principle of equity (in other words 'in the fair way' from the standpoint of morality rather than pure law). Speaking about jurisprudence, it should be specified that the Rus' Justice, in its later editions, sometimes explicitly referred to

---

[8] Oleg I. Chistyakov, *Russian Legislation of the 10th-20th centuries, Volume 1* (Russia, Moscow: Jurizdat, 1984), 199 and 233.

[9] For more details see e.g. Yaroslav N. Schapov, State and Church in Ancient Russia: X – XIII centuries (Russia, Moscow: Nauka, 1989).

[10] Maxim A. Isaev, *History of the Russian State and Russian Law* (Russia, Moscow: Statut, 2012), 40.

precedent practices of resolving similar cases by former princes, e.g. knyaz Yaroslav, his offspring (Yaroslavichi), or knyaz Vladimir Monomach.

In addition, *Rus' Justice* contained quite elaborate rules of court procedure. Accordingly, all litigations had a distinctly adversarial nature. Legal proceedings were triggered by the claimant. The litigating parties, the claimant and the respondent, were deemed equal in terms of their rights. Third parties could be involved in the process for testimonies or as witnesses. The proceedings were always open to public and conducted orally. Ordeal practices were quite frequent to sustain the party's position or serve as a piece of evidence.

The litigation was triggered by "call" ('*zaklich*'), an oral public announcement of the essence of the dispute or crime. The call was always made in a public place, such as a market or similar location. The next stage was called '*swod*'. Basically, this meant a meeting and was quite similar to a modern face-to-face meeting of opposing parties to present their positions.

In a scenario where the opponent party was unknown, or in case of a crime, an investigation stage would be triggered by the courts. In the 11th-12th centuries CE there were no professional investigators. Therefore, the investigation was carried out by public servants specifically appointed on a case-by-case basis by the secular rulers, the archbishop, or a secular judge. The injured party, his/her relatives, community members and even volunteers could also take part in an investigation. Evidence accepted by the court included the testimonies of eye witnesses and hearsay testimonies, physical evidence, oaths and ordeals.[11]

---

[11] S.G. Zagoryan. "Evolution of the evidentiary process in Russia in the pre-revolutionary era," *Legal Journal of Criminalistics: yesterday, today and tomorrow*, no. 1 (2019): 17.

2.3 THE FEUDAL PRINCIPALITIES OF ANCIENT RUS' (1200-1500 CE)

By the end of the 12th century CE, the importance and powers of *'vetche'*, the meeting of urban community members, significantly decreased. Such meetings retained the right to call and replace the prince or princess and resolve on certain issues of war and peace[12], but lost nearly all judicial powers due to the ever-growing importance of clerical courts on the one hand, and principal (secular) courts on the other. Old nobility (*'boyar'*) were given the privilege of movng from one principality to another, with the option to change their sovereign, but retained all the rights and privileges granted due to their social status.

The role of *Rus' Justice*, the ancient set of codified rules and customs, still persisted. For some time, this document continued to evolve, expanding with new provisions, including those regulating the amounts of various court fees.

During the 13th-14th centuries CE, judicial powers focused on the following aspects – (1) matters relating to state and so-called public interest (tried by the court of the prince with or without the participation of clerical judges), and (2) matters which the boyar nobility were free to hear independently. Court procedure for those who lived on state land was different from court procedure for those who lived on land privately owned by a noble (boyar) family or the church. Clerical courts never sentenced people to death. In a scenario, if the committed crime had to be penalised by death and were to fall under the jurisdiction of a clerical court, it had to be referred to a secular court for trial. If a particular matter fell into several categories at a time or related to the territories of several lands or principalities, an ad hoc court of shared competence was convened, consisting of a representative of the prince or church (or both) and a representative of the particular feudal party.

---

[12] Vladimir P. Zhuravlev, Vladimir V. Fortunatov, *History of election in Russia* (Russia, Saint Petersburg: Deviz Editorial House, 2011), 64.

Such courts were called "*smestnye sudy*", which literally means 'mixed courts' or 'joint courts'.[13]

For a number of reasons Ancient Rus' was divided into several feudal principalities by the 13th century CE. Among all the principalities of the Ancient Rus', the most elaborate in terms of jurisprudence and court systems were those located in the north; that is, the capital cities of Novgorov and Pskov, respectively. The *Legal Codes of Novgorod and Pskov* were adopted in the said principalities, based mostly on the ancient Rus' Justice and existing common law, however the codes were already more sophisticated and complex.

The *Legal Code of Novgorod* was more illustrative in terms of explaining the court system and procedures of that period. According to this legal code, judicial powers were shared between the meeting of the urban community ('*vetche*'), the noble council consisting of the boyar, the prince ('*knyaz*') and the archbishop, as well as officials specifically appointed by the prince. Some judicial powers also belonged to professional unions and guilds ('*tsekha*'). Additionally, the Legal Code of Novgorod contained a list of court professions and court officers, including the bailiffs, court secretaries and so on. The prince could not hear a case without a special official called '*posadnik*'. Posadnik would participate in court hearings together with another official appointed by the prince (or the princess), called '*namestnik*'. Namestnik had the casting vote in the event there was no unanimity in resolving the case. Furthermore, the institute of appeal was already outlined within the Legal Code of Novgorod. The court of appeal was represented by a panel consisting of both the abovementioned officials (posadnik and namestnik) and a jury made up of 10 persons (including the nobility – the boyar, as well as the most respected people of other social classes). The judgment cast in the course of this appellate procedure was final.[14]

---

[13] Alexander R. Andreev, *Russian statehood in terms: IX – beginning of XX century* (Russia, Moscow: Kraft+, 2001), 763.

[14] Mikhail F. Vladimirskiy-Budanov, *Overview of the history of Russian law* (Russia, Rostov-on-Don: Fenix, 1995), 107.

Disputes between the secular and the clergy were tried by the city magistrate, together with a representative of the archbishop. The servants and courtiers of the prince or the princess had to submit their disputes to jurisdiction by the nobility (*boyar*) and such cases were tried in the principal palace. Appeal was also possible. The prince had to hear the appeal case personally, together with one of his officials (posadnik). The judgment was final.[15]

Commercial disputes between merchants were tried by the prince's officials. Disputes of artisans and craftsmen related to their professional activities were tried by so-called public courts, composed of representatives of the relevant guild and the most distinguished members of the local community.[16]

The *Legal Code of Pskov* absorbed many of the provisions of the *Rus' Justice* but upgraded and supplemented them, thus becoming quite a lengthy and elaborate document for its time. It comprised 120 articles, including provisions for civil and commercial law, family law, criminal law and court procedure. In the preamble, the Pskov court charter contained a list of its sources, including the rulings and decrees of princes adopted over a period of nearly 150 years, resolutions passed at the *vetche* (community meetings) of Pskov, customs and local traditions. The court procedures specified by the Legal Code of Pskov were quite similar to those set forth by the *Legal Code of Novgorod*, except for the fact that the court powers of the prince and his public officials were broader than those of the Novgorod Principality.

The period between the 13th-15th centuries CE was quite dramatic for the Russian principalities. One by one, many Russian rulers lost battles against the great khans of the Golden Horde and thus formally became their vassals, except for some territories in the North. Those territories did not enjoy a peaceful life for long, however, because Lithuania and Poland decided to benefit from the situation and

---

[15] Oleg I. Chistyakov, *Russian Legislation of the 10th -20th centuries, Volume 1* (Russia, Moscow: Jurizdat, 1984), 378.
[16] Ivan D. Belyae, *History of the Russian Legislation* (Russia, Saint Petersburg: Lan', 1999), 76.

spread their dominance, including Catholicism, over the Northern principalities of Russia. Still, the Russian Orthodox Church, Russian law and courts remained mostly intact. The Mongol Yassa of Genghis Khan and subsequently the Sharia rules of the Golden Horde experienced almost no recognition in Russian law[17], save for the practice of imposing physical penalties for certain crimes, including penalties which could inflict severe physical trauma or handicap the convict. Such penalties (including amputation and other types of mutilations) were an absolute novelty in Russian criminal law, which previously had always pertained to monetary compensation to the victim or the victim's relatives, rather than a 'blood price' which had be paid by the convict, according to the Mongol legal tradition.

Sharia rules were applicable to some extent in disputes involving Russians and Mongols. In such a scenario, a Mongol judge of the Golden Horde had to try the case alongside his Russian colleague. The disputes between Russian princes were subject to the jurisdiction of the supreme court of the Golden Horde and were tried personally by the Great Khan in his imperial seat. All other disputes or crimes not involving any Mongol parties fell within the exclusive jurisdiction of the Russian secular or clerical judges.[18]

In the territories of Russia occupied by Lithuania, the *Rus' Justice* had effect, together with the provisions of the *Magdeburg rights* (or Magdeburg Law), originally applicable in towns of the Grand Duchy of Lithuania.

The Russian principalities eventually conquered back their freedom in the 14th-15th centuries CE from both their northern neighbours (Lithuania and Poland) and the Golden Horde. In the 15th century CE, the ruler of Muscovy (the Grand Duchy of Moscow) defeated the Great Khan of the Golden Horde and spread Russian jurisdiction over the Khanate of Kazan. The Golden Horde was split into a number of smaller kingdoms, which then either became allies of Russia and integrated into

---

[17] Ramil G. Guseynov, "The influence of the Mongol-Tatar Yoke in the development of the Russian State and Law," *Issues of Russian Justice*, no. 3 (2019): 19.
[18] Ludmila V. Dudkina, *History of law and state of Russia* (Russia, Moscow: Allel, 2010), 196.

the Russian State, or were dispersed. Lithuania and Poland were absorbed by the Russian Empire at a later stage.

2.4 MUSCOVY AND RUSSIAN TSARDOM (1500-1700 CE)

The historical victory of the Grand Duchy of Moscow (the so-called *Muscovy)* over other Russian princes, its neighbours from the Baltic Sea and the Great Khan of the Golden Horde, enabled Muscovy to regain Russian lands which had been occupied by external invaders and to extend its jurisdiction over a large number of newly conquered territories. It is quite impressive that during the indicated period of time the reunited Russian state grew by approximately 35,000 kilometers per year. [19] Muscovy established a strong centralised system of state power, concentrated in the hands of the ruler (the Grand Duke), and significantly reduced the powers of boyar nobility. From that moment on, the boyar were merely consultants to the ruler and served him as he decided. They could easily be deprived of all their privileges and possessions at the ruler's discretion. The Grand Duke of Muscovy, Ivan IV, became the Tsar of all Russia. Omitting numerous breathtaking moments in Russian history of that time it should be noted that between the 15th and 17th centuries CE, the Russian court system and jurisprudence succeeded in reaching a new level in its evolution.

Thus, as a result of a large-scale codification, new codes on court procedures were adopted between 1497 and 1550 CE. These codes summed up all previous sources of law, including the *Rus' Justice*, previous legal codes and court practices, and turned the existing customs, common law and jurisprudence into a form of codified legal provisions.

The *Court procedure code of 1497* (a.k.a *Sudebnik* of 1497) was adopted by the Grand Duke of Muscovy Ivan III, who married the niece of the last Byzantine Emperor. He ensured that, in course of his reign, Russian state territory greatly

---

[19] Richard Pipes, *Russia under the old regime* (USA, New York: Charles Scribner's Sons, 1974), 83.

increased (for that, he was also called "Collector of the Russian lands"), had the famous Moscow Kremlin reconstructed in red bricks and took over the Byzantine imperial coat of arms (the double-headed eagle) following the fall of the Byzantine Empire. The red brick Moscow Kremlin and the coat of arms survive to this day. At present, they are the official residence of the Russian President and the official coat of arms of the Russian Federation respectively.

According to the *Court Procedure Code of 1497,* judicial power was not always separate from executive power, meaning that the Grand Duke, the boyars and other functionaries of the Grand Duke had quite a broad competence to hear cases. They in fact formed the highest court.[20]

Administrative courts were established as an integral part of the relevant ministries ('*prikazy*') and tried certain cases, subject to the competence of the relevant ministry, unless the case fell within the jurisdiction of the highest court (e.g. treason and other crimes against the State). Clerical courts continued to exist in parallel.

The *Court Procedure Code of 1497* was divided into four parts and set forth the rules for the highest court (part 1), regional and local courts (part 2), general rules of civil procedure and civil law (part 3) and additional provisions regarding court procedures (part 4). This code introduced the practice of taking written minutes of court hearings, formalised the participation of a jury in legal proceedings, and provided that judges had to take the oath before accepting their service. The legal costs of court proceedings had to be borne by the plaintiff. Legal proceedings were adversarial. The concept of insolvency was introduced as a self-standing court procedure.[21] The legal process distinguished between private cases (when the proceedings could be triggered by a private party only) and public cases (when the process could be initiated by a public authority or the injured party).

---

[20] E.I. Osadchuk, "Sudebnik of 1497 as the landmark of the Russian feudal law," *Actual Problems of Humanities and Life Sciences*, no. 8 (2013): 220.
[21] Ludmila V. Dudkina, *History of law and state of Russia* (Russia, Moscow: Allel, 2010), 271.

Crimes were tried in terms of public trial and had some features of inquisition proceedings in terms of the possibility to use torture and ordeal. The court decisions in all types of proceedings had to be unanimous. Otherwise, such cases had to be reported to the Grand Duke for his final judgment.

Last, but not least, the *Court Procedure Code of 1497* guaranteed that everyone had the right of equal access to justice and imposed liability on judges who refused to accept claims, provided these were filed in compliance with established procedures.[22]

The *Code of 1550* (a.k.a. *Sudebnik of 1550*) was adopted within the period of the Russian Tsardom. It is believed to have been inspired by Tsar Ivan IV, who was quite controversial and one of the most debated historical figures. The legal philosophy standing behind this document was greatly influenced by the ideology of the Russian Orthodox Church at the time. The idea of imperial continuity due to direct blood kinship of the Russian Tsar with the Byzantine Emperors, the ever growing territory, ethnic and cultural multiplicity made the Russian Tsardom more and more similar to an empire. This, along with fidelity to the Orthodox faith in the pure undistorted form practiced in the Byzantine Empire before its collapse, led to a new broader and more ambitious perception of Russia and the role that it naturally had in international politics of the time. All these factors had a great influence on the legal philosophy and legal culture of Russia. [23]

---

[22] Marat R. Zaguidullin, "Liability in Russian legal proceedings according to the court procedure codes of 1497 and 1550" in *Report to the University of Kazan, Department of Humanities and Social Sciences,* no. 1, (2019).

[23] The postulates such as "Moscow is the third Rome and there shall be no forth one" pointing at the direct succession of Russia to the Great Roman Empire (the first Rome) and the Eastern Roman (Byzantine) Empire (the second Rome) in terms of the Russian geopolitical goals and imperial ambitions, vital importance of the Russian Orthodox faith, and the unity or even quasi parental relationship between the Russian ruler and the Russian folk (not in the sense of the Russian ethnos but meaning all the people living under the Russian jurisdiction), where a father protects and cares about his children but also has the power to correct and punish them if they misbehave or disobey, originated in the 15th - 16th centuries and lasted throughout the whole continuing period of existence of the Russian state in whatever form it existed. Even the Soviet Union, which first proclaimed fierce atheism, did its best to destroy the Church and prosecuted thousands of priests, monks and believers, had to admit that the State won't survive if the faith is missing. Thus, on September 4, 1943, Stalin met the highest clergy. Since that moment on the Church was left in peace, priests and

The *Tsar Code* was enacted by the first Russian ad hoc parliament of feudal estates, the so called Hundred Chapter Council or '*Stoglavy Sobor*', convened in Moscow in 1551 and consisting of the boyars and the highest clergy. The Tsar Code revised and expanded the provisions of the Court Procedure Code of 1497. Compared to the Code of 1497, the Tsar Code was a much better structured document, divided into thematic sections, with all provisions numbered, which made the references within its text more comprehensive and logical.

The *Tsar Code* contained a list of sources on which it was established. Among the sources, the Tsar Code named customs, common law, the Rus' Justice, various charters and decrees previously issued by princes of the past, the Code of 1497 and the Legal Code of Grand Duke Vasiliy III (the latter is quite a disputed document, as neither the original nor copies survived to the present date).[24]

In terms of judicial procedure and jurisprudence, the *Tsar Code* provided for a clear vertical structure of secular courts, starting from the lowest instance in situ, the local courts (in rural communities), up to the court of the Tsar who had the supreme judicial power of reviewing the decisions of any lower courts, save for cases falling within the competence of or ever existing in parallel clerical courts (all family law issues and religious matters).

Decisions of the clerical courts were final and not subject to any appeal or review. Among the novelties of the Tsar Code the following should be mentioned. '*The law shall not apply retroactively*' was proclaimed as the general principle of law. The practice of granting tax immunities was abolished. The judges became subject to penal liability for improper performance of their duties, acting *ultra vires* or breaking their oath. Jail and imprisonment (for a certain period or a lifetime) were included in the list of penalties imposed for certain crimes.[25]

---

other prisoners of faith were released and amnestied, the new Patriarch of Moscow and all the Russias was elected, and religious living was revived.

[24] Maria D. Chupova, "Forgotten legal codes of the past," *Lex Russica*, no. 2 (2017): 185.

[25] Konstantin K. Korablin. "Evolution of punishment in the Legal Code of 1550," *Education and Law*, no. 11 (2020): 305-306.

The regulation of court proceedings were still very similar to those set forth in the *Court Procedure Code of 1497*. The process became more formalised. The parties had to be called in process by official summons. A claim could be raised by anyone against any individual notwithstanding the social class of the parties involved. A certain category of servants ('*kholopy*'), previously not acknowledged as having legal capacity, obtained this through the *Tsar Code of 1550*. From that moment on, Kholopy could sue or be sued. The age of full legal capacity for any social class in civil and criminal law was set forth as 14 years old for men and 12 years old for women.

The extinction of the Rurik dynasty in the late 16th century CE plunged Russia into the turmoil of a long political crisis which brought anarchy, lawlessness, and famine that killed nearly a third of the whole population, and all that was topped with dramatic battles for the throne among the various relatives of the defunct dynasty, the boyars and numerous external invaders wishing to abolish the Russian Orthodox Church, take over Russia and place their own candidate as the new puppet-tsar - or just annex the Russian territory and govern it directly.

The so-called Time of Troubles (a.k.a. *'Smutnoe vremya'*) occurred in the 17th century, when popular discontent became so great that it resulted in the creation of a volunteer army of Russia built up of an incredible variety of different misfits including commoners, peasants, merchants, Cossacks, aristocrats and even some representatives of the old Russian nobility, the boyars. As a result, the Polish, Lithuanian, Swedish regular troops and German mercenaries were crushed by the Russian volunteer army, while the rest of them fled. The whole of Russia's public council was convened in the year 1613 to commemorate liberation and independence. The new ruling dynasty, the Romanovs, was elected by the said convention.

In 1649, another nationwide public council had to be called in order to sum up and codify all the legal provisions of Russian law known and applicable at that time, notwithstanding whether they were in oral or written form, and add up the rulings and legal developments which the new dynasty had managed to generate so far. The draft document was prepared by the *Special Drafting Commission* that included selected officials of the *Boyar Duma* (ancestor of the Russian parliament) and the most reputed scholars of the time, both secular and clerical. In addition to purely Russian laws and customs, the drafting commission also analysed the laws of jurisdictions related to Russia either in the sense of traditions (such as Byzantine and Roman Law documents) or geopolitics (a mixture of rules previously applied on Russian territories under foreign rule prior to their liberation and reunification with the Russian Tsardom, or foreign laws and regulations of newly conquered territories, e.g. the *Lithuanian statute of 1588*. Provisions compatible with the spirit of Russian law and Russian legal philosophy of the time were synthesised in the draft new code of Russia. As a result, a single codified act called the *Council Code of 1649* was adopted by the public council. This document was one the most durable legal instruments in Russian history. Many of its provisions managed to survive up to the mid-19th century.

The Council Code 1649 turned out to be quite a lengthy document consisting of nearly one thousand articles divided into 25 sections. It was the first Russian code officially published in a printed form (all previous codes were handwritten and were notified to the public orally in public places and churches).[26] In total 2400 copies were published and spread throughout Russia, including its most distant territories. Taking into account the cost of book printing at that time, this was an extremely generous gesture on the part of the Tsar.

The court structure and legal proceedings were stipulated in section X of the *Council Code 1649*. The Code outlined the court system throughout the country. There were three levels of courts. The lowest level included the local courts in rural communities and cities. The upper level was represented by the courts

---

[26] Dmitry A. Savchenko, "The making of the Council Code: historical experience of modernization of national legislation," *Journal of the Novosibirsk State University of Economics and Management*, no. 3 (2013): 214.

established at different public offices in the capital (*'prikazy'*). The highest court consisted of the *boyar duma* (the boyars holding official positions within the Tsar's consultative council) and the Tsar himself. Cases concerning civil matters were triggered at the initiative of a private party (the claimant), who had to pay a court fee so that the court would accept to hear the case on its merits. Legal proceedings on public law matters (such as penal law cases) could be triggered by a private party or a public authority.

The defendant was called to court by summons handed over by court officials (the bailiffs). The defendant had the right to neglect the summons no more than twice, each time for a legitimate reason (such as illness, physical absence, or similar). If the defendant neglected the call for a third time, the case had to be resolved automatically in favour of the claimant. Legal costs were borne by the defendant. All legal proceedings were held as per the protocols. The court judgment was executed in the form of a charter (*'gramota'*), which was handed over to the parties.

The Code also introduced the concept of fault or guilt (in criminal matters) and outlined aggravating and mitigating factors. Many new provisions covering different branches of law were integrated into the Code; not all of them were progressive from a contemporary point of view (for example, the Code created the possibility of turning some categories of peasants into serfs who had no self-standing legal capacity). However, the Code did respond to the needs and challenges faced by the State at that time. If assessed in general, it should be admitted that the *Council Code 1649* upgraded Russian law, and in fact resulted in a more comprehensive and rational structure, laying the foundation for upcoming new developments in Russian law and jurisprudence.

2.5 IMPERIAL ABSOLUTISM IN RUSSIA (1700-1850 CE)

The Russian Tsardom did not turn into the Russian Empire in the blink of an eye. There were many contributory factors, including large scale administrative, social and military reforms, some of which were inspired by the outcomes of a European tour made by the Russian Tsar Peter I incognito. The apogee occurred with the Russian victory over Sweden of Carl XII in the Great Northern War which proved that Russia, previously still regarded as mostly a regional power, turned into one of the most powerful states of the time. Tsar Peter I (a.k.a. Peter the Great) became the first Emperor of the Russian Empire in 1721.

Victory over Sweden, and the adjoining of a large part of Poland and the Baltics as war trophies to the territory of the Russian Empire later on were very important from a strategic point of view, and endorsed the growing political and economic ambitions of the Russian State. As collateral benefit, this also gave a sort of moral relief after years of mischief and humiliation which the Swedes, the Poles and the Lithuanians had caused to Russians during the Time of Troubles.

In terms of courts and jurisprudence of that period, many attempts were made to modernise the court system and separate judicial and executive powers. Not all the aspirations were easily achieved. The most progressive scholars of the time opted to implement the models of Western Europe. The Swedish and Prussian law models were taken as samples; however these proved to be inconvenient and too distant from the spirit of Russian law. Thus, Swedish and Prussian legal influence was mostly present in the realm of Russian military statutes and regimental regulations of the time.

The newly built judicial system inspired by German law had to turn back to Russian realities and adapt significantly. Thus, big rural settlements and small cities got their own sole judges, bigger cities had local courts consisting of presiding judges and a panel of legal assessors. In the regional centres (capitals of provinces), governors had the authority to preside in court as well as to suspend any judicial act for a legitimate reason. Suspension of legal enforcement of a court act by the resolution of a governor without cause could result in the personal liability of the governor. This practice lasted almost until 1775, when another attempt was made to keep judicial and executive powers fully separate.[27]

In parallel with ordinary courts, military courts and admiralty courts were established to resolve relevant specific cases in those niche areas. Depending on the social class (estate) of the parties, cases had to be tried in different court chambers.

Based on the analysis of numerous legislative acts of the time, including province charters and Imperial Decrees, it is possible to conclude that by the late 18th century, the following court system was formed which distinguished people by their social class and estates. The noble class (aristocracy) had to bring their cases to the lower court ('*uezdny sud*') and could appeal to the upper court of the province. The city commoners, craftsmen and merchants would bring a case to the city magistrate and would then be able to appeal to the upper magistrate of the province. The peasants had to deal with their cases in a specific chamber of the lower court in their district and could appeal to the relevant chamber of the upper court of the province. Internally, the courts were divided into sections for civil and criminal matters. The highest judicial instance of appeal for all courts was the Senate, a special supreme state authority having its seat in the newly constructed capital of the Russian Empire, Saint Petersburg.[28]

As regards court procedure, through the 18th century it varied from a purely written form with no physical presence of the parties and no oral pleadings in the early 18th century, to an adversarial form of the court process with each party presenting

---

[27] Svetlana A. Knyazeva, *History of the Russian State and Law* (Russia, Moscow: AST Editors, 2012), 164.
[28] V.A. Tomsinov, "Court system in the Russian Empire of the XVIII – mid XIX centuries," *Journal of the Moscow State University, Series 11 – Law and Jurisprudence*, no. 3 (2016): 3-4.

its case both in writing and then orally at the court hearing, acting in person or represented by a proxy. Progressive thinking of the *Age of Enlightenment* also spread through the territory of the Russian Empire and had a great influence on Russian legal philosophy of the time. Thus, starting from the mid-18th century the ideas of individual liberty, separation of the state from the church, tolerance and humanism in general started to actively circulate within Russian high society.[29]

Gradual improvement of juridical techniques, which differed a lot from what was within the documents of the past yet still remaining in effect, logically led to the initiative of the new Emperor Nicholas I to systemise the existing corpus of Russian law and adopt the new Code of Laws of the Russian Empire set forth in up-to-date legal style and language and reflecting the actual realities in the State.

More than three hundred thousand various legal acts had to be reviewed and protocolled. Those acts formed the so-called *Collection of the Russian legislation.* Each act of the Collection was accompanied by an annotation which had no legal effect, however it assisted in interpretation of the relevant act. All laws and regulations that the legislative commission decided to leave in effect formed fifteen volumes of the Code of Laws submitted to resolution and adoption by the State Council, a multifunctional legislative authority which was the predecessor of the modern Parliament. The *Code of Laws* started to apply on January 1, 1835. At the same time the first endeavours to introduce constitutional monarchy in Russia emerged.[30]

---

[29] Unfortunately, not so many of those intellectuals, philosophers and other Enlightenment adepts, who had lived in palaces for generations and circulated in illustrious literary salons, cosy ball rooms or Masonic lodges were ready to spread the admired ideas of Enlightenment over the generations of their own serfs and their descendants even after the emancipation, which was one of many reasons why the civil war after the collapse of the Russian Empire was so brutal and was fought with no mercy.

[30] Leonid V. Karnaushenko, "Problems of management and administration in the Russian Empire in constitutional drafts of early XIX century," *Society, Environment, Development (Terra Humana)*, no. 3 (2009): 33.

2.6 RUSSIAN CONSTITUTIONAL MONARCHY (1850- 1917CE)

The second half of the 19th century was a period of crucial reforms in the Russian Empire, which brought the long-expected emancipation of serfs, proclamation of vital human rights, a boost of industrialisation and other numerous developments within Russian society and the State. The amount of stock companies established in Russia within the short period of 1856-1860 exceeded the aggregate amount of commercial entities established in Russia over the previous 20 years.[31]

The emancipation of serfs and the process of them becoming free peasants was a complex and poignant issue which generated discussions among – (1) members of the Imperial government, (2) scholars of law, (3) intellectuals of the time and (4) landlords (not necessarily of a noble origin). Several models were discussed for obtaining this noble objective. In the end, the crucial point that emerged after such debates was whether to liberate the peasants individually or together with the land slots to which they were tied. A pilot project of individual landless emancipation showed a high risk of proletarianisation of the peasants and the progress of revolutionary and anarchic ideas among the liberated former serfs. Finally, a balance was found between the *liberal model* of unconditional release of the serfs with their real estate (houses and land slots), supported by the Russian Emperor Alexander II, and the *conservative model* supported by a number of Imperial ministers and the landlords owning land in the provinces with the most fertile soils, who insisted on liberating the serfs with no land, or at least with a full compensation paid to the landlord for those land slots transferred to peasants.

A compromise was found by combining the progressive ideas of emancipation and a compensated real estate transfer where the compensation to landlords had to be paid 20% by peasants and 80% from the state budget. This amount was provided to the peasants by the State as a loan at 6% p.a. for a period of 49 years,

---

[31] Maxim A. Isaev, *History of the Russian State and Russian Law* (Russia, Moscow: Statut, 2012), 413.

with the archaic forms of self-governance of the liberated peasants found in ancient Russian law, including rural communities (*'obshina'*), collective liability of the community members (*'krugovaya poruka'*), collective possession of the arable farmland by the community, regular or extraordinary meetings of community members (*'skhod'*) and the relevant powers of the community over its members which would last until they pay off the all debts.[32]

At almost the same time, namely in 1864, a significant judicial reform commenced in the Russian Empire which was triggered by the adoption of four Acts aimed at improving and modernising the Russian court system. Those Acts were the *Regulations on establishment of Judicial Authorities*, *Regulations of Civil Proceedings*, *Regulations of Criminal Proceedings*, and *Regulations of Punishments Imposed by Justices of the Peace (or magistrates)*. Courts were totally separated from the executive branch. The principle of equality of the parties was proclaimed. Court hearings were open to the public. It should be pointed out that practices of ordeals or any other physical impact on litigation parties or others involved in the process had already been abolished in the 18th century. In course of the 1864 judicial reform this rule was once again sustained as a fundamental principle of personal inviolability.

Attorneys-at-law were recognised as self-standing professionals who had to meet a set of qualification criteria – (1) have a professional diploma, (2) hold a degree in law, (3) be of Russian citizenship, (4) a minimum five years' experience of legal practice, (5) solid financial solvency, (6) no criminal records or restriction in a legal capacity, and (7) a successful result at the bar exam. The guild of Russian advocacy was established.[33] Similar criteria applied to judges. Being a judge became a profession per se and could not be exercised on a part time basis. Candidate judges had to comply with all formal criteria, pass a qualification exam

---

[32] L.A.Muravyeva, "Emancipation of serfs in Russia: reasons, implementation and the meaning," *Financial University Journal*, 6, no. 2 (2012): 48-49.

[33] Ekaterina I. Osadchuk, "History of origin and legal profession development in imperial Russia" in *Scientific notes of Orel State University*, Department of humanities and social sciences Vol. 4, no. 54, (2013).

and receive an official appointment to serve in a certain district or province by a governmental decree. The status of a judge was a life-long appointment terminated only by death or a justified professional disqualification with no further possibility to qualify in any other legal profession.[34] The institution of trial by jury was formalised, scrupulously regulated and had a widespread application for both civil and criminal matters. The qualification criteria for general prosecutors and bailiffs were ascertained and systemised.[35]

The principle of social class or 'estates' jurisdiction with separate courts and estates chambers was abolished. Instead, a unified court system was introduced throughout the whole Empire for all its subjects, notwithstanding their social class.

The lowest judicial units were represented by magistrates (literally *'judges of peace'*) who were competent to resolve on civil matters of small claim amounts as well as minor crimes sentenced by not more than one year of jail or a fine in an amount of up to three hundred rubles. Each magistrate was assigned to serve in a particular circuit. Several circuits constituted a district (*'uyezd'*).

District courts had the general competence to resolve on a variety of civil and criminal matters. The composition of the panel of judges, as well as the need to involve a jury depended on the gravity of the criminal case, or the amount of the civil claim. Normally, the panel would include three judges. When a jury was involved, there would be one judge who was authorised to pronounce the sentence or draw the civil judgment.

The decisions of district courts could be appealed to judicial chambers formed within provinces. So basically, judicial chambers could be considered 'regional

---

[34] N. N. Smirnova, "Establishment of judiciary in the Russian Empire," *Herald of Russian State University of A.I. Herzen*, 74, no. 1 (2008): 454.
[35] Nadezhda N. Efremova, "Evolution of the Russian jurisprudence (judicial reforms of XVIII-XIX centuries)," *HSE University Journal*, no. 2 (2008): 47.

courts'. Apart from appeal functions, they were also competent to resolve on certain high crimes.

The supreme judicial authority of the Russian Empire at that time was the Senate. It was the instance of the second appeal (*'cassation'*) for the lower courts. Within the Senate there were the Department of Cassation for civil cases and the Department of Cassation for criminal cases. Grounds for review in cassation included the discovery of new facts and circumstances not previously known in the course of proceedings in the lower courts or 'explicit violation of the sense and spirit of material law' by lower courts. At a later stage, a special Disciplinary Commission for judges was also established within the Senate, authorised to resolve on the professional disqualification of judges. Special Commissions could be formed within the Senate to try extraordinary cases; for example, assassination of or assault on the Emperor or members of the Imperial Family.[36]

Special courts, such as military courts and admiralty courts, continued to exist in parallel with the abovementioned courts of general competence and were subject to their own *Regulation of 1867*. These special courts exercised a very precise scope of powers limited to disciplinary offences committed by soldiers and officers of the various corps. Minor offenses were tried by the regiment court. Severe crimes and appeals were heard by district military courts. Cassation appeals had to be submitted to the Supreme Military Court in Saint Petersburg. The judges of said Supreme Court were appointed directly by the Emperor.[37]

The above judicial system continued to exist with no significant changes until the Russian Empire fell in 1917. Finland, Poland, Estonia, Latvia and Lithuania, formerly integral parts of the Russian Empire, became independent. Over the next couple of years, the Imperial Family, many relatives of the Romanov dynasty and

---

[36] Andrey V. Kalinichenko, "Senate as a part of judicial system of the Russian Empire" in *Report to the Kuban State University*, No. 4857497, Thesis Department, (2011).

[37] Igor V. Zozulya, "Military Justice in the Russian Empire: from courts martial to military tribunals of the beginning of the XX century", *Science Innovations Technologies*, no. 67 (2010): 41-42.

people of their circle, a lot of representatives of former state establishment and many civilians were brutally killed. Millions of people were forced to emigrate to save their lives.

2.7 RUSSIA DURING THE SOVIET ERA (1917-1991)

The revolutionary powers in Russia were so stupefied with their success that they managed to destroy the whole structure of the supreme state authorities of the Russian Empire within just a few months of the revolution. The State Duma (the parliament of the Russian Empire), the State Council and the Provisional Government, put in place by the old Russian establishment with the aim of ensuring at least some sort of civilised transfer of state powers, were dissolved after Russia was proclaimed a federal republic. Many statesmen were executed or killed with no sentence or trial. Civil War broke out.

The Bolsheviks created the Revolutionary Military Council (*'Revvoensovet'*) which, together with the All-Russian Central Execute Committee, accumulated the full scope of state powers in the newly proclaimed Russian Republic. Companies and enterprises were nationalised. Private ownership of land was banned. The State established a monopoly on grain. Private trade in essential goods was prohibited. Public powers *in situ* were exercised by local units of said Revolutionary Military Council. Judicial powers were exercised by Court Martials, revolutionary tribunals or so-called peoples' courts (*'narodny sud'*), where cases were often tried purely on the basis of revolutionary ideals. Thus, justice ceased to be the prerogative of professional judges and was no longer based on law. Summary justice was also practiced.

The Crimea peninsula, last stronghold of the monarchist White Army, fell in 1920. Siberia and the Far East territories had become part of the Soviet Union by 1922. By 1923, the Civil War was over. According to various studies and estimations, the civil war resulted in between 10 to 17 million casualties, mostly civilians.

Around 2 million people were forced to emigrate.[38] After the civil war was over, supporters of the new regime started a large-scale cleansing and prosecuted anyone who could be identified as an ideological adversary.

Fierce rejection of all previous laws and legal structures, as rudiments of the 'old regime', which were inconsistent with the philosophies of Russian military communism, resulted in a legal vacuum. The Soviet State had to take a step back to the legal heritage of the defeated Russian Empire. Thus, according to the *New Economic Policy* introduced by the Bolsheviks leader Vladimir Lenin in 1921, private individuals were again allowed to freely carry out economic activities, own small enterprises, own and possess movables and real estate (save for land). Promissory notes and bills of exchange started to circulate again.

A large part of transactions, contracts, and many other legal concepts in the realm of nearly all branches of law originating from the period of the Russian Empire had to be re-integrated into the corpus of Soviet law. However, these were always subject to the new primary governing principles of constant state control and compliance with the postulates of *Marxism and Lenin's socialism.* The time interval between the end of the Civil War in Russia and the beginning of the Second World War was a period of intense legislative activity in the young Soviet state, when a lot of decrees, legal codes and even several editions of the new *Soviet Constitution* were adopted.

On 22 June 1941, Nazi Germany started a war of annihilation against the Soviet Union,[39] attacking it with a colossal force of millions of German and their allied troops, thus unleashing the most destructive military campaign in history.[40] The

---

[38] N.A. Pocheshkov, Zh. O. Abregova, and R.M. Shkhachemukhov, "Population losses during the Civil War in Russia (1917-1922): the debatable space of historical demography," *Modern scientific thought*, no. 6 (2020): 64.

[39] Barry Grey, "Seventy-five years since the Nazi invasion of the Soviet Union," available at, <https://www.wsws.org/en/articles/2016/06/22/pers-j22.html>, accessed on 10 September, 2021.

[40] Geoffrey Roberts, "The 75th anniversary of Operation Barbarossa: The Nazi invasion of the Soviet Union," available at <https://www.sott.net/article/320566-The-75th-anniversary-of-Operation-Barbarossa-The-Nazi-invasion-of-the-Soviet-Union>, accessed on 25 October, 2021.

German Hunger Plan was aimed at exterminating a large part of the Soviet population by starvation and the extinction of its industries.[41] Besides, according to the Nazi General Plan *Ost*, over 70 million Russians had to be eliminated in order to give *Lebensraum* (living space) to Germans.[42]

This deadly war required mobilisation of all the military and economic resources of the Soviet Union. Soviet laws passed during that period of time were all designed to support that goal. Penal laws became harsher in order to address desertion, looting, espionage and collaboration with the enemy, money forging, disclosure of state secrets or other confidential data and the unauthorised circulation of weapons. Labour laws had to be amended in order to enable women, pensioners and minors to replace men in workplaces and at industrial sites. Due to hideous human losses and a huge number of orphans and street kids, family laws and adoption laws had to be reviewed and supplemented accordingly. The scope of administrative law became significantly broader in order to encompass the regulation of war-related challenges, including the status of war refugees, displaced persons, victims of war and their evacuation, housing, allowances, etc.

Despite the initial aspirations of the Nazi leaders and their allies, in May 1945, the Soviet Army captured Berlin. Hitler and some of the Nazi establishment committed suicide. Many others ended up in the Nuremberg Tribunal; some were sentenced to death as war criminals, or jailed. Quite a number actually fled and managed to escape punishment. In August 1945, the Soviet Army liberated China and North Korea from Japanese occupation and brought the war nearer to its end.

The post-war period revealed colossal devastation in the European part of the USSR, de-population, a ubiquitous shortage of everything, a war-related surge of banditry, street crimes and illicit trade, and the terror activities of clandestine

---

[41] Timothy Snyder, "The Reich's forgotten atrocity," available at, < https://www.theguardian.com/commentisfree/cifamerica/2010/oct/21/secondworldwar-russia>, accessed on 23 October, 2021.
[42] André Mineau, *Operation Barbarossa: Ideology and Ethics against Human Dignity* (Amsterdam-New York: Editions Rodopi B.V., 2004), 180.

fascist cells and Nazi collaborators still present in the country. All these factors emphasised the new challenges which Russia had to face right after World War Two, including the very disappointing fact that yesterday's Western allies were already considering the option of starting a new war against the Soviet Union.[43]

The above circumstances had a decisive impact on the legal philosophy, laws and the entire state system of the Soviet Russia. Functions and competencies of the police, investigators, prosecutors, law enforcement organisations, and courts were upgraded and structured in a more efficient way. War-period justice was no longer possible. Once again, justice became the exclusive prerogative of state courts overseen by professional judges. No punishment was possible, save that based on verdicts cast by a competent court after an official public trial based on the rule of law.

In parallel, the national laws of the Soviet Union experienced considerable influence from the impressive evolution of post-war international law generated within the newly established legal system of the United Nations Organisation, founded by the Soviet Union together with the Allies and several other countries. All democratic fundamental principles of law stipulated in the *UNO Charter,* the *Universal Declaration of Human Rights*, the milestone provisions of the *international humanitarian law conventions* and many other international law documents were integrated in the laws of the USSR.[44]

In 1964, both the *Civil Code and the Penal Code 1964* were adopted, which were imbued with general ideas of the liberalisation of the economy (to the extent possible in the state-planned economic system), the enhanced protection of human rights, equality before the law, the prohibition of discrimination, milder

---

[43] There are a lot of studies on this matter, see for example Jonathan Walker, *Churchill's Third World War: British plans to attack the Soviet Empire 1945* (London: History Press, 2017).
[44] The UNO statute was ratified by the *Decree of the Presidium of the USSR Supreme Council* on 20.08.1945 with immediate direct effect and integration in Soviet law, the four Geneva humanitarian conventions of 1949 were ratified by the Decree of the Presidium of the USSR Supreme Council on 17.04.1054 with immediate direct effect and integration in Soviet law, all subsequent protocols to them were also ratified and integrated in Soviet law in the 70s.

provisions on liability in general and increased age thresholds for imposing penal liability.

The system of courts included courts of general competence, courts for commercial disputes, arbitration courts and so-called comrades' courts (a special form of a collective justice, with court members elected for a short period of time not exceeding two years and competent to deal with minor offences and small claims).

In 1977, the new *USSR Constitution* was adopted, which stated that the Soviet people were the only source of power, whereby the basis of the Soviet Union lay in the unity of the workers, peasants and intellectuals (*'intelligentsia'*). Later on, mostly due to growing disagreement between the Soviet people and the State establishment, this Constitution (which in fact did contain many reasonable and even progressive legal provisions) started to appear nothing more than clichés. The annulment of *Article 6 of the USSR Constitution* (related to the governing role of the Communist Party) and the election of the first and only President of the USSR (Michael Gorbachev) in 1990 did not change much.

Gorbachev's *perestroika,* [45] combined with poor leadership, created the prerequisites for a new revolution in 1991 as a result of – (1) general fatigue and irritation in Soviet society, (2) the rise of nationalism, stimulated by local governments in many ethnic Soviet republics, (3) the collapse of the *Warsaw Pact* system, which illustrated that *'people's friendship'* was just a myth, mostly believed in by Russians, (4) exhausting bureaucracy, (5) persisting censure, state frontiers still remaining closed for much of the Soviet population (save for a special caste of communist party elite, diplomats and selected individuals), and (7) creating an illusion that the grass was always greener on the other side (mostly in Western Europe and the USA).

---

[45] It means the policy or practice within old Soviet Union of restructuring or reforming the economic and political system.

The initial idea of preserving and reforming the Soviet Union was put to a vote at the *USSR referendum of 1991*. It was indeed supported by the majority of the Soviet population, according to the referendum results,[46] but these results were ignored due to a sequence of events (surprisingly similar to a coup d'etat) which came immediately afterwards and destroyed the Soviet Union. The announced arrival of genuine democracy and a free market economy in fact turned out to be – (1) a new colonisation campaign bringing about plunder through the privatisation of state property and state enterprises, (2) nationwide fake insolvencies aimed solely at asset drain, (3) the creation of an oligarchy, (4) a broadening of corruption, (5) colossal unemployment, (6) an immense growth of criminality, (7) a brain drain, (8) severe impoverishment of the population, (9) a tremendous demographic gap, (10) outbreaks of terrorism, and (11) other inherent experiences of living in a brand new reality, to which Russia still had to adapt.

2.8 CONTEMPORARY RUSSIA (1991-PRESENT)

In 1991, the Soviet Union ceased to exist. Russia was transformed into the Russian Federation, pretty much as we know it today. Pursuing a doctrine of sovereign continuity, Russia became the legal successor to the Soviet 'empire', accepting all rights and obligations of the Soviet Union. External debts and international obligations of both the USSR and former Soviet republics which became sovereign were also assigned to Russia,[47] basically allowing those countries to start a new chapter with a positive balance, whereas Russia found itself close to financial ruin. However, it retained the status of a permanent member of the UN Security Council, with a right of veto and the nuclear power of the whole former USSR.

---

[46] Edward W. Walker, *Dissolution: Sovereignty and the Breakup of the Soviet Union* (Lanham: Rowman & Littlefield, 2003), 137.
[47] Arsen G. Avsharov, *External economic policy of the Russian Federation* (Russia, Saint Petersburg, Piter Editorial House, 2012), 213.

Considering the numerous difficulties and challenges of the transition period faced by the newly proclaimed Russian Federation, at least the legislative transformation of Soviet law into Russian federal law had to be gradual to avoid a legal vacuum and paralysis of the whole legal system. The legislations of the Soviet era continued to remain in effect for quite a long period of time. Even now, thirty years later, there are still quite a number of acts and various bylaws of the Soviet period that apply in the Russian Federation and form an integral part of modern Russian law.

The early 1990s was a period of research and general openness to all types of societies and legal cultures, mostly Western, which positioned themselves as developed democracies in the thought process of Russian scholars. Numerous legislative experiments and attempts to transplant foreign laws directly into the Russian legal framework were made. For example, despite the fact that Russian law pertains to the Roman law family, there were attempts to introduce the Anglo-Saxon concept of trusts and split property into Russian civil law. Naturally, it did not work out due to factors involving purely juridical, plus cultural and social relevance. At present, a law of trust management is present in modern Russian law, but it is quite distant in its legal nature from classical trusts in the meaning of English law.[48]

A number of fundamental legislative acts were adopted in the mid-late 1990s, aimed at addressing the new political, economic and social developments in the Russian Federation. These acts managed to integrate those legal structures which had proven to be efficient and successful in the past and were compatible with new Russian realities, combined with up-to-date jurisprudence. The most important laws of the mentioned period include the *Constitution of the Russian Federation of 1993* (still in effect, as amended in 2020), federal constitutional laws that regulate the modern judicial system of the Russian Federation and its state

---

[48] Svetlana V. Chugunova, Konstantin G. Ryndin, "An introduction to trust management in Russia," *Trusts & Trustees*, 14, no. 5 (2008): 278.

apparatus, several legal codes (varying on the branch of law), including those of court procedure, together with some other federal laws and bylaws.

The Constitution of 1993 (the initial edition), being the supreme Act in the hierarchy of Russian law, proclaimed the supremacy of the general principles of international law and international treaties made by the Russian Federation (or inherited from the Soviet Union) over its national laws and guaranteed protection of all rights and freedoms known and recognised universally. It also outlined the current state structure and the core principles on which it is based, provided for the distribution of powers amongst the Federation, its subjects and autonomies, set forth the status and competences of the President, the Government, the Federal Assembly (the Parliament of the Russian Federation consisting of the State Duma, the lower chamber, and the Council of the Federation, the upper chamber), the system of courts and general prosecutors, and the system of municipal authorities.

The Constitution was amended in 2020, after the draft new edition was approved in the nationwide referendum of 1 July 2020. These amendments highlight the quintessence of the legal philosophy of present-day Russia, as compared to the status quo of 1993 when the said Constitution was originally adopted.

Thus, general principles of international law and international treaties made by the Russian Federation still form an integral part of its legal framework and prevail over domestic legislation, but Russia can now decline to abide by the resolutions of any international authorities made within the scope of said international treaties, if they are in conflict with the provisions of the Constitution of the Russian Federation.

At the same time, in practice, quite a number of international law documents are directly applicable in Russia. Ratification is not always needed. For example, regulations and other legal acts adopted by supranational authorities of the

Eurasian Economic Union (in which, at present, membership is held by Armenia, Belarus, Kazakhstan, Kyrgyzstan, Russia and where Moldavia, Uzbekistan and Cuba are observer states) have a direct effect in the Russian Federation and form part of its national legislation.

Furthermore, the *Constitution 1993*, as amended in 2020, acknowledges the uninterrupted existence and legal continuity of Russian statehood through the whole history of Russia in whatever its form, name or title, counting more than one thousand years. Before 2020, only legal succession to the Soviet Union was emphasised.

In addition, a new provision was added by the amendments of 2020, stipulating that the Russian ethnos is officially acknowledged as the 'ethnos constituting the State'. This was added as a supplement to the numerous sections from the old Soviet constitution and customs pertaining to issues of ethnic, national, cultural pluralism and diversity, protection of minor ethnicities, guarantees of their rights, freedoms, languages, cultural heritage, and so forth. These sections, as discussed earlier, were already present in the Constitutions from the Soviet era and the initial edition of the Constitution of the Russian Federation of 1993, but the "Russian issue" was always modestly put aside. Despite the fact that it may seem natural and self-explaining that the Russian ethnos has been in all senses contributing significantly to the State over the past centuries, this thesis has never been enshrined in law (neither in the period of the Russian Empire, nor in the period of the Soviet Union) until now, in particular in its present form.

Protection of Russian minorities as well as Russian-speaking *compatriots* (people of common Soviet heritage, including those having Soviet or Russian citizenship in the past or their descendants) living abroad is proclaimed as one of the priorities of the Russian Federation.

As a result of the amendments of 2020, state officials at a federal or regional level, and some other categories of people forming the Russian political establishment, faced prohibition of foreign citizenship or a residence permit in any third state, as well as any bank accounts, real estate or other assets abroad, which came as a rather unpleasant surprise for quite a number of them.

Another distinctive feature of the 2020 Amendments worth mentioning, is that in addition to already existing articles specifying that the Russian Federation is a secular state where religious organisations are separated from the State and absolute freedom of religion is guaranteed (where anyone can manifest any religion or belief, or practice none), a new provision was added, stipulating that the Russian Federation preserves the memory of ancestors who transferred to subsequent generations their ideals and faith in God.

Chapter 7 of the Constitution, dedicated to the Russian judicial system and public prosecutors, is quite illustrative from the standpoint of the synthesis between the laws of monarchic Russia and those of the Soviet Union in the modern law of the Russian Federation. The court system in Russia is governed by a number of fundamental principles which can be summed up as follows – (1) judicial power is separated from legislative and executive powers, and can be exercised by courts only, (2) no other authority is competent to dispense justice. Prosecution is vested on public prosecutors only, (3) the status of a judge and that of a prosecutor are recognised on a nationwide basis, (4) throughout the whole immense territory of the Russian Federation, there is a unified system of courts built up in a clear hierarchical order. Russian law distinguishes between constitutional, administrative, civil, commercial and criminal legal procedures. All court proceedings are freely accessible to the public, save for some matters covering certain of the most serious crimes, or those involving confidential information protected by law or state secrecy.

The contemporary Russian court system includes magistrates, courts of general competence, courts for commercial disputes, specialised courts (such as military courts, the Patent court), the Supreme Court of the Russian Federation, constitutional courts of the federal subjects and the Constitutional Court of the Russian Federation[49].

Quite similar to the Russian Empire, magistrates in the Russian Federation are competent to hear minor crimes and administrative offenses, civil claims for small amounts in dispute and some family law cases.[50] Decisions of a magistrate may be appealed in the district court of general competence.

In short, courts of general competence are authorised to try a variety of civil, criminal and administrative cases. These courts are the most numerous in the Russian Federation, present in practically each town or district.[51]

In legal nature, military courts in Russia also belong to courts of general competence, but their main focus is on cases involving servicemen and the military. Still, military courts are regulated *inter alia* by a separate federal law.[52]

Courts for commercial disputes (a.k.a. state arbitration courts) are federal courts competent to try commercial disputes between legal entities or individual entrepreneurs, administrative cases involving said parties, recognition and enforcement of the judgments of foreign courts/awards of international arbitration institutions, as well as insolvency cases.[53]

---

[49] *Federal Constitutional law No.1-FKZ* dated 31 December 1996, as amended on 8 December 2020, "On system of courts in the Russian Federation", Article 4.

[50] *Federal law No.188-FZ* dated 17 December 1998, as amended on 1 July 2021, "On magistrates in the Russian Federation", Article 3.

[51] *Federal Constitutional law No. 1-FKZ* dated 7 February 2011, as amended on 8 December 2020, "On courts of general competence in the Russian Federation", Article 1.

[52] *Federal Constitutional law No. 1-FKZ* dated 23 June 1999, as amended on 8 December 2020, "On military courts in the Russian Federation".

[53] *Federal Constitutional law No. 1-FKZ* dated 28 April 1995, as amended on 8 December 2020, "On state arbitration courts in the Russian Federation".

The Patent court is a specialised court handling IP claims and other disputes in the realm of IP law.[54] It is a novelty in modern Russian law; this court never existed in the past, although the necessity of establishing such a specialised court was subject to lively discussion among legal practitioners and scholars from the late Soviet period.[55]

Constitutional courts of the federal subjects are optional and may be established in certain federal subjects (e.g. republic, region, autonomy within the Russian Federation). All of them are subordinate to the Constitutional court of the Russian Federation, located in Saint Petersburg (its seat is a reference to the former imperial capital). Constitutional courts have a narrow scope of competence limited to the verification of constitutional consistency of all legal acts and laws, as well as handling private claims concerning an alleged violation of the Constitution of the Russian Federation.[56]

Court procedure in Russia is governed by the relevant legal codes including the *Civil Procedure Code, the Arbitration Procedure Code, the Code of administrative offenses, the Penal Procedure Code and federal constitutional* laws (for constitutional courts only).[57]

Roughly described, the stages of court proceedings normally include the lowest instance (magistrate or district court of general competence or state arbitration court, depending on the case, its nature and jurisdiction), which can be followed by one or two appeals in the upper courts (appeal and/or cassation), once again, depending on the case, its nature and jurisdiction. Sometimes a so-called special

---

[54] *Federal Constitutional law No. 1-FKZ* dated 31 December 1996, as amended on 8 December 2020, "On system of courts in the Russian Federation", Section 26.1.

[55] Artem A. Brodskiy, "Court for IP disputes in the system of Russian state courts," *Scientific Magazine*, 38, no. 4 (2019): 64.

[56] *Federal Constitutional law No. 1-FKZ* dated 21 July 1994, as amended on 1 July 2021, "On Constitutional Court of the Russian Federation".

[57] *Civil Procedure Code No. 138-FZ* dated 14 November 2002, as amended; *Arbitration Procedure Code No. 95-FZ* dated 24 July 2002, as amended; *Code of administrative Offenses No. 195-FZ* dated 30 December 2001, as amended; *Penal Procedure Code No. 174-FZ* dated 18 December 2001, as amended.

appeal is possible, which is called 'revision based on facts previously unknown', a procedure existing in Russian law since the mid-19th century. The highest judicial authority is the Supreme Court of the Russian Federation. There are a limited number of cases which can be brought to the Supreme Court of the Russian Federation for original decisions. In general the Supreme Court reviews the decisions of all the subordinate courts in civil, commercial, administrative and criminal matters.[58]

Legal professions (such as attorneys-at-law, judges, prosecutors, bailiffs) are subject to a number of qualification criteria, are officially sworn into office and may be disqualified for life for a set of particular causes. Thus, parallels can be drawn again with the legal philosophy of the late Russian Empire and the Soviet period, which demonstrated a similar approach in regulating these matters.

When it comes to court process, very schematically described, the process still has imprints from past experience within the Russian system. In particular, in public law cases, the process can be triggered by either the private party concerned or the respective public authority. The process is adversarial. The parties have equal rights. Attorneys-at-law play a very important role, and the whole case may be easily overruled if the party's right to be properly protected was violated. The list of admissible evidence is strictly regulated by law. Investigation and legal enforcement can be carried out only by competent public authorities. A trial by jury is usual and sentence is always rendered by professional judges.

In private law, the process is triggered by the party concerned. Rulings and clarifications of the Supreme Court of the Russian Federation, as well as judgments cast by courts in cassation may be deemed as case law or case practice, still with some reservations. Such case practice may be (and usually is)

---

[58] *Federal Constitutional law No. 3-FKZ* dated 5 February 2014, as amended on 2 August 2019 "On Supreme Court of the Russian Federation".

taken into consideration by all courts of the Russian Federation, but they are not legally bound by it.

The oldest branches of Russian material law, such as civil law, reveal in some aspects a very deep integration of the most archaic forms of law, such as customs, in the modern legal framework of the Russian Federation. According to the clarifications of the Supreme Court of the *Russian Federation provided in 2015,* customs may regulate civil rights or the contractual obligations of the parties to the extent that such customs are not in conflict with the core elements of Russian civil law (summed up in Article 1 of the RF Civil Code) and other existing laws of the Russian Federation.

3 FINAL COMMENTS

Russian jurisprudence and Russian law both represent a living matter that is capable of evolving and adapting to a variety of external and internal factors. The evolution commenced more than one thousand years ago and during the process absorbed all existing legal material, starting with archaic forms of the original juridical behavior and customary practices of Slavic tribes who formed up the Russian state.

Jus gentium and international treaties made by Russia since the very beginning of its statehood have always played a significant role in developing its legal framework and continue to hold important positions in the hierarchy of sources of law in the Russian Federation.

Actuality of the key postulates of Russian law and Russian legal consciousness verbalised some five centuries ago can be easily traced through to the present day in current jurisprudence and legal system. In addition, these postulates still have a great influence on the external and internal politics of the Russian Federation and are appropriately reflected in its Constitution and many other laws.

The doctrine of uninterrupted legal continuity of the Russian state over the whole period of its sovereignty determines the integrity of Russian legal materials and stipulates that Russian law and jurisprudence should be analysed and assessed in the context of Russia's historical background.

BIBLIOGRAPHY

- Alexander R. Andreev, *Russian statehood in terms: IX – beginning of XX century* (Moscow: Kraft+, 2001).

- André Mineau, *Operation Barbarossa: Ideology and Ethics against Human Dignity* (Amsterdam-New York: Editions Rodopi B.V., 2004).

- Andrey V. Kalinichenko, "Senate as a part of judicial system of the Russian Empire" in *Report to the Kuban State University,* No. 4857497, Thesis Department, (2011).

- N. Sakharov, *History of Russia from ancient times till present* (Moscow: Prospect, 2021).

- Arsen G. Avsharov, *External economic policy of the Russian Federation* (Saint Petersburg, Piter Editorial House, 2012).

- Artem A. Brodskiy, "Court for IP disputes in the system of Russian state courts," *Scientific Magazine, 38,* no. 4 (2019): 64-65.

- Arbitration Procedure Code No. 95-FZ dated July 24, 2002, *Collection of the Laws of the Russian Federation,* no. 30 (2002), 3012.

- Barry Grey, "Seventy-five years since the Nazi invasion of the Soviet Union," *WSWS* (2016)

- Civil Procedure Code No. 138-FZ dated November 14, 2002, *Collection of the Laws of the Russian Federation,* no. 46 (2002), 4532.

- Code of administrative offenses No. 195-FZ dated December 30, 2001, *Collection of the Laws of the Russian Federation,* no. 1 part 1 (2002), 1.

- Dmitry A. Savchenko, "The making of the Council Code: historical experience of modernization of national legislation," *Journal of the Novosibirsk state university of economics and management,* no. 3 (2013): 209-221.

- Edward W. Walker, *Dissolution: Sovereignty and the Breakup of the Soviet Union* (Lanham: Rowman & Littlefield, 2003).

o Ekaterina I. Osadchuk, "History of origin and legal profession development in imperial Russia" in *Scientific notes of Orel State University, Department of Humanities and Social Sciences* Vol. 4, no. 54 (2013):

o E.I. Osadchuk, "Sudebnik of 1497 as the landmark of the Russian feudal law," *Actual Problems of Humanities and Life Sciences*, no. 8 (2013): 218-222.

o Federal constitutional law No. 1-FKZ dated December 31, 1996, "On system of courts in the Russian Federation," *Collection of the Laws of the Russian Federation*, no. 1 (1997), 1.

o Federal law No. 188-FZ dated December 17, 1998, "On magistrates in the Russian Federation," *Collection of the Laws of the Russian Federation*, no. 51 (1998), 6270.

o Federal constitutional law No. 1-FKZ dated February 7, 2011, "On courts of general competence in the Russian Federation," *Collection of the Laws of the Russian Federation*, No. 7 (2011), 898.

o Federal constitutional law No. 1-FKZ dated June 23, 1999, "On military courts in the Russian Federation," *Collection of the Laws of the Russian Federation*, no. 26 (1999), 3170.

o Federal constitutional law No. 1-FKZ dated April 28, 1995, "On state arbitration courts in the Russian Federation," *Collection of the Laws of the Russian Federation*, no. 18 (1995), 1589.

o Federal constitutional law No. 1-FKZ dated July 21, 1994, "On Constitutional Court of the Russian Federation," *Collection of the Laws of the Russian Federation*, no. 13 (1994), 1447.

o Federal constitutional law No. 3-FKZ dated February 5, 2014, "On Supreme Court of the Russian Federation," *Collection of the Laws of the Russian Federation*, no. 6 (2014), 550.

o Geneva Convention for the amelioration of the condition of the wounded and sick in armed forces in the field, dated 12 August 1949, Decree of the Presidium of the USSR Supreme Council dated April 17, 1954, *Collection of the Laws of the USSR and Decrees of the Presidium of the USSR Supreme Council of 1938-1975, vol. 2 (1975)*.

o Geneva Convention for the amelioration of the condition of wounded, sick and shipwrecked members of armed forces at sea, dated August 12, 1949, Decree of the Presidium of the USSR Supreme Council dated April 17, 1954, *Collection of the Laws of the USSR and Decrees of the Presidium of the USSR Supreme Council of 1938-1975, vol. 2 (1975)*.

o Geneva Convention relative to the treatment of prisoners of war, dated August 12, 1949, Decree of the Presidium of the USSR Supreme Council dated April 17, 1954, *Collection of the Laws of the USSR and Decrees of the Presidium of the USSR Supreme Council of 1938-1975, vol. 2 (1975)*.

- Geneva Convention relative to the protection of civilian persons in time of war, dated August 12, 1949, Decree of the Presidium of the USSR Supreme Council dated April 17, 1954, *Collection of the Laws of the USSR and Decrees of the Presidium of the USSR Supreme Council of 1938-1975, vol. 2 (1975)*.

- Geoffrey Roberts, "The 75th anniversary of Operation Barbarossa: The Nazi invasion of the Soviet Union," *Sott*, June 16 (2016).

- <http://hdr.undp.org/en/content/human-development-index-hdi>, accessed on November 18, 2021.

- Ivan D. Belyaev, *History of the Russian legislation* (Saint Petersburg: Lan', 1999).

- Igor V. Zozulya, "Military Justice in the Russian Empire: from courts martial to military tribunals of the beginning of the XX century," *Science Innovations Technologies*, no. 67 (2010): 40-47

- Jonathan Walker, *Churchill's Third World War: British plans to attack the Soviet Empire 1945* (London: History Press, 2017).

- Konstantin K. Korablin, "Evolution of punishment in the Legal Code of 1550," *Education and Law*, no. 11 (2020): 305-311.

- L. A. Muravyeva, "Emancipation of serfs in Russia: reasons, implementation and the meaning," *Financial University Journal, 6*, no. 2 (2012): 42-53.

- Leonid V. Karnaushenko, "Problems of management and administration in the Russian Empire in constitutional drafts of early XIX century," *Society, Environment, Development (Terra Humana),* no. 3 (2009): 30-33.

- Ludmila V. Dudkina, *History of law and state of Russia* (Moscow: Allel, 2010).

- Marat R. Zaguidullin, "Liability in Russian legal proceedings according to the court procedure codes of 1497 and 1550" in *Report to the University of Kazan, Department of Humanities and Social Sciences,* no. 1, (2019).

- Maria D. Chupova, "Forgotten legal codes of the past," *Lex Russica*, no. 2 (2017), 184-207.

- Maxim A. Isaev, *History of the Russian State and Russian Law* (Moscow: Statut, 2012).

- Mikhail F. Vladimirskiy-Budanov, *Overview of the history of Russian law* (Rostov-on-Don: Fenix, 1995).

- M.V. Bibikov, "Russo-Byzantine treaties" in *Big Russian Encyclopedia*, Vol. 29, ed. Yu. S. Osipov and S. L. Kravetz (Russia, Moscow: BRE, 2015), 75-76.

- Nadezhda N. Efremova, "Evolution of the Russian jurisprudence (judicial reforms of XVIII-XIX centuries)," *HSE University Journal*, no. 2 (2008): 34-50.

- N.A. Pocheshkov, Zh. O. Abregova, R.M. Shkhachemukhov, "Population losses during the Civil War in Russia (1917-1922): the debatable space of historical demography," *Modern scientific thought*, no. 6 (2020): 63-68.

- N. N. Smirnova, "Establishment of judiciary in the Russian Empire," *Herald of Russian State University of A.I. Herzen, 74*, no. 1 (2008): 453-456.

- Oleg I. Chistyakov, *Russian Legislation of the 10th–20th centuries*, Vol. 1. (Moscow: Jurizdat, 1984).

- *Penal Procedure Code No. 174-FZ* dated December 18, 2001, *Collection of the Laws of the Russian Federation*, no. 52 part 1 (2001), 4921.

- Prof. R.L. Hachaturov, "Common law in the history of old Russian law," *Report to the Togliatti State University,* TSU Department of history and theory of law, Vol. 1 (2010).

- Ramil G. Guseynov, "The influence of the Mongol-Tatar Yoke in the development of the Russian State and Law," *Issues of Russian Justice*, no. 3 (2019): 16-23.

- Richard Pipes, *Russia under the old regime* (New York: Charles Scribner's Sons, 1974).

- S.G. Zagoryan. "Evolution of the evidentiary process in Russia in the pre-revolutionary era", *Legal Journal of Criminalistics: yesterday, today and tomorrow,* no. 1 (2019): 16-19.

- Svetlana A. Knyazeva, *History of the Russian State and Law* (Moscow: AST Editors, 2012).

- Svetlana V. Chugunova, Konstantin G. Ryndin, "An introduction to trust management in Russia," *Trusts & Trustees, 14*, no. 5 (2008): 277-283.

- Timothy Snyder, "The Reich's forgotten atrocity," *The Guardian*, Oct. 21 (2010).

- United Nations Charter dated June 26,1945, ratified by the Decree of the Presidium of the USSR Supreme Council dated August 20, 1945, initially officially published in *State Herald of the USSR*, no. 147, now recorded in *Collection of the Laws of the USSR and Decrees of the Presidium of the USSR Supreme Council, vol. 2 (1975).*

- V.A. Tomsinov, "Court system in the Russian Empire of the XVIII – mid XIX centuries," *Journal of the Moscow State University. Series 11 – Law and Jurisprudence,* no. 3 (2016): 3-24.

- Vladimir P. Zhuravlev, Vladimir V. Fortunatov, *History of election in Russia* (Saint Petersburg: Deviz Editorial House, 2011).

o   V.V. Chernih, G.A. Tsykunov, "Legal Customs of Ancient Russia as source of law," *Journal of the East-Siberian Institute of the MIA of the Russian Federation, 84*, no. 4 (2017): 175-182.

o   Yaroslav N. Schapov, *State and Church in Ancient Russia: X – XIII centuries* (Moscow: Nauka, 1989).

o   Yu. V. Ruzmanov, M. A. Eldin, "The influence of the Byzantine legal culture on Russia and the Russian political and legal space," *Eurasian Union of Scientists, 76,* no. 7 (2020): 69-77.

CHAPTER 3

THE HISTORICAL DEVELOPMENTS OF CHINESE CIVIL LAW OVER THE CENTURIES, AND A NEW CIVIL CODE 2021

Prof. Xiaojuan Shi

98

1 INTRODUCTION

The connection between Chinese traditional culture and modern civil law culture has seen many twists and turns over the centuries. The development of civil law lasted more than a hundred years from amendments to the laws in the last few years of the Qing Dynasty until the birth of the *Civil Code of the People's Republic of China 2021*.

"Fracture-preliminary, connection-deviation, deep integration" could be a way to discuss civil law culture in China. *"Fracture"* refers to draft civil legislation in the late Qing Dynasty. In the *Draft of the Civil Law of the Qing Dynasty* 1911, property law content embodied the principles of rule of law, as found in western law. However, in the *Draft of the Civil Law of the Qing Dynasty 1911*, the codes concerning personal rules did not absorb western civil law rules; on the contrary, they embodied the rituals of traditional Chinese culture. However, this Code maintained the feudal character of civil law and the influence of foreign laws can easily be seen. The *'preliminary connection'* embodied in civil legislation refers to civil laws during the period of the Republic of China. [1]

There were two laws of the "Civil Law of the Republic of China" – the *Draft Civil Code 1925*, which referred to the draft of Civil Law of the Qing dynasty and later the *Draft Civil Law 1931* that was based the *German Civil Code 1896*. [2] Therefore,

---

[1] The Republic of China refers to the regime from 1911 to 1949.

[2] Refers to German Civil Code signed by the German Emperor Wilhelm II on 18 August 1896, and promulgated on 24 August 1896 (see "*Imperial Law Gazette*" 1896, p. 195), and was implemented on 1 January 1900.)

attempts to draft civil code were made on the basis of the transplantation of ideas and code from western civil law systems into Chinese civil legislation. Insufficient attention was given to traditional Chinese culture in these two codes immediately after the founding of the new Republic of China at the end of the Qing Dynasty.

On the other hand, after the founding of the People's Republic of China (hereinafter 'PRC') in 1949,[3] the attempt to draft civil code in 1956 was influenced by laws from the Soviet Union. Legal scholars refer to this as the *"deviation"* that was embodied in civil legislation, and accordingly was the main reason as to why these drafts failed in the PRC.

However, there was a further attempt to draft code in 1964 which was influenced by civil laws from Germany. In later years, there was again an attempt to deeply integrate modern Chinese cultural characteristics with a modern civil law system by legislators in contemporary Chinese civil legislation. These combined features are reflected in the new *Civil Code of the People's Republic of China 2021*. According to scholars, this is an example of "*deep integration*" referring to the in-depth integration of modern Chinese culture in civil code. This is a revolutionary civil code based on attempts made over centuries by legal scholars and politicians, in particular, after the market reforms of 1978 and the drafting of individual legislations on various aspects of civil law.

The complete "*Civil Code of the People's Republic of China*", hereinafter known as the *Civil Code 2021,* was promulgated and adopted at the third meeting of the 13th National People's Congress of China on 28 May 2020. On the same day, Chinese President Xi Jinping signed *Presidential Order No. 45* to promulgate the Civil Code. On 1 January 2021,[4] the Civil Code 2021 was officially implemented in China. The new *Civil Code 2021* deeply integrates the two cultures and presents distinctive characteristics of both traditional Chinese culture and modern times.

---

[3] New China refers to the People's Republic of China established in 1949.
[4] *Civil Code of the People's Republic of China* is implemented on 1 January 2021 (hereinafter referred to as new "*Civil Code 2021*").

This chapter is composed of six parts. The first part will discuss the characteristics of civil law (Chinese law) in Chinese history. The second part will discuss the evolution and changes to civil law in Chinese legislation before 1949. The third part of the Chapter is about the evolution of, and changes to, civil legislation in China after 1949. The fourth part will discuss the legislative features of the "Civil Code of the People's Republic of China". The fifth part highlights important aspects of the "Civil Code of the People's Republic of China". The sixth part has been placed in Appendix A, which gives an overview of the main highlights of Civil Code 2021.

2 CHARACTERISTICS OF TRADITIONAL CHINESE LAW V/S CHARACTERISTICS OF CIVIL LAW

According to scholars, the "*Civil Code of the People's Republic of China*" (the new "Civil Code"),[5] hereinafter called 'Civil Code 2021', was not completely detached from the history and legal culture of Chinese civil law. From the perspective of legal culture, the drafting of the Chinese civil law system did pay attention to the spiritual temperament of Chinese traditional culture as well as to the requirements of modern civil law. Another issue that was particularly relevant to the drafting of the new code relates to the *cultural relevance* of the Civil Code to Chinese society.

For decades, there has been a desire for a new modern civil code in China that could follow examples of successful civil law cultures from around the globe. This necessitated a movement to codify existing civil law available in any form in modern China and interlock it with the rich heritage of traditional Chinese culture where they exhibited common values relevant to society. Accordingly, integration

---

[5] The Civil Code of the People's Republic of China was promulgated and passed on 28 May 2020, and came into effect on 1 January 2021. It is called as the *New Civil Code* by Chinese scholars.

between these two sets of values from the two cultures was to be the key to success for the new *Civil Code 2021*.

Any kind of law or legal phenomenon is a legal reflection of the culture of a particular society. China's legal system began in the Xia Dynasty in the 21st century BCE. Since then, among the various laws, civil law had been the law relevant to managing private life within society. At a cultural level, in spite of thousands of years of history, the feudal society of China lacked the basis for the growth of civil law and accordingly there was no independent systemic civil law in ancient China.[6]

The cultural foundations from the "*Fa Jing*"[7] to the "*Laws of the Qing Dynasty*"[8] were formed. The characteristics of Chinese legal culture were such that civil law codes and criminal law were not separated in the ancient legal system, and all laws were integrated. In fact, there was a dominance of criminal codes within the ancient Chinese legal system.

2.1 CODIFICATION

Beginning with the first systematic code of feudal society "*Fa Jing*"[9], formulated by Li Kui during the Warring States Period of ancient China, there were other similar codes in all later dynasties in ancient China. This can be seen from the examples – (1) the "Law of Qin", after the unification of China by Qin Shihuang, [10] (2) the

---

[6] For example, the code of the Tang Dynasty "*Yonghui Law*", the code of the Song Dynasty "*Song Xingtong*", and the code of the Ming Dynasty "*Daming Law*" all embodied that the criminal legal system and the civil legal system were mixed together in one code.

[7] "*Fa Jing*" is the first relatively systematic feudalized grammar in Chinese history. The "Law Classics" is a statutory code composed of all laws, and the main components were still predominantly the rules necessary for criminal law.

[8] Qing Dynasty : The time of the Qin Dynasty was from 1644-1911 CE.

[9] Li Kui was a famous law researcher in ancient China. In 407 BCE, Li wrote and completed the first written code of law in ancient Chinese history, "The Book of Laws".

[10] Qin Shihuang was the founding emperor of China's unified Qin Dynasty, who unified China in 221 BC.

"Law of Han", formulated in the Han Dynasty, [11] (3) the "Law of Jin", formulated at the end of the Cao Wei Dynasty, (4) the "Kaihuang Law"[12], formulated by Emperor Wen of the Sui Dynasty, and so forth. With such codes, a systematic pattern of Chinese feudal codes began to emerge in ancient China.

Twelve chapters of "*Zhenguan Law*", "*Yongwei Law*" and "*Kaiyuan Law*" formulated among the various laws during the Tang Dynasty, [13] had profound influence on later generations of Chinese society. In order to understand the ancient Chinese legal system, the author would recommend reading "*Tang Law Commentary,*" Song Dynasty's "*Song Xing Tong,*" Ming Dynasty's "*Da Ming Law,*" and Qing Dynasty "*Da Qing Law*". [14] Any further detail about such ancient codes is beyond the scope of this Chapter.

2.2 CRIMINAL LAW AS THE PREDOMINANT LAW

From BCE 400, in the Zhanguo Period, Li Kui's "*Fa Jing*", the basic structures of the codes compiled in the Qin, Han, Tang, Song, Ming and Qing dynasties, were predominantly drafted on criminal law, but had elements of relevant civil law, procedural law, and administrative law. The contents of the law in these Codes were often not divided into categories, or were often not codified based on the object and nature of issues at hand. In fact, most of these legal rules were compiled in chronological order and were often comprehensive in structure. These issues were the same, even for the legal forms,[15] other than the Basic Code.

---

[11] The time of the Han Dynasty was from 202 BCE-220 CE.

[12] "*Kaihuang Law*", "*Zhenguan Law*" and "*Kaiyuan*" are statutory laws of different periods in ancient China.

[13] The time of the Tang Dynasty was from 618-907 CE.

[14] The time period of the Qin Dynasty was from 1644-1911 CE.

[15] *Legal form* refers to the form of legislation. In ancient Chinese legislation, laws were not classified according to the object and nature of adjustment, such as civil legislation and criminal legislation. But in a law, there are civil laws, criminal laws, and administrative laws. Most of these laws were compiled in chronological order, and the structure was often comprehensive.

2.3 EMPHASIS ON ETHICS AND THE COMBINATION OF ETIQUETTE WITH LAW

In ancient China, rituals occupied an important position within ancient laws. Accordingly, for the purposes of governance and law enforcement, social ethics were significant and considered as the foundation of governance. *Etiquette* was not only a code of ethics, but also a legal code. In terms of jurisprudence and in the judicial system of that time, this "original code of ethics" of law enforcement meant that in addition to legal rules, family ethics and social ethics were also considered by the legal system when implementing law for society. This was a major feature of traditional Chinese law.

In ancient judicial practice, in specific cases regarding conviction in cases where sentencing was needed, the emperors advocated the concept of "jurisdiction from the original ethics". Pursuant to this concept, the authorities had to strive to be in line with legal principles, sentiments and reasons, and these two concepts were synchronized. The working of such a concept can be seen from these examples – (1) the "Spring and Autumn Jueyu"[16] system in the Han Dynasty, and (2) the Ming Dynasty Emperor Zhu Yuanzhang, who was known for his harsh enforcement of laws. It was known that Zhu Yuanzhang was once a "*Xiaozi Qufa*".[17] On analyzing various ancient cases, it is apparent that law enforcement was actually a process pursuant to which the code of social ethics further penetrated into activities associated with the trial of cases.

---

[16] The "Spring and Autumn Jueyu" : "Spring and Autumn" is a classic book from Confucian times, which is said to have been revised by Confucius. Spring and Autumn Jueyu means that in ancient China, when the Chinese judges tried cases, they used the spirit of the book "Spring and Autumn" to make judgments in accordance with Confucian teachings.

[17] "Xiaozi Qufa" refers to an individual who was found to be very respectful and filial to his parents during the execution of the law, or a person who violates the law because he was filial to his parents. In both cases, even if the person had violated the law, a pardon could still be obtained. With reference to ancient times, the *criminal motive* was important in any case, and if it turned out that the criminal motive was to respect and protect the elders, the sentence could be lightened for the accused.

2.4 APPLICATION OF LAWS BASED ON ETHNICITY

In ancient China, the laws of the Chinese legal system were unified and laws across the country were implemented in accordance with the laws of the dynasty that was in power. However, for ethnic minorities and special regions, there were provisions within the laws that were different from the main laws. For example, in the Tang Dynasty, there were different legal management systems for the *Sogdians* [18] in the western regions of the Chinese empire, which were implemented in accordance with the status of naturalization and non-naturalization of such people. The legal system of the Yuan Dynasty was a pluralistic amalgamation of laws that included Mongolian law, Han law and a portion of Hui law. Another example was from the Qing Dynasty, when it had formulated many separate laws and regulations according to the needs of ethnic minority areas such as the Hui Law and Mongolian Laws. These laws played a certain role in maintaining the unity of the country.

2.5. IDEALIZATION OF LAW (LEGAL IDEALS)

Ancient Chinese legislations had a tendency to introduce idealisation to varying degrees, which could often turn an idealised and excessively *high moral obligation* into a legal obligation. The main function of this concept was correct orientation, and more often than not such concepts remained out of touch with the actual populace's expectations and needs. Accordingly, it was not recognised by the common people.

However, when deeply analysed, the fundamental purpose of ancient Chinese legislation and formulation of laws was not really meant for implementation to help society, but as a political ornament. This purpose was, in fact, further influenced

---

[18] The *Sogdians* were originally an ancient people who lived in the Amu Darya and SyrDarya in Central Asia and spoke an Eastern Iranian branch of the Iranian language group.

by the idealistic moral philosophy of Confucianism, but the real purpose was to reflect the rationality and effectiveness of the dynasty that was in power at that time.

2.6 VARIOUS FORMS OF ANCIENT CHINESE LAWS

From a legislative point of view, the biggest feature of Chinese legal tradition was that laws were supposed to be seen as coming from the emperor, and laws enacted by the emperor had different connotations of nationalism associated with them. In the dynasties of China, law code was used as its basic code, and it was supplemented by legal forms such as *Ling*, [19] *Geshi*,[20] *Li*,[21] and *Shu*,[22] which constituted a relatively comprehensive and detailed legal system. There were many forms of law, and they complemented each other.

2.7 DEVELOPMENT OF THE CULTURE OF PUBLIC LAW

As discussed earlier, Chinese laws focused predominantly on criminal law, the need for the law to manage the organisation of bureaucracy in the empire, and laws that were necessary for the administration of law within the Chinese empire. In fact, even administrative law emerged in the shape of criminal law in ancient China, but it had significant attributes of public law. In addition, even the civil legal rules that pertained to issues of marriage, debt, and land-house relationships were also drafted in the nature of public law, and this public law also had the characteristics of criminal law. Therefore, further development of the state led to

---

[19] *Ling*: In ancient China, an order was an instruction from a higher-level official to a lower-level official.

[20] *Gesh*: In ancient China, the format was in the form of rules governing the handling of administrative affairs and the trial of civil and criminal cases by officials.

[21] *Li*: In ancient China, precedent was formed after officials had tried civil and criminal cases. However, this precedent must be distinguished from the way common law precedents used to work. Any further discussion is beyond the scope of this book.

[22] *Shu* : Royal refers to the order issued by the ancient Chinese emperor or the emperor's detailed explanation of the legislation.

the development of public law and thus the process of criminialising traditional Chinese law also gradually evolved.

2.8 THE LEGAL SYSTEM WAS CLOSED TO NEW IDEAS

Although China's legal system and legal thought and jurisprudence has undergone several major changes and developments over the past four thousand years, the mutual inheritance relationship was still very obvious. Especially since the Western Zhou Dynasty,[23] the traditional Chinese legal system had historical origins and structural forms. Since then, no substantive changes have taken place in terms of concepts, terms, and spiritual principles. It can be said that for some scholars, the evolution of law was consistent and had successfully passed the test of time.

Another manifestation of this aspect where the legal system was closed was its aversion to new ideas. This closed system even rejected the new form of the Chinese legal system, because legislators in all eras often thought that their codes were complete, and could be used in all scenarios and legal matters. These scholars prohibited interpretation and comparison by other scholars, and any criticism was of course a no-go area.

The above school of thought despised foreign legal culture and placed their own codes at the centre of all analysis. In ancient China, in fact, foreigners were called "*Huawai ren*"[24] and "*Man yi*"[25] , which could clearly be termed as xenophobic in the current politically correct world.

---

[23] Zhou dynasty was from 1046-221 BCE; Western Zhou Dynasty was from 1046-771 BCE.
[24] "*Huawai ren*" is the general term for foreigners in the laws of Chinese feudal society.
[25] "*Man yi*" is the name given to a few ethnic groups in ancient China.

3. CHANGES IN CHINESE HISTORY AND ACCOMPANYING CIVIL LAW

In traditional Chinese law, as discussed earlier, civil law and criminal law were not segregated and were, in fact, deeply integrated. In the later years of the Qing Dynasty, the desire to have a civil code emerged. Accordingly, the codification of modern Chinese civil law had its beginning in the late Qing Dynasty.

3.1 EMERGENCE OF REVISION OF LAWS IN THE LATER YEARS OF QING DYNASTY (1904-1911)

The law slowly started to evolve during the period 1904-1911. Until the beginning of the 20th century, in the Qing Dynasty, the civil legal relationship was still restricted by criminal law and Confucian moral rules known as etiquette. With the outbreak of the Opium War in 1840,[26] thousands of years of the traditional Chinese culture of etiquette were strongly impacted by the culture of rule of law from the West.

For this reason, from the later years of Qing Dynasty until the early years of the Republic of China, several generations of insightful people such as Gong Zizhen,[27] Wei Yuan,[28] Kang Youwei,[29] and Liang Qicha[30] began to reflect upon the ideological shortcomings of traditional Chinese culture. Accordingly, these learned scholars advocated the modern western legal concept of freedom and equality,

---

[26] Opium War: Usually the Opium War refers to the First Opium War. Britain often refers to it as the First Sino-British War or the "War of Commerce". Historians in China consider it to be an unjust war of aggression launched by Britain against China from 1840 to 1842, and it could be considered as a modern Chinese war. A few scholars consider it as a beginning of the history of the humiliation of the Chinese people.

[27] Gong Zizhen (1792-1841) was a thinker, poet, writer and pioneer of reforms in the Qing Dynasty.

[28] Wei Yuan (1794-1857) was an enlightenment thinker, statesman, and writer during the Qing Dynasty. Modern China slowly advocated learning from the West and accordingly understand the concepts from the West. He was involved in this subtle process and was an advocate of this way of thinking.

[29]Kang Youwei (1858-1927) was an important politician, thinker, educator, and representative of the bourgeois reform movement in China in the later years of the Qing Dynasty.

[30] Liang Qichao (1873-1929) was a politician, thinker, educator, and historian of modern China, and was a representative of the modern Chinese reform movement, but was also a neo-legal scholar.

and called for its implementation within Chinese political laws. The comprehensive reform process obliged the Qing Dynasty's government to passively carry out legal reforms. Accordingly, the Qing Government established the Law Amendment Hall on 15 May 1904. According to a decree from the highest authority in the Qing Dynasty, the Qing government finally decided to employ western laws as a model to amend and reform ancient Chinese laws.

The post-Qing government and the 1908 Revised Law Museum hired Japanese scholars Shida Kataro, [31] and Matsuoka Yoshimasa[32] as consultants to draft civil law. Shen Jiaben,[33] Wu Tingfang,[34] and Yu Liansan[35] chaired the process of revision of ancient laws. By 1911, the *"Draft Civil Code of the Qing"* was completed. This was the first civil code in the history of China's legal system, which could not be promulgated and implemented due to the fall of the Qing Dynasty on 12 February 1912. The *"Draft Civil Code of the Qing Dynasty"* included five parts – (1) General Provisions (2) Creditor's Rights, (3) Property Rights, (4) Relatives, and (5) Inheritance. The *Draft Civil Code of the Qing Dynasty* finally broke through the traditions of the ancient Chinese legal system and, as a result, the traditional Chinese legal system was replaced by a legislative model of the western continental legal system.

---

[31] Shida Kataro (1868-1951) was a Japanese jurist, and was hired by the Qing government in 1902 to participate in the revision of modern Chinese civil and commercial laws.

[32] Yoshimasa (1868-1951) graduated from the Tokyo Imperial University Law Department in 1892. In 1906, he was hired as a legal adviser by the School of Law. He may be considered as the first person to teach civil procedure law in China.

[33] Shen Jiaben (1840-1913) was an official and jurist in the late Qing Dynasty and was the representative of the new legalists that emerged in China. He participated in the reforms of the late Qing Dynasty, presided over the formulation of a series of codes such as *"The Civil Law of the Qing Dynasty"* and the *"Draft of the Commercial Law of the Qing Dynasty"*, and put forward a series of legal reform proposals. He can be considered as a pioneer in the modernisation of China's legal system.

[34] Wu Tingfang (1842-1922) was an outstanding diplomat and jurist in the late Qing Dynasty and early Republic of China. In 1874, he studied in the United Kingdom and entered the University of London's School of Law to study law and obtained the qualifications of doctorate & barrister. After the outbreak of the Revolution of 1911, Wu Tingfang made great contributions following the destruction of the monarchy and the reforms that were needed for the judicial system. He founded China's first modern law school.

[35] Yu Liansan (1841-1912) was a politician of the later years of the Qing Dynasty. He was appointed as Minister of Law Amendment in 1907.

3.2 THE CHARACTERISTICS OF THE "DRAFT CIVIL CODE OF THE QING DYNASTY"

The "*Draft Civil Code of the Qing Dynasty*" not only copied the legal principles and provisions from capitalist countries, but also attempted to maintain the feudalistic code based on "*Gangchang Mingjiao*".[36] On closely analysing these codes, it appears that there was an attempt to maintain both feudal characteristics as well as protecting the interests of imperialists from the west. The attempt to combine both the contents of capitalism and feudalism into one that highlight the struggle and compromises reached between old and new legal thoughts. In fact, the *kinship and inheritance* chapters were drafted by the Law Amendment Hall in conjunction with the conservative etiquette school of thought. The system and style of these codes had a deep-seated feudalistic colour and retained the spirit of many feudalistic laws.

3.3 THE INFLUENCE OF GERMAN CIVIL LAW 1896 ON CHINESE CIVIL LEGISLATIONS (1912 -1949)

During the period of the Republic of China, the civil code for China was drafted twice. In the spring of 1922, representatives from the *Beiyang government*[37]

---

[36] *Gangchang Mingjiao* was a set of norms set up by ancient Chinese society to maintain and strengthen the feudal system and for people's thoughts and behaviors.

[37] Beiyang Government – The Republic of China (1911-1949) had three different types of government during the period: The *Provisional Government of the Republic of China* (from 10 October 1911 to 6 October 1913). On October 10, 1911, an event occurred in Wuchang, Hubei, southern China, aimed at overthrowing the Qing Dynasty and which could be classed as a mutiny against the Qing government. After the mutiny, Sun Yat-sen returned from the United States, and advocated the overthrow of the monarchy that led to the establishment of a Republic. Sun Yat-sen was elected as the interim president of the Republic of China. It was then the turn of the *Beiyang Government of the Republic of China* from 1913 to 1928 to take power. After Sun Yat-sen was elected as the interim president of the Republic of China, his military power was quite limited, but Yuan Shikai, a former minister of the Qing government, had a large army. Sun Yat-sen negotiated with Yuan Shikai in order to reduce the massacres and violence in the new Republic and conceded the post of President to Yuan Shikai for the benefit of the new Republic. After Yuan Shikai forced the Qing emperor to abdicate, Yuan Shikai was elected President of the Republic of China in October 1913. Thereafter, there was the *Nanjing Government of the Republic of China* from 1928 to 1949; Refer also, to footnote 41 of this Chapter.

proposed to withdraw consular jurisdiction at the Washington Conference[38] in the United States, and the conference decided to send representatives from various countries to China for investigation into different kinds of laws at the material time. The Beiyang government rectified then existing laws and required the Law Centre to compile civil and criminal codes. It then referred to the *Draft Civil Code of the Qing Dynasty* and the latest legislation in various countries to investigate the civil and commercial customs of various provinces in China. Accordingly, the first "*Draft Civil Code 1925*" of the Republic of China was completed between *1924 and 1925*. The Ministry of Justice of the Beiyang Government issued an order to Chinese courts at all levels in November 1926 to use the *Draft Civil Code* as a legal principle in their judgments, even though this Code had not yet been formally promulgated.

After the Nanjing National Government was established, legal exchanges between China and foreign countries became more frequent.[39] In June 1927, the then Nanjing National Government set up the Legislative Affairs Bureau to draft various important codes and, in 1929-1930, they completed drafting the various parts of the Civil Code 1930. The Republic of China extracted their version of civil code from the contents of *German Civil law 1896*. The influence of German law can be seen from sections of this Civil Code – (1) the inheritance of civil legislation, and (2) the inheritance of civil law doctrine. This Civil Code was, at the time of the Republic of China, different to the draft code that was drafted in the later years of the Qing Dynasty, as it directly referenced German civil law. From a scholar's point of view, this new code embodied the characteristics of an independent school of thought and had a direct reference to a foreign law.

---

[38] In August 1921, the United States invited the four powers of Britain, France, Italy, and Japan to send representatives to the United States to discuss the issue of an arms reduction. At the same time, in order to solve post-war issues in the Pacific Far East, the United States also invited four major countries including China, the Netherlands, Belgium, and Portugal, as well as the top five countries including Britain, the United States, France, Japan and Italy. A total of nine countries participated in that meeting.

[39] *Nanjing National Government* – The National Government faced off with the *Beiyang Government* from 1925 to 1928. After the successful Northern Expedition, it became the only legal government representing China and thereafter survived from 1925 to 1949.

The legislation "*Civil Law of the Republic of China 1931*", comprising civil code that had direct reference to German law, was enacted and promulgated by the Nanjing National Government in 1931. The Civil Law of the Republic of China was the first civil code officially promulgated and implemented in Chinese history.

In 1949, the Nanjing government lost control of mainland China and retreated to Taiwan. From 1949 to the present day, the Civil Law of the Republic of China has been applied in Taiwan.[40]

4 COMMUNIST REVOLUTION AND THE FOUNDING OF THE PRC (1949)

After the Communist revolution, the People's Republic of China was established. All laws were strongly influenced by the laws of the former Union of Soviet Socialist Republic ('USSR'). Following the founding of the People's Republic of China (New China) on October 1, 1949, the "*Six Laws*"[41] of the Nanjing National Government were abolished, and the Civil Law of the Republic of China was consequently not applicable in Chinese jurisdiction.

After New China abolished the "Six Laws", the functions of law were replaced by the policies and guiding documents of the Communist Party of China and the state at that time. Accordingly, most of the civil laws and regulations were also included in the policies of the party and the state.

---

[40] See Zhenmin's Xie, *Legislative History of the Republic of China*, (Beijing: China University of Political Science and Law Press, 2000), 747·749, 755.

[41] The "six laws" refer to the *Constitution, Civil law, Criminal law, Civil Procedure law, Criminal procedure law, and Administrative law* promulgated and formulated during time of the Nanjing Nationalist Government.

4.1 CIVIL LEGISLATIONS IN THE FIRST TWO DECADES (1949-1977)

The new civil laws that were drafted in this decade were mostly transplants of the laws from the former USSR. A few examples of such laws that were promulgated but heavily influenced by USSR laws are given below.

4.1.1 The Marriage Act of 1950

During this period, China promulgated the Marriage Law in 1950, which was also the first civil basic law promulgated after the founding of New China. The Marriage Law took the "freedom of marriage and equality between men and women" as its legislative guiding spirit, and constituted the principles of marriage law, marriage, rights and obligations between husband and wife, the relationship between parents and children, divorce, child-rearing and education after divorce and property after divorce.

The basic framework of this Act comprised 27 articles that were divided into eight parts, along with supplementary regulations. Although the content of this law was not detailed enough, it embodied the values of modern marriage law such as "the freedom of marriage between men and women, monogamy, and equality of rights between men and women". The prevailing social atmosphere of equality played a vital role in bringing those concepts into the Act.

4.1.2 The First draft of the Civil Code 1956

In 1954, the Standing Committee of the National People's Congress tasked a committee to draft the civil law and began a process to compile the first civil code of the People's Republic of China. In *1956, the Draft Civil Code 1956* was completed. However, for various reasons, the process to draft the Civil Code was interrupted.

During this period, China's civil legislation was kept relatively simple. Due to the influence of factors such as the economic system being placed under the planned economy, the civil law of the former Soviet Union became almost the only possible reference point for China's civil legislation to follow. Scholars referred regularly to the *Soviet Russian Civil Code 1922* for guidance. In terms of specific provisions, the draft of civil law at that time only stipulated the statute of limitations, but not the acquisition of the statute of limitations, and emphasized the special protection of socialist common property, etc., all of which reflected the absorption and reference of Soviet civil law.

Although this draft was based on the *Soviet Russian Civil Code 1922*, this Soviet Code was itself drafted to a certain extent after taking guidance from the *German Civil Code 1896*. As scholar Liang Huixing said, "The first draft of the Civil Code of the People's Republic of China, and the subsequent civil legislation and civil law theories are still in common with civil law in the civil law system, especially the German Civil Code 1896. They have the same basic concepts, basic principles, basic systems and principles."[42]

4.1.3 The Second Draft Civil Law 1964

The second draft of civil law drafted by the People's Republic of China was drafted and completed by the country's highest legislature in July 1964. But it was not promulgated and implemented. The draft adopted a three-part system that was different from both German civil law and Soviet civil law. It comprised three parts – (1) "General Principles," (2) "Property Ownership," and (3) "Property Circulation." Furthermore, the issues of relatives, inheritance and infringements were all excluded from the draft civil law.

---

[42] Liang Huixing is a famous civil law Chinese scholar in the new China.

Chinese scholars generally believe that during this period, New China lacked the foundation for the formulation of a civil code – that is, the requirement of social space for equal subjects and the political autonomy of general public conditions. For ten years, the *"Cultural Revolution"* [43] interrupted almost all inheritance of extra-territorial law. During the Cultural Revolution, the inheritance of German civil law by mainland China was on hold. Sun Xianzhong[44] said that was why the status quo of the Chinese Civil Code and the Main Issues had to be considered.

4.2 CIVIL AND COMMERCIAL LEGISLATIONS (1978-2017)

Since the end of the *Cultural Revolution* in 1979, the People's Republic of China has carried out reforms of the economic system and has gradually begun to develop into a market economy. At the same time, the construction of China's legal system resumed, and a lot of work was done to codify the China's civil law. However, these efforts resulted in many separate laws. These separate laws were not only influenced by the European Code, but over the years were also significantly influenced by common law from countries such as England & Wales, the US and so forth.

The enactment of a series of separate laws in the past 40 years in fact laid the foundation for the compilation of the Civil Code of the People's Republic of China in 2021. The *"Civil Code of the People's Republic of China 2021"* is by far the largest basic law of the People's Republic of China. It includes the general provisions and six sub-sections of real rights: contracts, personality rights, marriage and family, succession and tort liability, as well as supplementary provisions. There are in total 1,260 articles and more than 100,000 words.

---

[43] The *Cultural Revolution* took place in mainland China from May 1956 to October 1976. It brought serious disasters to the Chinese country and people of all ethnic groups.

[44] Sun is a famous civil law scholar; he is also a member of the *Constitution and Law Committee* of the National People's Congress and is a member of the Chinese Academy of Social Sciences.

In the construction of the civil law system following the reform and opening up in 1978, the People's Republic of China not only carried out the compilation of civil code, but also formulated special civil law and the construction of commercial law. In this regard, China's legislation truly made great progress in a short span of time.

Under China's civil and commercial integration system, commercial law, as a special civil law, has an extremely important position in the civil law system and value in China's national economic development. Since 1978, the People's Republic of China has successively implemented company law, partnership law, sole proprietorship law, foreign investment enterprise law, securities law, bankruptcy law, insurance law, maritime law, bill law, and, to maintain transaction order, anti-monopoly law, the *Enactment of the Anti-unfair Competition Law*, and so forth.[45] A landmark *General Principles of Civil Law 1987* was promulgated for the first time in Chinese history.

These laws have become an important part of the integration of civil and business aspects in the civil law system. In addition, the field of intellectual property law has been drafted in a short span of time. Intellectual property law is also the most important special law of civil law, including individual intellectual property laws such as copyright law, trademark law, and patent law.[46] In another civil law legislation related to the protection of civil rights, the legislature has enacted a large number of protection of rights laws, such as the *"Law on the Protection of the Rights and Interests of the Elderly", "Law on the Protection of Minors", "Law on*

---

[45] *General Principles of the Civil Law of the People's Republic of China* (promulgated in 1987), *Company Law of the People's Republic of China* (promulgated in 1993), *The Partnership Enterprise Law of the People's Republic of China* (promulgated in 2007), *Law of the People's Republic of China on Sole Proprietorship Enterprises* (promulgated in 2000), *Foreign Investment Law of the People's Republic of China* (promulgated in 2020), *Securities Law of the People's Republic of China* (promulgated in 1999), *The Bankruptcy Law of the People's Republic of China (promulgated in 2007)*, *Insurance Law of the People's Republic of China* (promulgated in 2003), *The Maritime Law of the People's Republic of China* (promulgated in 1993), *The Negotiable Instruments Law of the People's Republic of China* (promulgated in 2004), *Anti-Monopoly Law of the People's Republic of China* (promulgated in 2008), *The People's Republic of China Anti-Unfair Competition Law* (promulgated in 2019).

[46] *The Copyright Law of the People's Republic of China* (promulgated in 1991), *Trademark Law of the People's Republic of China* (promulgated in 1983), *Patent Law of the People's Republic of China* (promulgated in 2009).

the Protection of the Disabled", "Law on the Protection of Women's Rights", and the "Law on the Protection of Consumer Rights".[47] This constitutes another series of special laws in civil law.

5 LEGISLATIVE FEATURES OF THE CIVIL CODE OF THE PEOPLE'S REPUBLIC OF CHINA

The *Civil Code of the People's Republic of China 2021* was the first law after 1949 to take its name from the founding of the People's Republic of China. It was also the first civil law in Chinese history to be named as a "*Civil Code*". To have a civil code was the long-cherished wish of several generations in New China. After more than 70 years of exploration and practice, the Civil Code of the People's Republic of China was a landmark achievement in the establishment of rule of law in China. The Civil Code of the People's Republic of China 2021 can truly be considered a milestone in the history of China's rule of law, which ushered in a new era of China's civil legal system.

The Civil Code of the People's Republic of China 2021 is a compilation of the separate civil laws and commercial laws promulgated in the previous forty years.

5.1 DRAWS ON FOREIGN LAWS AND INTEGRATION WITH CHINESE CHARACTERISTICS

---

[47] *Law of the People's Republic of China on the Protection of the Rights and Interests of the Elderly* (promulgated in 2013), *The Law of the People's Republic of China on the Protection of Minors* (promulgated in 1992), *The Law of the People's Republic of China on the Protection of Disabled Persons* (promulgated in 2008), *The Law of the People's Republic of China on the Protection of Women's Rights and Interests* (promulgated in 1992), *The Consumer Protection Law of the People's Republic of China* (promulgated in 1994).

5.1.1 Reference to the German Civil Code

Chinese civil law has always drawn on lessons from the German civil code and civil law theory. Accordingly, the spirit of German Civil Code was integrated into the new Code and reflected in the style of compilation adopted in the *Civil Code of the People's Republic of China 2021* ('Civil Code 2021').

The codified characteristics of German Civil Code were consistent with Chinese legislative traditions. After 1949, the year in which the People's Republic of China was founded, China's civil legislation showed signs of becoming more open to the concept of utilising the experience of other countries' civil law. Accordingly, China's separate civil laws were mostly created around German laws. For example, Article 230 of the "Property Law" promulgated in 2007 listed many provisions concerning security real rights, which were also formulated on the basis of articles 273 and 320 of the *German Civil Code 1896*. These salient features were absorbed by the new "Civil Code" in its property rights section due to the fact that legislative efficiency, legislative cost, and legal stability had passed the test of time in Chinese society.

5.1.2 Lessons from Anglo-American law

The section concerning law of contracts within the Civil Code of the People's Republic of China 2021 was drafted based on experience gained from China's "*Contract Law of the People's Republic of China 1999*". Contract Law 1999 played an important role within the Chinese contract system in international commerce. Therefore, many important codes with the new Civil Code were directly adopted from the "*United Nations Convention on Contracts for the International Sale of Goods 1980*" ('CISG'), "*General Principles of International Commercial Contracts 1994*," "*European Contract Law 2008*" ('ECO'), and from Anglo-American common law principles of Contract Laws.

5.1.3 Drafting of code in line with national conditions and legal practice

During the compilation process, the *Civil Code of the People's Republic of China 2021* carefully studied – (1) Roman law traditions, and (2) the beneficial results of foreign civil code compilation, especially the reference and absorption of the *French Civil Code 1807,*[48] the *German Civil Code 1896,*[49] and the *Swiss Civil Code 1907.*[50] During the process of in depth analysis, the focus was on the issues of *concepts, regulations and technology.*

However, China had experience of importing foreign concepts over the last few years, and a few of these had even been localised, taking into account their suitability for Chinese society. China did not blindly copy foreign concepts, ideas, systems, and legislative techniques of civil law, but attempted to bring in these concepts based on – (1) actual national conditions, (2) the integrity of the Chinese legal system, (3) the complexities involved in the future process of localisation, (4) issues of modernisation, and (4) potential administrative issues of legalising the compilation of the civil code.

The system framework and structure of the new Civil Code implemented on January 1, 2021, even though borrowed largely from the experience of German and French civil laws, ensured it did not copy certain practices of other countries, such as German property rights. The concepts from behavioral theory instead advocated that China's model for any change of property rights should conform to China's national conditions and legal practices.

This proposition was also adopted by the Chinese legislature and embodied in property law. For example, in terms of land rights, Chinese scholars proposed

---

[48] The *French Civil Code* which was a collection of 36 bills. After the promulgation of the code, it was not officially named the *Napoleonic Code* until 1807.
[49] The *German Civil Code* has been revised many times since, such as the Modernization Law of the Obligation Law, the Medical Contract, the Lease Law, and the Consumer Protection Directive. However, the Civil Code of the People's Republic of China draws more on its style and structure.
[50] The draft of the *Swiss Civil Code* was reviewed and approved on 10 December 1907, and came into effect on 1 January1912.

systems pertaining to land use rights with Chinese characteristics, such as rights for construction on land and related land contractual management rights, which have effectively realised an organic combination of socialist public ownership and market economy in the past few decades in China.

These legislative suggestions also highlighted the importance of Chinese characteristics and Chinese elements for the new civil code. In addition, many rules in the *Tort Liability Law* within the new code also reflect distinct Chinese characteristics – (1) the Tort Liability Law achieved a correct combination incorporating a preventive function while strengthening the remedial function, (2) the Tort Liability Law properly arranged general terms and conditions in the new Code. The new Code helped to illustrate catalogued relationships and, accordingly, effectively coordinated the highly abstract and moderately specific relationships in society, (3) the Tort Liability Law enriched mechanisms for new cause of actions in tort liability and expanded their visibility in society in relation to the bearing of responsibility, and so forth.

5.2 ADAPTATION OF THE NEW LEGISLATIVE MODEL

The new *Civil Code 2021* adopted a model whereby there was no longer segregation of civil and commercial law in the legal system. Accordingly, it integrated the following – (1) civil law and commercial law, (2) civil law and intellectual property law, and (3) the convergence of civil law and administrative law in the legislative model. The new Civil Code 2021 reflected the systemic, comprehensive, and basic characteristics of China's new philosophy in this Civil Code.

5.3 THREE INNOVATIONS OF THE NEW "CIVIL CODE"

The new "Civil Code" had three important innovations in the legislative system - (1) manifestation in the independent compilation of personal rights, (2) manifestation in the independent compilation of tort liability, and (3) manifestation in the independent compilation of the general rules of contract along with the general rules of the law of debt.

5.4 EMPHASIS AND AN ALL-ENCOMPASSING NATURE FOR THE CONFIRMATION AND PROTECTION OF CIVIL RIGHTS

The new *Civil Code 2021* has a total of 1,260 articles that are divided into seven parts. It includes general provisions, real rights, contracts, personality rights, marriage and family, succession and tort liability.

The new *Civil Code 2021* is built around the recognition and protection of civil rights through the rigorous logical system employed in its drafting. As Wang Liming, chairman of the Civil Law Research Association of the Chinese Law Society and a reputed Professor at Renmin University of China, said, "The new "Civil Code" is a declaration of rights protection".[51] Along with the specific content and boundaries of the law, the new code also gives individuals the protection to be able to exercise and claim their rights easily from illegal infringement by others. The Civil Code not only widely affirms the property rights of various subjects to meet people's material life needs, but also widely recognises peoples' personal rights to follow their spiritual life pursuits.

---

[51] "Civil Code is a Declaration of Rights Protection," *Guangming Daily*, 24 May 2020, 3rd edition.

6 HIGHLIGHTS OF LEGISLATION IN NEW CIVIL CODE 2021

Although the *Civil Code 2021* is codification rooted in segregated laws, yet it has a series of new regulations within the code based on new concepts and schools of thought. A full breakdown of the new Civil Code 2021 is attached as an Appendix to the chapter for the benefit of readers.

In the author's opinion, it may be that the *French Civil Code 1807* could be considered as the best model civil code of the 19th century, similarly the *German Civil Code 1896* could be considered as the model civil code of the 20th century. Accordingly, scholars in China wish China's new *Civil Code 2021* to be considered as the model civil code of the 21st century for other civil law jurisdictions.

6.1 THE CODE'S IMPACT ON THE PROTECTION OF VARIOUS RIGHTS IN PURSUIT OF A QUALITY OF LIFE

This code strengthens the protection of personal rights by organising them independently and drafting them afresh for Chinese society. The new Civil Code lists three rights – life, health, and body – and emphasises their importance within the code. Additionally, within the code, there are regulations for the prevention of sexual harassment. Lastly, the new code has stipulated a system of injunctions, deletions, corrections and so forth to provide remedies for the violation of rights. A few of the new items that are included in the new code are – (1) the protection of property rights and the rights of owners of those properties,[52] (2) the protection of

---

[52] Article 207 of the *new Civil Code* and ownership of buildings is differentiated to protect people's rights to their own real estate, including exclusive rights, co-ownership, and joint management rights.

rights pertaining to residence,[53] and (3) addressing the issue of risks within society by strengthening liabilities under law of tort.[54]

6.2 NEW CIVIL CODES FOR NEW AGE OF INFORMATION

In the new age of social networks and an interconnected world, the most serious challenge which exists within the justice system is in relation to the protection of personal privacy, personal information and other personal rights. The new Civil Code has comprehensively responded by drafting effective new personal rights rules. Article 1032 of the new *Civil Code 2021* has given primacy to rights of privacy that include – (1) the private life of a person and private space, (2) private activities, and (3) private information that should not be known to others.

The new code has strengthened the protection of personal information.[55] The new *Civil Code 2021* draws on relevant provisions of the EU's *General Data Protection Regulations 2016* and uniformly summarises the seven acts listed in the *General Provisions of Civil Law 2017*. The Civil Code 2021 was formulated in two stages – the first stage was to complete formulation of the General Provisions of the Civil Law of the People's Republic of China in 2017, and the second to complete formulation of the chapters of the new Civil Code. The two are combined to form the new Civil Code 2021, which was implemented on 1 January 2021.

The content of the *Civil Law General Provisions became the General Part of the Civil Code of the People's Republic of China 2017*, whereas other separate laws that existed previously in China, and the judicial interpretation of the previous

---

[53] The new Code adds provisions for the right of residence to protect the right of residence of the people, which is conducive to fully guaranteeing people's livelihood and realising the people's expectations for a better and happy life. The establishment of the housing rights system provides important legal support for the realisation of "housing" for all people.

[54] The tort liability clause adopts a combination of compensation for loss/damage pursuant to tort liability, issues of insurance and social assistance to provide relief for the victims. Accordingly, the Code fully demonstrates the *spirit of welfare* for the populace.

[55] Article 1034 of the new *Civil Code 2021* provides comprehensive regulations on personal information.

separate laws by the Supreme People's Court of China, accordingly became chapters of the sub-rules of the Civil Code of the People's Republic of China. The new code has recognised various kinds of data, original and non-original, which are considered a property within the code.

It also recognises that data and network virtual property can be protected as property. With the help of digital technology, a large number of new business formats, new technologies, and new industries have evolved, and data protection is extremely important. Data itself is also a property, and if the data is original, it may also be protected by intellectual property rights. Facial and voice rights of a person in light of the advent of Artificial Intelligence are also protected. Furthermore, this code contains rules regarding research on human genes and human embryos, and a system for this has been established.

6.3 NEW CIVIL CODES FOR THE PROTECTION OF THE ENVIRONMENT AND ECOLOGY

The 21st century is facing a serious ecological crisis, and the environment for human survival and development is encountering severe challenges. Protecting the ecological environment is a question for China and the times to which the new Civil Code must respond. The new *Civil Code 2021* could be termed the "Green Civil Code". Article 9 of the General Principles of the new Civil Code stipulates: "Civil entities engaged in civil activities shall be conducive to resource conservation and protection of the ecological environment." This is the basis for establishing green principles as civil activities within the Chinese society.

There are as many as 18 clauses directly related to resource and environmental protection in the various divisions of the new *Civil Code 2021*, which are mainly reflected in three aspects – (1) the ecological boundary of property rights is established within the details of property rights, (2) in relation to contractual obligations; the ecological boundary during the performance of the contract is stipulated by the code, and (3) the tort liability comprises seven articles, and accordingly this code comprehensively stipulates that the onus of responsibility for environmental pollution and ecological damage falls on the stakeholders.

6.4 CIVIL CODE FOR GLOBALISATION AND THE NEEDS OF A MARKET ECONOMY

New *Civil Code 2021* has added rules for e-commerce that include e-shopping and online trade. It also has included rules for providing 'Guarantees' along with rules for movable property and registration systems.

7 FINAL COMMENTS

The civil laws and a few of the commercial laws that the People's Republic of China has enacted, promulgated and implemented in the past 70 years have now been codified and incorporated into the new Civil Code 2021. This comprehensive code comes after centuries of attempts that included the transplantation of German civil code, the influence of Soviet laws, attempts to reform after the Communist revolution, attempts to use examples of civil codes from around the world and integrate them with Chinese characteristics with cultural relevance, and so forth. Although one of the legislative features of the Civil Code 2021 is to strengthen the integration of civil and commercial laws, there are still a large number of separate commercial laws that have not yet been incorporated into Civil Code 2021.

Therefore, it is still work in progress, and these separate codes continue to be applied in the form of separate laws, such as the *Company Law of the People's*

Republic of China 1993,[56] the *Securities Law of the People's Republic* of China 1999,[57] and the *Maritime Law 1993 of the People's Republic of China*.

However, there is still an ongoing debate amongst Chinese scholars and lawyers, as to whether there is the need for a separate "*Commercial Code*" in the future.

BIBLIOGRAPHY

- Sun Xianzhong, *The Inheritance of China's Foreign Civil Law* (Beijing: Law Press, 2003).

- Zhenmin Xie, *The Legislative History of the Republic of China (Volume 2)* (Beijing: China University of Political Science and Law Press, 2000).

- Lihong Zhang and Fuping Gao, *Civil Law Codification and Anti-codification* (Beijing: China University of Political Science and Law Press, 2008).

- Xianyi Zeng and Xiaogeng Zhao, *The History of Chinese Legal System,* 4th ed. (Beijing: Peking University Press-Higher Education Press, 2018).

- "*Civil Code of the People's Republic of China*", Adopted at the Third Session of the Thirteenth National People's Congress on May 28, 2020 [Notes: This translation is for reference only. In case of discrepancy between the English translation and the original Chinese text, the Chinese text shall prevail.]

APPENDIX A TO THE CHAPTER

Overview of the main contents of the Civil Code of the People's Republic of China

Book One – General Part

Chapter I General Provisions (Article 1- Article 12)

Chapter II Natural Persons

Section 1 – Capacity for Enjoying Civil-law Rights and Capacity for Performing Civil Juristic Acts (Article 13- Article 25)

---

[56] This law has been promulgated in 1993 and has been amended 5 times by 2021.

[57] This law was promulgated in 1999 and has been amended three times in 2013.

CHAPTER 4

UKRAINIAN NATIONAL LEGAL SYSTEM – THE IMPACT OF HISTORY AND, RECENTLY, OF ENGLISH LAW ON ITS DEVELOPMENT

Attorney Svitlana Sergeyeva

1. INTRODUCTION

The term "legal system" has three meanings in legal science, namely: 1) as a type of law; 2) as a synonym to the terms "law" or "legislation"; 3) as a group of legal systems.

Contemporary legal theory distinguishes broad and narrow approaches to the definition of a legal system. The broad approach, describes a multi-faceted national legal system, which is united by the common origin of – (1) sources of law, (2) the main legal terms, and (3) the methods and manner of its development. On the other hand, the narrow approach to the legal system definition comprises a national legal system which exists within a jurisdiction.

Outstanding Ukrainian scholars have determined a legal system as the centre of all legal phenomena, which are present in a particular state or a group of states.[1] According to these scholars, a legal system could also be a centre of interconnected and coordinated legal means that are dedicated to regulate public relations, as well as legal phenomena, which occur as a result of such regulations. A few of the legal means in any legal system are: legal norms, legal principles, sense of justice, legislation, legal relations, legal offices, legal techniques, legal culture, the state of legality and its deviations, law order, and so forth.[2]

According to N.M. Onishchenko, a legal system is a component of the regulatory ordered side of legal life – the process of creation and reproduction of legal relations, which occurs between persons due to serving particular interests, and legal life is an uninterrupted process of activity of numbers of individuals, who direct their efforts at the resolution of socially important issues using a system of legal means.[3]

There is a point of view in literature that a legal system is the centre of interconnected and interacted legal phenomena, created by a society and, where necessary, mediated by a state, dedicated to unite persons into a single society by specific means and methods. This will also regulate their relations, with the aim of self-preservation of society and its progressive development.

Contemporary legal literature of Ukraine also contains a definition of the legal system as a polysystemic, complex group of internally coordinated,

---

[1] P.M. Rabinovych, Osnovy zahalnoi teorii prava ta derzhavy *[Basics of general theory of law and state]* (Lviv: Krai, 2007), 118.

[2] O. F. Skakun, *Teoriia derzhavy i prava [Theory of the State and Law]* (Kharkiv: Konsum, 2001), 236.

[3] N. M. Onishchenko, *Pravova Systema: Problemy Teorii [The legal System: Issues of the Theory]* (Kyiv: The Institute of State and Law named after V.M. Koretsky of the National Academy of Sciences of Ukraine, 2002), 352.

interdependent, socially homogeneous legal phenomena, which belong to normative, institutional and ideological levels of legal reality, and have regulatory-organising and stabilising influences on public relations, with the aim of the harmonious development of society.[4]

Taking into consideration the aforementioned definitions, scientists have determined the following main features of a legal system, namely: systemic, cyclicality of functioning and sequence of the development of legal processes in the system, integrity, combination of statics and dynamics, continuity, clarity, as well as internal order.

The aim of a legal system is reasoned by the social system, thus legal regulation shall be considered as a function of a legal system. The aim of a legal system is a predictable and desirable result, which may be fully or partially reached as a result of the functioning of the aforementioned system - in other words legal order, which is necessary to reach the aim of a social system.

Summarising the above discussion on legal systems, the following definition of the term "legal system of society" may be proposed: *it is an integral, resistant interaction of subjects of law, structurally organized by legal norms, which ensures the achievement of proper legal order as a necessary condition of social system functioning.*

Legal literature contains differing points of view regarding the elements of a legal system. M.I. Matuzov outlines such elements as approaches, relations, establishments, conditions, institutions, regimes, processes and statutes.[5] Ch. Varga includes into the composition of a legal system of society a system of law

---

[4] O. M. Sadovska, *Pravova Systema Italii: zahalnoteoretychna characterystyka osnovnych elementiv [Legal system of Italy: general theoretical characteristics of the basic elements]* (Kharkiv: National University of Internal Affairs, 2001), 25.
[5] N. I. Matuzov, *Pravovaya systema i lichnost [Legal system and Individual]* (Saratov, Saratov University, 1987), 294.

comprising legislations, real possibilities and the functions of legal regulations.[6] S.S. Alekseev defines objective (positive) law, legal ideology (sense of justice), and judicial (legal) practice as elements of the legal system.[7]

Several authors have included into the structure of a legal system the arrangements of law, legislation, legal institutes and establishments, legal concepts, principles, symbols, legal policy, ideology and culture, as well as legal practice within the jurisdiction.

Professor P.M. Rabinovych includes in the composition of a national legal system the following – 1) different legal acts and the activity of respective subjects devoted to the creation of such acts; 2) different kinds and manifestations of sense of justice; and 3) the state of legality and its deviations.[8]

N.M. Onishchenko considers that the elements of the a legal system are – (1) the law as a system of norms, which are created and protected by a state, (2) legislation as a form of expression of the mentioned norms (regulatory acts), (3) legal principles, (4) legal establishments, which implement the legal policy of a state, (5) judicial and other legal practices, (6) the mechanisms of legal regulation, (7) law enforcement processes (including acts of application and interpretation), (8) the rights, freedoms and responsibilities of citizens (law in its subjective meaning), (9) legal activities, (10) the system of legal relations formed in society, that is, legality and legal order, (11) legal ideology (sense of justice, legal doctrines, theories, legal culture, etc.), (12) subjects of law (individual and collective), (13) systemic connections, which ensure the unity, integrity and stability of the system, (14) other legal phenomena (legal liability, legal personality, legal status, regime,

---

[6] C. Varga, *Is Law a system of enactment?* (Acta Juridica Academiae Scienliarum Hungaricae, 1984), 413-416.

[7] S. S. Alekseev, *Obshchaia Teoryia Prava [General Theory of Law]* (Moscow: Prospekt, 2009), 576.

[8] P.M. Rabinovych, *Osnovy zahalnoi teorii prava ta derzhavy [Basics of general theory of law and state]* (Lviv: Krai, 2007), 118.

guarantees, legal interests, etc.), which create the "infrastructure" of a legal system.[9]

American scholars L. M. Friedman and G. M. Hayden distinguish three groups of legal phenomena, namely – 1) a structure, which includes principles of the legal system, and legal establishments, 2) "essence", which includes the norms and samples of peoples' behaviour, which are fixed in decisions and other acts (instructions), 3) "legal culture", which means peoples' attitudes towards law and the legal system, ideals, and so forth.[10]

Based on the various positions available in legal literature, the following elements of a legal system may be proposed: (1) law (the system of norms), (2) legislation (as a form of expression of norms), (3) legal establishments, which implement the legal policy of a state, (4) judicial and other legal practice; 5) mechanisms of legal regulation, (6) the law enforcement process (including acts of application and interpretation of law), (7) the rights, freedoms and responsibilities of citizens (subjective law), 8) the system of legal relations, (9) legality and legal order, (10) legal ideology (sense of justice, legal doctrines, legal culture), (11) subjects of law (individual and collective), (12) systematising connections, and (13) other legal phenomena (legal liability, legal status, etc.), which create the "infrastructure" of a legal system.

Thereby, it follows that the structural organisation of a legal system is created by institutional, functional and normative components, which are necessary for the legal system's existence as an integral phenomenon, and are reasoned by the main features of its internal composition. It is interesting to analyse that subjects of law create institutional components, functional components are represented by the complexity of connections between subjects of law, which in turn become legal

---

[9] N. M. Onishchenko, *Teoretyko-metodolohichni zasady formuvannia ta rozvytku pravovoi systemy [Theoretical and methodological principles of establishment and development of the legal system]* (Kyiv, 2002), 10.
[10] L. M. Friedman and G. M. Hayden, *American Law: An Introduction* (Oxford: Oxford University Press, 2017), 7-21.

relations through the activities of subjects (in the majority of cases). The normative part of a legal system means such complexities of regulatory means (normative regulators) are mediators in the occurrence and existence of connections between subjects. Hence, institutional components are determinative for normative and functional ones.

The functioning of a legal system is in indissoluble connection with the vital activity of a particular society. In this regard, it is appropriate to affirm that a legal system is intrinsic to a particular society, which has reached a level of statehood, and the presence of a bespoke legal system in a state is caused by the fact that each country has its own legal customs, traditions, legislation, jurisdictional authorities, peculiarities of legal mentality and legal culture, which are created historically.

A legal system is a subsystem of a social system, and may only function within such a system in accordance with relevant objectives and aims, which it is intended to address. The general evolution of a legal system is a component of the development of society as an organic system (its formation as an integral part), which flows within particular general patterns.

The current stage in the development and functioning of national legal systems is caused by their close interaction and interdependence, which eventually leads to convergence. It also leads to the elimination of distinct borders between them. In particular, one of the ways of legal convergence is an extension of the system of sources of law, the application of principles of law in legal practice of national legal systems based on such as the *Romano-Germanic* tradition, or on *common law*.

In recent years, recognition through EU integration was a very important step for Ukraine. Therefore, in 2014 Ukraine signed the *Association Agreement* with the EU. From that moment on, the focus of attention was turned on the necessity of ensuring EU laws were integrated into national legislation and that involved hundreds of European normative acts, whilst at the same time determining economic, political and other rules were fit for purpose. The principal issue was to ensure the gradual integration of the Ukrainian legal system with the system of *Roman Dutch* tradition and to ensure it became the principle of rule of law.

Thus, Ukraine borrowed the principle of rule of law from the common law system. Besides, there is a discussion in the national jurisprudence regarding judicial precedent as the source of law. The relevance of scientific research within such chapters is caused by objective issues, faced by the legal systems of the world, connected with the processes of globalization, and leading to the mutual borrowing of elements from different legal systems.

The necessity for major judicial reform forced Ukraine to regulate the status of the judiciary as an independent and unbiased institution, which guaranteed respect for the rule of law and justice. One of the probable ways to achieve this aim was through the precedent system, borrowed from the common law system where the decisions of higher courts are binding on lower court decisions in Ukraine.

Undoubtedly, answering the above objective involves the issue of granting a few lawmaking functions to judiciary, and will involve the volume of cases in such courts and how the judiciary will exercise their discretionary power under the new system. In order to achieve this objective, it is necessary to take into consideration the respective experiences of other developed states, such as England.

There is no doubt within Europe, English law is a classic example of the successful implementation of judicial precedent, and therefore analysis of this principle can provide an opportunity to identify both positive and negative aspects of the precedent system.[11]

---

[11] B. V. Malyshev, *Sudovyi Pretsedent u Pravovii Systemi Anhlii [Judicial Precedent in the Legal System of England]* (Kyiv: Praksis, 2008), 10.

2 THE EVOLUTION OF THE UKRAINIAN LEGAL SYSTEM

The Ukrainian legal system is of the global complex, integrating category, which reflects the legal organisation of society and integral legal realities. [12] The Ukrainian national legal system developed in spite of the complicated conditions it was subjected to as a result of – (1) the absence of independence during significant periods of history, (2) the geopolitical position of Ukraine, and (3) the effect of conflicting ideologies from the European Union and Eastern concepts.

The development of the national legal system may be divided into two periods – (1) that prior to the declaration of independence in 1991, and (2) that following the attainment of independence; a period characterized by the adoption of the *Constitution in 1996*, which not only guided the Ukrainian population in building an independent, democratic, social and law-governed state, but also secured the main legal basis for furthering economic, political, social and cultural development, and prioritising ways of reforming the various institutions. [13]

2.1 RELEVANT HISTORICAL EVENTS IN THE EVOLUTION OF THE LEGAL SYSTEM

Undoubtedly, the current national identity of the legal system of Ukraine was influenced by a range of historical events that led to evolution into its current form. It is therefore obligatory to consider the various historical events leading up to the formation of Ukraine. Undoubtedly, all such historical events and sources have influenced the evolution and development of Ukrainian law in its current form.

---

[12] Yu. S. Shemshuchenko, *Pravovi Systemy Suchasnosti [Contemporary Legal Systems]* (2012), 224.
[13] V. P. Nahrebelnyi, "Zakonodavcha Tekhnika ta Efektyvnist Pravotvorennia v Ukraini" ["Legislation Technique and the Efficiency of the Law-making in Ukraine"] in *Chasopys Kyivskoho Universytetu Prava [The Chronicle of the Kyiv University of Law]*, 5, no. 3 (2003), 5.

2.1.1 Events prior to the Declaration of Independence

2.1.1.1 *"Rus' Justice"*

Agreements that were concluded between *Kievan Rus* and Byzantium dated 907 CE, 911 CE, 944 CE and 971 CE are considered to be one of the first written sources of law. These agreements contained rules of criminal, civil, procedural and international law. The treaties have references to the law of *Kievan Rus*, which was a compendium of oral archaic law. An analysis of the above-mentioned sources gives insight into the mixed *Rus-Byzantium law*.[14]

"Rus' Justice" played a very important role among sources of law in Ukraine, being the first and most important document in the history of law and state. It also had a great impact on the development of the legal systems of the Grand Duchy of Lithuania and the Kingdom of Poland, which once included a major part of Ukrainian territory.

"Rus' Justice" is the most prominent compendium of ancient laws, a very important source for research into the medieval history of law and the public relations of Kievan Rus and neighboring Slavonic nations. It is the most ancient code of *Kievan Rus*, created during the 11th-12th centuries CE and obtained its title in 1072 CE.

"Rus' Justice" regulated a wide range of public relations, including rules regarding the status of a person and his/her rights and freedoms. In particular, it contained widely regulated issues of ownership and inheritance. A series of rules ensured there would be – (1) an absence of capital punishment, torture or a heavy-handed approach during interrogations, (2) the restriction, and eventually the prohibition,

---

[14] S. V. Kivalov and Yu. M. Oborotov, *Vstup v Ukrainske Pravo [Introduction into Ukrainian Law]* (Odesa: Yurydychna literatura [Legal Literature], 2005), 6-7.

of blood vengeance, and (3) different legal mechanisms to protect life, honour and the dignity of a person. Scholars have distinguished three versions of the *"Rus' Justice"*, namely – (1) the Short Edition, (2) the Extensive Edition, and (3) the Abridged Edition. An approximate date of the adoption of the document within Ukraine was 1016 CE; however, some sources suggest the adoption date to be 1036 CE.

The oldest, Short Edition of *"Rus' Justice"* is connected with the name of Yaroslav the Wise, who created the code regarding the order in Novgorod (*"Yaroslav's Law"*). Its second part was *"The Law by Yaroslav's sons"*, which was adopted on the basis of a meeting between Yaroslav's sons - Izyaslav, Svyatoslav and Vsevolod – in the year 1072 CE at Vyshhorod. Thereafter, the code was supplemented by *Princes' Statutes*, as well as statutes from the Church, following Christian jurisprudence. Researchers assume that the Extensive Edition was created during the reign of Volodymyr Monomakh (after 1113 CE). The third, the Abridged Edition, was created in the 12th century, approximately.

Therefore, *"Rus' Justice"* regulated relations between persons in society by means of rules that governed that society. Comparing *"Rus' Justice"* with Roman and Graeco-Roman (Byzantine) law, the following comments could be made in relation to the influence of Byzantine law:

2.1.1.1.1 Polish-Lithuanian period (14th-16th centuries CE)

The legal system of the Grand Duchy of Lithuania (namely the *Statutes of Lithuania*) had a great impact on the development of legal thoughts and the understanding of law. Thus, the granting of "privileges" on the rights and freedoms to Ukrainian gentry, lower-middle class, clergy and eventually *Cossacks*[15] by

---

[15] The name Cossack means anyone who could not find his appropriate place in society and went into the steppes, where he was acknowledged as having no authority. In European sources, the term first appeared in a dictionary of the Cuman language in the mid-13th century. It was also found in Byzantine sources and in the instructions issued by Italian cities to their colonies on the Black Sea

Lithuanian and Polish Kings and Dukes, the Statutes of Lithuania, as well as the new status of Ukrainian lands, had an impact on the development and evolution of law in ancient Ukrainian lands.

As a result, the *Statutes of Lithuania (1529, 1566 and 1588)*, especially the *1588 Statute*, which is recognized as the most completed code in Europe by many contemporary researchers, declared a range of new approaches to the status of a person.

In this way, *Statutes* established a unity of legislation applicable to all nationals of the state. Its importance lies in the fact that all subjects were equal before the law. However, it could be argued that the above mentioned provision was just like a general declaration. Limited liberality was declared, but was limited towards the *Christian religion* only. It was prohibited to enslave a free person, as well as to marry a woman against her will. Arrest without relevant legal grounds, and punishment without a court decision were also declared to be unacceptable. The right to legal assistance was granted under these *Statutes*. The elective judiciary and the concept of separation of a court from an administration were provided long before this concept gained a foothold in other countries. Since *Rus' law* was one of the major sources of the Statutes, the latter were never considered by the Ukrainian population to be a creation of a foreign legal culture, but as their own "ancient law".[16]

---

coast, where it was applied to armed men who were engaged in military service in frontier regions and protected trade caravans traveling the steppe routes. By the end of the 15th century CE, the name acquired a wider sense and was applied to those Ukrainians who went into the steppes to practice various trades and engage in hunting, fishing, beekeeping, the collection of salt and saltpeter, and so on.)

[16] M. H. Khaustova, *Derzhavne Budivnytstvo ta Mistseve Samovriaduvannia [State Building and Local Government]* (2011), 65.

2.1.1.1.2 The Impact of Magdeburg Law on the territory of Ukraine (13th-18th centuries CE)

Magdeburg Law is one of the most famous systems of feudal town law, created in the 13th century CE in the German town of Magdeburg, according to which economic activity, socio-political life, property rights, and the legal status of citizens are regulated by their own system of legal rules. It was a collection of *German laws* translated into Polish. In the middle of the 14th century CE, Magdeburg Law had spread to such cities as Lviv, Kyiv, Kamianets-Podilskyi, Zhytomyr, Lutsk, Vinnytsia, Kaniv, Sniatyn, Dubno, Ostroh, Kovel, Berestechko, Bratslav, Sanok, Korsun and Pereiaslav, and had a huge impact on the development of the local governments of these cities.

According to the law, certain Ukrainian cities were granted the right "to litigate and consult each other". Towns that were utilsing *Magdeburg Law* were excluded from the jurisdiction of local administration (magnates, voivodes, vicegerents, and so forth), and accordingly these cities created their own local government authorities, namely magistrates. Additionally, sources of Magdeburg Law determined the organisation of handicraft industries, trade, the order of election and activity of local governments, and corporations of artisans and merchants.

2.1.1.1.3 The Cossack Hetmanate (the Zaporizhian Host) (16th-18th century CE)

The activity of Ukrainian hetmans is a unique example in Europe. Historically, the Ukrainian nation gained independence from Poland as the result of an uprising. The successful uprising was led by Hetman of Zaporizhian Host Bohdan Khmelnytsky, and accordingly renewed its sovereignty by creating the Cossack Republic. The territory of the Cossack Republic incorporated almost the whole area of contemporary Ukraine. In 1649 CE, *the Treaty of Zboriv* was signed, which approved the autonomy of the Cossack State. As a result of this Treaty, European states recognized Ukraine as a state and a subject of international law with its own territory and borders.

The *Treaty of Pereyaslav* of 1654 CE, which has references in detail in Bohdan Khmelnytsky's "*Pereyaslav Articles*", ensured the Cossack Republic retained all rights and privileges of Cossacks and their officers, the authority of a hetman, and so forth. In addition, the Treaty also had great importance in the development of the national legal system of that period. During his reign, Hetman Ivan Vyhovsky adopted the *Treaty of Korsun* with Sweden in 1657 CE, as well as the *Treaty of Hadiach* in 1658 CE. Both these treaties also had a prominent effect on the development of the legal traditions of Ukraine.

"*Pacts and Constitutions of Rights and Freedoms of the Zaporizhian Host*" was written and adopted by Hetman Pylyp Orlyk in 1710 CE. Historical sources have also referred to the same document by another title - "*the Constitution of Pylyp Orlyk*". This Constitution established the principle of the separation of powers between the legislative (Cossack General Council), the executive (hetman, regiment and squad chancelleries) and the judicial (the system of squad, regiment, town courts, general court) branches of government, as well as creating a parliamentary-hetman Cossack Republic. In particular, the document also – (1) limited powers to tax subjects, (2) established immutable rules regarding the protection of women – Cossacks' widows, as well as Cossacks' wives and orphaned children, and (4) obliged a hetman to ensure obedience to inviolable civil rights.

2.1.1.1.4 Influence due to the protection of other states (19th- 20th century CE)

In the 19th-20th centuries CE, Ukraine came under the protection of various states (the Russian Empire, the Austria-Hungarian Empire, Poland, Czechoslovakia and so forth) which resulted in the Ukrainian legal system experiencing the influence of many different legal systems, hence various legal concepts from those systems were absorbed by its own legal system.

More than 70 years of Soviet Ukraine (in the early 20th century) gave a grounding to determine the legal system of that period as of a *socialist character*. In 1917, revolution in Russia and Ukraine caused unprecedented attempts by the authorities to fundamentally alter society. This resulted in traditional legal values being outlawed.

Active participation of Ukraine in the processing and adoption of important international law acts in the field of rights and freedoms of a person in the 20th century must be emphasized. This means that specific concepts from Ukraine were reflected in the following International Conventions – the *Universal Declaration of Human Rights (1948, the International Covenant on Civil and Political Rights (1966),* the *International Covenant on Economic, Social and Cultural Rights (1966),* as well as the *International Convention on the Elimination of All Forms of Racial Discrimination (1965),* etc.

According to scholars, the right conditions for the creation of the contemporary national legal system of Ukraine occurred after the proclamation of the *Declaration of State Sovereignty of Ukraine dated 16 July 1990 and the Act of Declaration of Independence of Ukraine dated 24 August 1991.*

The Declaration of State Sovereignty of Ukraine dated 16 July 1990 and the *Application of the Verkhovna Rada of Ukraine* provided, in "To Parliaments and Nations of the World" dated 5 December 1991, that "a new, democratic, law-governed state is willing to join the family of civilized countries, and aims, inter alia, to ensure the rights and freedoms of a person and a citizen, and undertakes to strictly adhere to universally recognized principles and rules of international law, as well as international standards in the field of the rights and freedoms of a person".

Decisively, the declaration of Independence of Ukraine on 24 August 1991 heralded a new stage in Ukrainian history. This event gave new substance to the rights and freedoms of citizens of Ukraine. Hence, on 12 September 1991, the Law of *"On Succession of Ukraine"* was adopted, according to which the Constitution of the Ukrainian SSR, as well as laws of the Ukrainian SSR and other acts, adopted by the Verkhovna Rada of the Ukrainian SSR, still in force in the territory of Ukraine prior to the adoption of the new Constitution were still valid, on the proviso that they did not contradict the laws of Ukraine adopted after the declaration of independence of Ukraine.

The Affiliation of Ukraine to the Council of Europe on 9 November 1995 was the next important step, which had a further impact on the development of rights and freedoms of a person and a citizen in Ukraine. Thus, Ukraine adhered to European conventions in the field of rights and freedoms of a person and undertook to implement European Union norms into national legislation.

Adoption of the *Constitution of Ukraine in 1996* also had an important influence on the format of an independent Ukrainian legal system. The Constitution fixed the main legal principles of the state and its further economic, political, social and cultural development. The Constitution of Ukraine qualitatively defined the new status of a person and a citizen in Ukraine.

According to Article 3 of the *Constitution 1996*, an individual, his/her life and health, honour and dignity, inviolability and security shall be recognized in Ukraine as the highest social value. The State shall be responsible to the individual for its activities. Affirming and ensuring the human rights and freedoms of a person shall be the main duty of the State. Taking into consideration this concept, the current Constitution of Ukraine devotes Chapter II to the rights, freedoms and duties of a person and a citizen. This Chapter is one of the most important in the Constitution and contains approximately one third of its articles.

The current Constitution of Ukraine implemented all the main provisions of international instruments regarding the rights of a person and, above all, of the *Universal Declaration of Human Rights, the International Covenant on Civil and Political Rights, as well as the International Covenant on Economic, Social and Cultural Rights*, which are some of the greatest achievements for humanity in the 20th century.

It is an important fact that the Constitution of Ukraine not only proclaims rights and freedoms, but additionally provides a dedicated system ensuring that suitable guarantees are available to citizens of Ukraine in respect of those rights and freedoms. This is shown by the presence and balance of the systems of such institutions as the *institute of the President of Ukraine, the Verkhovna Rada of Ukraine* (legislative body), executive and local authorities, courts of all jurisdictions, prosecution, as well as the *Institution of the Ukrainian Parliament Commissioner for Human Rights*.

The right to apply to international guarantees, along with national ones, is provided in the Constitution of Ukraine. According to Article 55 of the Constitution of Ukraine, after exhausting all domestic legal instruments, everyone shall have the right to appeal for the protection of his/her rights and freedoms to the relevant international judicial institutions or to the relevant bodies of international organisations to which Ukraine is affiliated as a member or as a participant in the process. The Constitution does not see its subjects going abroad to seek redress as something to frown upon, because freedom and the guarantees related to it are very important.

The Ratification of the European Convention on Human Rights on 17 July 1997 was a fundamental step by Ukraine in this regard. As a result, each citizen of Ukraine is entitled, and has the possibility, to apply to the European Court of

Human Rights to protect his/her violated rights, as proclaimed by the European Convention on Human Rights.

It is noteworthy that the norms of the Constitution of Ukraine are directly applicable to its citizens. Consequently, recourse to a court for the protection of the constitutional rights and freedoms of an individual and a citizen is available directly, on the basis that the Constitution of Ukraine shall be guaranteed.

Nowadays, the Constitution of Ukraine is the basic law in Ukraine, which has a superior legal force over other laws. Thus, the Constitution is the basis for the development of the entire system of national legislation. The Constitutional Court is one more important element in the mechanism for the protection of the rights and freedoms of an individual and a citizen of Ukraine. The Court controls and protects the foundations of the constitutional system, the main rights and freedoms of an individual and a citizen, and ensures the rule of law and direct action of the Constitution on the whole territory of the state.

The Constitutional Court has the following powers – (1) to resolve issues of compliance of regulatory acts or their parts with the Constitution of Ukraine; (2) to interpret constitutional norms in the consideration of particular cases, and (3) to officially interpret the Constitution and laws of Ukraine, which are mandatory for all subjects of law.

The introduction of the Special Institute of the Ukrainian Parliament Commissioner for Human Rights was an innovation for Ukrainian governmental and legal systems to deal with issues pertaining to the protection of human rights and freedoms. Accordingly, *Article 55 of the Constitution of Ukraine* proclaims the right of individuals to apply to the Ukrainian Parliament Commissioner for protection of their Human Rights. *Article 101 of the Constitution of Ukraine* provides parliamentary control, through an appointed Commissioner, over observance of the constitutional rights and freedoms of an individual and a citizen. The status, functions and competence of the Ukrainian Parliament Commissioner for Human Rights are provided by the law of Ukraine "*On the Ukrainian Parliament Commissioner for Human Rights*", which was adopted by the Verkhovna Rada of Ukraine on 23 December 1997. While drafting this law, Parliament took into account the experience of European states regarding the institution of ombudsmen.

Hence, at the current stage of development of Ukrainian Law, sources of law in Ukraine include – (1) regulatory instruments (the Constitution, laws, and subordinate acts), (2) international treaties, (3) legal custom, (4) judicial practice, including practices of the European Court of Human Rights, (5) legal doctrine and (6) general principles of law.

In recent years, an interesting legal phenomenon has developed in the Ukrainian legal system. Even though judicial precedent is not considered to be a source of law in Ukraine, in the last few years explanations from the Supreme Court regarding some issues of particular categories of cases for courts of inferior jurisdiction, as well as judgements of the court of superior jurisdiction, are considered as binding according to hierarchy within the court system of Ukraine. In other words, the court of first instance, when making a decision in a case, will have to analyse judicial practices of the Supreme Court and must comply with them. This phenomenon has been influenced by the common law system, in particular that of England & Wales.

As a result, these days, when giving legal advice, every attorney-at-law in Ukraine needs to consider the judgments and comments from a superior court on the same or similar issues.

This tendency clearly testifies to the fact that the Ukrainian legal system has started to borrow features from the common law system, which is considered a complex legal system. This evolving nature and the influence of common law systems will be discussed in the following paragraphs.

3 IMPACT OF ENGLISH LAW ON THE UKRAINIAN LEGAL SYSTEM

3.1 KEY FEATURES OF THE COMMON LAW SYSTEM

The most essential features of the system of common law are – (1) judicial precedent as the main source of law, (2) the division of law into common law and equity law. The development of common law occurred around the time of the Norman Conquest in 1066 CE. Common law was supplemented by equity law in the 15th-18th centuries CE. Accordingly, (1) courts may seem to have a law-making function due to inherent flexibility, but within limits when they apply the law in courts, (2) judgements take the lead in the formation and development of law, (3) there is a casuistic character to judicial precedent, i.e. it shall apply only to the resolution of similar cases, (4) there is an importance to procedural law, along with substantive law and (5) there is an absence of the clear differentiation of law into branches and (6) relatively less prominence is accorded to codified laws, as compared to civil law systems such as those of Germany or France.

The group of legal systems affected by English law includes those of England & Wales, Canada, Australia, New Zealand, and other legal systems of the British Commonwealth of Nations (54 member states). The legal systems of Northern Ireland and Scotland, as well as the province of Quebec (Canada), do not belong to system following English law. The legal system of the USA pertains to American law and is based on the common law system.

One of the key landmark features of English law is that it was relatively uninterrupted and consistently evolved, unlike many civil law systems. During its long history, English law did not face great disruptions and transformations, as was the case in many other countries, inter alia, in France in 1793 or in the Russian Empire (to which Ukraine was affiliated) in 1917. England has been saved from the division of its laws into pre- and post-revolutionary legislation, and it has never experienced current law and its institutes differing to any great extent from their historical roots and traditions. It developed independently, transformed into a modern legal system and, accordingly, has a great influence on the commercial laws of the world.

However, despite the rapid development of legislation, the principle, according to which statutory provision comes into legal effect by courts, comes into existence only after its application by the courts.[17] Therefore, as a rule, English legislation is applied following its interpretation by courts. The English doctrine of interpretation consists of rules, presumptions, rules of linguistics, laws on interpretation, precedents and additional means and approaches. Such a system of tools of interpretation obliges an interpreter to creatively analyse statutory provision in accordance with particular legal relations, to identify optimal solutions not only on the basis of the statutory text, but grounded on equity law and common law. The English doctrine of interpretation approves principle, which is interesting to many of us, namely: law should always be interpreted rationally (*lex est aliquid rationis*).[18]

By virtue of the peculiarities of the English legal system, the difference between its legal theory and history is almost unnoticeable. Therefore, analysis of English law, as a rule, is similar to the research of its history.

Judicial practice is the main source of English law. Judicial practice in England not only applies the law, but creates legal rules that can be applied to future cases.

---

[17] A. Kh. Saydov, *Sravnytelnoe Pravovedenye (Osnovnie Pravovie Systemi Sovremennosty) [Comparative Law - the Main Contemporary Legal Systems]*, edited by V. A. Tumanova (Moscow: Yuryst, 2003), 250.

[18] E. N. Tonkov, *Tolkovanye Zakona v Anhlyy [Interpretation of Law in England]* (Saint Petersburg: Aleteiia, 2015), 10.

The rules, contained in the judgements, shall then apply during further consideration of similar cases. The rule of precedent, which obliges English judges to comply with judgements rendered by their predecessors, was established from the first half of the 19th century CE. The study of judicial practice presumes knowledge of the main principles of the English judicial system. There is a division into senior justice, which is conducted by senior courts, and subordinate justice, which is conducted by a number of subordinate courts. Particular attention is always paid to the operation of senior courts, since they not only consider specific cases, but create a precedent to be followed. Statutory instruments are another source of English law, along with judicial practice. Customs are a third source of English law, along with judicial practice and statutory instrument. However, it has quite secondary significance, and its application is limited.

Another noteworthy feature of the English legal system is that rule of law is the fundamental constitutional principle. According to its requirements, all are equal before the law, thereby the law is the sole (or the main) source of legal norms. The state acts in legal fields as one of the subjects of law, along with private persons. Thus, both the state, which protects public interests, and particular individuals, who protect their own private interests, shall establish their cases before the court each time when they go to the law. According to the rule of law principle, English courts do not stand for the state. Therefore, in the context of the practice of law, nobody can condemn judges for being in collusion with policy-makers.

The main purpose of the rule of law principle is to ensure human rights and freedoms, primarily in relation to the executive and organs acting on behalf of the authorities. From the very beginning, the concept of rule of law ensured a mechanism against the tyranny and despotism of monarchical regimes and authoritarianism to prevent the application of formal law to achieve anti-legal goals. The constitutional principle of rule of law aimed – (1) to "bind" state authority by law, (2) to establish reliable legal protection against state's unjustified invasion into human lives, and (3) to create the conditions necessary for the realisation and protection of human rights and freedoms.[19]

The aim of rule of law is not just a formal mechanism to ensure order as provided by laws and other statutory acts that are adopted by the state, but more importantly it is aimed at securing the approval of order, thereby restricting the absolutism of the state. These objectives are achieved by placing the executive authority under societal control and establishing respective legal mechanisms. In other words, even for values and beliefs, from the point of view of legal technique, law is not always a magic bullet for ensuring rule of law is maintained in the society.[20]

English law, as opposed to Ukrainian law, is characterised by the absence of strict classification into branches, however, basic branches continuously evolve. English law demonstrates a high level of development of legal process, on the basis of which substantive branches of law have evolved in the English Legal system.

Despite certain changes within contemporary circumstances, case law still retains its position in the English legal system. It continues to be an independent and meaningful source of law. Rules of case law directly regulate a range of the most important institutes of current English law, including contract law, law of obligations and other legal institutes. Precedents accompany the practice of legislative execution, since courts are obliged to interpret, clarify and develop provisions of statutory law. Actually, in England, statutory law loses its significance and could not apply without case law.

---

[19] "Verkhovenstvo Prava" ["Rule of Law"] in *Zakonodavchyi Biuleten [Legislative Bulletin]* (Kyiv: 2005), 5-6.
[20] Y.Bytiak, L.Voronova, A.Hetman, Y.Hroshevyi, A.Zakaliuk, V.Komarov, N.Kuznietsova, N.Onishchenko, O.Petryshyn, O.Pohribnyi, *Pravova Systema Ukrainy: Istoriia, Stan ta Perspektyvy [Legal System of Ukraine: History, Current State and Prospective]* (Kharkiv: Pravo, 2008), 151.

3.2 THE IMPACT OF ENGLISH LEGAL SYSTEM ON UKRAINIAN LAW

As discussed in the above section, there is an attempt in the Ukrainian legal system to adopt features of English Law. Accordingly, the key features of English Law are also evolving in Ukrainian Law. Notwithstanding the impact of English Law, Ukraine still belongs to the Roman Dutch civil law legal system. As a result, the high pace of legislative activities in Ukraine demonstrates – (1) an absence of pattern, (2) a certain amount of randomness, (3) the absence of a scientifically-based system of legal acts, and (4) the absence of mechanisms for the implementation of such legislations. These further result in a need to frequently amend and supplement these laws.

It is submitted that in order to resolve these deficiencies, the English law feature of robust judicial precedents should be further adopted and become an official source of law.

4 FINAL COMMENTS

It is submitted that even though English law is a model law and its influence is increasing, nevertheless, probably due to Ukrainian circumstances and its legal history, the key features of the English legal system are unlikely to be incorporated in the Ukrainian Law. However, there are rational reasons for the English legal system to influence and probably further impact judicial and legal reforms in Ukraine.

Accordingly, very recently on 11 June 2021, the President of Ukraine signed the *Decree No. 231/2021 "On the Strategy of the Development of the Judiciary and Constitutional Justice for 2021-2023"*. The strategy defines priorities for (1) the improvement of legislation devoted to the judiciary system, (2) the status of judges, (3) judicial proceedings and other institutes of justice, as well as prescribing priority measures regarding the improvement of the operation of legal institutes.

The document also describes issues within the legal system, which must be resolved in coming years to further improve judicial authority and justice.

BIBLIOGRAPHY

o S. S. Alekseev, *Obshchaia Teoryia Prava [General Theory of Law]* (Moscow: Prospekt, 2009).

o L. M. Friedman, and G. M. Hayden, *American Law: An Introduction* (Oxford: Oxford University Press, 2017).

o M. H. Khaustova, *Derzhavne Budivnytstvo ta Mistseve Samovriaduvannia [State Building and Local Government]* (2011).

o S. V. Kivalov, and Yu. M. Oborotov, *Vstup v Ukrainske Pravo [Introduction into Ukrainian Law]* (Odesa: Yurydychna literatura [Legal Literature], 2005).

o B. V. Malyshev, *Sudovyi Pretsedent u Pravovii Systemi Anhlii [Judicial Precedent in the Legal System of England]* (Kyiv: Praksis, 2008).

o N. I. Matuzov, *Pravovaya systema i lichnost [Legal system and Individual]* (Saratov: Saratov University, 1987).

o V. P. Nahrebelnyi, "Zakonodavcha Tekhnika ta Efektyvnist Pravotvorennia v Ukraini" ["Legislation Technique and the Efficiency of the Law-making in Ukraine"] in Chasopys Kyivskoho Universytetu Prava [The Chronicle of the Kyiv University of Law], 5, no. 3. (2003): 5.

o N. M. Onishchenko, *Pravova Systema: Problemy Teorii [The legal System: Issues of the Theory]* (Kyiv: The Institute of State and Law named after V.M. Koretsky of the National Academy of Sciences of Ukraine, 2002).

o N. M. Onishchenko, *Teoretyko-metodolohichni zasady formuvannia ta rozvytku pravovoi systemy [Theoretical and methodological principles of establishment and development of the legal system]* (Kyiv: 2002).

o P.M. Rabinovych, *Osnovy zahalnoi teorii prava ta derzhavy [Basics of general theory of law and state]* (Lviv: Krai, 2007).

o M. Sadovska, *Pravova Systema Italii: zahalnoteoretychna characterystyka osnovnych elementiv [Legal system of Italy: general theoretical characteristics of the basic elements]* (Kharkiv: National University of Internal Affairs, 2001).

o Kh. Saydov, ed. V. A. Tumanova, *Sravnytelnoe Pravovedenye (Osnovnie Pravovie Systemi Sovremennosty) [Comparative Law (the Main Contemporary Legal Systems] (*Moscow: Yuryst, 2003).

o   F. Skakun, *Teoriia derzhavy i prava [Theory of the State and Law]* (Kharkiv: Konsum, 2001).

o   Yu. S. Shemshuchenko, *Pravovi Systemy Suchasnosti [Contemporary Legal Systems].* (Kyiv: Yurydychna dumka [Legal Thought], 2012).

o   E. N. Tonkov, *Tolkovanye Zakona v Anhlyy [Interpretation of Law in England]* (Saint Petersburg: Aleteiia, 2015).

o   Varga, "Is Law a system of enactment?" in *Acta Juridica Academiae Scienliarum Hungaricae*, (1984), 413-416.

o   "Verkhovenstvo Prava" ["Rule of Law"] in *Zakonodavchyi Biuleten [Legislative Bulletin* Kyiv], (2005), 5-6.

O   Y.Bytiak, L.Voronova, A.Hetman, Y.Hroshevyi, A.Zakaliuk, V.Komarov, N.Kuznietsova, N.Onishchenko, O.Petryshyn, O.Pohribnyi, *Pravova Systema Ukrainy: Istoriia, Stan ta Perspektyvy [Legal System of Ukraine: History, Current State and Prospective]* (Kharkiv: Pravo,2008).

CHAPTER 5

JAIN JURISPRUDENCE & ITS IMPACTS ON THE PRACTICE OF LAW IN INDIA

Dr. Malay R. Patel

1 INTRODUCTION – OUTLINE: JAINISM AND DIFFERENTIATION FROM HINDUISM

1.1 SUMMARY OF THE CHAPTER

Religion is the very foundation of human life; it is not simply a set of beliefs, it is also a way of life, as followers of a particular religion follow a particular way of life. With this moral obligation on adherents to follow certain rules & customs, it is natural that religion enters the realm of law, whereby a person is compelled to follow and not break the rules established by a state (i.e. any country). Accordingly, it is self-evident that law and religion are inextricably linked, because prior to the notion of any state or democracy, the populace was obligated to perform religious responsibilities and could even assert religious rights. Thus, religion had a critical role in preserving law and order in ancient communities around the world.

As an introduction to readers, since ancient times the Jain community - followers of Jainism - has been a vibrant economic group in India.[1] Jains are the adherents of Jain *religion/philosophy*. Despite being a religious minority [2] in India (representing only 0.4 percent of the total population of India according to the census carried out in 2011),[3] they are dispersed throughout the length and breadth of the Indian sub-continent, making significant contributions to trade and

---

[1] David Hardiman,"Usury, dearth and famine in western India,"*Past & present* 152 (1) (1996): 113-156.

[2] The Government of India granted minority status to the Jain community in India on January 20, 2014, in accordance with Section 2(c) of the National Commission for Minorities (NCM) Act (NCM), 1992. After Muslims, Christians, Sikhs, Buddhists, and Parsis, the Jain community, with a population of 7 million people (0.4 percent of the population according to the 2011 census), became the sixth "national minority" Though Jains enjoyed minority status in 11 Indian states, including Uttar Pradesh, Madhya Pradesh, Chhattisgarh, and Rajasthan, community representatives filed a plea with the Supreme Court of India in 2005, which was backed by the National Minorities Commission. The court left the choice to the central government in its ruling.

[3] C. Chandramouli, & Registrar General, "Census of India 2011,"*Provisional Population Totals, New Delhi: Government of India* (2011): 409-413.

commercial activities in the country.[4] Based on recent surveys and some scholarly research on the Jain community, we can estimate the relative affluence of Jains in India; one such survey conducted by the International School for Jain Studies highlights the following facts: [5]

- ♦ 96% are literate (both males and females), with 60% holding a graduate degree; and
- ♦ 54% of males and 22% of females want to run their own business; and
- ♦ The average per capita income of Jains in India is 4.9 lakhs, which is 2.4 times greater than the per capita GDP for India (as at March, 2019).

Apart from the findings of sociological surveys, the entrepreneurial and progressive zeal among Jains in India is also evident from academic research - an empirical study conducted in 2013 suggests that Jains are 25.5% more likely to be self-employed, compared to Hindus in India.[6]

In this chapter, the author will discuss the evolution of Jain law in India, which emerged out of Jain religion/philosophy. The author will also examine how the Jain religion, as a way of life, has influenced political systems in India. In addition, while exploring the roots of Jain law, the author will analyse the modern relevance of Jainism and Jain law, and will also examine links and connections of some elements of Jainism to the Indian legal system, drawing support from Jain religious/philosophical texts. At the conclusion of this chapter, the author offers a method for measuring the extent to which concrete legal systems have become equitable and fair, thus promoting general pleasure and societal peace, with imprints from Jain philosophy. A similar method may be used to classify legal actors, stakeholders and institutions.

---

[4] Sinclair Stevenson, *The heart of Jainism, Vol. 2* (Humphrey Milford, Oxford University Press, 1995).
[5] *National Report – A sociological study of the Jain community* (International School for Jain Studies, 2019).
[6] David B. Audretsch, Werner Boente, and Jagannadha Pawan Tamvada, "Religion, social class, and entrepreneurial choice," *Journal of Business Venturing* 28, no. 6 (2013): 774-789.

In summary, this chapter is structured into four sections. Section 1 gives an overview of the purpose of the chapter, followed by a brief introduction to the Jain religion, highlighting its key differences to the Hindu religion. In Section 2, the historical evolution of Jain law and traces of Jainism in India's ancient political structure are presented; along with these historical aspects, the uniqueness of Jain law and a few Indian court judgments reflecting the distinctness of the Jain religion are given. Section 3 discusses the broader impact of Jain principles on Gandhi's political ideology, general law and the Indian constitution, along with the *Jain code of conduct*. Finally, in Section 4, the reformation of law & legal systems through the routes of Jain philosophy are discussed, along with a hypothetical measurement scale of *'Jainification'*. The author has coined this word 'Jainification', which aims to show the how the Jain principles of *Ahimsa, Aparigraha and Anekantavada* have become infused into the legal systems, by measuring the degree to which tangible legal systems have become equitable and fair, promoting overall happiness and social harmony.

1.2 WHAT IS JAINISM?

Jainism, which began in India, is one of the world's oldest faiths/philosophies. Jains, those who practice Jainism, are devout devotees of the *'Jina'*, the subjugator, the spiritual conqueror, the one who has conquered all earthly emotions and wants. A *'Jina'* is a common human being who has attained *'KevalGnan'* - ultimate knowledge of the cosmos – by his or her own efforts. According to Jain philosophy, *'KevalGnan'* is a permanent, everlasting, absolute knowledge of the soul that allows a person to attain *'Moksha'* - salvation (the soul's ultimate release from the recurring cycle of life and death).

According to Jainism, salvation is the ultimate objective of human existence. In Jainism, salvation is not contingent on a deity's compassion; it does not believe in the existence of a god, or in god's creation of the world. Rather than a god or collectivism, it emphasises individualism in the sense that each and every soul may perfect its real dharma (nature), i.e. perfect knowledge, limitless power, unbounded joy and so forth. According to Jain philosophy, the primary impediment to attaining such perfect knowledge is karmic bonds (an attachment to worldly wants), which may be freed by severe austerities, non-violence, and self-torture. Jains believe in 24 'Jinas',[7] of which Lord Mahavira (599-527 BCE) was the last. Jainism has been extensively described and studied by scholars like Dundas in 2002,[8] and Jain in 2010.[9]

According to various texts, the major vows and tenets of Jainism are as follows:

I.   *Ahimsa* (Non-violence)

II.   *Satya* (Truth)

III.   *Achorya* (Non-stealing)

IV.   *Bramhacharya* (Celibacy)

V.   *Aparigrapha* (Non-possessiveness)

VI.   *Anekantvada (Multiplicity of views)*

1.3 HOW JAINISM IS DIFFERENT FROM HINDUISM?

Hinduism is the most followed religion/philosophy in India. According to India's 2011 Census, 966.3 million people have identified themselves as Hindu, accounting for 79.8 percent of the country's population. India has the world's largest Hindu population, accounting for 94 percent of the global Hindu population. The Indian subcontinent is the birthplace of four of the world's major religions: Hinduism, Buddhism, Jainism, and Sikhism—all of which are collectively known as Indian religions/Dharmas.

---

[7] In Jain literature, *Jinas* are often referred to as *Tirthankaras* - they are enlightened souls who have achieved omniscience and who assist other souls in order to free them from the cycles of repeated terrestrial existences, i.e. reincarnation.

[8] Paul Dundas, *The Jains* (London: Routledge, 2003).

[9] Kailash Chand Jain, *History of Jainism* (New Delhi: DK Printworld, 2010).

Due to various social and cultural similarities, some scholars believe that Jainism is a branch of Hinduism[10] and that Jain Law is the same as Hindu Law, which is incorrect. There are also some scholars who have propagated a theory that Jains are, in fact, Hindu dissenters. In this regard, Luniya's argument (1967)[11] can be useful; he argued that both Jainism and Buddhism were not new faiths, they emerged as a result of the disappointment of some 'Hindus' with the Vedic Hindu religion.

In a true sense, we cannot argue that Jains are really the dissenters, as to date the majority of the Hindu creed in India remains unchanged. However, when there is a divide within a religious group the variations occur mainly in the interpretation of a few specific theological issues, while most of the ordinary mode of living in that territory remains more or less the same. Thus, superficially, it appears that Jainism and Hinduism are the same because of their many similarities in everyday life, but philosophically and theologically the religions/philosophies are different.

If one were to compare Hinduism and Jainism, then it would be observed that, in fact, the contrasts between Jainism and Hinduism are significant; their similarities are limited to a few specifics, with the exception of those that pertain to the ordinary way of life as mentioned earlier. If rituals are thoroughly examined, it will be observed even ceremonies that appear to be similar in appearance are, in fact, distinct in terms of their intended outcome. Jains believe that the world is everlasting, but Hindus believe that it was created by a divine being. It is not the eternal and eternally pure God who is worshipped in Jainism, but rather those Great Ones who have realised their lofty ideals and gained Godhood themselves. In contrast, in Hinduism, worship is dedicated to a Lord who serves as both creator and ruler of the universe, one who maintains the universe but can also destroy the Universe.

---

[10] Helmuth Von Glasenapp, *Jainism: An Indian religion of salvation*, Vol. 14 (New Delhi: Motilal Banarsidass Publ., 1999).
[11] Bhanwarlal Nathuram Luniya, *Evolution of Indian culture, from the earliest times to the present day* (Agra: Lakshini Narain Agarwal, 1967).

Worship has a different meaning in Hinduism than in Jainism. In Jainism, a kind of idoltory is practiced; no food or other offerings are made, and no petition for boons is performed to the Deity. In Hinduism, purpose is attained by the will of certain divine creatures who must be appeased. However, there are also profound disparities between Hinduism and Jainism when it comes to their holy texts. The holy texts of Jains are called *Agama,*[12] which are 45 in number. In contrast, the holy texts of Hindus are 4 Vedas and 18 Puranas, which were orally transmitted by memory for many generations and written down for the first time around 1200 BCE or even earlier; all printed versions of Vedas that are available in modern times are in the Sanskrit language and are believed to have been written in the 16th century CE. Hindus do not accept any writings from the Jains, and the Jains do not accept any Hindu writings. Consequently, the Jain scriptures do not include any of the 4 Vedas (*Rig Ved, Sam Ved, Atharva Ved and Yajur Ved*) or the 18 *Puranas.*[13]

Furthermore, no section of either the Jains' or Hindus' holy scriptures is solely social in nature; they are intermixed with theology and philosophy, so the relevance of social ritual fluctuates in accordance with their religious/philosophical significance. Ordinary social similarities are to be expected between societies that have co-existed over a long period of time, much more so when inter-marriages have occurred, as they have between Jains and Hindus. Numerous social rituals are shared by Jains, Hindus, and Muslims in the Indian subcontinent,[14] despite their lack of religious significance.

---

[12] Jain Agama's are also known as *Dvadasangi, Upadesa, Vacana, Aptavani, Pravacana, Siddhanta, Sruta, Sutra, Sutta* etc. They are written in the Prakrit language. There are various forms of ancient language Prakrit: - *Ardha Magadhi, Paisachi, Maharashtri,* etc. and they are considered as the languages of the masses spoken in North India during ancient period.

[13] The 18 Puranas are *Agni Purana, Skanda Purana, Matsya Purana, Shiv Purana, Linga Purana, Vishnu Purana, Bhagavata Purana, Naradeya Puran, Garuda Purana, Padma Purana, Varaha Purana, Brahmanda Purana, Brahmavaivarta Purana, Markendeya Purana, Bhavishya Purana, Vamana Purana and Brahma Purana.*

[14] Pakistan and Bangladesh were partitioned from India on the basis of religion. For the sake of completeness, even after that, imprints of Hinduism, Jainism and Buddhism cannot be removed from these countries partitioned from India on the basis of religion.

Many traditions are passed down from group to group, most notably in imitation of rulers. These differences and traditions have led to considerable legal distinctions between Hindus and Jains, as observed through documented evidence.[15]

2 JAIN LAW – HISTORICAL EVOLUTION, DISTINCTIVENESS AND THE PRACTICES OF JAIN RULERS

2.1 THE HISTORY AND EVOLUTION OF JAIN LAW

According to Jain legends, the first '*Jina*' of the present era of human cycle, Rishabhadeva,[16] is said to have brought the concept of a work culture and the advent of urbanisation to this world several millennia before the beginning of the Christian era. Before, learning more about Rishabhdeva, it is important to shed some light on the concept of time as per Jain philosophy. According to Jainism, time is beginningless and eternal. The *Kalachakra*, the cosmic wheel of time, rotates ceaselessly.

The wheel of time is divided into two half-rotations, *Utsarpini* or ascending time cycle and *Avasarpini,* the descending time cycle, occurring continuously after each other. Utsarpini is a period of progressive prosperity and happiness where timespans and ages are on an increasing scale, while Avsarpini is a period of increasing sorrow and immorality with a decline in timespans of the epochs. Each of this half time cycle consists of innumerable periods of time (measured in *sagaropama* and *palyopama* years as per Jain scriptures) and further sub-divided into six *aras* or epochs of unequal periods.

---

[15] Champat Rai Jain, *The Jaina Law* (Delhi: Devendra printing & publishing Company Limited, 1926).
[16] Pandit Phulchand Sastri *Adi Purana (2 volumes)* Hindi translation *(published by Bhartiya Jnanapith Delhi) Vol 1 page 362;* See also, Helen Johnson *Jain Saga (3 volumes), English translation of TriŚasti-Ślākāpuruṣa 16 (Sixty-three luminary persons) by Acharya Hemchandra* (Acharydev Shrimad Vijay Ramchandra Surishwar Jain Pathshala, Ahmedabad).

Currently, the time cycle is in Avasarpini or descending phase. In *Utsarpiṇi*, the order of the eras is reversed. Starting from *duhṣamā-duhṣamā*, it ends with *suṣamā-suṣamā* and thus this never-ending cycle continues. Each of these *aras* progresses into the next phase seamlessly without any apocalyptic consequences. The increase or decrease in the happiness and lifespans of people, and general moral conduct of society changes in a phased and graded manner as time passes. No divine or supernatural beings are credited with, or responsible for, these spontaneous temporal changes, either in a creative or overseeing role – rather human beings and creatures are born under the impulse of their own karmas. Twenty-four *Tirthankaras* appear in every half, the first Tirthankara founding Jainism each time. In the present time cycle, Rishabhadev is credited as being the first Tīrthaṅkara, born at the end of the third half (known as *suṣama-duṣamā ārā*).

Name of the Ara	Degree of Happiness	Length of Aras
Susama-Susama	Utmost happiness and no sorrow	400 trillion sagaropamas
Susama	Moderate happiness and no sorrow	300 trillion sagaropamas
Susama- Duhsama	Happiness with very little sorrow	200 trillion sagaropamas
Duhsama-Susama	Happiness with little sorrow	100 trillion sagaropamas
Duhsama	Sorrow with very little happiness	21,000 years
Duhsama-Duhsama	Extreme sorrow and misery	21,000 years

Source: Based on Jain Scriptures

Table 15 – <u>Jain Time Cycle</u>

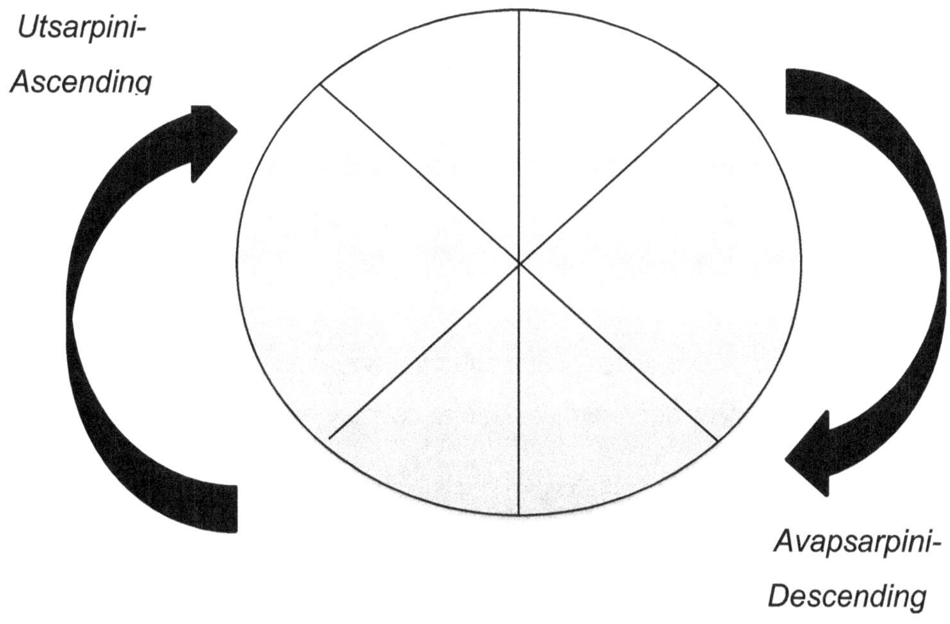

Figure 1: <u>Utsarpini & Avapsarpini (Time cycle of Jains)</u>

Jain literature further narrates that Prince Rishabhadeva was a gifted, foresighted, and hardworking gentleman. Although the exact time line of Rishabhadeva is debatable, it seems that, about the fourth or third century BCE, Rishabhadeva became popular as the first Jina, the first Tirthankara, and the founder of Jainism.[17] He had a deep understanding of human psychology. During his father's rule, the populace was only structured into random nomadic clans. Rishabhadeva divided them into three communities, according to their virtues, occupations, and vocations - *Kshatriya* for defence, *Vaiśya* for trading and professions and *Śūdra* for menial labour. Looking at the necessities of the time and society, he informed

---

[17] Kailash Chand Jain, *History of Jainism,* (New Delhi: DK Printworld, 2010), 7; See also, Helmuth Von Glasenapp, *Jainism: An Indian religion of salvation,* Vol. 14 (New Delhi: Motilal Banarsidass Publ., 1999), 16 where as an estimate it was provided that Rishabhadev existed around 592.704×10^{18} years ago.

them that they needed to labour (be busy with economically profitable things) to produce food, exchange surpluses with others, and live in communities.

As a result of such efforts, he asked them to choose one of six types of activity, namely '*Asi*' (the making of, and serving with weapons, i.e., armed forces), '*Masi*' (earning through writing/accounts, etc.), '*Kṛṣi*' (agriculture), '*Vanijya*' (trade), '*Vidhya*' (education or arts teaching), and '*Shilpa*' (arts and crafts by hand), in order to earn enough money to meet their own needs as well as to support others. To achieve this, he provided them with the necessary expertise.

Prince Rishabhadeva also developed social security, criminal justice systems, and many skills that enhanced human society in the domains of knowledge, the arts, entertainment, administration, and so on. His contributions are claimed to include pottery, architecture, music, and dance. He instilled in people the ideals of family, collaboration and community living, as well as punishment for non-compliance. He taught farming to some, and the trade of storing and trading agricultural produce to others, thus establishing the first agriculture-based culture. He created alphabets, languages, and numerals, as well as writing instruments. He developed martial arts for self-defence and taught them to people with powerful bodies.

People of the time came to regard Rishabhadeva as their king/leader, having seen the effects of his endeavours on society. As a result, individuals began to establish business premises and lived as communities in town/city units or groupings by each activity. As a result, Indian historians argue that he was the father of Indian urbanisation.[18] Rishabhadeva ruled his people and opened new frontiers of knowledge for many years.

Over time, Prince Rishabhadeva began to believe that his subjects were living a happy life. On the other hand, he believed material wellbeing provides only ephemeral pleasures/happiness. In spite of achieving success in his mission, he

---

[18] B.N Mukherjee, *The Foreign Names of Indian Subcontinent* (Mysore: Society of India, 1981); See Also, Sunil Khilnani & Abhay Kumar Dube, *Bharatnama* (New Delhi: Rajkamal Prakashan, 2001).

began to wonder about actual, long-lasting bliss. In order to achieve this goal, he considered giving up his worldly pursuits and becoming free to pursue true and permanent happiness. As a result, he divided his kingdom equally among his 101 sons, with the eldest son, Bharat, receiving the capital city. He then gave up his worldly possessions and became a recluse.

In later years, he acquired real insight, unlimited knowledge, and pleasure after arduous self-sacrifice and penance. He went on to teach people about the importance of voluntarily giving up or sharing their financial prosperity for the benefit of the community's overall personal and social well-being introducing, for example, charity/philanthropy, belief in non-violence in all circumstances, and a set of vows/rules to be followed based on non-violence in order to stay happy. He was able to attain unlimited knowledge on holy Mount Kailash. This could be considered as the first imprint of a philosophy of non-violence in the ethos of the Indian subcontinent.

Later, his eldest son, Bharat, began a quest to re-unify the fragmented estates granted to his siblings and to enlarge his dominion so that he could become world's monarch. During the time of Bharat, scholars are of the view that Jain law is likely to have emerged. Thus, Jain law is an independent part of jurisprudence and its original author, the first legislator, was Bharat. It may be of interest that the original name of India for many centuries (even BCE) was Bharat as well.

The entire Jain law was composed at one time and hence lacks the characteristics that distinguish judge-made law. However, it is possible that minor changes, not impacting its essential principles, have been made to it from time to time due to community needs and human interactions over the centuries.

The primary sources of Jain jurisprudence are written in the Prakrit language known as *Agama* or *Siddhanta*. Early 'Jain law' was solely monastic law, which continues continued to grow via commentary and extra regulations/customs, and most importantly was free from any state influence. It blossomed according to the needs of the community.

2.1.1 Sources of Jain Law

Jain Law was originally part of the '*Upasakadhyayana Anga*', which has since been lost. Its current sources are mostly through the books listed below:[19]

- The *Bhadrabahu Samhita* – The book was possibly written between 1601 to 1609 CE. It is based on the '*Upasakadhyayana Anga*'.

- The *Arhan Niti* – It cannot be ascertained who is the author or during what period he lived, but it appears that this book is not very old, compared to other books.

- The *Vardhamana Niti* – Written in 1011 CE by author Amitagati Acharya in the reign of Raja Munj,[20] the book contains several verses which are identical to those in the *Bhadrabhahu Samhita*. Under this context it would be appropriate to assume that both these books were prepared using detail from earlier books.

- The *Indranandi Jina Samhita* – This book, by Vasunandi Indranandi, is based on *Upasakadhyayana*, a book which was originally lost. It is to be noted however, that although seemingly lost, there are some stray fragments of the *Anga Upasakadhyayana*, which have survived to the present day. By also looking to some additional stray fragments from secondary sources, we can postulate the profound message in this text pertaining to law in the few introductory verses of the book, which state: -

---

[19] Champat Rai Jain, *The Jaina Law* (Delhi: Devendra printing & publishing Company, Limited, 1926), 1-17.
[20] A Raja is the Indian sub-continent's equivalent of the Monarch of the state.

Law should be known for living in this world. *Dharma* (Duty) is of two kinds; first is that for laymen involving the householder. Second is that for ascetics. These are founded on the principle of increasing purity. In Bharatvarsha, in Kosala Country, in Saketa (Ayodhya) Rishabhadeva, the Lord of Jinas was born. The Laws for Karma Bhumi were preached by Him. His Son Bharata Chakravarti, the kings of kings, laid down the rules of conduct, charity, punishment, inheritance and partition. This Samhita being arranged by Vasunandi Indranandi is authoritative. [21]

♦ *Traivarjikacara* – Composed in 1611 CE by Bhattaraka Somasen.

♦ The *Adi Purana* – This book was composed by Jinasena Acharya in the ninth century CE.

These are the ancient law-related books which are still available now, although none of them contains the entire law; however, it is sufficient for our legal understanding of ancient times regarding references to Jain law.

The world-renowned scholar on Jainism, Peter Flügel, describes the uniqueness of Jain Law through four interpretations, as follows:

i.   In its broadest meaning, the term "Jain law or also referred to as Jaina law" refers to the concepts and practices of the Jain religion.

ii.   In a more particular sense, it refers to the entirety of Jain monastic and lay traditions' norms and legal codes.

iii.   The 'personal law' of the Jain laity is the focus of the current Indian legal system. The word 'Jain law' was used in Anglo-Indian case law to refer to both the written 'Jain scriptures' on personal law and the unwritten

---

[21] *Indranandi Jina Samhita* verses 52 to 55, p.105.

'customary rules' of the Jains, i.e, the social standards of Jain castes and clans.

iv.   Jain personal law was subsumed into the statutory *'Hindu Code'* in 1955/1956, and was only tangentially recognised by the legal system in the form of residual Jain *'customs'* that must be shown in court.[22]

Due to the merging of Jain personal law with Hindu Law, accordingly it could be argued that, in the current context, Jaina law retains evidence of legal and social reconstruction. In the nineteenth century, the community was indirectly forced by the British India Government to actively employ the formal procedures in place which could benefit the masses, thus while there was an existing Jain Law, it was merged with Hindu Law.

Jain law has a distinct legal position, which is presently recognised by the legal system as Jain custom under the vast range of topics in Hindu law. This scenario confirms the existence of Jain Law. Despite the fact that it is no longer officially recognised in its birth place, India, Jain law has the ability to thrive as a mostly unofficial law in the context of set rules that are recognised by the government of India. As per Chiba,[23] this situation is true for Jain Law in both India and the United Kingdom, where there is a lot of scope for re-igniting thoughts on Jain Law. There is also a scope to assert the distinctive characteristics of Jain law and the Jain way of life. However, this distinctive characteristic cannot be directly endorsed or propagated by the Jain community as they are a minority in most places in which they currently reside.[24]

---

[22] Peter Flügel, "A short history of Jaina law," *International Journal of Jaina Studies* 3, no. 4 (2007): 1-15.

[23] Chiba Masaji, ed., *Asian Indigenous Law: in interaction with received law* (London: Taylor & Francis, 1986).

[24] Werner Menski, "Jaina law as an unofficial legal system" in *Studies in Jaina History and Culture* (London: Routledge, 2006), 435-453.

In the past, there were many cases in British India where Hindu Law was enforced on Jains in 1867 CE, such as – (1) Mahabeer *Prasad v. Mussamat Kundun Koer,* 8 Weekly Reporter, page116), (2) *Chotay Lal v. Chunoo Lal,* I.L.R.,4 Calcutta,744, (3) *Bachebi v. Makhan Lal,* I.L.R., 3 Allahabad, 55, (4) *Periammnani v. Krishnasami,* I.L.R.,16 Madras,182), and (5) *Mandit Koer v. Phool Chand*, 5 Calcutta Weekly Notes 154. All these cases were decided according to Hindu Law and, according to a few religious scholars, were wrong in so much as the Jain practice was held not to have been proved in those cases.

The above-mentioned cases are quoted from Barrister C.R. Jain's 1926 exemplary work on 'The Jain Law'. According to Jain's 1926 research, there are quite a few instances in which Jain, as plaintiffs, have believed that they were treated unfairly due to the omission or neglect of even fundamental Jain law principles. The inclusion of Jain principles would have likely aided efforts to keep conflicts out of official courts to the greatest extent feasible. This issue needs to be observed further, and only then would it be clear whether or not this is still a problem today in the current Indian context, and what the ramifications have been for the Jain populace over the decades in the land of the birth of Jainism.[25]

2.2 HISTORICAL TRACES OF JAINISM ON INDIA'S POLITICAL STRUCTURE

Although no comprehensive research has been carried out to examine the impact of the Jain faith on India's political history, it can be claimed that Jain academics and monks have had a significant impact on the country's cultural and political history. Many Indian historians and philosophers believe that portions of India's spiritual heritage originated with the warrior or ruling class (*Kshatriya*) and later spread to the Brahmin or priestly elite. This viewpoint is supported by a thorough examination of India's ancient Jain rulers, such as Lord Risbhadeva until Lord

---

[25] Champat Ray Jain, *The Jaina Law. Madras: C.S. Mallinath* (The Jaina Gazette, 1926), 14-15.

Mahavira; in fact all of the Jain Tirthankaras in this human cycle were born and nurtured in the Kshatirya (warrior) class.

During the lives of each Tirthankara, several Jain monarchs ruled different parts of Bharat (the ancient name for India that spanned from current day Afghanistan to current day Myanmar). Several monarchs with large kingdoms, who lived during the period of the Tirthankaras adopted an austere Jain lifestyle later in their lifetimes. In fact, these monarchs made major contributions to the spread of the Jain religion/philosophy. Unfortunately, little historical data are known on many of them today, despite the fact that information about kings during and after Lord Mahavira's time is abundant. They rose to prominence in part as a result of their contributions to the spread of the Jain religion. It is important to analyse the important kingdoms in ancient history and their monarchs, who were strong believers in Jainism, to fully comprehend the imprints of Jainism on current Indian law.

- **Other monarchs, including King Chetaka (5th Century BCE)**

Lord Mahavira's first lay follower (non-monk) follower was King Chetaka. He was the leader of a federation of eighteen kingdoms and a powerful and fearless monarch of Vaisali. He promised himself that he would only allow his daughters to marry acceptable Jain bachelors. He had to fight a terrible war with Kunika, the king of Magadha, at one point, to defend the honour of his beliefs and his subjects. King Udayana of Sindhu Sauvira, King Pradyota of Avanti, King Satanika of Kausambi, King Dadhivana of Campa, and King Srenika of Magadha were all sons-in-law of King Cetaka and devout adherents of Jainism.[26]

- **King Srenika and King Kunika (543-491 BCE)**

In Jain literature, ruler Bimbasara, the historically renowned king of Magadha, is known as King Srenika. His stories are well-known among Jains. King Kunika, Srenika's son, was likewise a fervent follower of Lord Mahavira. Eighteen

---

[26] Dr. Pannalal Jain, *Uttarapurana of Acharya Gunabhadra* (New Delhi: Bhartiya Jnanpith, 2015).

provincial kings and rulers of non-mainstream castes (for example, rulers of the Licchavi and Malli clans) greeted Lord Mahavira's nirvana with great excitement, as did Kunika's son, Udayana, who was a Jain devotee like his father. This implies that Jain philosophy had a strong effect on all of these monarchs.[27]

■ Chandragupta Maurya: Emperor of the Mauryan Empire in India (321-298 BCE)

Chandragupta Maurya was a Jain follower who eventually became a monk as a student of Acharya Bhadrabahu in his later years. He travelled with the Acharya across the state of Mysore in South India. In the latter portion of his life, he performed arduous spiritual penance in the cave of Sravana-Belagola. Chanakya, his chief minister and advisor, was born and nurtured in a Jain family and was a devout follower of Jain Dharma throughout his life. [28]

■ Emperor Ashoka (273-232 BCE)

Chandragupta's grandson was Ashoka, who had a major influence on present day India. His contributions to the non-violence movement are well known. Despite being a recognised Buddhist, the ideals of non-violence preached by Ashoka were more in accordance with Jain doctrine than Buddhist philosophy, according to the book *Jainism; or, the Early Faith of Asoka*.[29] His proclamations to cease killing animals and birds, to stop destroying forests unnecessarily, and to outlaw animal killing on auspicious dates and festive occasions seem to be more aligned with Jain ideals.[30]

---

[27] Girish Prasad Singh, *Early Indian Historical Tradition and Archaeology: Purāṇic Kingdoms and Dynasties with Genealogies, Relative Chronology and Date of Mahābhārata War*, Vol. 3. (New Delhi: DK Printworld, 1994), 164.

[28] L. D. Barnett, "An Advanced History of India. By RC Majumdar, HC Raychaudhuri, and Kalikinkar Datta. pp. ix, i, 1081; 10 maps. London: Macmillan and Co., 1948," *Journal of the Royal Asiatic Society 81*, no. 1-2 (1949): 103-104.

[29] E. Thomas, *Jainism; or, the Early Faith of Asoka* (London: Trübner and Co., 1877).

[30] Nayanjot Lahiri, *Ashoka in ancient India* (London: Harvard University Press, 2015).

■ **Emperor Samprati (224-215 BCE)**

Emperor Samprati was the grandson of Emperor Ashoka. He went to his mother with great delight after winning a war, but was taken aback when he saw tears in her eyes instead of joyful smile. When he inquired about the source of her melancholy, she stated:

> A triumph won via the indiscriminate death of innocent beings is not a real win. The ultimate symbol of triumph is peace, which can only be achieved via non-violent methods.[31]

Samprati converted to Jainism after hearing these words, under the guidance of the renowned Jain monk Arya Suhasti. He built several Jain holy places to assist the spiritual activities of Jain followers in culturally and socially impoverished areas of the nation, in order to propagate Jain faith. He took on a number of important initiatives for the improvement of disadvantaged places, and dispatched a number of instructors to promote Jain teachings there. Many historians and researchers believe that Samprati produced many stone inscriptions that are attributed to Asoka.[32]

■ **Emperor Kharavela Kalinga's (177-152 BCE)**

Emperor Kharavela ruled in the second century BCE and was the most powerful ruler of the time. The Jain faith developed greatly during his reign. As a consequence of his efforts, a grand gathering of Jain monks and academics was held, and the Jain community bestowed upon him the titles of Eminently triumphant (*Mahavijayi*) Khema Emperor and King of Ascetics (*Bhishu-Raja or Dharma*). Kharavela made important contributions to the Jain faith and was an extraordinarily famous emperor of India.[33]

---

[31] Parveen Jain, *An Introduction to Jain Philosophy: Based on Writings and Discourses by Ācārya Sushil Kumar* (New Delhi: DK Printworld (P) Ltd, 2019), 284.

[32] John Cort, *Framing the Jina: Narratives of Icons and Idols in Jain History* (London: Oxford University Press, 2010).

[33] Nabin Kumar Sahu, *History of Orissa from the Earliest Time Up to 500 AD, Vol. 1.* (Bhubnaeshwar: Utkal University, 1964).

■ **Ganga Dynasty Kings (350-550 CE)**

Ganga kings founded their empire in South India in the third century CE. They reigned over a large territory until the eleventh century. The monarchs of the Ganga were all devout Jains. The first ruler, King Madhava, was also known as Komgani Varma. Acharya Simhanandi was his teacher. During King Madhava's reign, the Jain faith became the official religion of his empire. Marasimha, another dynasty monarch, conquered a number of lesser kingdoms while living an opulent and indulgent lifestyle. But, in the end, he gave up everything and chose an austere existence. He departed this world in 975 CE, according to the inscription on his memorial stone, in a profoundly spiritual condition after taking a Samadhi marana vow from Acharya Ajitsena. The women of this dynasty were likewise devout Tirthankara devotees.[34]

■ **The Kalacuri Dynasty and King Kalabharavamsi (550-625 CE)**

During this period, the Kalacuri dynasty was the most powerful lineage of monarchs in the core of the subcontinent, with Tripuri city as its capital. The splendour of its authority peaked in the eighth and ninth centuries CE. The rulers of the Kalacuri dynasty were all devout Jain believers. Some descendants of this bloodline are still thought to exist in Nagpur and the surrounding districts. They go under the moniker Jain Kalara.[35]

■ **King Sivakoti (650- 900 CE)**

In South India, Sivakoti was the ruler of Kanchi. After hearing the inspirational lectures of the renowned Acharya Samantabhadra, King Sivakoti [36] became a student of his and contributed significantly to the spread of the Jain faith in South India.[37]

---

[34] Krishna M Kumari, *Social and Cultural Life in Medieval Andhra* (New Delhi: Discovery Publishing House, 1990).

[35] Nagendra Kr Singh, *ed. Encyclopaedia of Jainism, Vol. 1* (New Delhi: Anmol Publications Pvt. Ltd., 2001).

[36] R. S. Mugali, *The Heritage of Karnataka* (Hong Kong: Hesperides Press, 2006).

[37] Sarat Chandra Ghoshal, ed., *Āpta-mīmāṁsā of Āchārya Samantabhadra, Vol. 13* (New Delhi: Bhartiya Jnanpith, 2002).

- ### **Vanaraja Chavda and King Chalukya (746- 780 CE)**

Mularaja was a devotee of the Jain faith, as were many other reigning families in Gujarat. Aside from the aforementioned monarchs, other notable figures include King Vanaraja of the Chavda dynasty, who was a pupil of Acharya Silaguna Suri. The kings of the Chalukya dynasty, which succeeded the Chavda dynasty, were also Jain adherents. [38]

- ### **King Ama (749-753 CE)**

The renowned Acharya Bappabhuti, a student of Acharya Siddhasena, ordained this great Gwalior ruler in the Jain religion.[39]

- ### **Rulers of the Rastrakuta Dynasty and Amoghhavarsa (800-878 CE)**

The monarchs of the Rastrakuta dynasty were also powerful rulers of their time and devout followers of the Jain religion. During their reign, the faith prospered greatly. Among these rulers, Amoghavarsa is particularly notable. A famous disciple of Acharya Jinasena, the Jain faith thrived under his rule. Amoghavarsa was a famous scholar who wrote the well-known text 'Pranottara Ratna Malika' (Assembly of the Most Important Questions and Answers). He commanded the kings of the lesser kingdoms of Anga, Banga, Magadha, Malava, Citrakuta, and Bedi. He reigned over Gujarat and the southern states. During the final few years of his life, he rejected his kingdom and its comforts and became a monk. Indra, Amoghavara's son, was also a devout follower of the Jain religion and he too became an ascetic in his later years.[40]

- ### **Chamundaraya (940- 89 CE)**

Chamundaraya was a well-known South Indian figure who served as an excellent counsellor and minister to King Marasimha the second. Camundaraya remained

---

[38] John E Cort, *Jains in the world: Religious values and ideology in India* (London: Oxford University Press on Demand, 2001).

[39] Shyam Manohar Mishra, *Yaśovarman of Kanauj: A Study of Political History, Social, and Cultural Life of Northern India during the Reign of Yaśovarman* (New Delhi: Abhinav Publications, 1977).

[40] O. Pertold, "" Reu BN:" History of the Rashtrakûtas (Book Review)," *Archív Orientální 6*, no. 2 (1934): 422.

the chief minister to King Marasimha's son, Rajamalla, and rose through the ranks of the military forces to become commander-in-chief. Chamundraya was a devout Jain devotee. Nemicandra, his spiritual guru, was a profoundly committed ascetic. Chamundaraya composed the Trisasthi-Laksana text in Kannada and oversaw the construction of Lord Bahubali's world-famous idol in Sravana-Belagola.[41]

■ Hoyasala dynasty kings (1116-1343 CE)

The Jain faith was followed by many monarchs, rulers, ministers, and commanders of the Hoyasala dynasty's troops in the Karnataka area of South India. Sudatta Muni, His Holiness, was the kingdom's spiritual leader. Initially, he served as a spiritual counsellor to the kings of the Calukya kingdom. He presided over the foundation of of an independent kingdom in 1116 CE.[42]

■ Siddharaja Jayasimha (1092-1142 CE)

Despite the fact that King Jayasimha was not formally initiated into the Jain religion, he had a strong affection for it. The respected Acharya Hemchandra, who composed the grammar treatise known as the "*Siddha-Hema- Sabdanusasana*" (Command over words according to Hemachandra) at the behest of Jayasimha had a big effect on him. [43]

■ King Kumarapala (114 -1173 CE)

Kumarapala was the King of Gujarat and an excellent pupil of the renowned Acharya Hemchandra, who had a lifelong commitment to the Jain faith. He popularised non-violence by forbidding hunting, meat consumption, and other violent actions. His historical contributions are well-known; Acharya Hemchandra and Kumarapala are responsible for the integration of Jain philosophy into

---

[41] Edward P. Rice, *History of Kannada Literature* (New Delhi: Asian Education Services, 1982), 17-45.

[42] Sailendra Sen, *Textbook of Medieval Indian History* (New Delhi: Primus Books, 2013).

[43] Asoke Kumar Majumdar, *Chaulukyas of Gujarat: A Survey of the History and Culture of Gujarat from the Middle of the Tenth to the End of the Thirteenth Century, No. 4* (Bombay: Bharatiya Vidya Bhavan, 1956).

Gujarat's culture and social life. The awarding of the title of Supreme Arhata (*paramarhata*) to Kumarapala was a great honour, and it was both inspiring.[44]

2.3 Jainism in India (14th CE-20th CE)

From the 13th century onwards especially, Muslim monarchs' conquests and reigns in various parts of India resulted in the widespread destruction of Jain and Hindu temples. Jain monks, in particular, [45] *Digambar* monks, were required to dress appropriately when attending royal courts or moving in public. During the period 1075-1613 CE, four monks widely known as *Dadagurus* (literally meaning patriarch and religious instructor) gained widespread popularity in India for motivating a number of different types of people living at that time to be followers of Jainism. These Dadagurus were said to possess supernatural abilities that enabled them to shield their disciples from both natural and human-caused adversity.

Numerous Jain reformers, such as Lokashah in Gujarat (founder of the Sthanakavasi Shvetambar sect) and Bhikku in Rajasthan (founder of the Terapanth), stressed on the issue of monks' strict adherence to non-violence and eliminated distinct monks' quarters. Similarly, a number of householders, such as Banarasi Das and Todarmal, were outspoken critics of excessive material contributions in worship and religious activities, as well as the monks' extravagant lifestyles, leading to additional splits within Jainism.

From the 18th century to 1947 CE, Britain controlled every aspect of policy making in India. As a result, thoughts and ideas from western civilisation began to infiltrate the country. This also assisted Indian faiths & philosophies relative to Islamic rule in India, and accordingly culture, arts, and history to flourish once again. British

---

[44] Bhanwarlal Nathuram Luniya, *Life and culture in medieval India* (Indore: Kamal Prakashan, 1978).
[45] The two main sects of Jainism, *the Digambara* and the *Shvetambara sect,* likely started forming about the 3rd century BCE and the schism was complete by about 5th century CE. These sects later subdivided into several sub-sects such as *Sthānakavāsī* and *Terapanthis.*

education was promoted amongst the masses. Finally, it seems Mahatma Gandhi was profoundly inspired by two people – his mother and religious instructor Shrimad Rajchandra (a Jain laity, who virtually lived as a monk in Gujarat). Gandhi used non-violence and truth as his weapons in the fight for the country's freedom from British control, as opposed to violent revolutions or wars to gain independence, as was the case in others parts in Asia such as China or Vietnam.

During this time period, there were important publications of Jain newspapers in a variety of languages. Religious organisations such as the *Digambara Jain Mahasabha, the Shvetambara conference*, and the Young Jains association were established and thrived. Jains began establishing their own schools and institutions, where they taught religion alongside other disciplines. Additional socially beneficial organisations, such as orphanages, widow rehabilitation centres, hospitals, clinics, and enhancements to pilgrimage sites' amenities, were built. In the twentieth century CE, monk Shanti Sagar restored the Digambar Jain monastic tradition. Kanji Swami, a convert from the Sthankavasi tradition to the Digambar tradition, is another contemporary reformer. He criticised the Digambar monks' behaviour and highlighted the need to study spiritual books.[46]

2.3 UNIQUENESS OF JAIN LAW

In order to analyse this aspect of Jain Law, a comparative analysis is needed with other faiths. A few highlighted points are as follows:

- ◆ Unlike their Hindu counterparts, Jains do not adopt their faith for spiritual wellbeing.[47]
- ◆ Having or not having a son does not make a man spiritually worthy or otherwise.[48]

---

[46] The write-up is based on the writings in Shugan C Jain, "Jainism' (for young inquisitive)," *International School for Jain Studies, New Delhi,* (2018): 13-15.
[47] *Sheo Kaur Bai v. Jeo Raj* 25 C.W.N.273.
[48] Bhadrabahu, 8 and 9.

- There are significant discrepancies between Hindu and Jain law regarding the rights of female heirs. Females can inherit completely in Jain law; under Hindu law, women are only entitled to a life estate.

- According to Hindu law, absolute ownership is reserved for male heirs. In Jain Law, a woman is shown in all her splendour as the better half. Even her son is considered as insignificant in her presence.

- A woman's wealth (*Stridhan*) - that is, whatever is received by the bride at the time of marriage - is all her wealth. And after the marriage, whatever is given to her by her father-in-law's family is also regarded as (Stridhan), her wealth. Her own wealth is not liable to division at a partition, like ancestral property. A woman is the absolute owner of her wealth and may give it away during her life to anyone. After the death of a woman, her wealth will go to her daughter and, in the absence of a daughter; it will go to her son. If she dies childless her wealth will go to her husband.

- It is the duty of the elder brother to act like a father toward younger brothers. The guardianship of sisters up to the time of their marriage devolves, in the absence of a father, on their elder brothers. In the absence of a father or elder brother, the mother will be guardian of the children. Jain Law recognises the right of a man to arrange for the management of his property by means of the testamentary appointment of a trustee, who will protect his widow as well as the estate.

- According to Jain Law, a son is solely entitled to be a part of the grandfather's wealth. He has only the right of maintenance over the father's immovable property, while the father has complete control over his moveable goods.

- Furthermore, whereas Hindu law favours jointness (Joint Family), Jain law, while not forbidding jointness, advises separation (Nuclear family) in order to promote Dharma (merit).

- Even jointness under Jain Law is more akin to a tenancy in common than a joint estate under the Mitakshara in Hindu Law.

◆ Jain Law would have the son thrown out and disaffiliated if he is opposed to Worldly and Religious duties (Dharma) and is incorrigible. However, according to Hindu law, this is not possible.

There are many such differences between Jain Law and Hindu Law, thus it is incorrect to assert that Jainism is a subset of Hinduism, or that Jain Law is identical to Hindu Law.[49]

2.4 THE CHRONOLOGICAL ORDER OF VARIOUS JUDGMENTS IDENTIFYING JAINISM AS A SEPARATE RELIGION

A few judgements from various courts in India are as follows:

- **1927-** Madras High court in *Gateppa v. Eramma and others* reported in AIR 19, Madras 228 held that "*Jainism as a distinct religion was flourishing several centuries before Christ*". Jainism, as an anti-authoritarian religion, rejects the effectiveness of numerous Hindu rituals and contradicts the Vedas, which constitute the basis of Hinduism.

- **1939 -** In *Hirachand Gangji v. Rowji Sojpal* reported in AIR 1939 Bombay 377, it was observed that "*Jainism prevailed in this country long before Brahmanism came into existence and held that field, and it is wrong to think that Jains were originally Hindus and were subsequently converted into Jainism.*"

- **1951 -** A Division Bench of the Bombay High Court, consisting of Chief Justice Chagla and Justice Gajendragadkar, in respect of *Bombay Harijan*

---

[49] Champat Rai Jain, *The Jaina Law* (New Delhi: Devendra printing & publishing Company, Limited, 1926).

Temple Entry Act, 1947 (C.A. 91 of 1951) - Jains are distinct from Hindus in that they have their own religious entity.

- **1954** - In the Commissioner Hindu Religious Endowments, *Madras v. Sri Lakshmindra Thirtha Swamiar of Sri Shirur Mutt* reported in AIR 1954 SC 282, this Court noted that there are well-known Indian faiths such as Buddhism and Jainism that reject God. In contrast to Vedic religion, the Court acknowledged Jainism and Buddhism as two separate faiths practiced in India.

- **1968** - In *Commissioner of Wealth Tax, West Bengal v. Smt. Champa Kumari Singhi & Others* reported in AIR 1968 Calcutta 74, a Division Bench of the Calcutta High Court observed that:

  > Jains rejected the authority of the Vedas which forms the bedrock of Hinduism and denied the efficacy of various ceremonies which the Hindus consider essential. It will require too much of boldness to hold that the Jains, dissenters from Hinduism, are Hindus, even though they disown the authority of the Vedas.

- **1976** - In Arya Samaj Education Trust, Delhi & Others v. The Director of Education, Delhi Administration, Delhi & Others reported in AIR 1976 Delhi 207, it was held as follows: "*Not only the Constitution but also the Hindu Code and the Census Reports have recognized Jains to belong to a separate religion.*" In said judgement, the Court referred to the observations of various scholars in this regard. The Court quoted Heinrich Zimmer in "Philosophies of India" wherein he stated that:

  > Jainism denies the authority of the Vedas and the orthodox traditions of Hinduism. Therefore, it is reckoned as a heterodox Indian religion.

The Court also quoted J. N. Farquhar in Modern Religious Movements in India wherein he stated that "*Jainism has been a rival of Hinduism from the beginning*". In the said judgment, in conclusion, the Court held that "*for the purpose of Article 30(1), the Jains are a minority based on religion in the Union Territory of Delhi*".

- **2005** - The Supreme Court of India gave verdict that Jainism, Sikhism (and Buddhism) are distinct religions, but are inter-connected and inter-related to Hinduism, so these three are part of a broader Hindu religion, based on the historic background as to how the Constitution subsequently came into existence.[50]

- **2006** - The Supreme Court of India found that the "*Jain Religion is indisputably not a part of the Hindu Religion*".[51]

Therefore, there are numerous documented instances from the 19th and 20th centuries demonstrating the long-term influence of mediaeval codified Jain personal rules on Jain caste traditions. [52]

---

[50] Case No.: *Appeal (Civil) 4730 Of 1999 - Bal Patil & Anr v. Union Of India & Ors*, Date Of Judgment: 08/08/2005.

[51] *Committee of Management Kanya Junior High School Bal Vidya Mandir, Etah, Uttar Pradesh v. Sachiv, U.P. Basic Shiksha Parishad, Allahabad, U.P. and Ors., Per Dalveer Bhandari J., Civil Appeal No. 9595 of 2003,* decided on: 21.08.2006, Supreme Court of India, para 25.

[52] Vaibhav Jain & Sanjay Jain, "'Legal Aspect of Jain Religion as separate entity'," *IOSR Journal of Humanities and Social Science* (IOSR-JHSS) 19, no. 2 (2014): 08-19.

3 THE IMPACT OF JAINISM ON INDIAN POLITICAL IDEOLOGY, THE CONSTITUTION AND LEGAL SYSTEMS

3.1 THE REFLECTION OF JAIN PHILOSOPHY IN GANDHI'S POLITICAL IDEOLOGY

The political foundation of modern India was laid by the lead Indian freedom fighter, Mohandas Karamchand Gandhi, popularly known as Mahatma (Great Soul) Gandhi. Mahatma Gandhi's impact on the Indian independence struggle cannot be quantified with words. With the help of other independence fighters, he drove the British out of India. His thoughts and actions have inspired millions, and his battle movement and policies were non-violent. He was well known for his non-violent protests and played a key role in liberation movements in both India and South Africa. Due to his efforts, India was eventually freed from British colonial rule. Human rights were always important to him. With his philosophy of non-violence, honesty, tolerance, and social welfare, Mahatma Gandhi is without a doubt a genuine inspiration, not just for the previous generation but also for future generations.

Non-violence was the most valuable he impressed upon India to, and he also inspired other countries to adopt this principle. Today, in situations such as wars or conflicts in any nation, there is a reminder to stakeholders to consider using non-violence to resolve differences. Nowadays, the birthday of Mahatma Gandhi on 2nd October is celebrated as an international non-violence day. Non-violence made a significant contribution to the Indian independence struggle. Thus, the fundamental teachings of Jain philosophy in India are appreciated through Gandhian politics, in which Gandhi placed a strong emphasis on non-violence, peace, morality, and ethics in human existence.

Despite the fact that Gandhi did not claim his views to have been founded on any specific religion, the majority of his concepts were similar to those of Jainism. Non-violence is emphasised in both Jain and Gandhian ideologies, not just for humans but also for other living beings. Gandhi's concept of vegetarianism is the greatest illustration of his philosophy of peace for all living things. Both Jainism and Gandhi placed significant emphasis on morality and truth.

Gandhi advised movement leaders to adhere to moral principles and was able to lead the independence struggle using those moral principles. Gandhi's constructive program is one of the most significant documents demonstrating his perspective on Indian society and his constructive agenda helped to envision the idea of self-sufficient Indian communities. Self-sufficiency is also an indirect philosophy of Jainism; Gandhi's political views were therefore extremely similar to Jain philosophy.

Another worthwhile connection of Gandhi with Jainism can be gauged by his affiliation with Jain scholar, philosopher and poet 'Shrimad Rajchandra' (Raychandbhai).[53] Referring to him as Raychandbhai in his autobiography, *The Story of My Experiments with Truth*, Gandhi said:

> I have since met many a religious leader or teacher. I have tried to meet the heads of various faiths, and I must say that no one else has ever made on me the impression that Raychandbhai did. His words went straight home to me.... In my moments of spiritual crisis, therefore, he was my refuge....[54]

---

[53] Uma Majmudar, *Gandhi and Rajchandra: The Making of the Mahatma* (Lexington Books, 2020).
[54] Mahatma Gandhi, *My experiments with truth: An autobiography* (Jaico Publishing House, 2008), chapter-1 of Part- II, "Raychandbhai".

One more reference to Gandhiji's public acknowledgement of Shrimad Rajchandraji as his foremost spiritual guru can be noted from his letter to H.S. L. Polak from Pretoria Jail in South Africa, in which Gandhi wrote:[55]

.... The more I consider of his life and his writings, the more I consider him to have been the best Indian of his times. Indeed, I put him much higher than Tolstoy in religious perception. The books I have read [by Rajchandra] have afforded me the highest solace... Both Kavi [Rajchandra] and Tolstoy have lived as they have preached. Kavi [Rajchandra], though, writes from richer experience.

Mahatma Gandhi said of Jain philosopher Shrimad Rajchandraji, "*Such was the man who captivated my heart in religious matters as no other man has till now.*" Mahatma Gandhi in 'Modern Review', (June, 1930). [56]

3.2 CONNECTING *AHIMSA, APARIGRAHA AND ANEKANT* WITH JUSTICE, AGREEMENT AND RIGHTS IN CURRENT LEGAL CONTEXT

In this section of the Chapter, the main aspects of Jainism are discussed in the context of the current legal system in India.

3.2.1 Ahimsa

Ahimsa, or non-violence, is a basic characteristic and cornerstone of Jainism. An unshakable commitment to Ahimsa is a distinctive and distinguishing feature of Jainism. In Jainism, Ahimsa does not only refer to human compassion, it also refers to empathy, the desire to totally connect with other people, sentient species, and the entire universe. "*If you murder someone, you are killing yourself,*" Lord Mahavira said. Similarly, "*If you abuse someone, you are torturing yourself*" and "*If*

---

[55] This letter was written by Gandhi to H.S.L. Polak from Pretoria Jail in South Africa. The letter was dated April 26, 1909. Satish Sharma, *Gandhi's Teachers: Rajchandra Ravjibhai Mehta* (Gujarat Vidyapith, 2005), 5.

[56] *The Modern Review* was a monthly journal published in Calcutta.

you harm someone, you are injuring yourself." Accordingly, a prudent and educated person is aware of this and so abstains from killing, overwhelming, or torturing others.

Non-violence is central to Jainism. To put it another way, Jainism is a religion/philosophy of compassion, global love, and agreeableness. It is concerned with the well-being of all animals and plants, not just humans. It argues that the number of living things is infinite; all seemingly empty spaces in the cosmos are inhabited by tiny life. According to its principles, countless single-sense animals exist that are made out of the most fragile components of the elements: earth, water, fire, and air. Humans should avoid causing harm to water, air, and other natural resources, which would constitute an act of hostility toward them. For example, while new soil is alive, it becomes inert when baked. Fresh water from a well is alive but, when it is cooked or contaminated with another substance, it dies. While vegetables, trees, plants, and fruits all retain life, once dried, cut, or cooked, they expire. To avoid causing them damage, it is recommended that humans use them with discretion.

Among other things, worms, insects, and mammals contribute to ecological balance, thereby assisting humans. And domestic animals have long been a dependable ally in man's attempt to connect with them and in the process becoming more civilised. When viewed from their ultimate pure flawless state, all living beings are similar in nature. According to Jainism, one should see them as one's own self. Inflicting hurt on others is akin to self-inflicted anguish. Ahimsa, or non-violence, is a concept that evolved through reason and experience. It is a wholly empirical endeavour. It developed from the idea that all souls are equal - everybody desires to live, and none relishes death. Violence originates in the head, manifests itself via words, and eventually shows itself through actions. That is why it is said that mens' conflicts originate in their minds.

3.2.2 Aparigraha

All evil stems from possession. Possession does not just relate to the acquisition or accumulation of items; it also refers to the desire for and attachment to items. C. Rajagopalachari stated, "*Restraint is the defining characteristic of Indian culture.*"[57] This sense of ownership underpins all crimes, including violence, deceit, theft, sexual pleasure, and attachment. Today, we understand that a fundamental cause of the world's interminable sorrow is man's unrestrained need for possessions.

Man believes that acquiring something brings happiness. Ownership, on the other hand, has often been the cause of suffering and slavery. Possession establishes a connection between man and external objects. As a bee collecting honey from a flower often kills that bee in process, accordingly, a welfare-seeking man should cause the least amount of harm possible in this earthly existence. Thus, Lord Mahavira describes the five major vows, "*much as the wind sweeps over a burning fire, so ideal beings who keep these vows will pass over Samsara (transmigration) and attain eternal joy.*"[58] According to Lord Mahavir, passions and desires are unlimited and their only limit is the sky.

3.2.3 Anekant

Anekant is regarded as the spiritual core of Jainism. It is largely concerned with religious philosophy, particularly with ethical issues. It teaches that the kingdom of truth is approachable in a number of different ways. Additionally, it emphasises the need to not impose one's own beliefs or viewpoints on others, and instead attempting to reconcile them with one's own. Thus, when properly used, this notion teaches us how to transcend our generally restricted, self-centered, and

---

[57] See <https://www.livemint.com/Sundayapp/lxc7Scq8luW5agVMin669H/C-Rajagopalachari--Of-communism-culture-and- freedom.html>, accessed on 5th September, 2021.
[58] *Acharanga Sutra tr. Hermann Jacobi,* 2:15:24.

incomplete view of the world. It teaches us how to resolve disagreement and discord in our lives and how to foster concord and harmony in our communities via a broad and tolerant viewpoint and attitude toward others.

All elements of life should be governed by the Anekant ideal. It teaches us how to embrace the candid viewpoints of all free thinkers worldwide and, as such, this Jain philosophy establishes a foundation for current democracy. It fosters a sense of togetherness in the midst of diversity. It makes the assertion that it reconciles disparate or antagonistic statements, ideas, ideologies, systems, and religions, among others. Thus, Anekant ideals may prove to be an effective means of promoting world peace and harmony.

Jain scriptures, based on preachings of the principles of *Ahimsa, Aparigraha, and Anekant,* highlight the basic fact that every living being possesses inherent sanctity and dignity. Therefore, they must be respected in the same manner that one expects others to respect one's own dignity. Additionally, it highlights the necessity of remaining unattached to the world and maintaining a liberal and just mindset. The Jain sacred scriptures make it very clear that life is sacred regardless of species, caste, colour, religion, or nationality. The people fought for the notion of live and let live based on this principle, and it eventually gained support among the general population of today's India, influencing current law and even the foreign policies of the nation. Thus, Jain teachings convinced the population that practicing Ahimsa is a personal and societal virtue, indicating that Ahimsa had both positive and communal appeal.

When we examine the three fundamental principles of Jainism: Ahimsa, Aparigraha, and Anekant, we discover that all three systems of thought contain the universal ideals necessary for a crime-free, legitimate society. Individual emancipation is the goal of the Jain principles of Ahimsa, Aparigraha, and Anekant; as a result, it possesses a religious bent. Its objective is to spiritualise all facets of life, in order to better prepare individuals to accomplish their ultimate aim. Its primary tenet, which applies to both monarchs and commoners, is to do one's duties in the most compassionate manner possible.

If *Ahimsa, Aparigraha, and Anekant* are the three pillars of Jainism, then fairness, agreement, and right are the three pillars of law. Justice is usually connected with the rule of law, as achieving justice is the primary objective of the rule of law and legal systems. Justice is both a goal and an inherent characteristic of all legal systems. As Augustine once observed, a political community that is not governed by justice resembles a band of robbers.[59] To be justified, a legal system must be fair; it must be created and operated in accordance with justice. The most fundamental idea of justice, usually means that rights not to be deprived of any of the fundamental rights including of possession except in accordance with due process, is a topic of intense dispute. It is defined by the political community's fundamental ideas as well as society's own historical experience. As a result, as John Rawls phrased it, "*a well-ordered society is one that is successfully governed by a public conception of fairness.*" This public concept of justice is a culturally-evolving phenomenon that acts as an impetus for any genuine social order to exist.[60]

Law is formed in democratic society by general and specific agreements. In reality, legal systems and law are composed of an abundance of contracts, pacts, treaties, transactions, protocols, compromises, bargains, and settlements, as well as numerous other national and international agreements. A legal system is the product and evolution of a fundamental agreement (constitution) within political society that establishes a framework for developing enforceable general agreements (legislation), enforcing those agreements (executive authority), and resolving disagreements over those agreements (judiciary). Relevant ideas such as majority rule, social contract, and overlapping consensus, among others,

---

[59] Augustine, *De civitate Dei* 4.4, available at <http://www.thelatinlibrary.com/augustine/civ4.shtml *"Remota itaque iustitia quid sunt regna nisi magna latrocinia?"*>, accessed on 3 Oct 2021.
[60] John Rawls, *Justice as Fairness: A Restatement, ed. Erin Kelly* (Cambridge, MA, London: Harvard University Press, 2001), 31.

contribute to the connection and solidification of political communities, built on the concept of agreement. Agreements facilitate social integration and action coordination by recognising and protecting individual and collective rights. This is why Hans Kelsen viewed the idea *pacta sunt servanda* (agreements must be upheld) as the starting point or fundamental assumption of international law.[61]

In an environment of vehement disagreement, which is a common element of a varied society, it is critical that the law respects and acknowledges each individual. Respect for, and recognition of others is fundamentally expressed through a mechanism where an individual's rights are accepted, which is the third component of the legal triangle. Rights are defined as individual or collective interests that are legally protected by coercive institutions. Physical coercion becomes an integral part of legislation in order to protect rights (and public order), but is absent from other facets of reality. Individuals develop as human beings when they exercise their civil and political legal rights, participate in the legislative process, and finally contribute to the political community's consolidation. Without rights, a legal system is akin to a desert that is empty of sand.

Although law is a matter of justice, agreement, and rights, the fundamental pillars of Jainism – *Ahimsa, Aparigraha, and Anekant* all inspire an appreciation for the notion of law and legality. Human beings require both compassion and fairness. And justice and compassion are not diametrically opposed; genuine justice and compassion are compatible. Furthermore, compassion is a necessary requirement for the administration of justice. There can be no compassion without justice, and there can be no justice in its whole without care and compassion. According to Nicholas Wolterstorff, *"distorted love is love that perpetuates injustice"*.[62] Ahimsa is an embedded ideal in the Jain precept *Parasparopagraho Jivanam,* which translates as *"Living creatures offer service to one another."* Thus, non-violence strives not only to live and let live, but also to live and assist others in

---

[61] Hans Kelsen, *Principles of International Law* (Clark, NJ: The Lawbook Exchange, 2009), 316.
[62] Nicholar Wolterstorff, *Justice in Love* (Michigan: Eerdmans Publishing Company, 2011).

living. Hypothetically, if the Jain philosophy of Ahimsa were to be practiced by all of us, crime rates would be close to zero almost everywhere in the world!

Numerous legal systems view forgiveness as a type of justice-consistent love. In Jainism, forgiveness is the ultimate virtue; it includes relinquishing one's authority to administer justice. By acquitting the offender and therefore elevating them spiritually, forgiveness re-establishes order in its entirety. In case of debt condonation or remission in private law, the creditor forgives a debt by treating the debtor as if the obligation never existed. When a person condones money or any of his possessions, the Jain principle of *Aparigraha* is at work. If we look closely, the bulk of sins and misdeeds are committed as a result of our great passion for, and devotion to, worldly possessions. When we liberate ourselves from these worldly goods, the source of mainstream disputes vanishes. Consider why would we need law and legal institutions if we all suppressed our intense passions and behaved consciously and with the utmost prudence?

Additionally, there is a connection between Anekant and agreement. A contract always requires some degree of empathy and accommodation: a meeting or communion of the contracting parties' ideas. A sincere follower of Jainism is more likely to reach an accord because it allows a diversity of ideas and points of view. Anekant does not entail renunciation or a diminution of one's own beliefs, aspirations, or values. It helps us to comprehend and tolerate diametrically opposed and conflicting perspectives while maintaining the legitimacy of our own beliefs. Since it accepts numerous ways, and there is no one right view, Jainism is more a way of life or a philosophy, rather than a religion which is in the mold of monotheism, with a singular perspective.

Anekant encourages its adherents to research the thoughts and beliefs of their adversaries and adversarial parties. Additionally, Anekant does not assert that all arguments and points of view are valid; rather, it maintains that logic and evidence determine which points of view are accurate, in what aspect, and to what extent.

Democracy, free speech, religion, tolerance, and secularism all are legal expressions of the Jain philosophy of Anekant.

3.3 THE DIFFUSION OF JAIN PRINCIPLES IN THE INDIAN CONSTITUTION

Jainism places a premium on householders adhering to a Code of Right Conduct comprised of twelve vows, five *Anuvratas*[63] and seven supplemental vows known as Silavratas.[63] Among these twelve vows, the first vow of Ahimsa has been given precedence, and the following vows are all expressions of Ahimsa in some way. It is urged upon householders to follow these vows with the greatest care in their everyday lives so that *aticharas*, or breaches of these vows, may be avoided to a large degree. This implies that these vows must be kept as perfectly as possible. Clearly, these vows have significant social significance because they provide religious legitimacy to some of the most important public and private interests and rights protected by contemporary state laws.

One might argue that these pledges simply replicate the unwritten moral code of most great human civilisations, although making breaches more difficult. They also include the whole of contemporary society's legal limitations, such that one need only adopt them to avoid violating criminal legislation in any country. For instance, the vow of Ahimsa prohibits all crimes against people; even harming an animal is prohibited. Similarly, crimes against property are encompassed by the *Achorya* vow, i.e. non-stealing, when taken in its whole. Again, perjury, forgery, counterfeiting money, and all other associated crimes are prohibited by the *Satya* vow, i.e. honesty; and social misbehaviors are prohibited by the *Brahmacharya* fourth vow, i.e. chastity. Finally, the final vow of Aparigraha, namely abstinence from worldly attachments, cultivates a satisfied spirit, which is the true guarantee

---

[63] The *anuvratas* are a type of vow that are part of a layperson's 12 vows in Jainism. The anu vratas are also known as small vows or vows of a limited nature. The term is derived from the Sanskrit words anu, which means "common," "tiny," or "fine," *Vr,* which means "conduct" or "restraint," and rta, which means "order" or "oath." Because ascetics and monks strictly observe these same vows, they are known as the *maha vratas*, or "great vows." The layperson, on the other hand, observes an anu vrata only for a limited time and as moderately as his life circumstances allow.

of peace and a strong check on crime, as it crushes the propensity for law-breaking at the outset.[64]

Another confluence of Jainism and the Indian constitution happens when both entities emphasise equality among human beings. Lord Mahavira vigorously rejected the Hindu caste system. In the Indian Constitution, adopted on the 26 January 1950, the abolition of untouchability is included in article 17, equal protection of the laws for all is provided in article 14, and prohibition of discriminations on grounds of religion, race, caste, sex or place of birth is similarly provided in article 16.

Although the caste system remains in existence in India, discrimination is no longer regarded as legitimate under various laws and the constitution of India. The same may be said about discrimination against women. This great contribution to equality and rights for all is among the most valuable contributions that Lord Mahavira made, in addition to other rights that he espoused – respect for truthfulness and honesty, chastity, avoidance of passions, the encouragement to practice virtues and detachment and so forth.

In terms of Indian circumstances, it is emphasised that proper observance of these five primary vows will protect a man from virtually any provision of the Indian Penal Code. In this connection, Shri. A. B. Latthe,[65] a well-known author and social leader, demonstrated in a tabular format, as given below, that observing the five main vows without committing any of their associated faults or transgressions is practically equivalent to complete conformity with moral principles.

---

[64] Vilāsa Ādināth Saṅgave, "The Jaina path of Ahimsa," *Jainology monograph series* (1991).

[65] Ānnāsāheb Bahādur Laṭhṭhe (1878-1950), a lawyer, was the Dīvān of Chhatrapati Shahu (1874-1922), Mahārāja of Kolhapur. He was a major leader of the Non-Brahman Movement, and founder of the Dakṣiṇ Bhārat Jain Sabhā.

Chapter	Section	Substance of the Sections	The equivalent vows
I	1	Preamble	Command to take the religious texts of the Jain religion as an authority
II	6-52	Definitions	Sins and promises (vows) are defined
III	53-75	Punishments	Penance
IV	76-106	General Exceptions	There is no such thing as in until an action is motivated by passion
V	107-120	Abetment	The five vows and their faults.
VI	121-130	Offences against the State	Fault of vow of *Ahimsa* and *Achourya*.
VII	131-140	Offences against the Army and Navy	Fault of vow of *Ahimsa* and *Achourya*.
VIII	141-160	Offences against public tranquillity	The vow of *Ahimsa* and its faults.
IX	161-171	Offences committed by public servants	The vows of *Satya* with their faults.
X	172-190	Contempt of Court, etc.	Fault of vow of *Ahimsa* and *Achourya*.
XI	191-229	False statements etc.	Fault of *Satya* and *Ahimsa*
XII	230-263	False coinage etc.	Fault of vow of *Achourya* and *Satya*
XIII	264-267	Offences regarding Weights, etc.	Fault of vow of *Achourya* and *Satya*.
XIV	268-294	Offences against health, safety, etc	Fault of *Satya* and *Ahimsa*
XV	295-298	Offences against religion, etc.	Fault of *Satya* and *Ahimsa*
XVI	299-377	Offences against person	The vow of `*Ahimsa*' and its faults
XVII	378-462	Offences against property	The vow of `*Satya*' & '*Aparigraha*'
XVIII	463-489	Regarding false documents etc.,	Faults of *Satya* and *Ahimsa*
XIX	490-492	Regarding failure to perform services	The vow of *Satya*.

XX	493-499	Offences against marriages	Vow of `Brahmacharya'
XXI	499-502	Defamation	Vow of `Satya'
XXII	503-510	Intimidation	Vow of `Satya'
XXIII	511	Attempt to commit offences	The five vows.

Source: Modified from Sangve's book on the Jaina Path of Ahimsa (1991), p.72

Table 16 – <u>Vows in Jainism and Concepts of Offences</u>

3.4 THE JAIN CODE OF CONDUCT AND ITS IMPLICATIONS ON THE LAW AND LEGAL SYSTEMS

The sacred Jain texts have not only extolled the doctrine of Ahimsa's comprehensive and all-encompassing nature, demonstrating how the basic principle of Ahimsa is present in all five main and seven supplementary vows prescribed for the observance of Jain householders, but they have also emphatically emphasised the dire necessity of exercising the utmost care by Jain householders in actuality. According to the scriptures, the required twelve vows must be followed both in heart and in deed.

In this regard, it has been suggested that mental and behavioural flaws or errors in the observance of the *Vratas* be avoided. In the observance of vows, for example, when there is a loss of purity of mind, it is called '*atikrama*, i.e., contravention; when there is a craving for sensual pleasure, it is called '*vyatikrama*, i.e., violation; when there is laxity or idleness, it is called 'atichara' - that is, transgression. Whenever there is a breach, it is called '*anachara*', and in simple terms this means immorality.

Rationalisation is the key aspect of any law, which comprises subjects such as fairness, agreement and rights. The basic tenets of Jainism – *Ahimsa, Aparigraha and Anekant* and other related vows, support the concept of law and legality, at least inspirationally. The following are descriptions of the twelve vows proposed for laypeople in Jain scriptures:

1) *Ahimsa-* **Limited Violence Vow**
   ♦ In order to keep this vow, a person must not intentionally harm any living being (plants, animals, humans, etc.) or their feelings, either through thought, word, or deed, by himself or through others, or by approving such an act committed by someone else.

   ♦ In this case, intention refers to selfish motives, pure pleasure, and even avoidable negligence.

   ♦ One may use force to defend their country, society, family, life, property, or religious institute if necessary.

   ♦ Agricultural, industrial, and occupational living activities may involve injury to life, but this should be kept to a bare minimum through care and caution.

   ♦ There are four stages of violence described:
     ✓ Premeditated Violence: Knowingly attacking someone.
     ✓ Defence Violence: Intentional Violence committed in defence of one's life.
     ✓ Vocational Violence: Inflicting violence in the execution of one's means of subsistence.
     ✓ Committing violence in the course of daily activities is referred to as common violence.

All forms of premeditated violence are prohibited. A householder may engage in defensive and vocational violence as long as they maintain complete detachment. Common violence is accepted for survival, but even here, one must exercise caution when preparing food, cleaning the house, and so on. This explains the Jain practices of drinking filtered water, vegetarianism, not eating meals at night, and abstinence from alcohol. The foundation of Jain ethics is extreme non-violence.

2) ***Satya-*** Truthfulness Limited Vow

Truth is the second of the five limited vows. It entails more than simply avoiding deception. It is seeing the world for what it is and adapting to that reality. The vow of truth connects a person to their inner strength and capacities.

In this vow, a person promises not to tell lies, such as giving false evidence, denying the property of others entrusted to them, cheating other people, and so on. The vow is to be carried out in thought, action, and speech, either by doing it oneself or by enlisting the help of others. No one should speak the truth if it might cause harm or hurt the feelings of others; under these circumstances, people should remain silent.

3) ***Achaurya*** - Limited Vow of Non-Stealing

In order to fulfil this vow, a person must not steal, rob, or misappropriate the goods or property of others, including goods and property of nations and states. They must also not cheat or use illegal means to obtain worldly goods, nor must they do so through others or by approving such an act committed by others.

4) ***Brahmacharya*** - Limited Vow of Chastity

The primary goal of this vow is to conquer passion and prevent energy waste. Positively stated, the vow is intended to instill a sense of calmness in the soul. The householder must not have a sensual relationship with anyone other than their own lawfully wedded spouse under this vow. Excessive indulgence in all kinds of sensual pleasures should be avoided even with one's own spouse.

5) ***Aparigraha*** - Non-possession/non-attachment) Limited Vow:

The fifth limited vow is non-possession. As long as a person is unaware of the abundance of joy and peace that comes from within, they will try to fill their empty and insecure existence with the clutter of material acquisitions. According to Lord Mahavir, security derived from material possessions is a delusion. To rid oneself of this delusion, one takes a vow of non-possession and realises the perfection of the soul, imiting one's needs, acquisitions, and possessions such as land, real estate, goods, other valuables, animals, money, and so on.

Any surplus should be put to good use. One must also limit the number and quantity of food items or articles consumed on a daily basis. This Jain principle of limited possession for householders contributes to the equitable distribution of wealth, comforts, and other goods in society. Thus, Jainism contributes to the global establishment of socialism, economic stability, and welfare.

6) ***Dik Vrata*** - Vow of Limited Area of Activity:

This vow restricts one's worldly activities to a specific area in each of the ten directions: north, south, east, west, north-east, north-west, south-east, south-west, above, and below. A person abstains from committing sins in any location other than the limited areas of their worldly activity. This vow places a space limit on sins that are not restricted by the limited vows of non-violence.

7) ***Bhoga-Upbhoga Vrata*** - Consumable / Non-consumable Item Restriction vow:

In general, this sin is committed through the use or enjoyment of consumable (Bhoga) and non-consumable (Upbhoga) objects. Consumable items (Bhoga) refer to objects that are only used and enjoyed once, such as food and drink. Non-consumable items (Upabhoga) refer to objects that can be used and enjoyed repeatedly, such as furniture, clothes, ornaments, and buildings. By taking these vows, one should limit the use of these two categories of items in accordance with one's need and capacity.

8) ***Anartha-danda Vrata*** - Vow to Avoid Purposeless Sins:

One must not commit a sin or moral offence that is unnecessary or purposeless, as defined below:

- ✓ Thinking, talking about, or preaching evil or ill about others.
- ✓ Inconsiderate or unnecessary behaviour, such as walking on grass unnecessarily.
- ✓ Making or supplying attack weapons.
- ✓ Reading, or listening to, immoral literature are all examples of immoral literature.

9) ***Samayik Vrata*** - Meditation Vow for a Limited Time:

This vow entails sitting down for at least 48 minutes and focusing one's mind on religious activities such as reading religious books, praying, or meditating. This practice may be repeated several times throughout the day. It must be observed by the mind, body, and speech. The 48-minute meditation emphasises the significance of a life-long vow to abstain from all sinful activities and serves as a stepping stone to a life of complete renunciation. During Samayik, one contemplates the soul and its relationship to worldly actions (Karma). This meditation vow should be practiced by giving up affection and aversion (Rag and Dvesha), observing equanimity in all objects, thinking evil of no one, and being at peace with the world (Samayik).

10) ***Desavakasika Vrata*** - Activity Vow with a Limited Duration:
This vow establishes an additionalnew limit within the parameters established by Dik Vrata and Bhoga-Upbhoga Vrata. The general lifetime restriction on doing business in certain areas and the use of articles is further restricted to specific days and times of the week. This means that for a set period of time, no activity, business, or travel shall take place outside of a specific city, street, or house.

11) ***Pausadha Vrata*** - Limited Vow of living an Ascetic Life for a limited time period.
This vow necessitates a person living the life of a monk for one day. During this time, one should retreat to a secluded location, renounce all sinful activities, refrain from seeking pleasure from all objects of the senses, and exercise proper restraint of body, speech, and mind.

12) ***Atithi Samvibhaga Vrata*** - Limited Charity Vow
Monks, nuns, and pious people should be given food, clothing, medicine, and other items from adherents' own possessions. The food served should be pure and reverent.

3.5 IMPLICATIONS OF THE JAIN CODE OF CONDUCT

By observing these tenets, Jain lay adherents can live a righteous life, progress towards a fuller and more perfect existence, and conquer desire. Followers are taught self-control, love, and equanimity while earning wealth, supporting their family, and taking up arms to protect themselves, their family, and country from intruders if desperately necessary.

On one hand, self-regulated cautious behaviour prevents advocates from causing harm to themselves, their family, country, or humanity at large. On the other hand, by letting go of attachments, they gradually prepare themselves for ascetic life. If one delves deeper into the rules, it can be seen that the practice of limiting the number of things to be kept or enjoyed by individuals eliminates the risk of concentration of wealth at one point, which will help to reduce poverty and crime in society.

Individual desires are thus limited, resulting in an ideal society. Comparing these Jain codes of conduct, one can observe that law and legalities start with a conflict, and the majority of those struggles are pertaining to an unequal distribution of resources, disagreement caused by different belief systems, insensitive attitudes towards other living beings and insatiable greed. Under such conditions, just imagine if all of us across the globe were well mannered, displayed sound emotional self-regulation, and acted mindfully with the utmost caution, for what good reason would we need law and legal systems?

4 FINAL COMMENTS – POTENTIAL IMPACT OF JAINISM IN FUTURE LEGAL PHILOSOPHY IN INDIA

4.1 REFORMATION OF LAW & LEGAL SYSTEMS THROUGH THE ROUTES OF JAIN PHILOSOPHY

The majority of legal advances entail a degree of philosophy in the legal system in one way or another. Jain philosophy influences the evolution of legal systems in a variety of ways, including:

- Encouraging a higher code of conduct (*Ahimsa, Aparigrapha, Anekant*), which is beyond the boundaries of prevailing legal systems;

- Inspiring a reduction in coercion and oppression;

- Stimulating the primacy of human empathy and love;

- Prompting a stronger interaction between humans, non-human animals and the environment.

If the above listed points are pondered upon, Jainism, through its basic tenets, presents us with a fundamental truth before our very eyes. So, if we believe that we live in a systematic universe, then the reality of universal, unchanging, timeless truths follows directly from this fundamental truth. If this premise is valid, one may simply make a case for the existence of a higher code of conduct, as prescribed by Jainism.

This higher code of conduct would always take precedence over all other social, legislative, customary, and traditional laws.

It would remain the individual's responsibility to discover this set of laws through self-examination. Hypothetically, if all of us are mindful and self-regulated, and equally sensitive to the rights of all living beings, do we even need law to govern us?

Moreover, today's world is moving beyond political communities, new technologies are dematerialising, decentralising, and democratising the globe, and therefore under such circumstances a wider framework for action based on interdependence is vital for the future existence of all living beings on the earth.

Therefore, on the grounds of rationalisation and fairness, which legal systems require, we need to re-think, re-orientate, renew, re-form and re-imagine building, legal structures based on the Jain philosophy of *Ahimsa, Aparigraha and Anekant.*

If we all adopted such a higher Code of Conduct, as prescribed by Jainism, there would be no conflicts, no personal interests, no rights and there would be a perpetually prevailing oneness of all living beings.

4.2 LEVELS OF 'JAINIFICATION' IN LEGAL SYSTEMS

By infusing the Jain principles of *Ahimsa, Aparigraha, and Anekant* in legal systems, we can measure the degree of Jainification in legal arenas. It is recognised that the writing in this chapter is not purely scientific, in a true sense. However, it is written based on scientific temperament, because the fundamentals of science and technology also start with necessary and reasonable assumptions.

Based on the below mentioned table, Jainification (the application of Jain philosophy) can measure the degree to which legal systems have become equitable and fair in promoting overall happiness and social harmony. Similarly, legal actors and institutions can be categorised using the same pattern.

Level 3 **Complete Jainificatio n**	Legal systems not required	No personal desires	Communit -y of compassio -nates	No coercion or conflicts	Rights are surrende red voluntari ly	Higher sense of duty toward all living beings	Oneness of all living beings
Level 2 **Partial Janificatio n**	A logical and independ -ent legal system	Prevalence of common interests v. individual interests	Global law for basic human rights	No war is promoted, conflict is resolved by arbitration Use of selected weapons by local police and the military	Civil Rights Political Rights Collectiv e Rights	Moderat -e sense of duty towards all living beings	Equality of law Democracy and peaceful coexistence
Level 1 **No Jainificatio n**	No legal systems at all	Complete dominance by powerful people	Use of compulsio- n with all people	Free use of weapons Rampant war	No rights are given	Least sense of duty towards all living beings	No equality Exploitation of one another

Table 17 – <u>Jainification of Legal System</u>

BIBLIOGRAPHY

- o Arti Dhand, "The Dharma of Ethics, the Ethics of Dharma: Quizzing the Ideals of Hinduism," *Journal of Religious Ethics* 30(3) (2002): 347-72.

- o Asoke Kumar Majumdar, *Chaulukyas of Gujarat: A Survey of the History and Culture of Gujarat from the Middle of the Tenth to the End of the Thirteenth Century No. 4* (Bombay: Bharatiya Vidya Bhavan, 1956).

- o Bhanwarlal Nathuram Luniya, *Life and culture in medieval India*, (Indore: Kamal Prakashan, 1978).

- C., Chandramouli, and Registrar General, "Census of India 2011," *Provisional Population Totals,* New Delhi: Government of India (2011): 409-413.

- Champat Rai Jain, *Fundamentals of Jainism* (Meerut: Veer Nirvan Bharti, 1974).

- Christopher Key Chapple, ed. *Jainism and ecology: nonviolence in the web of life, Vol. 22.* (New Delhi: Motilal Banarsidass Publisher, 2006).

- David B.Audretsch, Werner Boente, and Jagannadha Pawan Tamvada, "Religion, social class, and entrepreneurial choice," *Journal of Business Venturing* 28, no. 6 (2013): 774-789.

- David Hardiman, "Usury, death and famine in western India," *Past & present* 152 (1996): 113-156.

- Edward P. Rice, *History of Kannada Literature* (New Delhi: Asian Education Services, 1982).

- E. Thomas, *Jainism; or, the Early Faith of Asoka* (London: Trübner and Co., 1877).

- Girish Prasad Singh, *Early Indian Historical Tradition and Archaeology: Purāṇic Kingdoms and Dynasties with Genealogies, Relative Chronology and Date of Mahābhārata War, Vol. 3.* (New Delhi: DK Printworld, 1994).

- Hans Kelsen, *Principles of international law* (New Jersey: The Lawbook Exchange, Ltd., 2003).

- Helmuth Von Glasenapp, *Jainism: An Indian religion of salvation, Vol. 14* (New Delhi: Motilal Banarsidass Publ., 1999).

- Jeffery D. Long, *Jainism: an introduction* (New York: Macmillan, 2009).

- John E. Cort, "Models of and for the Study of the Jains," *Method & Theory in the Study of Religion* 2, no. 1 (1990): 42-71.

- John E. Cort, *Jains in the world: Religious values and ideology in India* (London: Oxford University Press on Demand, 2001).

- John Rawls, *Justice as fairness: A restatement* (Cambridge: Harvard University Press, 2001).

- John Wesley Lowery, "What higher education law says about spirituality," *New directions for teaching and learning* 2005, no. 104 (2005): 15-22.

- John Witte Jr., "Law and religion: the challenges of Christian jurisprudence," *U. St. Thomas LJ* 2 (2004): 439.

- Kailash Chand Jain, *History of Jainism* (New Delhi: DK Printworld, 2010).

- Krishna M Kumari, *Social and Cultural Life in Medieval Andhra* (Discovery Publishing House, 1990).

- Lawrence A. Babb, *Understanding Jainism* (Edinburgh: Dunedin Academic Press Ltd, 2015).

- *L. D. Barnett,* "An Advanced History of India. By RC Majumdar, HC Raychaudhuri, and Kalikinkar Datta. pp. ix, i, 1081; 10 maps. London: Macmillan and Co., 1948," *Journal of the Royal Asiatic Society 81, no. 1-2* (1949): 103-104.

- Laxmi Mall Singhvi, *The Jain declaration on nature* (USA: Federation of Jain Associations in North America, 1990).

- Michael Tobias, *Life force: the world of Jainism* (Jain Publishing Company, 1991).Mohandas K. Gandhi, Trans. by Mahadev Desai, *An Autobiography: The Story of My Experiments with Truth* (Boston: Beacon Press, 1957).

- Nabin Kumar Sahu, *History of Orissa from the Earliest Time Up to 500 AD. Vol. 1* (Bhubneshwar: Utkal University, 1964).

- Nagendra Kr Singh, ed. *Encyclopedia of Jainism, Vol. 1* (New Delhi: Anmol Publications Pvt. Ltd., 2001).

- Natubhai Shah, *Jainism: the world of conquerors, Vol. 1* (New Delhi: Motilal Banarsidass Publisher, 2004).

- Nayanjot Lahiri, *Ashoka in ancient India* (London: Harvard University Press, 2015).

- Nicholar Wolterstorff, *Reason within the bounds of religion* (Michigan: Wm. B. Eerdmans Publishing, 1984).

- **Nicholar Wolterstorff,** *Justice in Love* **(Michigan: Eerdmans Publishing Company, 2011).**

- Pertold, "" Reu BN:" History of the Rashtrakûtas (Book Review)," *Archív Orientální* 6, no. 2 (1934): 422.

- Dr. Pannalal Jain, *Uttarapurana of Acharya Gunabhadra* (New Delhi: Bhartiya Jnanpith, 2015).

- Parveen Jain, *An Introduction to Jain Philosophy: Based on Writings and Discourses by Ācārya Sushil Kumar* (New Delhi: DK Printworld (P) Ltd, 2019).

- Paul Dundas*, Jains* (London: Psychology Press, UK, 2002*).*

- Peter Flügel*, "A short history of Jaina law,"* International Journal of Jaina Studies 3, no. 4 (2007): 1-15.

- Rafael Domingo, "Why spirituality matters for law: An explanation," *Oxford Journal of Law and Religion* 8, no. 2 (2019): 326-349.

o   Rama Shankar Tripathi, *History of ancient India* (New Delhi: Motilal Banarsidass, 2014).

o   R. S. Mugali, *The Heritage of Karnataka* (Hong Kong: Hesperides Press, 2006).

o   Sailendra Sen, *Textbook of Medieval Indian History* (New Delhi: Primus Books, 2013).

o   Sarat Chandra Ghoshal, ed., *Āpta-mīmāṁsā of Āchārya Samantabhadra,* Vol. 13 (New Delhi: Bhartiya Jnanpith, 2002).

o   Satish Sharma, *Gandhi's Teachers: Rajchandra Ravjibhai Mehta* (Ahemadabad: Gujarat Vidyapith, 2005).

o   Sinclair Stevenson, *The heart of Jainism, Vol. 2* (Humphrey Milford: Oxford University Press, 1995).

o   Shugan C. Jain, "'Jainism' (for young inquisitive)," *International School for Jain Studies*, (New Delhi, 2018).

o   Shyam Manohar Mishra, *'Yaśovarman of Kanauj': A Study of Political History, Social, and Cultural Life of Northern India during the Reign of Yaśovarman* (New Delhi: Abhinav Publications, 1977).

o   Sohan Lal Jain Gandhi, "The Jain Principle of Ahimsa (Non-violence) and Ecology," *Journal of Oriental Studies (Tokyo) 23 (2013)*: 166-177.

o   Sunil Khilnani and Abhay Kumar Dube, *Bharatnama* (New Delhi: Rajkamal Prakashan, 2001).

o   Thomas Reid edited by Haakonssen Knud, *Practical Ethics: Lectures and Papers on Natural Religion, Self-Government, Natural Jurisprudence, and the Law of Nations*, (Edinburgh University Press, 1990).

o   Uma Majmudar, *Gandhi and Rajchandra: The Making of the Mahatma* (London: Lexington Books, 2020).

o   Upendra Baxi, *"Conflicting conceptions of legal cultures and conflict of legal cultures,"* Journal of the Indian Law Institute 33, no. 2 (1991): 173-188.

o   Vaibhav Jain & Sanjay Jain. "'Legal Aspect of Jain Religion as separate entity'," *IOSR Journal of Humanities and Social Science (IOSR-JHSS)* 19, no. 2 (2014): 08-19.

o   Vilāsa Ādinātha Saṅgave, "The Jaina path of ahimsa," *Jainology monograph series* (1991), published in Solapur, India.

o   Zachary R. Calo, "Constructing the secular: law and religion jurisprudence in Europe and the United States," *Robert Schuman Centre for Advanced Studies Research Paper No. RSCAS 94(2014).*

CHAPTER 6

IMPACT OF HINDU JURISPRUDENCE ON LAWS OF INDIA

Assist. Prof. Shrut S. Brahmbhatt & Mr. Nilang Soni

1. INTRODUCTION

This chapter criss-cross through the evolutionary phase of the current Indian legal framework which is, to a large extent, derived from ancient Indian texts such as the *Vedas, Smritis, Upnishads and Arthasastra*. These sources, individually as well as collectively, were all secular and based on principles of *Dharma* (Natural Justice). The reflection of such principles in India's contemporary legal system is analysed with an examination of the ancient mechanisms that nurtured the evolution of modern laws. It is established in the conclusion that the ideologies and intent of current laws and legal frameworks are based upon ancient norms of morality, equity, justice, and non-violence which promote the governance of any civilised society.

The Indian legal framework is elaborated on through distinct parts of this chapter, which begins with an introduction to present-day law, the relevance of its basis on sacred texts and religious scriptures, and the historical evolution of law by tracing the highlights from ancient texts on modern laws, supported by various judicial pronouncements and precedents that remained the foundation for the development of laws, including the Indian Constitution. The notion and aim of the law, as well as the legal system is based on ancient principles. Accordingly, it is connected with the central idea of justice and morality emphasised in ancient Indian scriptures.

The progression of Indian law and legal systems has been contributed to by customs and religious practices, along with prescriptions to present legal as well as constitutional mechanisms referring to secular and common law system. The Honourable Apex court of India has emphasised that, in spite of the adoption of global legal standards, the roots of Indian law can be traced back to the culture, norms and classical religious practices of ancient times.

This is deliberated on further in parts of this chapter, along with an inspection of *Hindu Law* and ancient legal literature that demonstrate the conceptualisation of Indian Ancient Law and Modern Law. Alongside this, the relevance of *Islamic law and jurisprudence* contributing to legal aspects in medieval ages at the time of the advent of the Mughal Dynasty in the middle of the 16th Century is also discussed in this chapter.

2. EVOLUTION & SOURCES OF HINDU LAW

Hinduism is one of the oldest major religions across the globe.[1] Its existence has contributed to the progression of society, jurisprudence and other religions that were born out of this jurisprudence on the Indian sub-continent. Customs and practices evolved through this religion were not legislated by kings or any central authority, but in fact evolved from sages and philosophers, who acted as human agents to serve the divine purpose of God.[2]

Although the role of kings remained that of executors of such laws, they themselves had to abide by the same laws.[3] Despite this, they bestowed legal systems by implementing laws on the advice of the sages and philosophers appointed in their levees known as *Daarbaar.* Decisions were based on jurisprudence that had been authored by sages or philosophers. Such jurisprudence remained the primary source for the kings and levees and this will be discussed later in the chapter. The evolution of Hindu Law within the broader meaning of Law and Hindus or the *Vedic Civilization* is elucidated here below.

2.1 HINDU LAW WITHIN THE BROADER MEANING OF LAW

The laws primarily developed and followed in India evolved from *Dharmasastra* or holy principles based on 'righteousness'.[4] The identification of such laws can be traced taking into consideration multiple perspectives, for example the various sources, impacts, expression, and end results in each case. While it can be determined from such varied perspectives that the laws are based on nature, reason, religion or ethics, the sources could, in fact, be founded on customs,

---

[1] Wendy Doniger, *The Hindus: Alternative History* (New York: Oxford University Press, 2010).
[2] U. C. Sarkar, "Hindu Law: Its Character and Evolution," *Journal of Indian Law Institute* 2, no. 6 (1964): 213-235.
[3] Ibid.
[4] R. Lingat & J.D.M. Derrett, *The Classical Law of India* (Berkeley: University of California Press, 1973).

precedent and legislations. Impact is evaluated on the effect on lives within society; expression would involve formal expressions or authoritative applications; and the end result includes the aim or objective that is sought to be attained through specific codification of the law. Each of these parameters can be justified through Hindu Law, with appropriate reasoning embodied within *Dharmasatras* or Duties within Dharma.

Hindu Law has remained a vital element in the analysis of the evolution of the legal system of India, although due to poor record keeping in India during pre-modern times, it may sometimes not be distinguishable as such.[5] British colonial rule had a severe impact on the evolution of the Indian legal system;[6] however, the foundational principles that had existed for several millennia are still reflected in the contemporary legal system. This is illustrated in later parts of this chapter, wherein the reflections of Hindu laws are elucidated through precedents and decisions taken by courts.

2.2 HISTORY OF HINDU/ VEDIC CIVILISATION

The emergence of Hinduism and the Vedic civilisation can be traced back to earlier than 2000 BCE, as can be seen in the written records of the *Vedic Civilisation* in India.[7] Prior to this, the most controversial aspect dealt with the theory of invasion by Aryans into India around 1500 BCE. This theory has been propagated and deliberated by various scholars of law.[8] However in recent years, it has been rebutted by native scholars from the Indian sub-continent. It is evident from hymns in *Rigveda* (the oldest scripture in the world)[9] which enumerates God's wordings that this had greatly impacted Hindu Culture and society within

---

[5] Timothy Lubin, Donald R. Davis Jr and Jayanth K. Krishnan, *Hinduism and Law: An Introduction* (New York: Cambridge Press University, 2010).

[6] Tirthankar Roy & Anand V. Swamy, *Law and the Economy in Colonial India* (Chicago: University of Chicago Press, 2021).

[7] Raj Pruthi, *Vedic Civilization* (New Delhi: Discovery Publishing House, 2004).

[8] Shashi BhiushanSahai, *The Hindu Civilisation: A miracle History* (New Delhi: Gyan Publishing House, 2010).

[9] <https://bahaiteachings.org/rig-veda-worlds-oldest-scripture/>, accessed on 31 December 2021.

the Indian sub-continent. [10] The practices of two major dynasties, namely Suryavamsha, founded around 362 BCE, [11] and Chandravamsa, both mentioned within *Ramayana,* which was written around 500 BCE,[12] bear great relevance within Hindu culture in India. These dynasties, during their rule, naturally followed the norms prescribed within Vedas.

The Vedic concept of *Sanatana Dharma,* aiming to preserve peace, encouraged societies beyond the Hindu community to follow such principles. [13] The practitioners of law, kings and executors, mainly followed rules of the religion professed by them. Owing to the fact that India was primarily the homeland of Hindus and the majority of residents of the country were Hindus, naturally these practices were followed throughout the evolutionary phase within the sub-continent. Such customary practices built the roots of the modern legal system of present-day India and their reflection cannot be denied.

2.2.1 Dharma and Law

Ancient Indian civilians were governed by various classical and ancient texts that were followed rigorously by executors of law, even the kings. The central scheme and objectives of such literature lies within the concept of *'Dharma'.*[14] The ancient Indian language Sanskrit term *Dharma* is derived from another phenomenon *'dhri',* which means 'to hold together'.[15] The term *'Dharma'* stands for righteousness,

---

[10] Ibid.

[11] Bibek Debroy, *The Valmiki Ramayana* (New Delhi: Penguin Random House India Private Limited 2017), 3.

[12] N. Karpaha, Dr. D. Nagarathinam, L. Lakshmanan and Dr. R. Saravanan, "A Comparative Study of the Death of Vali from the Epic Ramayana and the Death of Julius Caesar from Shakespeare's Julius Caesar," *Language in India 20*, no. 7 (2020): 7-20, 8.

[13] Sita Ram Goel, *History of Hindu-Christian Encounters: AD 304 to 1996* (New Delhi: Voice of India, 2010).

[14] John Grimes, Sushil Mittal & Gene Thursby, *Religions of India* (New York: Routledge; Taylor and Francis Group, 2017).

[15] M. K. Sinha, "Hinduism and International humanitarian law," *International Review of Red Cross* 87, no. 858 (2005): 285-294, 285.

duty and law.[16] *Dharma* comprises religious obligations primarily, along with legal responsibilities. The legal mechanism enshrined under *dharma* includes multiple aspects such as legal principles and execution procedures, along with other general ceremonies such as purification, hygiene maintenance, dressing mode etc. It basically aimed to provide a path to lead life in an appropriate manner.

Ancient Indian society witnessed a time wherein *dharma* and law were considered to be similar. The *Dharma Sastras, Smriti, and Arthasastra* imbibed the notion of justice, law and religion in such a way that no distinction could be made between them at any particular moment. Justice and *'Dharma'* were equated with each other during the ancient period.[17] In spite of *Dharma* having a broader connotation, its most essential notion is justice and morality. Justice has been evaluated as a distinct part of morality with which legal provisions must conform.[18] The interconnection between law and *Dharma* in the Dharmasatras enumerates real progression of a common ethos that can guide society. This is possible only because the relationship between Hindu religion and law is unique, whereby law is considered an indispensable feature of *dharma* beyond being a mere part of it.[19] It can be said that *Dharma* has remained an integral part of law which can be evidenced from the matrimonial, succession and family laws of India. The foundations of these laws are based on the principles enunciated under dharmasastras.

The philosophy of Hinduism believing in the notions of *'unity in diversity'* and *'Vasudhaiva Kutumbakam'* ('world is a family') has continued to be followed in modern times in India and the surrounding regions; the development of Hindu Dharma as an inseparable part of this region has been observed since the 1980s. This reflects the values of Hindu law and customs as a development of universal

---

[16] D. R. Davis Jr, "Hinduism as a legal tradition, *Journal of the American Academy of Religion* 75, no. 2 (2007): 241-267, 241.

[17] N.C. Sen Gupta, *Evolution of Ancient Indian Law* (Calcutta: A. Probsthain, 1954), 336.

[18] H.L.A Hart, *The Concept of Law* (New York: Oxford University Press, 1972), 152-153.

[19] Donald R. Davis Jr., "Hinduism as a legal tradition," *Journal of the American Academy of Religion* 75, no. 2, (2007): 241-267.

Hinduism. It has more to do with a way of life, believing in certain perspectives when looking at the world. Indian Vedic literature has had a deep impact on its culture and thereby on modern-day legislations, since these traditions, customs and practices set a source of law for the legal system of the country.[20] The impact of Hindu jurisprudence has even been observed in places such as Indonesia and Cambodia.

Dharma shastras possessed deep roots in the origins and development of Burma, Cambodia and is still evident in modern day legislations. The word '*Manu*', which is the part of Hinduism being the originator of Hindu law can be also be clearly seen in these indigenous countries. The reason for this is because such sacred texts were written in the *Sanskrit* language and illuminating observations from the texts were also promoted by the preachers of Hinduism in these countries and, indeed, throughout the world in ancient times.

Hence, such texts of Hindu jurisprudence are highly regarded in these countries. Historically, the great scholars and writers - monks - accorded with the idea of Hindu jurisprudential text, *Manu smriti* which they found was crucial in understanding issues concerning property, civil and criminal codes at that time. Such similar connotations were also found in the Siamese version of *Manu smriti* in about 1614 CE. [21]

It is pertinent to mention that even the British, whilst they were ruling the Indian territories, had embraced principles from Hindu jurisprudence, in particular *dharma,* in laws they enacted. This assisted them in governing the colony in the best interests of the sustenance and welfare of society. The British were confronted with multifarious Indian local customs based on the principles of dharma. They recognised Indian religions and the notion of *dharma* judiciously when enacting statues. This is very well illustrated by one such principle, namely

---

[20] Martin Ramstedt, *Hinduism in Modern Indonesia* (London: Routledge Curzon, 2004).
[21] Low J., "On the Laws of Mu'ung Thai or Siam," *Journal of Indian Archipelago* I, (1847): 327-429, 329.

equity, based on the concept of fairness and righteousness - a central notion of Hindu Law - being reflected in various laws enacted by the British Empire. It also demonstrates how British law makers codified laws keeping in mind the core principles of *dharma.*

As far as independent India is concerned, constitution makers also linked up the concepts of *Dharma* to modern-day civil liberties and freedoms, since a paramount consideration was that ancient laws should provide a realistic approach for society.

The principles of natural law and *dharma* paved their way into the supreme authority of India via the pathway of fundamental rights enshrined within the Constitution.[22] Their interpretation can be seen through the prism of *dharma,* which was earlier embodied as a duty-bound legal system and is now actually a rights-based legal system with reasonable restrictions.

The Hindu jurisprudence concept of *'Raj Dharma',* which basically means the duty of the king towards his subjects, suggests that the King could not just make any rules as per his whims and fancies. Similar concepts can be seen in the present-day scenario, under *Article 368 of the Constitution of India, 1950,* which confers power on the legislators and parliament to frame and enact laws relating to any matter which is in the best interests of the citizens of India.

Although the procedure of such an approach has changed, the very essence and core foundations *vis-à-vis* the principles behind such an exercise remain the same and thereby, we can say that Hindu jurisprudence, through its principles of Dharma, plays a vital role in the administration of current day legislations and their pervasive impact in regulations meant to govern the personal life of the peoples of India.

---

[22] Article 12 to 35, *Constitution of India 1950.*

2.2.2 Hindu Law & Jurisprudence

Hindu Law and jurisprudence includes a framework of do's and don'ts created within the Hindu religion, primarily intended to regulate the conduct of those belonging to the Hindu religion. It has been commonly deliberated that neither the term *Hindu,* nor the definition of *Hinduism* were conceived or formulated by any Hindu.[23] The notion of *Hinduism* and the ideologies of its preachers promoted a prevalence of secularism in society. In fact an artificial dichotomy was created and religious demarcations were drawn upon only after the advent of the violent colonisation of the Indian sub-continent by Islamic empires between 12th-18th centuries.

Consequently, Hindu law never had a religious bias. Rather, it appreciated the concept of inclusiveness over being exclusive to a particular group of people and did not suggest that Hinduism was the only option for human salvation. This basic concept is very well reflected within the practices and notions of diverse Indian society. Contemporary Indian legislations, which are founded on the principles of Hindu laws and jurisprudence, are also secular by nature. Therefore, concept is secular and tolerance is inherent within Hindu jurisprudence and actually does not need the addition of concepts to make Indian society secular.

Sources of Hindu law and jurisprudence primarily include Vedas known as *shruti* and literatures known as *smritis.*[24] The four Vedas, namely *Rigveda, Samveda, Yajurveda, and Atharvaveda,* aim to convey knowledge and insights from ancient times that may be followed by future generations.[25] The thoughts contained within them portray an approach of righteousness. *Smritis* are literatures based on memories or remembrance, which include Manu *smriti*, Yajnavalkyasmriti, and

---

[23] C. J. Fuller, "Hinduism and Scriptural Authority in Modern Indian Law," *Comparative Studies in Society & History* 30, no.2 (1988): 225-248, 225.
[24] Domenico Francavilla, "The Hindu Tradition: A History" in *Routledge Handbook of Religious Laws* (New York: Routledge Publications, 2019).
[25] Frits Staal, *Discovering the Vedas: Origins, Mantras, Rituals, Insights* (New Delhi: Penguin Books India, 2008).

smritis of Vishnu, Narad, Parashar, Apastamba, Vashisht, Gautam, etc.[26] These *smritis*, despite being non-codified law and merely a literature authored by Sanskrit scholars of ancient times, remain a great source of Hindu law and jurisprudence. For example, the concepts of Hindu joint family as well as coparcenary[27], elucidating collective and individual rights over joint properties in Mitakshara and Dayabhaga families within the *Hindu Succession Act of 1956*[28] is nothing but a modernised version of commentaries authored by Vijnaneshwar[29] and Jimutvahan.[30]

Contemporarily, laws and policies in India are drafted and enforced by the basic arrangement model of India - that is, elected representative in the democratic union within Parliament create laws, enforce them and put them into affirmative practice by directing various state agencies. State agencies, such as the executive body of the state and the judiciary, need to make sure that the laws created by parliament are being followed and are not defied.

When the legislature creates laws or legislations, such laws are founded or drafted on the basis of certain values of morality, politics, rights & liabilities, history, societal benefit and so on and so forth. Classical Hindu law also followed a particular, yet dynamic, legal system with a unique combination of values, morality & politics. However, the ancient or classical Hindu laws founded and drafted by scholars of Vedas, who played a central role in the establishment of the legal systems outlined by the authors above, show that Hinduism and Hindu laws were never based on exclusion; rather, they were established on the grounds of inclusiveness. These laws undoubtedly differed from each other but were dynamic and diverse in practice between the communities.

---

[26] Geetanjali Srikantan, "Towards New Conceptual Approaches in Legal History: Rethinking 'Hindu Law' through Weber's Sociology of Religion" in Thomas Duve (ed.), *Entanglemens in Legal History: Conceptual Approaches* (Frankfurt am Main 2014), 102.
[27] Joint Heirship of the lineal descendants over Joint Family's Property.
[28] *Hindu Succession Act* 30 of 1956.
[29] Keshav Jha, "Sources of Hindu Law: A Comprehensive View," *International Journal of Research and Analytical Reviews* 6, no. 2 (2019): 592-595, 592.
[30] Ibid.

Currently, the prevailing laws of India are not entirely derived from ancient and classical Hindu methodologies, owing to several changes of legal administration in the country; however in the majority of cases, Hindu laws remain the guiding force behind the executed scheme or intention of the legislature, both in ancient and modern-day legislation. India, according to the Hindu jurisprudence of inclusiveness, has allowed the Constitution to have differing personal laws for minority groups, according to their own religious practices such as Islam or Christianity, although this has caused administrative issues within the judiciary and legal implementation. This is altogether another topic and beyond the scope of this chapter.

2.3 SOURCES OF HINDU LAW

Ancient Indian societies largely followed the Hindu religion; as a result, the law of the land was based on religious practices followed by Hindus. The practices mentioned within large scale literature and prevailing customs drove socio-legal matters of India. The laws enacted pre- and post- the advent of foreign rulers in India was based on Hindu laws. These laws were founded and developed on the basis of Vedic literature/scriptures that had an epistemological position in the different philosophical schools of thought within India. These literatures/scriptures remained large sources of Hindu law, which are independently deliberated further in subsequent paragraphs.

2.3.1 Vedas

Vedas, the scholarly ancient guides for Hindus, were considered a preliminary source on which to construct societal needs, while synthesising with religious and philosophical growth.[31] Despite their ancient origins, from around 1400 BCE until

---

[31] David Kinsley, *Hindu Goddesses* (California: University of California Press, 1988).

about 300 BCE,[32] their relevance to modern times is undiminished; rather, they have the potential to serve as a model for the path of life, even in modern times. The primary four Vedas - namely Rigveda, Yajurveda, Samveda and Atharvaveda - have remained a guiding source to Hindus in India. These Vedas, which are available in literary form in the contemporary world, existed earlier as *Shruti* (which means heard knowledge), disseminated through the generations.[33] Vedas are also called *Apauruseya*[34] and are said to come directly from God. Accordingly, they are treated as the ultimate authority to govern society. Collective analysis of the Vedas suggests that they are intended to protect the well-being of humans, and attempt to safeguard health, wealth, and the aptitude of Hindus to serve civilisation.

The Indian legal system frequently emphasises Vedas and its principles. Therefore, these are well reflected in many different judicial pronouncements, with a special emphasis on the significance of such scriptural authority. However, a stricter application of Vedas has not been observed by Indian Courts, and courts have frequently deviated from Vedic principles when carrying out reforms within society. In 1968,[35] the Supreme Court of India took a stand in one of the landmark judgments that, despite explicit permission allowing the sacrifice of animals including cows in Rig Veda, a law prohibiting their slaughter in Bihar cannot be overturned. The reason cited for the judgement was that revulsion against the custom of cow slaughter had started long ago and cows had achieved the sanctity and status of being *'Aghanya'*[36] since the beginning of the Gupta dynasty (240-550 CE), whereby people had started to respect these animals.

---

[32] Jacobus A. Naudé and Cynthia L. Miller-Naudé, *Sacred writings 1; The Routledge handbook of literary translation* (New York: Routledge Publications, 2018).

[33] N Ramanathan, "Shruti According to Ancient Texts," *Journal of Indian Musicological Society* 12, no. 3 (1981): 31-37, 31.

[34] Purusottama Bilimoria, "On the Idea of Authorless Revelation (Apauruseya)" in R. W. Perrett, *Indian Philosophy of Religion* (Netherlands: Kluwer Academic Publishers, 1989).

[35] *Mohd. Hanif Quareshi & Ors. v. The State of Bihar,* 1959 SCR 629.

[36] W Norman Brown, "The sanctity of the Cow in Hinduism," *The Economic Weekly* 16, no.5 (1964): 245-255, 245; *Aghanya* means not to be slain.

Hence, laws that did not adhere to Vedic norms were not considered detrimental on account of the transformation of society. In addition, the notion of a few scholars that principles of non-violence are a vital part of Brahmanical Hinduism has prevailed in Indian society. In another matter before the Apex Court of India, *Seshammal v. State of Tamilnadu,*[37] one of the issues involved questioned a feature of novel law passed by the state government, which allegedly surpassed the principles of *Agamas*. While the decision was in favour of the law passed by state government, the court clarified that the disputed feature of the law should, in principle, be in consensus with *Agamas* by reason of it being associated with religion which, in a general sense, should not be disturbed.

2.3.2 The Bhagavad Gita

Ancient Sanskrit literature comprises multiple versions of *Gita*, amongst which the most widely known edition is the Shrimad Bhagvat (Bhagvad) Gita, authored by sage Vyasa ji.[38] The Bhagavad Gita is considered to be the teachings of Lord Krishna, delivered during an epic war called *Mahabharata*.[39] It aimed to provide philosophical knowledge on ethics, conduct and devotion. This sacred text was followed by Hindus and its learning has been imbibed within tradition, converting it into customs lately followed by all. Accordingly, law and religion have been connected, and religion - that is, *Dharma* - is purported to have prevailed every time to protect the upright, whenever law or executors of law have failed in their duty to do so.

Hinduism and Bhagvad Gita individually and collectively intend a prevalence of equality and the progressive reformation of human beings.[40] This was well observed in a celebrated decision of the Supreme Court of India in *Sastri*

---

[37] *Seshammal v. State of Tamil Nadu* (1972) 2 SCC 11.
[38] Keith Hill, *The Bhagavad Gita* (New Zealand: Attar Books, 2009).
[39] Mahatma Gandhi, *The Bhagvad Gita: According to Gandhi* (California: North Atlantic Books, 2010).
[40] Juan Mascaro, *The Bhagavad Gita* (London: Penguin Publishing Group, 2003).

Yagnapurushadji and others v. MuldasBrudardas Vaishya and Another,[41] wherein the dispute was related to the restriction of entry by a traditionally proclaimed lower caste within the Hindu religion to the temples of one particular sect believed to be for upper-class members. While assessing the parameters of the case, the honourable court referred with the principles of Bhagvad Gita, and it was held that any such prohibitions would render an inequality in society.

Bhagvad Gita, along with other ancient literature, deliberated to maintain ethics and religious values along with self-control, as it possesses the capability to promote harmonious order in society. This literature is considered holy and guides individuals from and beyond the Hindu religion on various aspects of life. It has been used in courtrooms, for witnesses following the Hindu religion to take an oath which explicitly expresses its essentialness perceived by the community, before recording statements. In furtherance of this, as discussed above, it has remained a great source for law to interpret and understand legal connotations.

2.3.3 Upanishads

Upanishads, literatures concluding Vedas (discussed in §2.3.1), are revered and hold great significance in Hinduism.[42] Their speculations about humanity and the cosmos are respected and followed by Hindus and other communities across the globe. Upanishads bestowed the notion of rule of law, whose principles emphasise the importance of rules of natural justice, admire the process of law as most important and consider law stronger than and above its executors, even the kings. Despite having its roots in around the eighteenth century BCE,[43] its relevance to the modern world has remained intact and indeed has even been amplified.

---

[41] *Sastri Yagnapurushadji and others v. Muldas Brudardas Vaishya and Another* 1966 SCR (3) 242.
[42] Eknath Easwaran, *The Upanishads* (New Delhi: Nilgiri Press, 2009).
[43] V. Roebuck, *The Upanishads* (London: Penguin Publishing Group, 2004).

Upanishads are believed to be the first and preliminary sources of philosophical conclusions of Vedic literature. They add value to Vedas and elucidate to interpret complex notions of such literatures/scriptures, wherein the series of questions and answers by learned sages includes valuable inputs to govern matters of socio-legal, as well as political lives.[44] Their contribution to deduce the analytical concepts of Vedic literature has remained tremendously important.

3. HISTORY OF BHARATVARSHA (FORMER NAME OF INDIA)

India was formerly called *Bharatvarsha,* after having being known as *Aryavarta;*[45] there have been different views behind its name. One such view states that it is based on the gallantry of the legendry King, *Bharata Chakravarti,* ancestor of Pandavas and Kauravas.[46] The Land of Bharatvarsha was considered sacred, with the presence of sacred rivers, lakes, mountains, abodes of gods, and holy cities, each bearing their own unique history.[47] This land had been governed by kings, who accorded importance to Vedic literature and the religious beliefs of the public at large prior to the invasion of foreign entities, who ruled the pacifist nation violently and ruined the land that was once considered to be rich across the globe.[48] This nation had worshipped the realms of nature since the time of the Indus Valley Civilisation from 2300 BCE,[49] who are propounded to have achieved both flourishing trade and culture by adopting an advanced sense of civic culture.[50]

---

[44] E. Easwaran, *The Upanishads: Classics of Indian Spirituality* (New Delhi, Nilgiri Press, 2007), 2.

[45] Catherine Clementin-Ojha, "India that is Bharat…: One Country, Two Names," *South Asia Multidisciplinary Academic Journal* 10, no. 1 (2014): 1-21, 10.

[46] This can be derived from an excerpt of Vishnu Purana (2.3.1) which in *Sanskrit* language states, उत्तरंयत्समुद्रस्यहिमाद्रेश्चैवदक्षिणम्। वर्षंतद्भारतंनामभारतीयत्रसंततिः।।. Literal translation of the same is - "The country (Varsam) that lies north of the ocean and south of the snowy mountains is called Bharatam; there dwell the descendants of Bharata.

[47] Jugal Kishor Sharma, *Punya Bhoomi Bharat* (New Delhi: Suruchi Prakashan, 1993), 3.

[48] V. D. Mahajan, *Ancient India* (New Delhi: S. Chand Publishing 1962).

[49] Romila Thapar, *A History of India: From Origins to 1300* (London: Penguin Books, 1990), 1.

[50] Ibid.

The Pre-Vedic era witnessed the Kingship of Solar Emperor Manu's descendants, who began their rule by governing peacefully. In Treta Yuga, the solar dynasty aka Suryavansham was developed. This dynasty ruled India while increasing a feeling of unity alongside prosperity amongst residents.[51] This era was also known as the *first Vedic era,* the Rama reign, for almost thirty thousand years through several generations who passed on the ruling to Yadava in the *second Vedic era.* This era was governed by the lunar dynasty aka Chandravansham, wherein Pandvas and Kauravas fought the epic war of Mahabharata, ending Pandavas' reign. The post- Vedic period was known as Kaliyug, governed by the famous 'Mauryan and Gupta dynasties'[52] respectively.[53]

The period of Gupta dynasty rule saw a growth of literature. Following the Gupta Dynasty came the rise of the Hindu Empires of the Chalukyas and Cholas, and thereafter raiders from the Islamic Empires brutally invaded the Indian sub-continent.[54] Streams of such invaders came to loot enormous wealth from the pacifist country of *Bharatvarsha,* including Mughal emperors (famous invaders from Central Asia following Islamic jurisprudence) who changed the name of Bharat to 'Hindustan'.

They were followed by similar other foreign attackers, until finally the British colonised and called the nation as 'India'. The change of name was carried out on the basis of religion for the first time in the history of *Bharatvarsha*. The presence of foreign invaders affected several political and administrative affairs of the nation. Although the alien names and ideologies have been widely accepted due to centuries of colonisation, natives of the land retain their roots and never have forgotten their land's original ideologies, philosophies and jurisprudence.[55]

---

[51] Romila Thapar, "Cyclic and linear time in early India", *Museum International* 57 (2005): 19-31, 19.
[52] B. P. Sinha, *Dynastic History of Magadha* (New Delhi: Abhinav Publications, 1977).
[53] V. R. Dikshitar, *The Gupta Polity* (New Delhi: Motilal Banarasidass Publications 1993).
[54] P. K. Gautam, "The Cholas," *Journal of Defence Studies* 7, no. 4 (2013): 48-62, 52.
[55] Manu Goswami, *Producing India from Colonial Economy to National Space* (Delhi: Permanent Black, 2004).

3.1 GEOGRAPHICAL EXTENT OF BHARAT OVER CENTURIES

Ancient Vedic literature cites that the earth possessed Seven Dwipas, four of which surrounded the mountain Meru, which happened to be the land of Bharat Varsha. Natural entities such as mountains and rivers had great relevance in identifying geographical demarcations of the country. During its inception, way before the twentieth century, India's geographical limits extended all the way to Africa and Madagascar.[56] Since the nineteenth century, as proclaimed in *Rigveda*, in the east it extended to the Ganga River and in the west to the Kabul River; it also mentions the presence of the Himalayan mountains to the north and seas in the south.[57]

There exist dual concepts regarding the geography during the ancient era – the first is suggested by Vedic literature, as mentioned above, and the second is through evidence from the Harappan Civilisation which suggests how territories relied on living rivers. This underwent tremendous change during the evolution of India, due to the invasion and ingress of foreign rulers who divided Bharat into multiple units; presently what prevails is majorly post the partition of India into India, Pakistan and Bangladesh in 1947/1971.

3.2 GOVERNANCE THROUGH HINDU LAW

The impact of Hindu Law in the execution of judicial matters has been immense since ancient times. Individuals who were well-versed with *smritis* and legal procedures were appointed as *Nityukta*. The job specification of Nityuktas was to observe the relevant application of Hindu laws and methods prescribed in the scriptures.[58] Numerous writings exist from ancient times that were referred to as commentaries or *Nibandhas*and. These commentaries aimed to guide on legal

---

[56] Sanjeev Sanyal, *Land of Seven Rivers: History of India's Geography* (New Delhi: Penguin Books Ltd., 2012).
[57] Ibid.
[58] Ludo Rocher, "Lawyers in Classical Hindu Law," *Law and Society Review* 3 (1969): 383-402, 383.

parameters drawn within *dharmashastras*. The commentaries/scriptures/writings were used throughout the history of India by the various monarchs from different dynasties governing parts of Bharat such as the Magadha, Kalinga, Gonanda, Gandhara, Kuru, Pandyan, Chera, Chola from 600 BCE[59]-1700 BCE[60] to the most recent Maratha empire in 1674-1947 CE, as well as the Dogra Dynasty in the present day provinces of Jammu & Kashmir in 1846-1947 CE.[61]

Vedic literature entitles kings to govern a territory by referring to them as '*Rajan*', whose first and foremost duty is to observe prevalence of *Dharma* in consensus with such writings/scriptures.[62] This aspect is discernible from the approach of ancient emperors who preserved the essence of Hindu law during their governance. In the Northern part of *Bhartvarsha* during the period 320-185 BCE, when Emperor Ashok Maurya ruled, Kautilya's *Arthshastra* was followed to administer several socio-political matters.[63] Hindu law remained the foundation for the creation of the justice administration system and establishment of the hierarchy of authorities, such as Mantri Parishad, Adhyaksha, Sannidhata and so forth, during the Mauryan dynasty.

The influence of Sanskrit literature and Hindu law and jurisprudence is even evident in the sculptures created during this period. Historical evidence suggests that during this timespan, judicial procedures including the assessment of witnesses were in consonance with Hindu Law.[64] The principles of truthfulness being followed were held in high esteem, as reported by foreign visitors in this

---

[59] Ranbir Chakravarti, "Merchants and state society: some case studies from early historic period and the 'threshold times' (c. 600 BC to AD 700)," *Studies in People History* 6, (2019): 119-133, 119.

[60] J. Heitzman, "Temple urbanism in medieval South India," *The Journal of Asian Studies* 46, no. 4 (1987): 791-826, 793.

[61] Sumantara Bose, *Kashmir: Roots of Conflict; Paths to Peace* (Cambridge: Harvard University Press, 2005).

[62] Susheel Kumar Sharma & Vinod Kumar Singh, "Indian Idea of Kingship," *Indian Journal of Political Science* 71, no. 2 (2010): 383-398, 383.

[63] Klaus Schlichtman, *A Peace History of India: From Ashoka Maurya to Mahatama Gandhi* (New Delhi: Vij Books Pvt. Ltd., 2016).

[64] A. L. Basham, *The Wonder that was India* (Delhi: Picador India, 2004).

era.[65] This approach had its roots interwoven with Hinduism, as the previous dynasties in different regions had also followed Vedic literature while administering justice. The Karkota dynasty in Kashmir during the 7th century had also followed Hindu literatures to administer justice.[66]

The Southern regions of the country also followed Hinduism in a stricter sense throughout the ancient and medieval eras. The Pandyan dynasty, around 600 BCE,[67] followed Hinduism and the prevalence of *dharma* was considered high in the administration of law and justice. This dynasty worshipped Lord Shiva and followed Vedic literature when formulating norms and legal principles for society.

The prevalence of, and adherence to, Hindu literature can also be found during the Gupta dynasty's rule, between c. 240-550 CE,[68] wherein 'Brahmanical literature'[69] played a pivotal role in shaping the judicial system of the era. This dynasty showcased a liberal approach in welcoming, as well as coexisting with Buddhist and Jain communities. Administrative hierarchies were created in consonance with Vedic literature.

The implication and acceptance of Hindu law can even be witnessed while British rulers governed the country and administered through the King's courts in superior jurisdictions in Calcutta, Madras and Bombay.[70] The concepts of *Stridhana, Saptapadi, Mitakshara* and *Dayabhaga* Schools, Coparcenary, and Karta were recognised and implemented according to the Hindu texts. An updated version still continues in India.

---

[65] J. W. Mccrindle, *Ancient India: As described by Megasthenes and Arrian* (Delhi: Munshiram Manoharlal Publishers, 2000) 2.

[66] Pratapaditya Pal, "Bronzes of Kashmir: Their Sources and Influences," *Journal of the Royal Society of Arts* 121, no. 5207 (1973): 726-749, 728.

[67] Krishan Kumar, "Review Article; A Critical Study on the History of Pandyan Dynasty," *Journal of Advances and Scholarly Researches in Allied Education* 6, no.11 (2013): 1-3, 2.

[68] Patrick Olivelle and Donald Richards Davis, *Hindu Law: A New History of Dharmasastra* (Oxford: Oxford University Press, 2018).

[69] Hemchandra Raychaudary, *Political History of Ancient India: From Accession of Parikshit to the Extinction of the Gupta Dynasty* (New Delhi: Cosmo Publications, 2006).

[70] Thomas Andrew Lumisden Strange, *Hindu Law: Principally with reference to such portions of it as concern the Administration of Justice in the King's Courts, in India* (Madras: J. Higginbotham, 1864).

4. THE IMPACT OF HINDU LAW ON THE CONTEMPORARY LEGAL SYSTEM

Hindu law's key concepts, cultural and religious traditions must not be put down to the effect of a dominated past, but should be recognised as an underrated element as far as current or modern law-making processes are concerned. Hinduism and its principles were not only followed throughout the great history of the ancient and medieval eras' legal systems, but even post-independence in the newly-named country after foreign intruders had been driven back to their own lands. Modern laws have gone through several changes since its beginning, owing to various rulings since the Vedic era.

4.1 INFLUENCE OF HINDU LAW ON THE CONSTITUTION

The future course of Hindu law was preserved and safeguarded in the 1950s with the advent of the Constitution of India, which was the epitome of source of law in the post-colonial period of the country. Not only Hindu law, but numerous personal laws had to be in alignment and fine-tuned as per the constitutional scheme. One such minor scheme, yet the most significant example of the influence of Hindu law or principle on the constitutional scheme, is that of the *dharma* itself. The word *dharma* signifies an idealised duty (other than the notions of law and religion).

Idealised duty denotes an expectation that an individual shall strive to do the right thing at the right time. One can look at the lines of Article 51- A(j) of the *Indian Constitution, 1950* which states that *"it shall be the duty of every citizen, 'to strive towards excellence in all spheres of individual and collective activity so that the nation constantly rises to higher levels of endeavour and achievement"*. On the other hand Hindu law also talks about taking appropriate action and following one's duty being the aim of life, and not just attaining *Moksha*. The concept of individual duty also reflects the idea of the duties which are enshrined under the constitutional scheme of the Fundamental Duties under Article 51- A of the Constitution 1950.[71]

The Hindu Law Model is considered a tool of social engineering[72] in law and is highly regarded by scholars such as the Architect of the Constitution, Dr. Ambedkar, as well as eminent lawyers including Jawaharlal Nehru, the first Prime Minister of India. These scholars' belief in the Hindu Law Model is evident from the fact that the codification of Hindu Law took place in 1955 and 1956. It dealt with the provisions of various promulgated laws and attained the objective of social engineering which can be observed by analysing provisions such as the Criminalisation and Abolition of Hindu polygamy as well as a new regime of succession rights for Hindu widows. For example, The *Hindu Marriage Act 1955,* by the sheer implementation of section 11, prohibits any bigamous marriage and holds them void. In addition, if a person commits such an offence under the Act, he is then also covered under the provisions of sections 494 and 495 of the Indian Penal Code for the purpose of penal consequences. Moreover, Article 13 of the same *Hindu Marriage Act 1955* declares that any law which is inconsistent with the Fundamental rights enshrined in the *Constitution of India 1950* will be held as void. Therefore, it could be argued that the enactment of such statutes as well as the Constitution was intended to balance the approach of personal laws, and this is influenced by Hindu law's customs, spirit, principles and jurisprudence.

4.1.1 Secular Constitution and Hindu Law

India is a secular nation; this secular nature was accorded by way of the *42nd Constitutional amendment*, which inserted the word 'Secular' in the *Preamble of the Constitution of India 1950,* and thus a secular character as the epitome of source of law and rights in the post-colonial regime was born.

---

[71] Werner Menski, "From Dharma to Law and Back? Postmodern Hindu law in a Global World," *Heidelberg Papers in South Asian and Comparative Politics* 20 (2004): 2-21, 11.
[72] Werner Menski, *Hindu Law: Beyond Tradition and Modernity* (New Delhi: Oxford University Press, 2008).

Alhough the Honourable Supreme Court of India laid down connotations for the word 'secular' or 'secularism' within the domain of constitutional interpretation on several occasions, the 42nd Amendment reformed the predominantly political formulation to judicial adjudication.[73] In a general sense, the word 'Secular' means that there is no determined or official religion of the State. The State therefore treats all religions with equality and expressly grants religious freedoms to every individual and allows that every individual has the right to profess and practice the religion of their choice.

The reformation of religion and religious practices is strongly affected by secular ideas and the notion of emerging secular order is directly dependent on the concept of religion.[74] But even though India is a secular country by Constitution, it cannot in totality avoid the buzz of religious identity. In India, courts carry out the complex task of administering and implying notions of law and religion or customs by application and permission in a myriad of contexts, subjects of legislations and rules or regulations. For example, Indian legislation expressly grants the application of customs and religious practices in Family Law.

Similarly, electoral law prohibits the appeal of religion while campaigning for votes, while on the other hand, public law or laws of religious trusts guarantee the protection and promote the interests of religious communities for their welfare. Thus, the Courts of India have to adjudicate and administer balance between religious rights and the power of the State to interfere in matters related to religion.

Courts also have the power to regulate religious rights or, in a way, jurisprudence emanating from religion itself. There is another set of arguments from scholars that the Courts often tend to overlook Hindu traditions, customs and beliefs of the

---

[73] M Mohsin Alam, "Constructing Secularism: Separating 'Religion' and 'State' under the Indian Constitution," *Australian Journal of Asian Law* 11, no. 30, (2009): 29-55, 30.

[74] Marc Galanter, "Hinduism, Secularism, and the Indian Judiciary," *Symposium on Law and Morality: East and West; University of Hawai'i Press* 21, no. 4 (1971): 489-492, 490.

people, whilst it is preoccupied with processing and creating a uniform belief system in the heterogeneity of Hindu customs and religious practices.[75] However such contrary views do not change the actual conducti of the courtrooms wherein Hindu law has remained foundational.

Judicial interpretations have time and again widened the scope of religious protection, but they become restrictive when the test of "non-essential" and "non-obligatory" are put on them. The restrictive nature of judicial interpretations is further disliked by many when they are issued on the grounds of public morality, health and public order.[76] Even though India is secular in nature, the very constitution that put this in place also gives a right to protection of religious denomination and practice under Article 26 of the *Constitution of India 1950*. If, in any religion, the religious practice is found to be an essential and integral part of that religion then, in that scenario, the State will ensure its protection. Therefore, even though secular in nature, the State still at times has to regulate or restrict religious practices or customs associated after exercising the test of "essentiality" in the Court of law.

4.2 REFLECTION OF VEDIC PRINCIPLES ON PROCEDURAL ASPECTS

Law is equally applicable to all regions and subjects. Hindu laws are a form of positive morality and are administered, modified and altered by the Courts from time to time in order to protect its integrity and principles. For example, the *Hindu Marriage Act 1955* altered the nature of marriages that Hindus can enter into. Later, issues pertaining to adoption were governed by the *Hindu Adoption and Maintenance Act 1956*; for issues pertaining to succession the *Hindu Succession Act 1956* was promulgated. These are just some instances where Courts and legislators have prevailed upon the spirit of original law, if not the original letters of Hindu law.

---

[75] Derrett and Duncan's (1959: 38) criticism of the court for ignoring the 'customs and beliefs of people', while relying exclusively on orthodox and literary sources.
[76] *Ramji Lal Modi v State of Uttar Pradesh* AIR 1957 SC 620.

Therefore, such legislations can be considered to be modern sources of Hindu law and signify the evolution and development of Hindu law in its positive spirit. Accordingly, if in certain instances Hindu law or the Sacred texts/*Smritis* are unable to assist the courts in achieving any reasonable result due to conflict with Smritis, the principle of justice, equity and good conscience would prevail and this view was observed in the case of *Gurunath v. Kamlabai.*[77]

Hindu law not only affects the lives of Hindus, but also plays a crucial role as a catalyst of significant social change in personal laws for groups following other religions in India. This can be evidenced from the case of *ShayaraBano v. Union of India,*[78] popularly known as the Triple Talaq Case, in which it was determined that the practice of *Talaq-e-biddat* (the essential practice of Muslim personal law) was held to be unconstitutional. Now, the position of law is such that, irrespective of personal laws, any Indian ex-husbands will remain responsible for the maintenance of their Indian ex-wives. Such a practice of maintenance was established under provisions of Hindu law and the scheme of other penal laws.

So, it can be concluded that post-modern laws have been influenced or rather inspired by the Hindu concept of marriage as a sacrament, with its protective obligations and safeguards being rediscovered to further the agendas of social welfare and equity in all laws. Accordingly, Hindu law and jurisprudence is playing pivotal role in the Indian legal system and acting as a catalyst for dynamic change in the system of law.

4.3 THE CONSTRUCTION OF LAWS THROUGH HINDU CUSTOMS

In any society, customs play a significant role in jurisprudence and possess an influential role as a source of legislation. As such, customs have a deep impact on

---

[77] *Gurunath v. Kamlabai* 1955 AIR 206.
[78] *ShayaraBano v. Union of India* AIR (2017) 9 SCC 1 (SC).

the functioning of society and validate peoples' actions in society as well as societal acceptance. In the Indian legal system, it is not wrong to say that custom is a recognised source of law under the Indian Legal system regime. In fact, under Article 13 (3) of the *Constitution of India 1950,* any concept of law includes a connotation of customs and usages. The *Hindu Marriage Act 1955* defines custom as *"any rule that has been practiced continuously, consistently, and uniformly for a long time among Hindus in any local area, tribe, community, culture, group, or family, and has gained the force of law, provided that the rule is specific and not unreasonable or contrary to public policy."*[79]

Therefore, a custom is meant as an evolving standard of behaviour concerning a particular circumstance for members or stakeholders of society because of a passive or express approval of the community expressing it.[80] Customs are bifurcated into two streams, one with legal obligations and one without legal obligations and any customs which are of the utmost public importance attract an obligation of legal compliance. For example, the Hindu custom of shaving one's head on the occasion of the death of a father is not legally binding, but a marriage ceremony or custom for the solemnization of marriage is a legal obligation under section 7 of the *Hindu Marriage Act 1955.* Similarly, the transmission of property the death of the father under the obligations and provisions of the Section 10 of the *Hindu Succession Act 1956* and under the provisions of the *Transfer of Property Act 1882.*

But as we know that any law or provision of law is backed by the rationale and reasoning of meaningfulness and valid objective. Customs on the other hand, are often referred to as a conduct helping to maintain social order in the absence of a rule-making body. There may arise a situation wherein the status of customs is in conflict with written statutes. Customary rules are indistinct in nature, however it is reasonable to propound that Hindu law and jurisprudence did indeed originate

---

[79] The *Hindu Marriage Act 1955* [Act 25], §. 3(a)].
[80] Harikumar Pallathadka, "Relevance of Customs under Modern Hindu Law," *European Journal of Molecular & Clinical Medicine* 07, no. 06 (2020): 3222-3228, 3223.

from ancient texts or sacred scripts such as *Manusmritis, Upanishads, and Vedas,* as previously discussed in this chapter. To advance this contention, the authors submit that customs evolved as changes were required in society, were supplemented by the validation of members of society, and finally administered by Courts of law. Therefore, even though in today's modern legal system in India legislations and precedents are considered to be the epitome of the source and spirit of law, on the other hand, customs and customary practices hold the pivotal essence of cultural identity and hence also hold value as a source of law.

After rule of law was established in India, the codification of Hindu Law and legislations concerning subjects of Hindu law were recognised by the courts of law. It was further embodied in judicial pronouncements and then jurisprudentially developed in such pronouncements by the various Courts of India. Special provisions for particular customs also found their way into legislation for the purpose of accommodating minority communities.

Section 29 of the *Hindu Marriage Act 1955* retains customary grounds for a mode of divorce that were there before the enforcement of this Act. Thereby, if a custom allows parties to obtain a divorce, it will be valid even if it does not come under any of the grounds that are available to parties for obtaining a divorce under section 13, provided that such custom fulfils the required validity tests. In *Shakuntalabai v. Kulkarni,*[81] the Supreme Court of India held that an unbroken custom of divorce could be recognised under the law. Thus, a valid marriage can be dissolved by a customary mode of divorce. Besides, no provision of the Hindu Marriage Act 1955 such as – (1) one year's bar to divorce (the fair trial rule) under Section 14, (2) bars laid to divorce under section 24, or (3) any ancillary relief under section 24 or 25 would apply to such customary forms of divorce.[82]

---

[81] *Shakuntalabai v. Kulkarni* (1989 SC 1309).
[82] Dr Vijender Kumar, *Mayne's Treatise on Hindu Law and Usage* (New Delhi: Bharat Law House Pvt. Ltd., 2014): 17.

There has been a justified distinction between customs, civic or civil law and religious law. Though a custom was not recognised if it was in contravention of religious matters, in civil matters a custom contrary to written law was considered valid. Thus, any condemnation of a custom in Smritis would not affect the validity of customs regarding civil law matters.[83] Contrary to this, today the rule of law or a written law will prevail. For instance, section 5 of the *Hindu Marriage Act 1955* contains some essential conditions for a valid marriage. Two conditions under this section mention that the parties to marriage must not be within a prohibited degree of relationship with each other and should not be *sapindas*[84] to each other.

However, if there is a custom in the community to which the parties to marriage belong that allows such marriages in contravention of general laws, it can be considered valid in the eyes of law. Similarly, Section 7 allows for the customary rights of different communities to solemnize marriages that are a deviation from the general norms. Section 29(2) allows a party to obtain customary forms of divorce not covered in any of the grounds available to parties to obtain a divorce under the *Hindu Marriage Act 1955*.[85]

Secondly, it is propounded that while deciding a case involving issues of custom, the courts should not draw a chronological analogy of how the custom ought to be, rather they should seek evidence confirming the existence of the custom. A court should also not deduce the existence of a custom from the mere existence of another custom. Lastly, to be established as a binding law in a court of law, the custom has to fulfil the specific requirements of a valid custom.

---

[83] Ibid, p. 50.

[84] Sapindas are referred as relatives with prohibited degree of relationship for marriage under S. 3 (f) of Hindu *Marriage Act 1955*.

[85] P.J. Fitzgerald, *Salmond on Jurisprudence* (New Delhi: Universal Law Publishing Co. Pvt. Ltd., 2010): 12.

4.4 REFLECTION OF HINDU LAWS ON LEGISLATIVE PRINCIPLES

The *Constitution of India 1950* postulates separation between a secular domain administered by the State and that of a religious domain, and forbids interference in religious matters. Judicial pronouncements and observations have a far-reaching impact on regulations and conceptions of religious issues and practices. Thus, such interpretations have impacted the regular and day to day life of individuals in many cases. For instance, various definitions pertaining to religious connotations were given judicial colour in order to attain progressive realisation of Hindu law, philosophy, customs and practices.

The definition of worshipper and on what basis he would have – (1) the right to enter into legal proceedings, or (2) what *locus standi* would the worshipper have in a public interest litigation was a subject matter that was dealt with in a statute pertaining to temples in Tamil Nadu. Section 6 (15) (b) of the *Tamil Nadu Hindu Religious and Charitable Endowments Act, 1959* explains that it is *"a person who is entitled to attend at or is in the habit of attending the performance of worship or service in the temple, or who is entitled to partake or is in the habit of partaking in the benefit of the distribution of gifts thereat"* (quoted in *Chockalingam* 2010: §33). Thus, only worshippers at a given temple may petition a court about matters regarding that specific temple.

This may indeed sound restrictive to the public at large and the issue was settled by the High Court of Madras in one of its observations. It held that definition actually allows almost any person recognised as Hindu and claiming to be a worshipper to have *locus standi* in a local temple's dispute, without having ever been to that temple - reinforcing the trend to see Hinduism as a matter of an individual's choice within a larger national or global community of Hindus. But on the contrary, not many interpretations of court were observed to be as permissive. For example, the definition of "religious ceremony" was held by the Supreme Court of India to be a ceremony which ends as soon as offerings are made and thus, any act of collective offerings after this act of offerings was not a part of religious duty.[86] Such are the instances when the imposing legal observations would directly affect the way such litigations would decide the impact on the public and their religious life.[87]

Furthermore, the right to worship has been much in conflict as regards the theme of law and religion going hand in hand. In the case of *Kantaru Rajeevaru v. Indian Young Lawyers Association and Ors,*[88] which is popularly known as the *Sabrimala Temple Review Case*, the legal position with regard to the entry of women into the temple was in question. It was considered that the presence of women in the temple would deviate the deity from his state of celibacy, the assertion being that women would not be able to undertake the ritual of *Vrutham* forming major grounds for the denial of entry to women of menstruating age. The ritual of *Vrutham*isis is considered mandatory for pilgrimage to the Sabarimala Temple and includes leading the life of a Brahmachari and distancing oneself from one's family for a period of 41 days preceding the pilgrimage.

The petitioners in the case contended that such denial of entry into the temple is a direct violation of Article 25 of the *Constitution of India 1950* that expressly provides grant rights pertaining to the practice of religion of one's choice - and entering into the temple is one of the myriad ways through which a citizen or devotee can exercise such a right. Secondly, it was also argued that this practice was in direct violation to Articles 14 and 15 of the Constitution of India 1950 as it was discriminatory to women at large while giving men the right to entry based on gender. The Respondent in the same case contended that devotees of *Lord Ayyappa* constitute a religious denomination and retain the freedom to manage their own affairs in matters of religion. Thus, this was a case wherein there was

---

[86] *Shri Jagannath Temple Puri Management Committee represented through its Administrator and Ors. vs. ChintamaniKhuntia and Ors.* AIR 1997 SC 3839.
[87] Gilles Tarabout, "Ruling on Rituals: Courts of Law and Religious Practices in Contemporary Hinduism," *South Asia Multidisciplinary Academic Journal* 17 (2018): 1-20, 13.
[88] *Kantaru Rajeevaru v. Indian Young Lawyers Association and Ors* [2019] 8 MLJ 227.

clear conflict between the law and religion alongside the conflict between preservation and reformation.

Presently, the above case pertaining to denial of entry of women in that specific temple is pending before the court and has been referred to a larger bench. However, the judgment of two judges, Indu Malhotra, J and D.Y. Chandrachud, J., who rendered the dissenting and concurrent judgments in said case respectively, is crucial for understanding the position of such conflicts that frequently arise between religion and law. Justice Indu Malhotra found the worshippers of Lord Ayyappa to constitute a separate religious denomination and the custom of not allowing entry to women aged 10-50 years a practice essential to the religious traditions of the Sabarimala Temple. Justice Indu Malhotra also held the restriction was an essential practice as a NaishtikBrahmachari and was closely related to the worship of Lord Ayyappa. Justice Indu Malhotra considered it as an enabling provision that empowered the legislature to enact laws to dispel religious practices that are pernicious and oppressive in nature and she strongly affirmed that judicial review of religious practices ought not to be taken by courts of law since it would "negate freedom to practice one's religion with one's beliefs and faith."

On the contrary, Justice D.Y. Chandrachud viewed Article 25(2) to be reformatory in nature, in consonance with the constitutional objective to provide *"justice to those who are victims to traditional belief systems founded in graded inequality"* and guarantee to "protect the dignity of all individuals who have faced systematic discrimination, prejudice and social exclusion". Lastly, after deliberations on this matter, there is room for questions for the consideration of the Indian legal system, such as – (1) the denial of the entrance into the mosque and dargahs for Muslim women, (2) the female genital mutilation between Dawoodi Bohras and (3) the denial of entry into the Agyari of Parsi for women who are married to non-Parsi seeking equal attention, and so forth.

The deep roots of the discourse and engagement of law with religion in India are assumed by such engagement. As a result, legislations have evolved from Hindu practices and customs which can act as a source of law and eventually impact the day to day lives of people living in society.

5 FINAL COMMENTS

The Indian legal framework is the outcome of what was conceived during the Vedic era, as the earliest inhabitants of Indian sub-continent (*Bharatvarsha*) professed the Hindu religion. Hindu texts, scriptures, commentaries, literature and so forth have aided construction of the law of the land over millennia, although greater changes are evident as the concentration of law due to evolution within society has been broadened. Indian legal jurisprudence has evolved through the prism of the past and accordingly modern laws remain influenced by the principles of Hindu law and jurisprudence.

Historically, different religions dominated or fully controlled the legal systems of India, but today it is undoubtedly the Constitution of India that determines the scope and proportion of religion in the lives of an individual. In spite of this, in present-day India, the role of Hindu customs, religious practices, traditions and values continues to play a significant role, or a source of law. Therefore, the impact of Hindu law and jurisprudence on the Indian legal system and legislations can be observed with ease.

India is a secular democracy; the state does not have any official religion and does not create a wall of separation between religions. However, over the years, it has become evident that India does not need total exclusion of the Hindu religion, or any religion for that matter, from affairs of the State. The only requirement is that Constitution of India obligates the state – (1) to regulate religions if required, (2) to ensure the equality of all religions without any discrimination either directly or indirectly, and (2) any deviance from equality of religions needs to be adjudicated by the judiciary in India.

BIBLIOGRAPHY

o   L. Basham, *The Wonder that was India* (Delhi: Picador India, 2004).

o   Bibek Debroy, *The Valmiki Ramayana* (New Delhi: Penguin Random House India Private Limited 2017).

o   P. Sinha, *Dynastic History of Magadha* (New Delhi: Abhinav Publications, 1977).

o   J. Fuller, "Hinduism and Scriptural Authority in Modern Indian Law," *Comparative Studies in Society & History* 30, no.2 (1988).

o   Catherine Clementin-Ojha, "India that is Bharat...: One Country, Two Names," *South Asia Multidisciplinary Academic Journal* 10, no. 1 (2014): 1-21.

o   R. Davis Jr, "Hinduism as a legal tradition," *Journal of the American Academy of Religion* 75 (2007): 241. Donald R. Davis Jr., "Hinduism as a legal tradition," *Journal of the American Academy of Religion* 75, no. 2, (2007): 241-267.

o   Domenico Francavilla, *"The Hindu Tradition: A History"* in *Routledge Handbook of Religious Laws* (New York: Routledge, 2019).

o   David Kinsley, *Hindu Goddesses* (California: University of California Press, 1988).

o   Dr Vijender Kumar, *Mayne's Treatise on Hindu Law and Usage* (New Delhi: Bharat Law House Pvt. Ltd., 2014).

o   Eknath Easwaran, *The Upanishads* (New Delhi: Nilgiri Press, 2009).

o   Frits Staal, *Discovering the Vedas: Origins, Mantras, Rituals, Insights* (New Delhi: Penguin Books India, 2008).

o   Geetanjali Srikantan, "Towards New Conceptual Approaches in Legal History: Rethinking 'Hindu Law' through Weber's Sociology of Religion" in Thomas Duve (ed.), *Entanglemens in Legal History: Conceptual Approaches* (Frankfurt am Main 2014).

o   Gilles Tarabout, "Ruling on Rituals: Courts of Law and Religious Practices in Contemporary Hinduism," *South Asia Multidisciplinary Academic Journal* 17 (2018) 1-20.

o   H.L.A Hart, *The Concept of Law* (New York: Oxford University Press, 1972).

o   Hemchandra Raychaudary, *Political History of Ancient India: From Accession of Parikshit to the Extinction of the Gupta Dynasty* (New Delhi: Cosmo Publications, 2006).

o   John Grimes, Sushil Mittal & Gene Thursby, *Religions of India* (New York: Routledge; Taylor and Francis Group, 2017).

o   J. Low, "On the Laws of Mu'ung Thai or Siam," *Journal of Indian Archipelago* I, (1847).

o   Jacobus A. Naudé and Cynthia L. Miller-Naudé, *Sacred writings 1; The Routledge handbook of literary translation* (New York: Routledge Publications, 2018).

o   Juan Mascaro, *The Bhagavad Gita* (London: Penguin Publishing Group, 2003).

o   Jugal Kishor Sharma, *Punya Bhoomi Bharat* (New Delhi: Suruchi Prakashan, 1993).

o   J. Heitzman, "Temple urbanism in medieval South India," *The Journal of Asian Studies* 46 no. 4 (1987).

o   J. W. Mccrindle, *Ancient India: As described by Megasthenes and Arrian* (Delhi: Munshiram Manoharlal Publishers, 2000).

o   Keshav Jha, "Sources of Hindu Law: A Comprehensive View," *International Journal of Research and Analytical Reviews* 6 (2019): 592-595.

o   Keith Hill, *The Bhagavad Gita* (New Zealand: Attar Books, 2009).

o   Klaus Schlichtman, *A Peace History of India: From Ashoka Maurya to Mahatama Gandhi* (New Delhi: Vij Books Pvt. Ltd., 2016).

o   Ludo Rocher, "Lawyers in Classical Hindu Law," *Law and Society Review* 3 (1969).

o   M. K. Sinha, "Hinduism and International humanitarian law," *International Review of the Red Cross* 87 (2005).

o   Martin Ramstedt, *Hinduism in Modern Indonesia* (London: Routledge Curzon, 2004).

o   Mahatma Gandhi, *The Bhagvad Gita: According to Gandhi* (California: North Atlantic Books, 2010).

o   Manu Goswami, *Producing India from Colonial Economy to National Space* (Delhi: Permanent Black, 2004).

o   M Mohsin Alam, "Constructing Secularism: Separating 'Religion' and 'State' under the Indian Constitution," *Australian Journal of Asian Law* 11, no. 30, (2009): 29-55.

- Marc Galanter, "Hinduism, Secularism, and the Indian Judiciary," *University of Hawai'i Press* 21, no. 4 (1971): 489-492.

- N. Karpaha, Dr. D. Nagarathinam, L. Lakshmanan and Dr. R. Saravanan, "A Comparative Study of the Death of Vali from the Epic Ramayana and the Death of Julius Caesar from Shakespeare's Julius Caesar," *Language in India 20*, no. 7 (2020).

- N.C. Sen Gupta, *Evolution of Ancient Indian Law* (Calcutta: A. Probsthain, 1954).

- Purusottama Bilimoria, "On the Idea of Authorless Revelation (Apauruseya)" in R. W. Perrett, *Indian Philosophy of Religion* (Netherlands: Kluwer Academic Publishers, 1989).

- P. K. Gautam, "The Cholas," *Journal of Defence Studies* 7, no. 4 (2013).

- Patrick Olivelle and Donald Richards Davis, *Hindu Law: A New History of Dharmasastra* (Oxford: Oxford University Press, 2018).

- P.J. Fitzgerald, *Salmond on Jurisprudence* (New Delhi: Universal Law Publishing Co. Pvt. Ltd., 2010).

- R. Lingat & J.D.M. Derrett, *The Classical Law of India* (Berkeley: University of California Press, 1973).

- Raj Pruthi, *Vedic Civilization* (New Delhi: Discovery Publishing House, 2004).

- Romila Thapar, *A History of India: From Origins to 1300* (London: Penguin Books, 1990).

- Ranbir Chakravarti, "Merchants and state society: some case studies from early historic period and the 'threshold times' (c. 600 BC to AD 700)," *Studies in People History* 6, (2019).

- Shashi BhiushanSahai, *The Hindu Civilisation: A miracle History* (New Delhi: Gyan Publishing House, 2010).

- Sita Ram Goel, *History of Hindu-Christian Encounters: AD 304 to 1996* (New Delhi: Voice of India, 2010).

- Sanjeev Sanyal, *Land of Seven Rivers: History of India's Geography* (New Delhi: Penguin Books Ltd., 2012).

- Sumantara Bose, *Kashmir: Roots of Conflict; Paths to Peace* (Cambridge: Harvard University Press, 2005).

- Timothy Lubin, Donald R. Davis Jr and Jayanth K. Krishnan, *Hinduism and Law: An Introduction* (New York: Cambridge Press University, 2010).

- Tirthankar Roy & Anand V. Swamy, *Law and the Economy in Colonial India* (Chicago: University of Chicago Press, 2021).

o   Thomas Andrew Lumisden Strange, *Hindu Law: Principally with reference to such portions of it as concern the Administration of Justice in the King's Courts, in India* (Madras: J. Higginbotham, 1864).

o   U. C. Sarkar, "Hindu Law: Its Character and Evolution," *Journal of Indian Law Institute* 2, no. 6 (1964): 213-235.

o   V. Roebuck, *The Upanishads* (London: Penguin Publishing Group, 2004).

o   V. D. Mahajan, *Ancient India* (New Delhi: S. Chand Publishing 1962).

o   V. R. Dikshitar, *The Gupta Polity* (New Delhi: Motilal Banarasidass Publications 1993).

o   Wendy Doniger, *The Hindus: Alternative History* (New York: Oxford University Press, 2010).

o   W Norman Brown, "The sanctity of the Cow in Hinduism," *The Economic Weekly* 16, no. 5 (1964): 245-255.

o   Werner Menski, *Hindu Law: Beyond Tradition and Modernity* (New Delhi: Oxford University Press, 2008).

CHAPTER 7

THE YIN-YANG OF ISRAEL AS THE NATION-STATE OF THE JEWISH PEOPLE

Dr. Hadas Peled and Mr. Roy Katz

1 INTRODUCTION

1.1 SUMMARY OF CHAPTER

On 19 July 2018, the Knesset, the Israeli Parliament, passed the *13th Basic law: Israel as the Nation State of the Jewish People* ('Basic Law').[1] The final vote, in the early hours of a hot summer day, affirmed the bill with a slim majority.[2] The bill has been at the heart of a heated and long-standing debate among political leadership, group activists and civil society. Fifteen different petitions were filed by various civil society organisations. The hearing at Israel's Supreme Court was broadcast online. In July 2021, a mere three years following the passing of the law, a panel of eleven judges rendered a two-hundred-page decision, dismissing said petitions against only one dissenting opinion.[3]

The proclamation of Basic Law brought to the forefront of Israeli society issues pertaining to – (1) the role of Jewish traditions, (2) the jurisprudence of Judaism and its importance in law, (3) religion v secularism, (4) ethnicity, (5) the history of the Jewish nation,[4] (6) majority v. minority groups, (7) languages, (8) country of

---

[1] *Basic law: Israel as the Nation State of the Jewish People.*

[2] The Israeli Parliament ("the Knesset") has a total of 120 members. The bill was voted by a total of 119 members, with a return of 62 vs. 55 and two attestations. For a detailed analysis of the different members' voting patterns, and their affiliation to the different political parties, see the information published online on the Knesset website < https://main.knesset.gov.il/Activity/plenum/Votes/pages/vote.aspx?voteid=31013> accessed on 23 November 2021.

[3] HCJ 5555/18, *Hassoun v. The Knesset* and 14 other petitions, decision dated July 8, 2021.

[4] Abraham, the founder of the Jewish people, lived about 2000 BCE. He is even named in ancient clay tablets, dated around 1950 BCE in contracts between him and kings in Babylonia. Joseph, great-grandson of Abraham, led the Jewish people to Egypt. Jewish people were forced to live as slaves of Egyptian dynasties from around 1800 BCE to 1450 BCE. As the result of a plague that destroyed Egypt, another Jewish leader, Moses, led an exodus of the Jewish people out of Egypt to the land of Israel. Moses wrote the Torah with a prophecy of blessings and curses. The Jewish people lived in their land without a King for many years until King David's reign commenced in 1000 BCE. The descendants of King David continued to rule the land of Israel for another 400 years until 586 BCE. King Solomon, son of David, built the First Jewish Temple in Jerusalem. However, these 400 years of prosperity also led to corruption in society and it was captured by a Babylonian King and the Jewish people exiled to Babylonia in 600 BCE. Around 470 BCE, Persian ruler Cyrus captured Babylonia and allowed the Jewish people to return to Israel. In later years, Persia was

origin, 9) race (10) the rights of women, and so forth. These issues are subtly analysed from a prism of various factors including the history of Jewish people and Judaism.

1.2 INTRODUCTION TO THE BASIC LAW OF ISRAEL

Israel has no written constitution. Various attempts to draft a formal document since the founding of the state in 1948 have fallen short of the mark. Instead, Israel has evolved a system of basic laws. Basic laws enjoy semi-constitutional status. They take precedence over other Israeli legislations, guide the legal system in the absence of a constitution and require a special majority for any alteration or amendment.[5] The Jewish People Nation-State Basic Law specifies a strong legal-protection mechanism, requiring a supermajority vote on a basic law for any alteration or amendment of that basic law.[6]

Foreign observers may identify the enactment of the Jewish People Nation-State Basic Law as part of a global trend, whereby critique on secularism generates more affinity between religion and politics, while concerns over liberal disorder brought calls for a more illiberal religious order amid an anti-globalisation backlash connecting geopolitics, religion and ethnicity.

The authors, however, argue that the passing of the bill is related more to Israeli local intra-political struggles between political actors and interest groups than to

---

captured by Greek rulers who tried to force Greek worship upon the Jews. Around 60 BCE, Romans became the rulers and they deported Jewish people as slaves around the Roman Empire. In these different nations, Jewish people regularly suffered anti-semitic persecutions. Persecution of the Jews in dispersed lands was quite extensive, for example – (1) Spain, where all Jews were expelled in 1492, (2) across Western Europe, (3) Russia as a result of intense pogroms by the Tsars in the 1880's, (4) Nazi Germany, where extermination of Jews was ordered. In 1948, after many centuries, Israel, land of Jews, was established. After 1948, the struggle of the Jewish people did not end and they have fought many wars to survive as a nation; See also, <https://en.shalomfromg-d.net/2016/12/23/what-was-the-history-of-the-jewishpeople/?gclid=EAIaIQobChMI37nVju7Y9AIVRvIRCh3v1QtfEAAYASAAEgI0d_D_BwE>, accessed on 26 November 2021.

[5] Suzie Navot, *Constitutional law of Israel, vol. 557* (Netherlands: Kluwer Law International, 2007).

[6] *The Jewish People Nation State Basic Law,* Art. 11.

global geopolitical trends. In fact, a short time after the voting in of the law, the Israeli political system descended into a two-year political crisis involving four general elections.[7] Surprisingly, following the passing of the bill, it received relatively little attention in the media and did not play a central role in the subsequent four election campaigns.[8]

A compromise within the Israeli political system was achieved only after sometime, to which the Supreme Court rendered its decision (three years after the passing of the bill and the filing of petitions).

In short, proponents of the Jewish People Nation-State Basic Law upheld that its intention was to secure Israel's Jewish character in the praxis of law, and was necessary in light of increasing challenges to the notion of the Jewish state, and developments that tipped the balance between Israel's Jewish and democratic character. On the other hand, opponents argued that the law would obstruct the delicate balance and allow for the 'Jewish' element to take precedence over the 'democratic' element. In particular, the bill was heavily criticised by minorities, the *Druze community*[9] and Arab minority groups in Israel,[10] as well as by non-orthodox secular political parties.

---

[7] Meir Elran, et.al., The Israeli System: the Challenge of an Ongoing Political Crisis to National Security Foundations, INSS: Strategic Survey for Israel 2020-2021, INSS < https://www.inss.org.il/wp-content/uploads/2021/01/Chapter-2-compressed.pdf>, accessed on 25 November 2021.

[8] Spokesmen of Knesset, <The Knesset voted for Issac Herzog as the 11th President of Israel>, June 2, 2021 < https://m.knesset.gov.il/Activity/VipElect/pages/elections2021.aspx> (Issac Herzog, who played a central voice in opposing the bill, was later voted as the eleventh president of the state, without referring to the controversies surrounding the enactment of the bill).

[9] Kais M. Firro, "Druze maqāmāt (shrines) in Israel: From ancient to newly-invented tradition," *British Journal of Middle Eastern Studies* 32, no. 2 (2005): 217-239; See also, in addition, as of 2020, the Druze Minority in Israel included about 145,000 people, representing 1.6% of the population, source: central bureau of statistics, Population of Israel on the Eve of 2021, < https://www.cbs.gov.il/en/mediarelease/Pages/2020/Population-of-Israel-on-the-Eve-of-2021.aspx>, accessed on 28 November 2021.

[10] In 2020, the population by religion was roughly 18% Arab Muslim (1,636,000) and 2% (180,000) Arab Christian (source: central bureau of statistics, Population of Israel on the Eve of 2021, < https://www.cbs.gov.il/en/mediarelease/Pages/2020/Population-of-Israel-on-the-Eve-of-2021.aspx>, accessed on 28 November 2021.

The authors argue that the Jewish People Nation-State Basic Law represents an ongoing historical debate between the Jewish and Democratic elements of the Israeli state and society. These elements shaped Israel's history from its formation, and will continue to do so in the future.[11]

The chapter from hereon is organised as follows – in section two, the authors start by analysing the Basic Law: Israel as the Nation-State of the Jewish People bill and its legislative history. In the third section, the authors continue to discuss subsequent petitions and the Supreme Court's decision. The fourth and last section, against this backdrop, discusses the yin-yang elements of Israel as the Nation-State of the Jewish People, and the duality of competing ideologies and tensions between Jewish and secular composites, religious and liberal contradictory outlooks, and their religious and democratic nature.

2 THE BILL OF BASIC LAW – ISRAEL AS THE NATION-STATE OF JEWISH PEOPLE AND IT'S LEGISLATIVE HISTORY

The Basic Law, composed of 11 short articles, spells the formula agreed by the different political parties. A complete translation of the law is provided in *Annex A* to this Chapter.[12]

The basic principles of the bill state that the land of Israel is the historical home of the Jewish people, the State of Israel is their national home, and the right to self-determination in Israel is unique to the Jewish people. The bill formalises state symbols, declares Jerusalem (unified after 1967) as the nation's capital and lists national holidays. The bill confirms both secular and religious national holidays,

---

[11] Gideon Sapir and Daniel Statman, *State and religion in Israel: A philosophical-legal inquiry* (Cambridge: Cambridge University Press, 2019).

[12] *Basic Law: Israel as the Nation State of the Jewish People* (complete, unofficial translation of the final version of Basic Law: Israel as the Nation State of the Jewish People, passed by the Knesset on July 19, 2018, available at the website of the Knesset: <https://main.knesset.gov.il/EN/News/PressReleases/Pages/Pr13978_pg.aspx>, accessed on 23 October 2021. Complete translation of the text is provided in *Annex A* to the chapter.

including Independence Day and Memorial Day. The official rest day is the Sabbath, according to the Jewish tradition. Nonetheless, those who are not Jewish have the right to honour their own days of rest and holidays.

The concise wording of the law is the product of ongoing discussions and legislative processes. A mere reading of the law drops the barest hint regarding the struggle between the Jewish and Democratic conflict/duality. We therefore turn to discuss the long and short-term legislative history of this bill.

The bill raised particular concerns on three main issues: First, it defines Hebrew as the formal language of the state and Arabic as a language with special status. Secondly, it promotes Jewish settlements as a national value. This, according to opponents of the bill, maintains discrimination of Arabs and also undermines Arab minority rights to equality in land resources. Three, it confirms the right of Jewish people to immigrate to Israel. This right is not granted to other minorities.

2.1 THE LONG TERM LEGISLATIVE HISTORY OF THE BILL: THE ISRAELI DECLARATION OF INDEPENDENCE (1948)

Israel's *Declaration of Independence* (hereinafter referred to as "the Declaration") is regarded as an expression of the nation's vision and central beliefs. The Declaration is succinct, written in expressive, yet not flowery, language, while conveying the spirit of the dramatic period following the turmoil of the Holocaust (1939-1945) and achievements since the War of Independence. The Declaration addresses itself effectively to the future, defining the *yin-yang* elements of a Jewish and Secular Democratic state.

The Holocaust nearly wiped out a major proportion of the global Jewish population, and consequently ascertained the need to establish an independent state for the

Jewish People.[13] On 29 November 1947, the United Nations voted to adopt the Partition Plan dividing the land of Palestine, then under British rule, into a Jewish/Arab state.[14] Shortly after this vote, the British government decided that British rule would end on 14 May 1948 at midnight. The Declaration was proclaimed on the last day of the British Mandate, and read by David Ben-Gurion, the Executive Head of the World Zionist Organisation, Chairman of the Jewish Agency for Palestine, and soon-to-be first Prime Minister of Israel (hereinafter referred to as "Ben Gurion").

Ben-Gurion held a decisive weight on the drafting of the final version of the Declaration. [15] His pragmatic outlook appeased competing viewpoints and ideologies with the ultimate strategy of generating a broad united front among all political parties. In particular, these tensions involved the nature of the State as the Jewish State, and the duality between its secular non-conforming modern foundations and its Jewish roots.

In the decades before the Holocaust, a small group of non-conforming Jews called to leave the "old" Jewish ways and immigrate to Israel, to establish an independent state based on secular and national centred Judaism and Zionism.[16] These non-conforming views were criticised by the traditional rabbinical leadership, who objected to a "new" path for the Jewish nation. The debate regarding the traditional Jewish ways and the new wave of national-secular Judaism remained. This debate is reflected in the Declaration. Was it an "act-of-god" and "god's will" that enabled the foundation of the state, or was it attributed to the secular Jewish group, the "Zionists"?

---

[13] Yad Vashem Organization, <https://www.yadvashem.org/museum/holocaust-history-museum.html> (authoritative information about the Holocaust), accessed on 24 October 2021.

[14] United Nations, Future of Palestine, A/RES/181, 29 November 1947.

[15] Nir Nir Kedar, "Ben-Gurion's Mamlakhtiyut: Etymological and Theoretical Roots," *Israel Studies* 7.3 (2002): 117-133.

[16] Shlomo Avineri, "The Roots of Zionism," *The Wilson Quarterly* 7 (1976): 46-61.

The Declaration begins by affirming the land of Israel as the birthplace of the Jewish People, and its long-term biblical connections. It then accounts for the contribution of the Zionist movement in the revival of the state. Many of the Zionist leaders denounced the Jewish rabbinical establishment and tradition, and blamed their blindness for the upheavals in Europe. The Holocaust served as a pivotal factor in determining the right of the Jewish people to their homeland. The establishment of a Jewish state as the State of Israel is proclaimed *"By virtue of natural and historical right"*.[17] Thus, the Declaration recognises the *Jewish historical context* and the Zionist "new Jewish" model alike.

The next part of the Declaration spells the basic and common viewpoints of the Jewish State, (similar to France's Declaration of the Rights of Man and the Citizen, Britain's Magna Carta, and the US Declaration of Independence) and it provides:

> THE STATE OF ISRAEL will be open for Jewish immigration and for the Ingathering of the Exiles; it will foster the development of the country for the benefit of all its inhabitants; it will be based on freedom, justice and peace as envisaged by the prophets of Israel; it will ensure complete equality of social and political rights to all its inhabitants irrespective of religion, race or sex; it will guarantee freedom of religion, conscience, language, education and culture; it will safeguard the Holy Places of all religions; and it will be faithful to the principles of the Charter of the United Nations.

---

[17] The Declaration reads: "The Land of Israel was the birthplace of the Jewish people. Here their spiritual, religious and political identity was shaped. Here they first attained to statehood, created cultural values of national and universal significance and gave to the world the eternal Book of Books. After being forcibly exiled from their land, the people kept faith with it throughout their Dispersion and never ceased to pray and hope for their return to it and for the restoration in it of their political freedom. Impelled by this historic and traditional attachment, Jews strove in every successive generation to re-establish themselves in their ancient homeland. They made deserts bloom, revived the Hebrew language, built villages and towns, and created a thriving community controlling its own economy and culture, loving peace but knowing how to defend itself, bringing the blessings of progress to all the country's inhabitants, and aspiring towards independent nationhood.
In the Jewish year 5657 (1897 CE), at the summons of the spiritual father of the Jewish State, Theodore Herzl, the First Zionist Congress convened and proclaimed the right of the Jewish people to national rebirth in its own country. This right was recognized in the Balfour Declaration of the 2nd November, 1917, and re-affirmed in the Mandate of the League of Nations which, in particular, gave international sanction to the historic connection between the Jewish people and Eretz-Israel and to the right of the Jewish people to rebuild its National Home...." (See par. 1- 16 of the *Declaration*).

The Declaration adopts modern liberal values assuring freedom, justice and peace while citing historical Jewish sources as references. It assures the right to equality for all its inhabitants (as opposed to only Jewish inhabitants), and of social and political rights irrespective of religion, race or sex. Moreover, the Declaration specifically guarantees freedom of religion, which can also include freedom from religion, within the Jewish nation-state. Freedom of conscience, language, education and culture are enshrined as foundational principles of the Jewish nation-state.

In addition, religious members of the Jewish assembly insisted that the Declaration should specifically mention the God of Israel. Contrarily, many secular Zionists opposed any mention of God. Ben Gurion proposed that rather than refer to God, the Declaration would end with a mention of placing trust in *Tzur Yisrael*, The Rock of Israel, a biblical term used as a synonym for God, yet possessing different interpretations with a more secular stance.[18]

The Declaration affirms the foundations and the roots of the Jewish people in the state of Israel, while proposing a liberal order for the Jewish nation-state. This duality enabled common liberal values as the guiding principles of the religious Jewish State[19]

Ben Gurion, with his pragmatic outlook, led the adoption of the concise Declaration, thus avoiding a direct confrontation. Moreover, Ben-Gurion specifically recommended waiting before drafting a constitution. Ben Gurion's pragmatic outlook opted for a united front approach, which would support the efforts required for the establishment of the state.[20]

---

[18] Milton Viorst, *Zionism: The Birth and Transformation of an Ideal* (New York: McMillan, 2016).

[19] Hillel Somer, Dolev Keidar, Yaniv Roznai and Naama AbuLafia, Freedom of Religion and Freedom from Religion, policy paper submitted to the Constitutional Law Committee, September 13, 2005, available at: https://m.knesset.gov.il/Activity/Constitution/Documents/H19-07-2005_9-13-11_dat.pdf, accessed on 22 October 2021.

[20] Nir Kedar, *Ben-Gurion and the Constitution (Hebrew)* (Bar Ilan: University Press & Dvir Press, 2015).

Various attempts to draft a constitution since the founding of the state in 1948 have fallen short of the mark, resulting in the absence of a written constitution in Israel. Instead, Israel has evolved a system of basic laws and rights which enjoy a semi-constitutional status.[21]

For many years, the Declaration was cited as the main source for liberal and democratic interpretation and as a source for the Jewish roots of the state, where legal construction was required. The Declaration served as the reference point for interpretation while deciding controversies within society, and was absorbed into the Israeli legal system over the years through repeated court decisions,[22] as well as legislation such as the *Basic law – Human Dignity and Liberty*.[23]

Notably, the final version of the legislation did not refer to the Declaration, as we shall further explain in detail. However, the omission of the Declaration, although criticised, was not regarded as a decisive factor in undermining its importance or, conversely, to motivate the Supreme Court to intervene and require the amendment of the Basic Law.

2.2 THE SHORT TERM LEGISLATIVE HISTORY OF THE BILL FOR BASIC LAW

Over the years, repeated attempts to set the principles of Israel as the nation-state of the Jewish people have been unsuccessful. The bill for Basic Law ('Bill') had first been proposed in 2015 by the right-wing ruling party (the "Likud"). It returned to the discussion table in Parliament in 2017, with a series of more than 30 hearings by the legislative committee and repeated readings of the bill in Parliament between 2017 and 2018.

---

[21] Michal Tamir, "The Declaration of Independence as a Transitional Constitution: The Case of Israel," *Middle East Law and Governance* 8, no. 1 (2016): 57-89.

[22] HCJ 10/48, *Ziv v. Hamemune Bafoal Al Haezor Haironi* Tel Aviv, padi 1, 85; See Also, HCJ 726/94 *Clal Insurance Company Ltd. v. Minister of Finance,* padi 48 (5); *HCJ 10907/04 Solodoch v. Rehovot Municipality.*

[23] *Basic Law: Human Dignity and Liberty*, 5752-1992, Art. 1.

By comparison, other basic laws, such as the basic law of human dignity and liberty, were only brought to the discussion in Parliament ten times.

The heated debate was not confined to the Knesset but was repeated in the media and made public by academic groups, civil society organisations in Israel and abroad and various political parties. Consequently, several changes were introduced to the text of the bill during the legislative process.

2.2.1 A law without a "purpose"?

The "Purpose of the Bill" received considerable attention and criticism. The first bill introduced in the Preliminary Knesset Reading (May 2017) determined that its purpose was to safeguard Israel as the nation-state of the Jewish People and to enshrine in Basic Law Israel's value as a Jewish and democratic state in the spirit of the principles of the Declaration. This was heavily criticised by various groups. Jewish conservative parties complained about the equal emphasis on its nature as both Jewish and democratic state, and the reference to the Declaration which opted for a liberal interpretation of *Judaism*.[24]

In the First Knesset Reading, the Bill's "words of explanation" stated that the purpose was "to enshrine in a Basic Law the identity of the State of Israel as the nation-state of the Jewish people, and to add to the legislative array a series of clauses that deal with the fundamental characteristics of the state as a Jewish state. The suggested Basic Law will join existing Basic Laws that enshrine additional elements in the State of Israel's character as a Jewish and democratic state in the spirit of the principles within the Declaration of Independence."

---

[24] Arik Binder, "Yahadut Hatora is Angry About the Nation State Law: it shall not be promoted," (in Hebrew) *Maariv* 16 May 2018 < https://www.maariv.co.il/news/politics/Article-638443>, accessed on 20 October 2021.

The American Jewish diaspora (the largest concentration of Jewish population outside Israel) voiced deep concerns, and feared damage to the state-minority relations. Numerous Jewish organisations issued statements that referenced the rights of Israel's Arab citizens. [25]

Similar concerns were voiced within Israel itself. The Israeli Democracy Institute published analyses, saying *"the refusal to recognise the equality of members of minority groups who are its citizens also poses a threat to the internal Israeli discourse, already rife with exclusion and hatred of minorities and exacerbates Arabs' sense of alienation and loathing towards the regime and towards the concept of the Jewish state."*[26]

A particularly strong response came from within the Druze community. The Druze community has a special relationship with the state of Israel, which includes service in the Israeli military and is referred to as the "blood covenant." [27] Druze often deviate from criticism levied at the state by the wider Arab minority. In this case, however, three Druze members of the Knesset (from the parties of *Kulanu*, *Israel Betenu*, and *The Zionist Camp*) immediately filed the first Supreme Court petition against the bill, arguing that it violated basic rights, "deems that non-Jewish minorities have no status in the state" and "harms Druze members of the security forces, including Druze soldiers, as well as the Druze bereaved families who have been in fact exiled from their country despite their sacrifice for it.'" [28]

---

[25] For example, The American Jewish Committee, AJC Criticizes Knesset Adoption of Nation-State Bill, July 18, 2018 < AJC Criticizes Knesset Adoption of Nation-State Bill | AJC>; Jewish Council for Public Affairs, JCPA express disappointment on passage of Nation-State Law, July 18, 2018 <https://www.jewishpublicaffairs.org/jcpa-expresses-disappointment-on-passage-of-israels-nation-state-bill/>, accessed on 20 October 2021.

[26] The Israel Democracy Institute, Nation State Law Explainer, July 18, 2018 Nation-State Law Explainer - The Israel Democracy Institute (idi.org.il) <.https://en.idi.org.il/articles/24241>, accessed on 15 October 2021.

[27] Iman A. Hamdy, "The Druze in Israel: a less persecuted minority?," *Contemporary Arab Affairs* 1 July 2008; 1 (3): 407–416, doi: <https://doi.org/10.1080/17550910802164309>.

[28] Doron Matza, Meir Elran, Khander Sawaed, Ephraim Lavie, "The Arab Society in Israel and the Nation State Law," INSS Insight 1087 < The Arab Society in Israel and the Nation State Law | INSS>.

Following this heated debate, the final bill did not include any proclaimed reference to a purpose provision:[29]

> The deliberate omission of the Democratic nature, the Principle of Equality and the Declaration of Independence.

The bill introduced at the preliminary hearing included direct reference to "Jewish and democratic" as well as "in the spirit of the principles of the Declaration of Independence".

The final bill that was passed, however, did not include these words. This omission served as a basis for petitions to the Supreme Court. In contrast to how Israel is defined in its *Declaration of Independence*, the *Nation-State Law* defines the state in a distorted fashion according to opponents. It focuses exclusively on defining Israel as a Jewish state, yet ignores and even dismisses the fact that it is also a democracy. We shall revert to this important omission in the following section.[30]

2.3 JEWISH ARAB EQUALITY AND THE STATUS OF ARABIC LANGUAGE

When the State of Israel was founded in 1948, it accepted the existing legal system laid down by the British Mandate. Under the British mandate, Israel had three formal languages: English, Hebrew and Arabic.[31] This has been changed over the years.

Since the establishment of the state, Israeli legislation is published only in Hebrew, without providing formal translations of the legislation into Arabic or English.

---

[29] Alexander Yakobson, "Jewish Nation-State, Not This Law," *Israel Studies*, vol. 25, no. 3, Indiana University Press, 2020:167–84, <https://doi.org/10.2979/israelstudies.25.3.15>.

[30] Dov Waxman and Ilan Peleg, "The Nation-State Law and the Weakening of Israeli Democracy," *Israel Studies*, vol. 25, no. 3, Indiana University Press (2020):185–200, <https://doi.org/10.2979/israelstudies.25.3.16>.

[31] Yocheved Deutch, "Language law in Israel," Language Policy 4, no. 3 (2005): 261-285.

Traffic signs, however, appear in Hebrew, Arabic and English. Unsurprisingly, civil society organisations demanded the additional publication of materials in Arabic and English. Moreover, these translation rights were provided to Russian immigrants who came to Israel during the 1990s, and consequently, all main governmental services, in particular health services, include an unofficial translation into Russian.[32]

The bill, which was first introduced at the Knesset hearing, affirmed Hebrew as the national formal language, while assuring that Arabic has a special status in the state, and its speakers have the right to linguistic accessibility to public services, as determined by law. This provision was, however, heavily criticised. Numerous voices from Arab society stated their steadfast pride in their identity and in the belief that there is a future for Jewish-Arab partnership, requiring equal status for Hebrew and Arabic. Jewish journalists, activists and public figures joined in expressing a fear of the bill's negative ramifications on equality and Jewish-Arab relations in Israel.[33] Public Universities joined the protest as well.[34]

Subsequently, the bill presented at the first Reading was altered to include a confirmation that Arabic has a special status in the state. Its speakers have the right to linguistic accessibility to public services, as will be determined by law. Further, it included an undertaking that "This clause will not undermine the de facto status of the Arabic language." Additional critics remained with regards to the appropriate construction of "de facto" status. Therefore, the finally-adopted bill included a clearer confirmation opting for a status-quo, which accords the Arabic language a special status in the state, without however, affirming its equal status

---

[32] Bernard Spolsky, and Elana Goldberg Shohamy, *The languages of Israel: Policy, ideology, and practice* (Clevedon: Multilingual Matters Ltd. 1999).

[33] To name a few, these voices include writers and activists Odeh Bisharat, Abed L. Azab, Samah Salaime, Mohammad Darawshe, news anchor Lucy Aharish, Adv. Raghad Jaraisy, singer Mira Awwad, artist and activist Said Abu Shakra and many others., including for example, renowned conductor Daniel Barenboim, former Minister of Defense Moshe Arens, Rabbi Gilad Kariv, Tzipi Livni, Ben Dror Yemini, Prof. Mordechai Kremnitzer, as published on the popular Twitter platform.

[34] Tel Aviv University, Minerva Center, Language, Law and Justice, A series of Lecturers available at: <https://law.tau.ac.il/sites/law.tau.ac.il/files/media_server/law_heb/Minerva/Events/Language-Law-Justice2020.pdf>, accessed on 15 October 2021.

to Hebrew. This matter was addressed in most of the petitions, however, it was denied as a basis for court intervention.

2.4 REFERENCE TO SEPARATE COMMUNITIES/JEWISH SETTLEMENTS

Over the years, a series of petitions were filed against non-acceptance of Arabs within Jewish settlements.[35] In particular, such petitions were filed where the government provided incentives in the form of allocation of apartments or land, according to the bidders' background. The Supreme Court discussed a series of petitions, actually requiring closed Jewish settlement communities to consider applications on the part of Arabs. These decisions were constantly debated with proponents and opponents.[36]

The bill first presented at the preliminary hearing and the version at the First Reading included a provision which, according to the state, could allow a community, including members of a single religion or nationality, to maintain a separate communal settlement.

This stronger version of the Bill drew broad criticism, including from the Attorney General's office and President Rivlin for circumventing Supreme Court precedents and enabling discrimination on the basis of race, religion, sex, nationality, disability, personal status, age, parenthood, sexual orientation, country of origin, or political affiliation.[37] A President's open letter to the Knesset is a rare occurrence in Israeli democracy, since the President avoids intervention in the legislator's work to assure separation of powers. Ultimately, the final bill modified the text, according to which "The state views the development of Jewish

---

[35] Alexander Sandy Kedar and Oren Yiftachel, "Land regime and social relations in Israel," *Swiss human rights book* 1 (2006): 127.

[36] Aviad Bakshi, and Gideon Sapir, "Israel as a Nation-State in Supreme Court Rulings," in *The Israeli Nation-State* (Bar Ilan: Academic Studies Press, 2014) 164-190.

[37] President Reuven Rivlin, Public Letter to the Parliament, July 2018 < https://www.israelhayom.co.il/article/570267>, accessed on 20 October 2021.

settlement as a national value and will act to encourage and promote its establishment and consolidation." This provision was a source of contention for the different petitions.[38]

2.5 NON-REFERENCE TO JEWISH LAW AND THE LEGAL SYSTEM

The bill introduced in the preliminary hearing included a provision which was subject to wide criticism and was consequently excluded. That rejected provision provided:

> If the court is faced with a question for which it cannot find a legal precedent, it will rule on the basis of the principles of freedom, justice, righteousness and peace of the Jewish tradition.

The latter version of Bill presents an interesting feature, which is particularly telling in terms of the limitations of the Jewish tradition and its impact on the legal system. Although, in fact, existing legislation and judicial practice allows judges to refer to Jewish tradition while solving legal lacunas.[39]

Nonetheless, in the overall context and critique from all political parties, there was an agreement that the law should not include any reference to Jewish law as a source of law. Orthodox Jews complained that the excluded provision further undermined their rights and provided too much power for secular organs (courts) to interpret Jewish law in accordance with modern secular values.

Liberals complained that the formula undermined the "rule of law" and "freedom from religion" by referring to Jewish law as a source of binding reference.

---

[38] Gad Barzilai, "A Land of Conflict: Law as a Means of Hegemony," *Israel Studies*, vol. 25, no.3, Indiana University Press, (2020): 201–12, <https://doi.org/10.2979/israelstudies.25.3.17>.

[39] Brahyahu Lifshitz, "Israeli Law and Jewish Law—Interaction and Independence," *Israel Law Review* 24, no. 3-4 (1990): 507-524.

Minorities (Muslims, Christian) further supported such critics. Ultimately, the provision was deleted from the bill and was not included as of the first reading.

2.6 THE OMISSION OF RELIGIOUS FREEDOM AND CULTURAL HERITAGE

The *Preliminary Knesset Reading* of the Bill included a provision, according to which every resident of the state, regardless of religion or nationality, is entitled to strive to preserve their identity, culture, language and heritage. Sacred religious sites will be guarded against desecration or any other means of destruction; freedom of access will be guaranteed.

The text was highly criticised, in particular due to intra-Jewish disputes regarding freedom from religion, and the freedom of different Jewish groups to enjoy their freedom of religion. This long-standing debate was related to freedom of prayer at the Western Wall (known in Hebrew as the "Kotel"). The Western Wall is the most sacred site according to Jewish tradition. It is the only remnant of the temple house, the centre of Jewish tradition according to the Torah. The controversy relates to the claim of Women of the Wall, an international community of Jewish women who, since 1988, have sought freedom to conduct women-led Torah services in the women's section at the Western Wall. Its legal claims and political strategies raise questions about women's rights to equality within Judaism and under Israeli law, the nature of religious tolerance for non-Orthodox Jewish movements, and Israel's identity as a Jewish and democratic state.[40]

The Women of the Wall were not provided access to conduct their services at the Western Wall. In 1989, Women of the Wall petitioned the Supreme Court of Israel to challenge the Jewish orthodox group, supported by the government, to its mode of prayer. The organisation's petition was based on the constitutional right to

---

[40] Tanya Sermer, "Women of, for, and at the Wall: A Performative Analysis of Gender Politics at the Western Wall in Jerusalem," *Women and Music: A Journal of Gender and Culture* 23, no. 1 (2019): 48-74.

freedom of worship, their right of access to the Wall and their right to equality as women. It claimed that the Wall Administrator had acted beyond the limits of his statutory powers in denying them access. The case turned on the interpretation of a key provision of the Protection of Holy Places Law, enacted in 1967 to regulate access to Jewish and Muslim holy places on the Temple Mount and throughout the country. Since 1988, to date, the matter has not been finally resolved, despite several petitions and the nomination of several governmental committees, which did not yet implement an agreeable solution. [41]

Amid this long-standing debate regarding the Western Wall, which was repeatedly discussed by the Supreme Court, the Government, and the Knesset, the final version omitted any reference to religious freedom or cultural heritage.

3 PETITIONS TO THE SUPREME COURT

The Supreme Court was requested to rule on fifteen different petitions. Among those petitions – (1) thirteen of the fifteen Petitioners sought an injunction ordering the Respondents to explain why the Basic Law should not be void, (2) six Petitioners requested that the Basic Law be amended to include the principle of equality, and (3) five Petitioners requested that Respondents explain why sections 1(c), 4, and 7 of the Basic Law should not be repealed.[42] The Court had previously denied a petition to prevent entry into effect of the law before legislation procedures were completed.

It is important to note that over the last decade, there has been growing criticism of the function of the Judiciary in Israel. This criticism is addressed in particular at the Supreme Court, which is often required to intervene in disputes between competing political parties and group interests. The Israeli Democracy Index Survey indicates a continuing decline in public trust. It is in this context that the

---

[41] Shir Daphna-Tekoah and Rachel Sharaby, "Fighting for Equal Spiritual Voice: The Case of the "Women of the Wall"," *Frontiers in psychology* 10 (2019): 2199.
[42] See *Appendix A* to the Chapter for details on sections 1(c), 4, and 7 of the Basic Law.

Supreme Court rendered its decision. A large part of the 200-page decision was dedicated to constitutional doctrines, and to the authority of the Supreme Court, in the absence of a written Constitution, to annul or require an amendment in basic law to the nexus and balance of power between the judiciary and the legislature.[43]

3.1 THE MAJORITY OPINION – DISMISSING THE PETITIONS

Chief Justice E. Hayut wrote the opinion as part of the majority's decision. Hayut rejected the Petitioners' argument that the *Basic Law*, and at least some of its provisions, negated the fundamental values of the Israeli legal system and were therefore void. The Jewish People Nation-State Basic Law only safeguards and formalises rights related to the Jewish function of the country, without any ramifications concerning principles which are already embedded in Israeli society - specifically, its democratic nature and the prevalence of the right to equality.

Furthermore, Chief Justice Hayut left the question of the adoption of a comprehensive doctrine for the examination of the constitutionality of constitutional amendments open and vague until completion of the draft and the incorporation of all of Israel's basic laws into a complete Israeli constitution. Chief Justice Hayut clarified that this conclusion did not infer that the authority of the Knesset in its role as a constituent assembly was without boundaries. At this stage of the Israeli constitutional enterprise, maintained Hayut that *the Knesset could not eliminate, merely by a basic law, the core principle of Israel as predominantly a Jewish and democratic state.* This principle, she determined, derives from constitutional texts and frameworks that have been developed since the foundation of the state.

In determining that the basic law in question did not violate the character of Israel as a Jewish and democratic state, Hayut refrained from making a determination

---

43 Assaf Likhovski, Assaf, "The Rise and Demise of Constitutional Duties in Israel," *American Journal of Legal History* 61, no. 1 (2021): 90-120; See also, Gal Ariely, "Israel's Regime Conflicting Classifications," *The Palgrave International Handbook of Israel* (2021): 1-16.

regarding the court's authority to exercise a judicial review of the constitutionality of basic laws. The authors' discussion therefore focuses on the ramifications of the decision for Jewish-Democratic duality.

Chief Justice Hayut further rejected the Petitioners' claim that the Basic Law altered the existing balance or created any additional preference for the state's Jewish character as compared to its democratic character. She maintained that the Jewish traits of the state, such as its flag and instituted emblem, Holocaust remembrance, recognition of Jerusalem as its capital, etc., had already been regulated in primary legislation and developed in court decisions rendered since the establishment of the state. As such, in the words of Chief Justice Hayut, the law, "did not introduce anything new, but merely stated the obvious: that the State of Israel is the nation state of the Jewish people."[44]

Additionally, Chief Justice Hayut rejected the petitioners' claim that the Basic Law's omission of a commitment to equal treatment of all citizens inflicted severe damage to the democratic character of the state. She noted that the Basic Law constitutes only "one chapter of the future constitution." The principle of maintaining equal social and political rights for all citizens, regardless of religion, race, or gender, was expressed in the state's Declaration of Independence and recognised by the Supreme Court as a fundamental constitutional principle which is intertwined with Israel's basic legal concepts.

Finally, Chief Justice Hayut claimed that the passing of the law did not lead to a drastic change in the constitutional regime in Israel. Chief Justice Hayut held that the Basic Law did not include operative provisions that confer personal rights on individuals on the basis of their national affiliation. This conclusion is derived from the wording, legislative history, and objectives of the Basic Law. In addition, the learned Chief Justice maintained that, in cases where a conflict arises between competing components of the state's identity, the balancing of Jewish and

---

[44] *HCJ 5555/18*, section 13.

democratic values will be accomplished by means of respect for both values and synthesis and harmony.[45]

In fact, this line of interpretation was approved by a majority of nine justices and their views are as follows:

I. *Justice I. Amit* supported the Chief Justice's decision, however, while adding some clarifications on the balance between Jewish and Democratic elements, referring to the principles enshrined in the Declaration, including the right to equality, as embedded in the Israeli legal system and culture.[46]

II. *Justice O. Fogelman* also supported the Chief Justice's decision, regretting any "hard feelings" the law brought to the Arab minority. He tried to appease any such feelings by explaining that the law only explains the Jewish elements of the Jewish identity, without changing the substance of the democratic elements that govern the rights of the Arab minority. He stated that he regretted that the right to equality was not specifically enshrined in the wording of the law.

However, on the basis of legal interpretation and the long legislative discussion, he affirmed that its prevailing status was not impaired. He opined that a better phrasing of the bill would include direct reference to the right of equality as it reflects the underlying principles and functions of society and legal culture.[47]

III. The Honourable Justice D. Barak Erez explained that the law, per se, does not confer upon rights already granted. The Jewish People Nation-State Basic Law discusses the ethos and, as much as the bill generated public

---

[45] *HCJ 5555/18*, sections 19-22.
[46] Ibid, Sections 1-3.
[47] *HCJ 5555/18*, ss 1-3.

discussion, in future cases, the court will not hesitate to intervene when rights are violated in practice.[48]

IV. While Justice D. Mintz and Justice N. Solberg joined the Chief Justice's decision, they made an interesting addition to the discussion, in that they discussed Jewish sources for the principle of equality and democracy as integral to Jewish religious law ("halacha").[49]

The first rabbinical leaders to perform formal rabbinical roles at the foundation of the state of Israel advocated publicly for such views. According to Rabbi Ben-Zion Meir Uziel (an important rabbinical scholar and leader, 1880-1953), the foundation of the state of Israel was designated to re-establish Jewish law as part of the legal culture.

In the same way as Jewish people require equal rights as minorities while living outside Israel, they should recognise such rights of equality for those other minorities living within Israel.[50] According to Rabbi Yitzhak Yazek Halevi Herzog (an important rabbinical scholar and leader, 1888-1953), the foundation of Israel is also based on the United Nations' Decision, along with a recognition of the right to equality for minorities.

Rabbi Yehuda Amital (1924-2010), who was appointed as a minister by the late President Shimon Peres on a mission to reduce tensions between religious and non-religious groups in Israeli society, believes that the *Declaration of Independence* is also a significant legal source for Jewish law.[51]

---

[48] *HCJ 5555/18*, ss 1-2.
[49] *HCJ 5555/18*, ss 7-9.
[50] Hellinger, Moshe, "Individual and Society, Nationalism and Universalism in the Religious Zionist Thought of Rabbi Moshe Avigdor Amiel and Rabbi Ben Zion Hai Uziel," *Jewish Political Studies Review* (2003): 61-121.
[51] Yehuda Amital, "A Torah Perspective on the Status of Secular Jews Today," *Tradition: A Journal of Orthodox Jewish Thought* 23, no. 4 (1988): 1-13.

The *Torah*, which forms the religious foundation of the Jewish people, specifically instructs in many instances about such duties. For example, *"the foreigner residing among you must be treated as your native-born."*; *"Because you were tourists in Egypt. I am the Lord your God."*[52]; *"Do not mistreat or oppress a foreigner, for you were foreigners in Egypt."* [53]

Judaism specifically recognises equality toward minorities as an underlying principle. Moreover, Jewish sages recognised the principles of democracy. They endorsed the principles of general election as the most suitable and appropriate system for governance. These principles assume the principle of equality.

Another layer of this argument is linked to the universal application of the Torah and its principles to each and every man and woman. This humanitarian principle is repeated in the Torah. *"In his own image, God created mankind in his own image. In the image of God, he created them; male and female he created them"*.[54] This implies an obligation. Every man or woman has the duty to safeguard the principles of equality. The duty to safeguard human lives is also linked to this principle, including a prohibition on taking human life.[55]

Therefore, according to Justices Solberg and Mintz, the principle of equality is embedded in the Jewish way of thinking, and integrated within the legal system through such interpretation.

3.2 THE DISSENTING OPINION

Justice G. Karra (of Arab-Christian origins), wrote a dissenting opinion, claiming that the Basic Law denies the democratic identity of the state and rattles the foundation of the constitutional structure; therefore the law should be null and void.

---

[52] *Leviticus* 19, 34.
[53] *Exodus* 22, 21.
[54] *Genesis* 1, 27.
[55] *Genesis* 9, 6.

According to Justice Karra, the determination of the Arabic language as special and not formal disregards the accepted "balancing formula" of the state's dual identity as "Jewish and democratic".[56]

Further, he asserts the law disregards the existence of the indigenous minority, citizens of the state - the Arabs and the Druze - who are referred to as "present absentees": "present" for the purpose of harming their language and "absent" by virtue of their exclusion from the law.[57]

Further, the exclusion of the values of equality and democracy from the Constitution violates the principles of equality, which has not yet been constitutionally enshrined. The omission of the "principle of equality" and "democratic" characteristics from the law's wording undermines the feelings and rights of the Arab minority and necessitates amendment of the law to embed these principles in an obvious and clear manner.[58]

Justice Karra did not accept the "declarative reading" doctrine advocated by the majority decision. Even a declarative meaning is inconsistent with the manner in which other basic laws are interpreted and applied. According to Justice Karra, the law has operative legal implications, such as providing constitutional protection for discriminatory legislations and decisions that may be made by other governmental authorities or legislative auspices.[59]

---

[56] "Adalah Petition to Israel's High Court of Justice Proposed Basic Law: Israel— The Nation State of the Jewish People," *Israel Studies*, vol. 25, no. 3, Indiana University Press, 2020: 229–39. <https://doi.org/10.2979/israelstudies.25.3.20>.

[57] Ilan Troen and Natan Aridan, "Introduction to Adalah Petition to Israel's High Court of Justice," *Israel Studies*, vol. 25, no. 3, Indiana University Press, 2020:228–228, <https://doi.org/10.2979/israelstudies.25.3.19>.

[58] Doreen Lustig, "'We The Majority…': The Israeli Nationality Basic Law," *Israel Studies*, vol. 25, no. 3, Indiana University Press, 2020: 256–66, <https://doi.org/10.2979/israelstudies.25.3.22>.

[59] *HCJ 5555/18*, ss. 1-12.

4 ONGOING DISCUSSON – THE YIN-YANG OF ISRAEL AS NATION-STATE OF THE JEWISH PEOPLE

The *Basic Law: Israel as the Nation State of the Jewish People* reflects a widespread dialectic debate regarding the essence of the Jewish Nation State.[60] Yin-yang is a well-known Chinese philosophical concept, representing a process of harmonisation, ensuring a constant, dynamic balance of all things.[61] The authors have elsewhere noted in another article the similarity between Jewish and Chinese thinking in correlative thinking.[62] We therefore propose *yin*-yang, as a conceptually vivid symbol, explaining the intrinsic dualities in the Jewish People Nation-State.

Theologians, philosophers, historians and jurists may be at variance on the question, or even the very existence, of constant factors or structures making up the essence of the Jewish People and Judaism.[63] It is not only the philosophies that may change, but also historians' and jurists' views on the nature and historical function of earlier philosophical and theological expressions. The Basic Law of Israel as the Nation-State of the Jewish People should be read within this historical context. Ancient Jewish elements that have transcended into contemporary times are anchored in the law. For example, the symbols of the state, the Star-of-David, or the unique religious rest day, Shabbat, are accepted symbols of Judaism. The connection of the Jewish People to their historical roots and land, are once more anchored in the basic law. Perhaps, seen in the light of the tumultuous history of the Jewish people, such a decisive affirmation seems necessary and is able to generate a widespread consensus.

---

[60] Ilan Peleg, "Introduction to "Israel Dialectics"— The 2018 Basic Law: Israel as the Nation-State of the Jewish People," *Israel Studies* 25, no. 3 (2020): 132–34. <https://doi.org/10.2979/israelstudies.25.3.11>.

[61] Angus C. Graham, *Yin-Yang and the Nature of Correlative Thinking* (Singapore: The Institute of East Asian Philosophies, 1986).

[62] Hadas Peled et. al., *The Chinese Dream and the Jewish Dream: Understanding China in the 21st century through Ancient Chinese and Jewish Values* (Amazon: KDP, 2021).

[63] Daniel Frank and Oliver Leaman, *History of Jewish Philosophy* (London: Routledge, 2003).

However, an integral feature of the contemporary modern Jewish Nation-State includes a constant and active debate between its different elements and composition – Jewish and Democratic, secular and religious, traditional and modern. Within this context, the deliberate omission of the "purpose" section during the drafting and reading procedures is better understood. As noted by the Supreme Court decision, the basic law is only one step in the evolving discussion regarding the nature of Israel as the Jewish Nation-State. In fact, the omission of the purpose serves as a purpose, in that the purpose of the law is to assure constant discussion regarding the various yin-yang dualities.

4.1 RELIGIOUS/CIVIL FAMILY LAW

Constitutionalism is regarded as a key question in the formation of a Jewish nation-state. The functions of the religious and civil elements are under constant dialogue and duality. In particular, courts are often confronted with these questions in matters related to family law. Family law in Israel is governed by civil and religious law and adjudicated by both the civil court (Family Court) and the religious courts.

The rabbinical courts are part of Israel's official legal system. According to the *Rabbinical Courts Jurisdiction (Marriage and Divorce) Law 1953*, these courts have exclusive jurisdiction over matters of marriage and divorce for Jewish citizens or residents of Israel. There is no option for civil marriage in Israel, the only option available in Israel is to go through a religious marriage. Jewish couples who seek to divorce legally, even if they had a civil wedding outside of Israel, are still required to obtain a Jewish divorce through the rabbinical court. The rabbinical courts operate according to the *law of the Torah which is Jewish law* (*halacha*). Jewish law sometimes discriminates against women, since it is on occasions based on a perception of inequality of the sexes. [64]

Civil organisations constantly work to advance freedom of choice in marriage, to address situations where women face discrimination in the rabbinical courts, to change the reality in which women are forced to litigate in the rabbinical courts, and to increase the representation of women in key positions within the rabbinical court system, based on the belief that the inclusion of women in the system will lead to a change in how the law is applied to women.[65]

The Basic Law of Israel as the Nation-State of the Jewish People completely disregards such highly contentious questions. This omission is related to the constant and active yin-yang discussion and duality, rather than to admission of an agreed formula among religious and secular groups. This duality will continue to evolve and feature in the Israeli legal system for years to come.

4.2 DUTY TO PROTECT: MILITARY COMPULSORY SERVICE AND JEWISH PROFESSION EXEMPTION

Another important omission, which was completely disregarded in the drafting procedure, is related to – (1) constitutionalism, (2) the duty of mandatory military service, and (3) ultraorthodox Jewish exemption from military service. Israeli law subjects all male and female Israeli citizens and residents to a military draft at the age of 18. Mandatory military service is generally twenty-four to thirty-two months, with this period varying depending on the recruit's gender, age or professional training in medicine or dentistry.

---

[64] *HCJ 2232/03, A v. Tel-Aviv-Jaffa Regional Rabbinical Court* Decided: November 21, 2006; See also, Yitshak Cohen, *The Unique Family Law in the State of Israel* (Boston, USA: Academic Studies Press, 2021).

[65] Shifman, P. (1990), "Family Law in Israel: The Struggle Between Religious and Secular Law," *Israel Law Review,* 24(3-4), 537-552, doi:10.1017/S0021223700010062. See also, The Rackman Center, Faculty of Law, Bar Ilan University ,<https://rackmancenter.com/en/family-law-3/>, accessed on 10 October 2021.

Exemptions from the draft apply to female recruits under circumstances defined by law. Two groups within Israeli society, however, have also traditionally been exempted from the draft: ultra-Orthodox Jews (Haredi) and Israeli Arabs.

There has been a sharp increase recorded in the number of draftees who are exempt from serving in the Israeli Defence Forces due to the "torato omanuto" (Torah is his profession) arrangement, which exempts men from army service as long as they study the Torah on a full-time basis. As of 2020, 16% of Israelis are exempted from army service due to the "torato emunato" arrangement, and the numbers are constantly increasing. [66]

The deferral provided to *Haredi yeshiva* (Jewish Orthodox institutions of learning) students has been the subject of multiple public debates and Supreme Court decisions. The deferral often resulted in full exemption from the draft. At present, there is no statutory basis for the deferral nor for exempting *Haredi* from conscription.[67]

The widespread criticism regarding such an arrangement is not reflected in discussions regarding the Basic Law. However, it is an integral part of the yin-yang of Israel as the Nation-State of the Jewish people. Should modern Israel, which is located in the Middle East and faces existential threats, allow for such a broad exemption purely on the basis of Torah study?

---

[66] IDF: Increase in the number of draftees who are exempt from army service due to mental reasons or the "Torah is his profession" arrangement, December 6, 2020 <https://main.knesset.gov.il/EN/News/PressReleases/Pages/press161220x.aspx >, accessed 10 October 2021.

[67] David Ellenson, "The Supreme Court, Yeshiva Students, and Military Conscription: Judicial Review, the Grunis Dissent, and Its Implications for Israeli Democracy and Law," *Israel Studies* 23, no. 3 (2018): 197–206. <http://www.jstor.org/stable/10.2979/israelstudies.23.3.24>.

4.3 MAJORITY/MINORITIES AND THE RIGHT TO EQUALITY

Majority and minority conflicts, as well as the right to equality, have dominated discussion and criticism of Israel as a Jewish people's nation-state. The omission of the right to equality was highly criticised. However, it was not seen as critical in determining the respective rights and obligations. The *Declaration of Independence* was once more regarded, as a Constitutional source which is integrated in the Israeli legal system. [68] Minorities in Israel are developing political power and institutions are assuring their respective rights.[69] Within this context, the widespread criticism over the status of the Arabic language as formal or special, and the response, re-drafting the law demonstrates the assurance about de facto rights granted to equality of language, should not be impaired.

5 FINAL COMMENTS

Israel has no written constitution. Various attempts to draft this formal document since the founding of the state in 1948 have fallen short of the mark. Instead, Israel has evolved a system of basic laws and rights, which enjoy semi-constitutional status. Only seventy years after its founding, the Knesset, the Israeli Parliament, passed the Basic Law affirming the status of Israel as the Nation-State of the Jewish People. It took an additional three-year period for Israel's Supreme Court to dismiss fifteen petitions.

The long legislative process, the polarised widespread discussion within Israel and abroad, comprising strong condemnation alongside expressions of praise and support, reveals various dimensions and controversies surrounding the nature of

---

[68] Ilan Peleg, "Jewish-Palestinian Relations in Israel: From Hegemony to Equality?," *International Journal of Politics, Culture, and Society* 17, no. 3 (2004): 415-437.

[69] As'ad Ghanem, "The Political Institutions of the Palestinian Minority" in *The Oxford Handbook of Israeli Politics and Society*, Edited by Reuven Y. Hazan, et. al., (New York, Oxford University Press, 2021), DOI:10.1093/oxfordhb/9780190675585.013.24_update_00.

Israel as the Jewish People Nation-State, and the duality between its yin and yang - namely, the Jewish and democratic components. The petitions to the Supreme Court regarding the Basic Law mostly centred on majority/minority relations and the right to equality.

The concise law, in fact, left many of the topics of controversy outside its scope. For example, the yin-yang relations between Religious/Civil family law and the Duty to Protect: Military Compulsory Service and Jewish Profession Exemption. These are unique features of Israel, as the nation-state of the Jewish people, which allow for great diversity and open constitutional discussion among different groups in society. This is the essence of the yin-yang of Israel, as the nation-state of the Jewish people.

Theologians, philosophers, historians and jurists may be at variance on the question, or even the very existence, of constant factors or structures making up the essence of the Jewish People and Judaism. These questions will be re-visited in the future and may receive different responses, enabling the yin-yang duality. Thus, this chapter only serves as a guideline for conceptual thoughts and trends that will impact future discussions.

BIBLIOGRAPHY

Primary Sources

- *Basic law: Israel as the Nation State of the Jewish People.*

- *Basic Law: Human Dignity and Liberty.*

- *Exodus* 22, 21.

- *Genesis* 1, 27.

- *Genesis* 9, 6.

- *HCJ 10/48, Ziv v. Hamemune Bafoal Al Haezor Haironi Tel Aviv*, padi 1, 85.

- *HCJ 726/94, Clal Insurance Company Ltd. v. Minister of Finance*, padi 48 (5).

- *HCJ 2232/03, A v. Tel-Aviv-Jaffa Regional Rabbinical Court* Decided: November 21, 2006

- *HCJ 10907/04, Solodoch v. Rehovot Municipality*.

- *HCJ 5555/18, Hassoun v. The Knesset* and 14 other petitions, decision dated July 8, 2021.

- *Leviticus* 19, 34.

- United Nations, Future of Palestine, *A/RES/181*, 29 November 1947.

Secondary Sources

- "Adalah Petition to Israel's High Court of Justice Proposed Basic Law: Israel—The Nation State of the Jewish People," *Israel Studies*, vol. 25, no. 3, Indiana University Press, 2020: 229–39, <https://doi.org/10.2979/israelstudies.25.3.20>.

- Alexander Sandy Kedar and Oren Yiftachel, "Land regime and social relations in Israel," *Swiss human rights book* 1 (2006): 127.

- Alexander Yakobson, "Jewish Nation-State, Not This Law," *Israel Studies*, vol. 25, no. 3, Indiana University Press, 2020:167–84, <https://doi.org/10.2979/israelstudies.25.3.15>.

- Angus C. Graham, *Yin-Yang and the Nature of Correlative Thinking* (Singapore: The Institute of East Asian Philosophies, 1986).

- As'ad Ghanem, The Political Institutions of the Palestinian Minority in *The Oxford Handbook of Israeli Politics and Society* Edited by Reuven Y. Hazan, et. al., (New York, Oxford University Press, 2021), DOI:10.1093/oxfordhb/9780190675585.013.24_update_00.

- Assaf Likhovski, "The Rise and Demise of Constitutional Duties in Israel," *American Journal of Legal History* 61, no. 1 (2021): 90-120.

- Aviad Bakshi, and Gideon Sapir, "Israel as a Nation-State in Supreme Court Rulings," in *The Israeli Nation-State* (Bar Ilan: Academic Studies Press, 2014), 164-190.

- Bernard Spolsky, and Elana Goldberg Shohamy, *The languages of Israel: Policy, ideology, and practice* (Clevedon: Multilingual Matters Ltd. 1999).

- Brahyahu Lifshitz, "Israeli Law and Jewish Law—Interaction and Independence," *Israel Law Review* 24, no. 3-4 (1990): 507-524.

- Daniel Frank and Oliver Leaman, *History of Jewish Philosophy* (London: Routledge, 2003).

- David Ellenson, "The Supreme Court, Yeshiva Students, and Military Conscription: Judicial Review, the Grunis Dissent, and Its Implications for Israeli Democracy and Law," *Israel Studies* 23, no. 3 (2018): 197–206, <http://www.jstor.org/stable/10.2979/israelstudies.23.3.24>, accessed on 23 October, 2021.

- Doreen Lustig, "'We The Majority…': The Israeli Nationality Basic Law," *Israel Studies*, vol. 25, no. 3, Indiana University Press, 2020:256–66, <https://doi.org/10.2979/israelstudies.25.3.22>.

- Doron Matza, Meir Elran, Khander Sawaed, Ephraim Lavie, "The Arab Society in Israel and the Nation State Law," *INSS Insight* 1087 < The Arab Society in Israel and the Nation State Law | INSS>.

- Dov Waxman and Ilan Peleg, "The Nation-State Law and the Weakening of Israeli Democracy," *Israel Studies*, vol. 25, no. 3, Indiana University Press (2020):185–200, <https://doi.org/10.2979/israelstudies.25.3.16>.

- Gal Ariely, "Israel's Regime Conflicting Classifications," *The Palgrave International Handbook of Israel* (2021): 1-16.

- Gad Barzilai, "A Land of Conflict: Law as a Means of Hegemony," *Israel Studies*, vol. 25, no.3, Indiana University Press, (2020): 201–12, <https://doi.org/10.2979/israelstudies.25.3.17>.

- Gideon Sapir and Daniel Statman, *State and religion in Israel: A philosophical-legal inquiry* (Cambridge: Cambridge University Press, 2019).

- Kais M. Firro, "Druze maqāmāt (shrines) in Israel: From ancient to newly-invented tradition," *British Journal of Middle Eastern Studies* 32, no. 2 (2005): 217-239.

- Hadas Peled et. al., *The Chinese Dream and the Jewish Dream: Understanding China in the 21st Century through Ancient Chinese and Jewish Values* (Amazon: KDP, 2021).

- Ilan Peleg, "Jewish-Palestinian Relations in Israel: From Hegemony to Equality?," *International Journal of Politics, Culture, and Society* 17, no. 3 (2004): 415-437.

- Ilan Peleg, "Introduction to "Israel Dialectics"— The 2018 Basic Law: Israel as the Nation-State of the Jewish People," *Israel Studies* 25, no. 3 (2020):132–34. <https://doi.org/10.2979/israelstudies.25.3.11>.

- Ilan Troen and Natan Aridan, "Introduction to Adalah Petition to Israel's High Court of Justice," Israel Studies, vol. 25, no. 3, Indiana University Press, 2020:228–228, <https://doi.org/10.2979/israelstudies.25.3.19>, accessed on 20 October, 2021.

o Iman A. Hamdy, "The Druze in Israel: a less persecuted minority?," *Contemporary Arab Affairs* 1 July 2008; 1 (3): 407–416, doi: https://doi.org/10.1080/17550910802164309.

o Hillel Somer, Dolev Keidar, Yaniv Roznai and Naama AbuLafia, *Freedom of Religion and Freedom from Religion*, policy paper submitted to the Constitutional Law Committee, September 13, 2005, available at: < untitled (knesset.gov.il)>.

o Meir Elran, et.al., The Israeli System: the Challenge of an Ongoing Political Crisis to National Security Foundations, INSS: Strategic Survey for Israel 2020-2021, INSS < Chapter-2-compressed.pdf (inss.org.il)>>.

o Michal Tamir, "The Declaration of Independence as a Transitional Constitution: The Case of Israel," *Middle East Law and Governance* 8, no. 1 (2016): 57-89.

o Milton Viorst, *Zionism: The Birth and Transformation of an Ideal* (New York: McMillan, 2016).

o Moshe, Hellinger. "Individual and Society, Nationalism and Universalism in the Religious Zionist Thought of Rabbi Moshe Avigdor Amiel and Rabbi Ben Zion Hai Uziel" *Jewish Political Studies Review* (2003): 61-121.

o Nir Kedar, *Ben-Gurion and the Constitution* (Hebrew) (Bar Ilan: University Press & Dvir Press, 2015).

o Pinhas Shifman, (1990), "Family Law in Israel: The Struggle Between Religious and Secular Law," *Israel Law Review*, 24(3-4), 537-552.

o Shir Daphna-Tekoah and Rachel Sharaby, "Fighting for Equal Spiritual Voice: The Case of the "Women of the Wall"," *Frontiers in psychology* 10 (2019): 2199.

o Shlomo Avineri, "The Roots of Zionism," *The Wilson Quarterly* 7 (1976): 46-61.

o Suzie Navot, *Constitutional law of Israel,* Vol. 557 (Netherlands: Kluwer Law International, 2007).

o Tanya Sermer, "Women of, for, and at the Wall: A Performative Analysis of Gender Politics at the Western Wall in Jerusalem," *Women and Music: A Journal of Gender and Culture* 23, no. 1 (2019): 48-74.

o Yitshak Cohen, *The Unique Family Law in the State of Israel* (Boston, USA: Academic Studies Press, 2021).

o Yehuda Amital, "A Torah Perspective on the Status of Secular Jews Today," *Tradition: A Journal of Orthodox Jewish Thought* 23, no. 4 (1988): 1-13.

o Yocheved Deutch, "Language law in Israel," *Language Policy* 4, no. 3 (2005): 261-285.

Media Outlets

- o Arik Binder, "Yahadut Hatora is Angry About the Nation State Law: it shall not be promoted," (in Hebrew) *Maariv* May 16 2018 < https://www.maariv.co.il/news/politics/Article-638443>, accessed on 20 October 2021.

- o The Israel Democracy Institute, Nation State Law Explainer, July 18, 2018 Nation-State Law Explainer - The Israel Democracy Institute (idi.org.il) <.https://en.idi.org.il/articles/24241>, accessed on 15 October 2021.

- o IDF: Increase in the number of draftees who are exempt from army service due to mental reasons or the "Torah is his profession" arrangement, December 6, 2020 <https://main.knesset.gov.il/EN/News/PressReleases/Pages/press161220x.aspx >, accessed 10 October, 2021.

- o President Reuven Rivlin, Public Letter to the Parliament, July 2018 < https://www.israelhayom.co.il/article/570267>, accessed on 20 October, 2021.

- o Yad Vashem Organization, <https://www.yadvashem.org/museum/holocaust-history-museum.html> (authoritative information about the Holocaust), accessed on 24 October, 2021.

ANNEX A TO THE CHAPTER

The following is the complete, unofficial translation of the final version of "Basic Law: Israel as the Nation State of the Jewish People", passed by the Knesset on July 19, 2018.

Basic Law: Israel as the Nation State of the Jewish People

1. The State of Israel:

a) Israel is the historical homeland of the Jewish people in which the state of Israel was established.

b) The state of Israel is the nation-state of the Jewish people, in which it actualizes its natural, religious, and historical right for self-determination.

c) The actualization of the right of national self-determination in the state of Israel is unique to the Jewish people.

2. National symbols of the State of Israel:

a) The name of the state is Israel.

b) The flag of the state is a white background, with two blue stripes near the edges and a blue Star of David in the center.

c) The symbol of the state is the Menorah with seven branches, olive leaves on each side, and the word "Israel" inscribed at the bottom.

d) The national anthem of the state is "Hatikvah"

e) [Further] details concerning the issue of state symbols will be determined by law.

3. [The] unified and complete [city of] Jerusalem is the capital of Israel.

4. The Language of the State of Israel:

a) Hebrew is the language of the state.

b) The Arabic language has a special status in the state; the regulation of the Arab language is managed by state institutions or when facing them will be regulated by law.

c) This clause does not change the status given to the Arabic language before the basic law was created.

5. The state will be open to Jewish immigration and to the gathering of the exiled.

6. The Diaspora:

a) The state will labor to ensure the safety of children of the Jewish people and its citizens who are in harm's way or in captivity due to their Jewishness or citizenship affiliation.

b) The state shall act within the Diaspora to strengthen the affinity between the state and members of the Jewish people.

c) The state will act to preserve the cultural, historical and religious legacy of the Jewish people among the Jewish Diaspora.

7. The state views Jewish settlement as a national value and will labor to encourage and promote its establishment and development.

8. The Hebrew calendar is the official calendar of the state, and alongside it the secular calendar will serve as an official calendar. The usage of the Hebrew calendar and of the secular calendar will be determined by law.

9. National Holidays:

a) Independence Day is the official holiday of the state.

b) Memorial Day, commemorating those who fell in the wars of Israel and Holocaust and Heroism Memorial Day are official memorial days of the state.

10. The Sabbath and the Jewish Holidays are the official days of rest in the state. Those who are not Jewish have the right to honor their own days of rest and their holidays. Details concerning these matters will be determined by law.

11. This Basic Law may not be altered except by a Basic Law that gained the approval of the majority of the Knesset members.

CHAPTER 8

THE IMPACTS OF ISLAMIC & CUSTOMARY LAW DURING THE OTTOMAN EMPIRE ON THE CURRENT SECULAR LEGAL SYSTEM IN TURKEY

Attorney Tuğçe Ergüden

1 INTRODUCTION

Turkey is unique in the Muslim world as a country that has ensured their legal system is completely secularised. Throughout Turkey's history, there have been different legal systems, with states and nations influenced by it having their own separate legal structures. The Turks founded a state in 220 BCE and developed the structure of a unique and independent legal system.

This chapter endeavours to answer the question of which legal systems were implemented by Turks in the past and why they switched from old to new legal systems. In order to fully address this question, it is necessary to divide Turkish legal history into four main periods: *the pre-Islamic period*, the *period under the influence of Islam*, the *Tanzimat period* and the *Republic period*. The main purpose of making this distinction is to demonstrate the key events that have moulded the history of Turkish law. The acceptance of Islam by Turks was fundamental to these events, because it led to the adoption of Islamic law within their borders.

It is possible to see traces of Islamic law even when looking at current Turkish law. Likewise, the *secularisation* of the Republic of Turkey's laws first began by being influenced by westernisation movements that were adopted and declared as Tanzimat. However, it should not be forgotten that every period in this process carries traces of prior periods, making it necessary to examine each one in order to understand the current legal system.

Accordingly, Turkish law before Islam will be analysed with reference to the question of how this affected the Turkish legal system in subsequent periods. The period under the influence of Islam will be examined with reference to the Ottoman legal system, since the Turkish Republic is the successor to the Ottoman Empire. First, a distinction will be made between Ottoman law in the period before Tanzimat – *the Classical Period* – and afterwards.

The main reason for this distinction may be the reformist movements that started with Tanzimat and disrupted the understanding that had dominated the classical period, with attempts being made to adopt a western legal system. Secondly, the concepts of Islamic Law (*Sharia*), and Customary Law (*Orf'i Hukuk*) and the differences between these two types of law will be determined. Finally, the chapter will explain the issues that prevent Islamic law being applied in Turkey today.

The chapter will also examine the historical and sociological conditions leading to the *Tanzimat Edict*, the legal structures that were altered by the edict and its impact on the Empire's legal system. This will highlight the changes within Tanzimat's Edict that resulted in this period being unsuccessful.

Importantly, the Chapter will be concluded by focusing in detail on judicial reforms undertaken since the recognition of Turkey. Most of these reforms correspond to the initial two terms of the current ruling party – the AKP – spanning the period 2002–2011. A brief introduction will also be provided in this Chapter to the Turkish Constitutional amendments along with Turkey's membership in the European Union. Finally, the current debates on Turkey's existing constitution will be addressed in this Chapter.

2 EVOLUTION OF TURKISH LAW

2.1 TURKISH LAW BEFORE THE ARRIVAL OF ISLAM

It is understood, from information and documentation obtained through epigraphic and archaeological studies that the Turks, who established empires, states and principalities in different parts of the world before Islam, had a certain judicial system and understanding.[1] For example, in the Hun State, the judicial system took its legitimacy from the authority of *Tanrikurt*, and a certain excellence was established. The *Göktürk* Inscriptions, in the early 8th century, contained important information on state administration, criminal and private law. These inscriptions demonstrated that the Uyghurs had a certain legal awareness leading to related regulations. These regulations attached importance to the principles and legal rights of businesses, social commerce and social interaction.

---

[1] Hürol Erbay, "Eski Hukuk Sisteminden Yeni Sisteme Geçiş Ve Turk Hukuk Devrimi," *Sinop Üniversitesi Sosyal Bilimler Dergisi*, no. 2 (2018): 211-238.

Steppe life had a major impact on the formation of legislation in pre-Islamic Turkish communities. Due to the nomadic lifestyle – which was a necessity of steppe life – the Turkish Legal System consisted of rules regarding the preservation of life. The foundation of Pre-Islamic Turkish Law was shaped according to decades-old traditions and customs –*Töre*. Thus, former Turkish rulers, commanders and statesmen ruled their country, provinces and lands according to Töre. Security, food, war, hunting and their social life was organised according to Töre. No distinction was made between religions, men and women, domestic and foreign, and concepts were brought to the fore. From this point of view, Turkish customs historically had democratic, secular and universal constituents.

At this stage, it should be emphasised that the Turkish legal system of this era continued into the following years. In later years, with the widespread adoption of new Islamic beliefs and understanding, the Turkish legal system embraced Islamic law, however, it still maintained the old Turkish customs and traditions. Documented legislative procedures from the time of the ancient Turks were combined with legislation recognised by Islamic law, forming the *kanunname tradition.*[2]

2.2 THE INFLUENCE OF ISLAM ON TURKISH LAW

A turning point in the Turkish legal system occurred when Turkey embraced Islam as its religion from the 9th century onwards, which paved the way for the incorporation of Islamic values and norms into the Turkish legal system. When examining the history of Turkish law, it is impossible to ignore Islamic law because people have not abandoned their local and religious laws and customs, irrespective of whether these have been recognised in the modern legal system,. Currently, secular official and Muslim unofficial laws co-exist in the Turkish socio-

---

[2] Mustafa Sentop, "Tanzimat Dönemi Kanunlaştırma Faaliyetleri Literatürü," *Türkiye Araştırmaları Literatür Dergisi,* no. 5 (2005): 647-672.

legal sphere.[3] For example, Article 174/4 of the *Turkish Constitution 1982 (as amended)* states that only civil marriages performed by authorised marriage officers are allowed and recognised.

However, some marriages are still performed by *imams* (religious priests in Islam), without an official ceremony. Turkey's State Planning Organisation's statistical data from the 1990s shows that religious marriage ceremonies continue to be important in Turkey. In urban areas, the ratio of civil-only marriages to all subsisting marriages is 13.59%, the figure for religious-only marriages is 3.09%, whereas the ratio of couples who employed both civil and religious marriage ceremonies is 82.70%. In rural areas, the figures are 5.11%, 6.89% and 87.38% respectively.[4] This seems to demonstrate that Muslim Turks have assimilated secular law pursuant to the Constitution, but on their own terms. By combining the rules of two different normative orderings, they have been pragmatically successful in meeting the demands of both secular and religious laws.[5] Accordingly, it is critical to analyse how Turks consider and adopt Islamic law (*Sharia*) and how they apply it in practice.

Turks first encountered Islamic armies under Caliph Omar. Travels by Muslim merchants and conversion to Islam of the military and administrative staff of Abbasids paved the way for the acceptance of Islam in the Turkish nation.[6] In fact, it can be said that the Turks' adoption of Islamic law alongside their adoption of Islam was inevitable. Not only is the religion of Islam based on principles of belief and worship, but it is also a system that regulates all aspects of life, including law. That is why most nations that have accepted Islam have also adopted Islamic law as a pre-condition for its acceptance.

---

[3] İhsan Yilmaz, "Secular Law and The Emergence of Unofficial Turkish Islamic Law," *Middle East Journal,* no. 1 (2002): 113-131.
[4] B. Öztan, "MEDENİ KANUN'UN KABULÜNÜN 70'NCI YILINDA AİLE HUKUKU," *Ankara Üniversitesi Hukuk Fakültesi Dergisi* 44 (1995).
[5] Murat Şen, "The Historical Development of Turkish Law," *Hufs Global Law Review,* no. 2 (2014): 65-76.
[6] Murat Şen, "The Historical Development of Turkish Law," *Hufs Global Law Review,* no. 2 (2014): 65-76.

Whilst analysing Sharia law, the focus of this chapter is also on the *Ottoman Empire* rather than other Turkish states that have adopted Islamic law. There are three reasons for this: first, although Islamic law was in force over a large landmass for centuries, nowhere were Islamic courts' proceedings recorded as thoroughly, or records as fully preserved, as in the Ottoman Empire. Secondly, the empire was able to sustain itself over a long period of time, which allowed the judicial system to develop solid foundations.[7] Finally, because the Ottoman Empire was a long-standing state, existing from 1299 -1922 CE, it forced the legal system to adapt to the requirements of the times. During that period, the great reform movements experienced by the Ottoman Empire either brought innovations to the legal system, or led to further reforms of the judicial system, to ensure that such reforms responded to requirements. Such requirements were observed within the legal system after initiating the original reforms.[8]

2.2.1 Ottoman Law, as influenced by Islamic Law concurrently with the evolution of Customary Law

Before analysing Ottoman law it is essential to state that, upon the establishment of the Ottoman Empire, a new and original legal system was not introduced into the legal system. The founders of this state adopted a largely unified legal structure, along with many other concepts they inherited from the previously established Turkish and Islamic states. It is not accurate to say that they did not make any changes to this structure; indeed, the Ottomans incorporated changes and additions as necessary over the centuries. However, despite these amendments, Ottoman law was largely similar to the laws of other Islamic states that preceded or were contemporaries of the Ottoman Empire.[9] It should be noted

---

[7] Timur Kuran and Scott Lustig "Judicial Biases in Ottoman Istanbul: Islamic Justice and Its Compatibility with Modern Economic Life," *Journal of Law and Economics* no. 3 (2012): 631-666.

[8] Macit Akman, "The Closure Of The Sharia Courts" in *Social, Educational, Political, Economic And Other Developments Occurred In Turkey Between The Years Of 1923-193,* ed. Özkan Akman And Mustafa Murat Çay and Fatih Bozbayindir (Turkey: ISRES Publishing, 2018), 42.

[9] Mehmet Gayretli, "Tanzimat Sonrasından Cumhuriyet'e Kadar Olan Dönemde Kanunlaştırma Çalışmaları," *Ph.D diss.,* (Marmara University, 2008)

at this point that the Ottoman legal system is related to the *Classical period* since, in the later *Tanzimat period*, a great deal of change and transformation took place.

The legal system of the Ottoman Empire was founded solidly on the principles of Islamic law; however, it was not solely composed of Islamic law. In line with needs that emerged over time, additional necessary amendments were made, to the extent they were permitted by Islamic law. The Ottoman administration enacted decrees and laws, taking advantage of the wide discretion in regulatory power provided by Islamic law. When these arrangements, made by the will of the Sultan, reached a significant number over time, they were evaluated in their entirety, assessing the way they had come about, and hence started to be categorised as *customary law* (Örfi hukuk).

Before examining the difference between these two types of law, it should be explained why there is such a dichotomy. Islamic law has no provision to adapt in order to be applicable to the complicated and diversified requirements of any modern community.[10] As a matter of fact, Islamic law does not contain any provisions for the regulation of the sundry relationships of political institutions and commercial transactions, and the vast field of criminal law and jurisdictional rules is limited to the extent that they need to adequately serve the needs of society.

At the same time, there are only a few rules on public law in the *Qur'an,* such as the administration of, or internal structure of the state. Inevitably, it became impossible to govern an Islamic state with its ever-widening borders by enforcing only a few rules of public law. It is critical to appreciate that these customary laws were not independent of the religious laws; nonetheless they still possessed a secular character. Their co-existence for over 600 years during the period of the Ottoman Empire demonstrates that *Sharia* was indispensable in the Ottoman Empire and that customary law evolved over time within the limits that Sharia law allowed for within the legal system. It could be said that these two types of law

---

[10] Hıfzi Timur, "The Place of Islamic Law in Turkish Law Reform," *Annales De La Faculté De Droit D'Istanbul* no. 6 (2011): 63-74.

were not parallel and, in fact, had inherent harmony created for the welfare of Turkish society.

At this point, it is worth mentioning the basic differences between Customary Law and Sharia Law. The main difference between these two types of law is that the source of Sharia is a divine will that needs to be accepted above and beyond the human will, whereas the rules of Custom have no sacred meaning. Therefore, although obedience to Sharia was a legal obligation as well as a religious obligation, for Customary laws to remain in effect, these needed to be renewed or validated at the will of each subsequent Sultan.[11] Additionally, it should be noted that each of these types of law is focused on different, specific areas. In the area of private law, such as personal, family, inheritance, property, debts, and commercial laws, which are regulated in detail by Islamic law, Sharia legal principles have prevailed over customary laws. On the other hand, in the field of public law such as organisational, administrative, criminal, tax and so forth, Customary laws were dominant within the legal system.

The most important laws issued by the Sultans were laid down during the period of Sultan Mehmet the Fatih and Sultan Suleyman, the Magnificent. The law of the Fatih, which has a rather administrative character, not only covered rules imposed by the Sultan but also collated, determined and compiled the old rules. On the other hand, the rules of the *Kanuni period* were notable for not only being related to the administrative field, but also to the legal, criminal and procedural fields. Hence, rules made in that era were broader and more comprehensive. In the light of this information about the Ottoman legal system, it is understood that before the *Tanzimat period*, which will be discussed in following paragraphs, rules pursuant to religious law were broken. In addition, regulations made from time to time in fields that were different from legal fields related to private law such as personal, family, inheritance, property, debts, commercial law.[12]

---

[11] İbrahim Durhan, "Osmanlı Hukukunun Yapısı Üzerine Bir Etüt," *Erzincan Binali Yıldırım Üniversitesi Hukuk Fakültesi Dergisi*, no. 1 (1999): 215-232.
[12] Ertan, "Atatürk, Cumhuriyet ve Hukuk Sistemi," *Cumhuriyet Özel Sayısı*, no. 33 (1999): 743-757.

From the 17th century, there was a decline in the role of customary laws and, as a result, laws/rules could not be issued as a response to the needs and conditions of society during that time. Accordingly, the scope of customary law narrowed day by day with a contrasting expansion in the scope of religious law in Turkish society. Thus, the religious character of the state began to prevail over other matters.

This dual structure inevitably raises the question: Does the dual distinction in law mean that Islamic law was not fully implemented within the territory of the Ottoman Empire? Towards the end of the 9th century, the great Islamic scholars declared that Sharia had taken its final form and that the "Ijtihad Gate" – that is, the possibility of establishing new rules in Islamic law - was closed. Islam recognised a single law that regulated both public life and relations between individuals, based on religious orders, and that was Sharia. A Muslim ruler, whether he be a Caliph or a Sultan, could not assume the status of a lawmaker. As an Islamic state, the Ottoman State should have had no other laws than those provided by Sharia law. Moreover, as per this jurisprudence, customary law, as a rule, could not contradict Sharia and could not infringe this field of law.

In point of fact, in the Ottoman State, imperatives arising from the implementation of strict Sharia law partially eliminated the possibility of showing that customary rule actually neglected Sharia laws. As a result of strict implementation of Sharia law of this, customary legal arrangements which were incompatible with the Sharia law and even in violation of the strict Sharia law, had emerged. For example, adultery is a "*hadd*" offense regulated in Islamic criminal law, for which the penalty is specified as "face stick" or "stoning". In the provisions of the "*Kanuni Sultan Suleyman Law*" regarding adultery, a fine is stipulated for this offence. When such laws are being issued, a country's customs were generally kept in mind, but the authorities tried to prove that the regulation drafted were actually not often against the Sharia law. However, although customary law, which was contrary to sharia law, emerged due to the difficulties caused by implementation, the creators of customary law, which was important at that time, had to get the approval of the *Ulema* – persons with in-depth knowledge of *fiqh* and *Sharia* – to approve compliance of these rules with Sharia. Therefore, with this approval, while the legitimacy of customary law was left out of discussion, the moral effect of Sharia on society was transferred to customary law.[13]

When it came to courts in the pre-Tanzimat Ottoman Empire, since the Ottoman courthouse organisation was a continuation of the structure that had been developed during the first periods of Islam, they had great similarities with those of previous Islamic states. However, it is submitted that the Ottoman courthouse had a unique structure. From its establishment until the Tanzimat period, there was essentially a one-tier judicial system in the Ottoman Empire, and the authority where any legal dispute was resolved was the Ser'iyye courts. Apart from that, as private and authorised judicial institutions, there were councils, community courts, and consulates.[14] In addition to this, although there was no systematic appeal procedure in Ottoman law, it is evident that *Divan-i Humayun* had the duty of appeal.[15]

As can be seen in the following paragraphs in this chapter, the Ottoman Empire attempted to westernise the legal system rather than follow a strict version of Islamic law. At this point, it is essential to analyse what prevented Turkey from promulgating legislation or codification in complete accordance with the Islamic law.

Firstly, there was an absence of provisions in Islamic law sources for the complicated and diversified requirements of a modernising community. Additionally, the prevalent political concepts of modernising Turkey made it requisite for the state to extend equal status to all its citizens, regardless of

---

[13] İbrahim Durhan, "Osmanlı Hukukunun Yapısı Üzerine Bir Etüt", *Erzincan Binali Yıldırım Üniversitesi Hukuk Fakültesi Dergisi*," no. 1 (1999): 215-232.

[14] İbrahim Durhan, "Tanzimat Döneminde Osmanlı Yargı Teşkilatındaki Gelişmeler," *Erzincan Binali Yıldırım Üniversitesi Hukuk Fakültesi Dergisi* no. 3 (2008): 55-111.

[15] Mehmet Gayretli"Tanzimat Sonrasından Cumhuriyet'e Kadar Olan Dönemde Kanunlaştırma Çalışmaları," *Ph.D diss.*, (Marmara University, 2008)

religious differences, and to apply the same laws without discrimination. It was contrary to the democratic and humanitarian principles of that time this century to establish separate courts of justice exercising jurisdiction over different segments of the population in the same country on the ground of differences of religious affiliation, and consequently to hand down vastly varying court judgements to particular individuals in quite similar situations. Moreover, in Muslim countries, as previously was the case in Turkey, a great many Islamic codes and legal provisions have either been left untouched and disregarded, or have become impracticable in that, at some point in time, they have fallen short of meeting the requirements brought about by the continuous metamorphosis of communities, and have completely lost their ability to adopt.[16]

2.3 EVOLUTION OF JURISPRUDENCE IN THE TANZIMAT ERA

The Tanzimat Era was a turning point in the history of Turkey. It is considered to be the first official step in its attempt to become a modern state. In fact, the Tanzimat Era began with the announcement of the *Gulhane Restrict* (the Tanzimat Edict) in 1839 and ended in 1876, when the first western-style *Ottoman constitution 1876* was promulgated. The objective of this section of the Chapter is to find answers to the question of what changed within Turkish society with the Edict of Tanzimat. In this regard, one first needs to outline the reasons to enter such a process, the content and main characterisation of the Tanzimat edict, and the legal developments that have taken place in the post-Tanzimat era. Finally, it will be examined why this period was not successful and why the Ottoman empire came to an end.

---

[16] Hıfzi Timur, "The Place of Islamic Law in Turkish Law Reform," *Annales De La Faculté De Droit D'Istanbul* no. 6 (2011): 63-74.

2.3.1 Background of the Tanzimat Edict and the role of Western jurisprudence, in particular from France

What were the primary dynamics that lead to the "modernisation" of the Ottoman Empire? These can be classified under three headings: 1) changes in commercial, economic and social life, 2) the legal needs of society, and 3) external pressures.[17]

It all started with immense changes in commercial, economic and social life as a result of the Industrial Revolution. The revolution increased commercial and economic vitality in the western world and created a need to search for new markets for products manufactured in Western Europe. In this scenario, the Ottoman Empire attracted the attention of western traders due to its large market, and this resulted in many agreements being signed with western countries. Other states followed the *Balta Harbour Trade Agreement* signed with England in 1838 and, as a result, a revival of trade with Westerners began in the Ottoman Empire.[18] When these fresh developments brought commercial conflicts, new regulations were implemented, first in the courthouse structure and subsequently in the laws applied to resolve these new problems. As a result, commercial and mixed courts were established, and the Commercial Code was adopted in 1850.

Likewise, after the Tanzimat reform, an important change was made to regulations in the fields of tax, land and agriculture. Reforms in these areas constituted the basis of the Ottoman Empire's economy and, as a result, the legal system evolved systematically, an example of this being the *Land Code of 1858*.

Moreover, after the reforms introduced by Tanzimat, further modifications were observed in the social structure of the Ottoman Empire. The effects of a new education system, the increased participation of women in social life, the

---

[17] *Mehmet Gayretli, "Tanzimat Sonrasından Cumhuriyet'e Kadar Olan Dönemde Kanunlaştırma Çalışmaları," Ph.D diss.*, (Marmara University, 2008)

[18] Aydın Yetkin, "Osmanli Devleti'nde Hukuk Devletinin Gelişim Süreci," *Uluslararası Sosyal Araştırmalar Dergisi*, no. 24 (2013): 380-413.

development of women's rights, the publication of newspapers and magazines addressing women and the family, and the establishment of women's associations also necessitated parallel regulations in the field of law. The *Family Law Decree 1917* was promulgated to respond to this novel social situation.

When it came to the essential obligations of state in relation to citizens, such as the safety of life, property and honour, this resulted in the first edicts pertaining to such issues in the Tanzimat Edict and then in the *Reform Edict*. These edicts prescribed equal rights for all citizens. All of these edicts, along with other promised rights, required new regulations to be mandated. The *Criminal Code 1840*, which was issued right after the Tanzimat, and the *Criminal Laws 1851 and 1858*, resulted from such mandatory requirements for society.

Finally, in all the arrangements made after the Tanzimat, as well as the Tanzimat itself, the influence of western jurisprudence is frequently questioned by scholars in various debates. During this period, the influence of the western jurisprudence & philosophy can be clearly observed in activities involving the codification of laws in two ways. The mentality that first prepared and declared the Tanzimat, and guided developments until the end of the Ottoman Empire, took the West as an example to promulgate laws in every area of society. Therefore, it is vital to analyse the extent of the influence of western philosophy and jurisprudence over the new laws that were enacted. However, these influences were not the only reason; there were also external pressures on the Ottoman Empire to revise laws in line with other European states. There are various reasons for such external coercion to modify laws within Turkey.

After the Industrial Revolution began in Western Europe, there was a need for new markets in which to sell goods. To traders from Western Europe, the Ottoman State appeared to be a large, convenient and nearby market. The reduction of customs rates with Balta Port, and the treaties that followed, enabled western merchants to easily enter the Ottoman market. In this environment, the Ottomans recognised the need for adopting commercial legislation to ensure the smooth development of trade. It is therefore unsurprising that the first law influenced by western jurisprudence to be adopted was the *Commercial Code 1850*.

One of the reasons for coercion from Western European states was their desire to mould legislation in the great Ottoman Empire as a means to enhance their own reputation and influence. In the era of reform, the West not only tried to export western jurisprudence and philosophy to the Ottoman state, but also tried to export law wholesale.

Due to the prestige gained by the French in Europe with Civil Code in the field of codification in the 19th century, some countries had adopted this Code in their territories; this encouraged the French to also attempt to influence law within the Ottoman Empire. It is a known fact that when preparations began for civil law in the Ottoman Empire, especially during the preparation of the Mecelle, great demands were made on the Grand Vizier of the period, Âli Pasha, to adopt *French Civil Code.* As a result of these demands, Âli Pasha gave directions to the Sultan in line with the wishes of the French, but he was unable to convince the Sultan to follow this path. Even though the French were unsuccessful in exporting French civil code to the Ottoman Empire, nevertheless such demands were effective in driving the adoption of most Ottoman laws from France.[19]

2.3.2 The Announcement and Repercussions of the Tanzimat Edict

Islamic law continued to be a main part of the legal system until 3 October 1839. It was replaced by legal reforms with the enactment of the *Hatti Sharif of Gulhane 1839* and the *Imperial Edict 1856* of the Rose Chamber by Abdulmecid. The reform process continued until the proclamation of the Turkish Republic. The above mentioned *Gulhane Edict 1839* is often seen as one of the most important

---

[19] Mehmet Gayretli, "Tanzimat Sonrasından Cumhuriyet'e Kadar Olan Dönemde Kanunlaştırma Çalışmaları," *Ph.D diss.*, (Marmara University, 2008)

documents in modern Middle Eastern history, marking the beginning of an era of reforms in the Ottoman Empire. Through this mandate, the Ottoman Empire abandoned its classical concept of justice.

The Gulhane Edict consisted of five different sections. In the first part, it stated that Sharia had bound the Ottoman Empire since its establishment, and the state was strong and the people prosperous during this period. The second part noted that weakness and poverty had replaced the old power and prosperity, as there had been no respect and adherence to Sharia laws for the past 150 years. The third part stated that some new laws should be introduced to ensure good governance of the state. Section four outlined the general principles on which new laws should be based: the security of life, honour and property (civic rights) of each subject, tax adjustment and collection regularly, and the establishment of military service as a regular procedure. The fifth chapter stated how new laws would be based upon general principles and how they should be enacted.

Two important aspects of the *Gulhane Edict* should be noted. First, it was in no way to be construed as part of an Ottoman constitution that could be used to limit the powers of the Sultan. In principle, the Sultan himself had issued this Edict and could therefore also abrogate it at will. However, this edict could be considered a proto-constitutional document, as it included a promise by the Sultan to abide by any law enacted by the legislative machinery. Secondly, even though this declaration guaranteed individual rights as subjects of the Ottoman Empire, it neither challenged the sultanate nor exceeded its limits when introducing a comprehensive and novel system to replace the evidently malfunctioning Ottoman system.[20] Nonetheless, it further confused the subjects of the empire, both with its various ideologies and superficial rearrangements.

---

[20] Seda Unsar, "A Path-Dependent Analysis of The Ottoman Empire and Its Influence on The Foundation of The Turkish Republic," *The Turkish Yearbook Of International Relations* no. 33 (2002): 77-121.

There were positive developments that emerged from Gulhane Line and the Tanzimat period, though, and it can be considered as a step towards Rule of Law for Turkish society. Following these developments, a group emerged within Turkish society that slowly realised the dangers posed by the social and political regime. During this period, the Ottoman state was slowly dragged towards a process of constitutional administration. As a result, the Empire was gradually moving from the will of a single person, towards the collective decisions of parliament and the boards in performing state affairs and activities. Institutions were established from time to time as a result of this gradual change and the authority given to these institutions clearly demonstrated such a change happening in the Ottoman State.[21]

2.3.2.1 Repercussions of the Tanzimat Edict

Recognising that there was a need for comprehensive regulations for administrating the Empire efficiently, the Tanzimat administration created an infrastructure for the reforms in the *Meclis-i Vala-yi Ahkam-i Adliyye*. This assembly had been assigned the task of preparing laws and regulations, supervising their implementation and judging the top-level administrators.

The most important regulations after the Tanzimat were made in the field of law. It is possible to divide the legal regulations into two legalisation studies and the renewal of the judicial system.[22]

As proposed by the *Tanzimat Edict*, legalisation studies clearly stated the necessity and importance of new laws, the principles they would be based on, what kind of laws would be put into effect, and the conditions under which such laws should be drafted. Within this framework, studies of codification had been

---

[21] Aydın Yetkin "Osmanli Devleti'nde Hukuk Devletinin Gelişim Süreci", *Uluslararası Sosyal Araştırmalar Dergisi*, no. 24 (2013): 380-413.
[22] Ercimet Sarıay, "Tanzimat Sonrasi Kanunlaştirma Çalişmalarinin Kaynaklari Ve Metodolojisi", *Bayterek Uluslararası Akademik Araştırmalar Dergisi,* no. 1 (2019): 9-35.

started in accordance with the principles stipulated by the edict. For this reason, an intensive restructuring activity was carried out in almost every area of the law following the announcement of the Tanzimat. The legalisation movements followed three directions: indigenous/national (*Tedvin*), quotation/citation (*Codification*) and a *mixed* method.

The legalisation movements during the Tanzimat period started with the *Penal code* enacted in *1840,* which was amended three times – in 1850, 1854 and 1857. This code was influenced by French criminal law, but it was still largely within the framework of Islamic penal laws. However, its importance stems from the fact that an *Ottoman Kanun* was in the form of a secular western code for the first time in the history of Turkish people.[23] It was inevitable that this would be a first step law, since the very essence of the Tanzimat Charter was to ensure the 'life, property, and honour' of the Turkish people.

The first codification in the field of private law was evidenced in the area of commerce. From the first half of the nineteenth century, increasing commercial relations with western countries resulted in the need to make new regulations to adequately deal with problems encountered by merchants and the state. The *Commercial law* of the Tanzimat period was prepared with reference to French commercial law and was enacted in 1850.

Another important regulation was made in the field of civil law. *Mecelle-i Ahkam-ı Adliyye*, or *Mecelle* in short, which was prepared by Ahmet Cevdet Pasha and enforced in 1876, was the first civil law of the Islamic world. With many other laws enacted in addition to these laws, the Tanzimat period witnessed a rapid and widespread effort to draft new legislations.

Mecelle, based on Islamic law, had important deficiencies compared to other contemporary civil laws from Western European countries. Yet, it was a step

---

[23] İhsan Yılmaz and Hüseyin Gündoğdu, "Secular Law in an Islamic Polity: The Ottoman Case," *European Journal of Economic and Political Studies*, no. 2 (2013): 57-81.

forward for Turkey as there were previously no foundations for family and inheritance laws, and the laws on property were entirely inadequate to deal with issues arising in the modern world. From the dates of the introduction of laws mentioned above, we can say that following publication of the *Reform Edict 1856*, the tendency of the Ottoman state to follow western laws gained considerable momentum.

In this period, the most important codification in constitutional law was the preparation of the first written constitution in Ottoman and Turkish history,[24] the Ottoman constitution *Kanun-i Esasi* (*Ottoman Basic Law of 1876*) – one hundred years after the first written constitution of the United States. Even though the constitutional status of this edict was questionable, as there was no social contract between citizens and the Ottoman administration, the document was a big step towards a democratic constitutional state limiting the power of the Sultan.[25]

Although the constitution of a specific country was not taken as the basis for creating the content of the Basis of Law, the constitutions of many countries were consulted. Significant local contributions from various regions of the Ottoman Empire were also taken into account. It is submitted that it is more appropriate to mention that this *Kanun-i Esasi* constitution comprises of the mixed laws or atleast their significant influence. It is also necessary to draw attention to the democratic dimension of the Principle of Law. With the *Kanun-i Esasi*, for the first time in the Ottoman State, the State was officially organised into three units –legislative, executive and judicial.

In the judicial system, laws drafted using western legal techniques required the establishment of new courts.[26] Following the equality declared through the

---

[24] İbrahim Ülker, "Hukukun Genel İlkeleri Bağlamında Kanun-I Esasi'Deki Yargılamaya İlişkin Hükümlerin Değerlendirilmesi," *Selçuk Üniversitesi Hukuk Fakültesi Dergisi*, no. 2 (2013): 101-124.
[25] Akif Tögel, "Ottoman Human Rights Practice: A Model of Legal Pluralism," *Yıldırım Beyazıt Hukuk Dergisi*, no. 2 (2016): 201-220.
[26] Aydın Yetkin "Osmanli Devleti'nde Hukuk Devletinin Gelişim Süreci," *Uluslararası Sosyal Araştırmalar Dergisi*, no. 24 (2013): 380-413.

Gulhane Decree, and for all non-Muslims to be subject to the same rules of law, complex domestic legislation was required to implement these new concepts.

It was not possible for judges in existing courts to implement this Decree. The judges in existing courts had an Islamic law background and worked alone without assistants such as prosecutors and lawyers, and for them to apply the new laws was difficult since they were the product of completely different legal ideas to Sharia law. For this reason, the reformist statesmen of the Tanzimat tried to organise the existing Sharia courts, while at the same time attempting to set up the new courts with well-trained judges to assist with the implementation of new laws.

The result was that, rather than ending the existing judicial order, the newly established courts created a more complex judicial organisation.[27] The reason for such complexity arose due to the fact that the state was theocratic and had to constantly verify the Sharia courts and former privileges. Similarly, it had to preserve the communal courts and, finally, the Consular courts, as it could not abolish the capitulations. During the Tanzimat period, a *Nizamiye* ('regular') court system was created in the mid-1860s. Inspired by French law regarding legal sources and structure, the new courts were designed to address criminal cases and civil & commercial disputes.[28] The introduction of the new courts required a new division of labour in the judiciary. This heralded the end of the centuries-old rule of Sharia courts, which had been the backbone of the Ottoman judicial system. Thus, the creation of the Nizamiye court system signalled a remarkable change in the history of the modern Middle East.

It should not be forgotten that codification efforts during this period also have important significance in terms of Islamic law. Throughout history, Islamic law was

---

[27] İbrahim Durhan, "Tanzimat Döneminde Osmanlı Yargı Teşkilatındaki Gelişmeler," *Erzincan Binali Yıldırım Üniversitesi Hukuk Fakültesi Dergisi,* no. 3 (2008): 55-111.
[28] Avi Rubin "Legal Borrowing and Its Impact on Ottoman Legal Culture in the Late Nineteenth Century," *Continuity and Change,* no. 2 (2007): 279-303.

developed and implemented as case law. Especially in terms of private law, there was no law practice that can be compared with modern-day practice. However, post-Tanzimat, Ottoman codifications were important in showing that Islamic law was suitable for enactment and could also be functional as a law in itself.

The result effort of codification in this period in terms of Islamic law was that *fiqh*, the Islamic jurisprudence that had been inert for a long time, saw renewed development. This resulted in laws being made in various fields using *fiqh* as a resource, and it played an important role in reconsidering and systemising Islamic law in line with the needs of the day. An outdated understanding of the law, which was strictly bound to a single sect, and the practice of repeating the *ijtihad* and *fatwas* of the previous laws was replaced. There was a new understanding about the law, which could benefit from the wide scope of Islamic law, and could apply to all sects and jurisprudence, considering the conditions of the day.[29]

2.3.3 Why was this Period Unsuccessful?

Among the reforms of the Tanzimat period, the most comprehensive and important were undoubtedly the innovations made in the field of law. However, despite all efforts, the desired result in the field of judiciary and enactments could not be completely achieved. Perhaps the most important reason for this was the lack of unity and consistency within the newly developed legislation itself. On the other hand, the unity of law, which was already corrupted in the state, was thoroughly fragmented, and the understanding of sovereignty had been dealt a great blow with foreign states claiming the right to judge within Ottoman territories.

The application of Tanzimat that had set out to ensure legal unity could not prevent the legal system from breaking down further. Due to the preservation of old rules alongside the enactment of new laws, a strictly separated binary system

---

[29] Mehmet Gayretli "Tanzimat Sonrasından Cumhuriyet'e Kadar Olan Dönemde Kanunlaştırma Çalışmaları," *Ph.D diss.*, (Marmara University, 2008).

emerged in the field of law, as was also observed in almost every other field in the Empire.

For these reasons, efforts to gather the various elements under one roof and to implement the Ottoman ideology proved to be difficult and were, accordingly, inconclusive. The Ottoman State was also faced with the need to stay together in internal harmony to eliminate external pressure. In fact, some of the legal innovations carried out to solve problems in the Ottoman Empire initiated further issues. Due to the differences in mentality and the lack of a competent practitioner staff and infrastructure, each innovation needed structural changes by the Empire and such changes were not supposed to be temporary or superficial.

Hence, this legal reform process resulted in a few positive results as well as failures. First of all, these reforms, gained the Ottoman Empire time in their fight against western states, resulting in reduced external coercion, albeit for a while.[30] At the same time, for the first time in the history of the Ottoman Empire and even the Turkish-Islamic states, the Ottoman state switched to a constitutional monarchy. As a result, practices such as parliamentary control over the written constitution and administration came into force. Moreover, with the enactment of new laws and the understanding arising from these laws, legal inequalities were eliminated, and the idea of public service emerged.

It is submitted that the Tanzimat period should be evaluated in terms of the evolution of rule of law in Turkey, and accordingly should not be severely criticised in hindsight from a modern perspective. In this respect, it can be argued that the Tanzimat period was the first step in the evolution of rule of law in Turkey, even if there were insufficient powers of sanction and it was subject to reversals from authorities. The concept of codification was recognised and settled for the first time in its contemporary character. Judicial procedures were improved, and new

---

[30] Ali Sezdi, "Osmanli'nin Son Döneminden Cumhuriyet'in Kuruluşuna Hukukta Modernleşme Sürecinde Millileşme Tartişmalari Ve İslam Medeniyet Tarihindeki Yeri," Masters, (Ankara Üniversitesi, 2020).

courts established. For the first time, the status of Ottoman citizens was recognised within the structure of citizenship laws.[31]

3 TURKISH LAW AFTER THE ESTABLISHMENT OF THE TURKISH REPUBLIC

When the failures in modernisation during the Tanzimat Era coalesced with the First World War, the Ottoman Empire, which had lasted for about 700 years, suddenly came to an end. After its defeat in the First World War, the Ottoman Empire was brought to its knees. With the *Armistice of Mudros* signed on 30 October 1918 and the *Treaty of Sevres* signed on 10 August 1920, the Allies, under the leadership of Britain and France, aimed to divide and share Ottoman lands. The state administration and the Istanbul government did not have the will to refuse to sign these agreements, or to show any resistance.

Mustafa Kemal Pacha, hero of Gallipoli, did not accept the situation and launched a war of independence on 19 May 1919. A new revolutionary parliament named Turkiye Buyuk Millet Meclisi, ('TBMM'), the Grand National Assembly of Turkey, was founded in Ankara on 23 April 1920. On 20 December 1921, the TBMM finally ratified the *Teskilat-I Esasiye Kanunu (Constitution of 1921)* to be the first constitution of the newly emerging state.

The Constitution of 1921 was a relatively short document, comprising 23 articles, and did not explicitly abolish *Kanun-i Esasi*. The Sultan's rule ended when the first and second articles of this constitution came into effect. In these 23 articles, it was clearly laid out that that sovereignty would rest unconditionally with the nation and that the Grand National Assembly of Turkey would wield this authority on behalf of the people. However, the process of state formation required more detailed, rigid

---

[31] Temuçin Ertan, "Atatürk, Cumhuriyet ve Hukuk Sistemi" *Cumhuriyet Özel Sayısı*," no. 33 (1999): 743-757.

and permanent text. To meet this need, TBMM adopted a *new Constitution on 20th April 1924*. The Constitution of 1924 preserved the principle of national sovereignty and strictly prohibited any amendment to its first article, thereby ensuring that Turkey remained a republic.

The new *Constitution 1924* clearly repealed the *Kanun-i Esasî* and introduced the principle of supremacy of the constitution over other laws. However, the new Constitution did not establish a constitutional court to guard that principle. Since the Tanzimat, all subjects of the Sultan were equal before the law as Ottomans, regardless of race or religion. The Constitution of 1924 maintained the principle of equality while renaming the nation. Article 88 of the *new Constitution* provided, *"The name Turk, as a political term, shall be understood to include all citizens of the Turkish Republic, without distinction of, or reference to, race or religion."* The Constitution 1924 remained in force for 36 years, although the text was amended several times during that time.

TBMM granted the title Atatürk (Father of Turks) to Mustafa Kemal. Later, Mustafa Kemal managed to transform Turkish law and judiciary in a strong and conclusive way. With the passage of the *Judicature Reform Act 1924,* there were landmark reforms – judicial reforms, and abolition of the religious courts and the 'mixed courts'. French courts were taken as a model for the reorganisation of the Republican courts. The Court of Cassation became the primary court responsible for the review of questions of law.[32] Under it were courts of premier instance, the assize courts for resolving more serious panel cases, the summary courts, and the peace courts' justice.[33]

Under the Constitution of 1924, Islamic law was abrogated, and it was decided to adopt the secular codes of European countries. The first serious step towards establishing a new legal system was the opening of the Law School in Ankara in

---

[32] Aylin Özman, "Law, Ideology and Modernization in Turkey: Kemalist Legal Reforms in Perspective," *Social & Legal Studies*, no. 1 (2010): 67-84.
[33] Manley O. Hudson, "Law Reform in Turkey," *American Bar Association Journal*, no. 1 (1927): 5-8.

1925. This was an essential development because modern lawyers were needed to understand and apply the new legal system. In his speech at the opening of the school, Mustafa Kemal Pasha mentioned the need for new laws and stated that this institution was being opened to raise a new generation of lawyers. It was later, in 1926 that serious steps were taken to do this.

With laws taken from the West, the Turkish legal system had now entered a new era, with a new school of thought. Pursuant to this new school of thought, a few examples can be seen in the passage laws that followed: civil code from Switzerland, the penal code from Italy, and the commercial code from Germany. Also, administrative justice was re-organised using the experience of France. This meant that the legal framework was synthetically constructed through voluntary and imposed receptions, imitations, adaptations and adjustments.

The outcome was a new Turkish legal system moving towards an 'eclectic' and 'synthetic' legal system, directly borrowed and translated from and significantly replicating foreign models. It must be appreciated that it was not the first encounter of Turkish law with laws from the west. However, the new attempts could be differentiated from attempts made in the 19th century, when attempts to modify Turkish law had been piecemeal and remained strictly within the framework of an indigenous system of law. The reforms carried out pursuant to 1926 were totally different, as the old legal system was abrogated completely.

It is necessary to mention the factors that played a role in the orientation of the new Turkish state towards western law. Modernisation was a closely related issue, with the existence of the new Turkish state and the Republic. Atatürk observed that western countries were oppressing and exploiting under-developed countries. In order to prevent this fate for the Republic, he ensured that the new legal system was compliant with the standards of the West to pre-empt a similar fate. The new legal system took reasoning and science as a foundation, and he observed that development was only possible by establishing a model of society based on secularism.

For a secular state to be established, it was essential that all concepts relevant to the state be separated from religious rules. Therefore, religious rules in the legal system were abolished and laws were liberated from the influence of religion. Times were changing and it was recognised that existing laws were no longer meeting the needs of society. Therefore, it had become necessary to abolish or change the laws and procedures that were no longer suitable for the evolving community.

The multiplicity and confusion in the Ottoman legal system, which was imperial law, had to be eliminated because the new Republic of Turkey was a national state founded on very different principles. One of its most important goals was to ensure national unity. For this, differences such as religion, sect, belief and language had to be eliminated. Therefore, there was a need for a single legal system that would reflect equally on all citizens, apply to all and cover the whole country. The main purpose of Atatürk's principles though revolutionary at that time was to create a western-style nation society away from the *ummah* community – the whole community of Muslims bound together by the ties of religion. For this to happen, it was first necessary to eliminate the Arab-Islamic influence on society. However, when the system of law of one country is taken over by another, especially if it appears in the form of a code, two questions arise simultaneously: first, how are linguistic differences to be overcome by the translator; and secondly, how are the local courts to succeed in interpreting and applying an alien law?

Regarding linguistic difference, technical difficulties arose from mistakes in the translation of the code and the failure to observe a strict uniformity of terminology. Moreover, the code was translated into the Turkish language from French text, which was, in turn, was a translation from the original German text. Since the

French version of the Swiss Civil Code was by no means perfect, the Turkish text suffered from corresponding imperfections. [34]

Writers and the courts made many attempts to systematically eliminate the effects of these defects. Interpretation techniques were utilised to remedy mistakes in the translation of such codes from foreign law. Also, the legislature and courts made a valiant effort to fill gaps in the codes and adapt it to the structure of Turkish society. For example, the Swiss Civil Code provided for the protection of a person's name, although family names were not used in Turkey in 1925. A law for family names was enacted in 1934, requiring the compulsory registration of family names and making their use obligatory.[35]

1926 was also an extremely important year for Turkish legal reforms. During this year, the structure and nature of the Turkish legal system was completely changed, and Turkey entered a very different legal environment, as the result of importing many codes from western nations. The importance of the Civil Code is due to the fact that it was the most relevant law for human and social life. All life relationships that are important in private law are regulated by the Civil Law, from prenatal conception to the postnatal period.

It was inevitable that there would be gaps in the law which would cause serious problems within society. Indeed, adoption of the Civil Code constituted the beginning of a radical change in the field of civil law, freed the institutions and concepts of civil law from the necessity of relying on religious jurisprudence, and made laws secular. [36] Following adoption of the Civil Code, major changes occurred in the Turkish family structure. A new and advanced family order was created, which was of vital importance to a contemporary society. This included

---

[34] Umut Özsu, "Receiving' The Swiss Civil Code: Translating Authority in Early Republican Turkey," *International Journal Of Law In Context*, no. 1 (2010): 63-89.

[35] Hrfzi Veldet Velidedeoğlu, "The Reception of the Swiss Civil Code in Turkey," *International Social Science Bulletin*, no. 1 (1957): 60-65.

[36] Temuçin Ertan, "Atatürk, Cumhuriyet ve Hukuk Sistemi," *Cumhuriyet Özel Sayısı*, no. 33 (1999): 743-757.

marriage with a single woman instead of the practice of polygamy, converting the marriage contract from a religious to a secular structure, and attempts were made to introduce equality between men and women instead of the dominance of a husband in marriage. In 1937, secularism found a place in the legal history of the Republic for the first time through a constitutional amendment. This was also the last of Atatürk's revolutionary steps.

After the death of Atatürk in 1938, and with the new era of a multi-party system under President İnönü in 1945, things changed. The Constitution of 1924 predicted a representative and majoritarian democracy, which was not appropriate for the multi-party system introduced in 1946. Hence, capitalising on gaps in the constitution, the Democratic Party government became extremely authoritarian in the late 1950s. On the pretext of taking the country to a more effective democracy, a junta composed of young Turkish military officers staged a coup d'état on 27 May 1960.

Shortly afterwards, on 9 July 1961, a new constitution prepared by the Constituent Assembly was forced through in a referendum in which 63% of the voters were in favour.[37] Being drafted by the Constituent Assembly and approved by popular vote, the *Constitution of 1961* was unique in the legal history of Turkey. It was a long and detailed text, comprising 157 articles and 11 transitory articles. Unlike the Constitutions of 1876, 1921 and 1924, the rights and freedoms of individuals had a more prominent place in this version of the Constitution. The 1961 Constitution dealt with the real issue of rights and freedoms in Turkey and examined them in detail. In this constitution, many rights were given to the people, such as individual rights and freedoms. It was the most libertarian constitution in terms of rights, freedom and equality in Turkey. In this context, the 1961

---

[37] Halim Alperen Çıtak, "A Brief History of Turkish Constitutionalism," Lm-Dp.Org., 2021, <http://lm-dp.org/a-brief-history-of-turkish-constitutionalism/>, accessed on 20 June 2021.

Constitution can be classed as the most liberal constitution in the history of Turkish democracy.[38]

The *Constitution 1961* was substantially amended in 1971 and 1973, under the influence of the military, following the half-coup of 12 March 1971. The amendments were made to strengthen the executive powers of the government, restrict the scope of some rights and liberties of individuals, and weaken the role of the judiciary. The purpose of these amendments was to strengthen the state's authority, which terror and violence in society had eroded. However, these constitutional amendments failed to achieve the expected results.

Turkey faced an extreme polarisation between the extreme left and the right. The country was also plagued by terrorist movements, which threatened public order even more seriously than before, and faced several economic crises. Once again, the Turkish Armed Forces intervened and took power on 12 September 1980.[39] The intervention was carried out by the National Security Council, which was composed of the Chief of the General Staff and four commanders. The basic aim of the military government was to restructure the constitutional and legal order of the country and restore democracy. The National Security Council stayed in power longer than its predecessor and exercised extraordinary powers until November 1983, when general elections were held. During this period, they prepared a new constitution and adopted several hundred laws, which entirely restructured the constitutional and legal order of Turkey. Thus, Turkey inherited an authoritarian legacy, a legacy that proved difficult to eliminate.[40]

Unlike in the previous constitution, the military played a far greater role in preparing the Constitution of 1982. Members of the constituent assembly were

---

[38] Bilal Tunç, "Türk Anayasa Tarihinde 1961 Anayasası'Nın Yeri Ve Önemi," *Karadeniz Araştırmaları*, no. 67 (2020): 657-692.

[39] Halim Alperen Çıtak "A Brief History of Turkish Constitutionalism," Lm-Dp.Org., 2021, <http://lm-dp.org/a-brief-history-of-turkish-constitutionalism/>, accessed on 20 June, 2021.

[40] Serap Yazıcı, "UPDATE: A Guide to Turkish Public Law And Legal Research –Globalex," *Nyulawglobal.Org*, 2017, <https://www.nyulawglobal.org/globalex/Turkey1.html>, accessed on 2 July 2021.

directly appointed by the National Security Council (Millî Güvenlik Konseyi – the official name of the coup plotters). On 7 November 1982, the text was approved through a referendum by 91.37% of voters and entered into law. By the same referendum, Kenan Evren, the chairman of the National Security Council, was elected as President of the Republic. The transitional period envisaged by the new constitution terminated in 1987, and Turkey returned to a normal democracy.

Having 177 articles, the *Constitution 1982* is a more detailed and rigid text than its antecedents. Makers of the Constitution of 1982 projected a less participatory democracy and a de-politicised society while preserving the main principles and basic outline of the 1961 version, such as social state, the rule of law, equality, secularism, the supremacy of the Constitution, separation of jurisdictions, independence of judges, legality and liability of administration.[41]

The most important amendments made to this 1982 Constitution were the changes carried to synchronise them with the scope of the European Union (EU)'s harmonisation process. This process started with Turkey's application for full membership to the European Communities in 1987. It should not be forgotten that Turkey was the only Muslim country in the world that had turned to the West since the Tanzimat. In addition, Turkey was a country that had adopted secular and democratic principles, had common borders with the western world, and had chosen the West whilst by protecting its own cultural lifestyle values. Turkey first communicated its willingness to participate in the new enlargement process initiated by the EU in 1996.

At the 1998 Cardiff Summit, Turkey was included in the reporting system, which included other candidates. The first progress report examining Turkey's performance in terms of the Copenhagen criteria was published in 1998. At the EU Heads of State and Government Summit held in Helsinki on 10-11 December

---

[41] Halim Alperen Çıtak, "A Brief History of Turkish Constitutionalism," Lm-Dp.Org., 2021, <http://lm-dp.org/a-brief-history-of-turkish-constitutionalism/>, accessed on 20 June, 2021.

1999, Turkey was accepted as an EU candidate country on equal terms with other candidate countries.

At the 1993 *Copenhagen Summit*, the political criteria for membership declared that the candidate country must have 'ensured democracy, the rule of law, human rights, and the stability of institutions that guarantee the enumeration and protection of minorities.' These criteria were to be met by countries applying for candidacy before being admitted to full membership. The countries applying – Cyprus, Malta and Turkey - could then become EU members if they met the economic and political criteria required for full membership. At the Helsinki Summit, it was stated that accession negotiations with Turkey would be initiated once Turkey was able to meet the Copenhagen political criteria.[42]

The National Program, prepared by Turkey in response to the Accession Partnership Document, prioritised a comprehensive reform process. Turkey made the necessary arrangements for compliance with the Copenhagen Political Criteria, which were a pre-requisite for initiating accession negotiations with the EU. Changes covered various fields through constitutional amendments, the revision of basic laws and legislative harmonisation packages that served to approve more than one law at the same time.[43]

With these laws, known as EU harmonisation legislative packages and enacted to comply with the Copenhagen Political Criteria, freedom of expression, freedom of association, freedom of the press, personal security and freedom, protection of private life, equality of women and men and other fundamental rights and freedoms were defined. All EU standards were met by the new laws.[44]

---

[42] Mehmet Akif ÖZER, "Avrupa Birliği'Ne Tam Üyeliğin Eşiğinde Türkiye," *Yönetim Ve Ekonomi Dergisi*, no. 1 (2009): 89-105.

[43] Hakan Özdemir and Ahmet Çiftlikçi, "Conversion Of Constitutional State In Membership Process of Turkey To European Union (EU): About Arrangements Performed In Domestic Law From Helsinki Summit Until Today," *Fırat University Journal Of Social Science*, no. 1 (2015): 123-144.

[44] Haydar Efe and Seyfi Han "Contributions of The "Eu Adjustment Laws "To The Advancements Of Human Rights In Turkey," *Kafkas Üniversitesi İktisadi Ve İdari Bilimler Fakültesi Dergisi*, no. 4 (2012): 149-187.

Nine reform 'packages' were passed between February 2002 and July 2004. For example, the first package of harmonisation was adopted in 2002, in which four laws were amended. In the third harmonisation package, where changes were made in the thirteenth law, it became important to abolish the death penalty except in the case of threat of war, and lift the ban on broadcasting in different languages and dialects. Apart from the harmonisation packages, some basic laws were also renewed between 2001 and 2018. The first of these was contained in the *New Turkish Civil Code*, which entered into force on 1st January 2002. This code has been shown to respond to current needs, with adaptation to changes and developments in foreign legal systems. The renewed civil law included regulations for protecting the weak, ensuring equality, and widening areas of freedom.

On 23 November 2004, *law No. 5253* on associations was ratified. With the Association Law, restrictions were reduced, freedoms related to associations were expanded, and provisions were introduced to facilitate the activities of associations. On 1 June 2005, the *New Criminal Code* became law. By way of example, within it, innovations introduced with *law No. 5237* showed new crimes to have been included, and some types of crimes defined in law were changed. In addition, the importance given to individuals was emphasised in this new penal code. According to the determined legal value, crimes were listed as crimes against people, individuals, society, or the state. The *New Criminal Procedure Code 5171* was adopted on 1 June 2005. It regulated how to conduct criminal proceedings and the rights, powers and obligations of the persons participating in this process. Accordingly, new regulations were made within the framework of human rights and freedoms.

Other reforms were also introduced. One law renewed in this process was the foundations law. The new law on *Foundations (No. 5737)* entered into force on 27 February 2008. One of the innovations made in this law is directed towards community foundations belonging to minorities. To ensure the right to a fair trial in Turkey, *the Civil Procedure Law 6100* became law on 1 October 2011. The right to a fair trial requires that it be completed within a reasonable time. For this reason, changes were made to the law to ensure a faster and more efficient execution of trials. Another law that was renewed, to ensure its compliance with the Turkish Civil Code and to meet the needs of our day, was the Turkish Code of Obligations. The new *Turkish Code of Obligations (No. 6098)* was ratified on 1 July 2012 along with the *New Turkish Commercial Code*. New additions to the law included the obligation to transfer laws from the European Union into Turkish law, technological developments and the obligation to be a part of international markets in this context, and the removal of six zeros from the Turkish Lira.

Finally, it should be noted that other legal changes were made that fell outside the framework of harmonisation processes with the European Union. A number of reforms were made to the *1982 Constitution*. The amendment made to the 1982 Constitution with *law No. 4709* was the most significant change made to the Constitution so far. With the amendment to the section of the Constitution regulating fundamental rights and freedoms, limits of freedom of thought and expression were expanded and obstacles for citizens to use different languages and dialects in daily life were removed. In addition, with the amendments made in the general provisions, the 'general reasons for restriction', which are stated to be valid for all rights and freedoms in the Constitution were terminated. The practice of finding 'special reasons for restriction' related to each right and freedom in the European Court of Human Rights system was initiated.[45]

Thereafter, a lot of changes were made to the 1982 Constitution and such efforts to amend continue. All the changes described so far have a common point: the abolition of certain constitutional prohibitions, the enlargement of fundamental

---

[45] Hakan Özdemir and Ahmet Çiftlikçi, "Conversion Of Constitutional State In Membership Process Of Turkey To European Union (EU): About Arrangements Performed in Domestic Law from Helsinki Summit until Today, " *Fırat University Journal Of Social Science*, no. 1 (2015): 123-144.

rights and freedoms, the strengthening of rule of law guarantees, and the abolition or weakening of privileges given to the armed forces.

On 16 April 2017, another constitutional amendment was made which was quite different from earlier ones. Within this amendment, Turkey put an end to the parliamentary government system, which had been in practice since 1876, and adopted a presidential system. All aspects of the new government system came into force with the election of the President by the people on 9 July 2018. Notably, this system is different from the American model in several ways. While the American system is based on the strict separation of power between the legislative and executive branches, the new Turkish system is not.

3.1 2017 AMENDMENTS TO THE CONSTITUTION AND THEIR IMPLICATIONS

The 2017 amendments made the popularly elected president the most powerful actor in the field of legislative, executive and judicial branches, as wide powers were allocated to the executive branch. This meant the new system was based on the unity of powers, instead of the strict separation of powers. Thus, it is no exaggeration to refer to the new system as "Turkish-style presidentialism". The US model is based on a system of checks and balances from legislative and judicial branches, thus limiting executive power. In the new Turkish system, the legislature and the judiciary lack such powers. As a matter of fact, some powers that previously belonged to the legislature have now been given to the president, and the judiciary determine the fate of the country by submitting to the influences of the president.

At this point, in order to understand current Turkish law, we should ask whether the *1982 Constitution dated 7th November 1982 (No. 2709)*, is still in force. Under normal circumstances, nobody would think to ask such a question because this would seem to be an absurdity. However, this Constitution has not been repealed separately and explicitly, and it is, in fact, still in force today. This Constitution was accepted due to the referendum of 7th November 1982 and entered into being following publication in the *Official Gazette dated 9th November 1982 (No. 17863)*. Subsequently, there was no revolution or government coup in Turkey, and therefore the Constitution was not repealed.

One of the underlying reasons for this dilemma is that although the domestic version of the 1968 Constitution pre-supposes the parliamentary government system and there was no change in the Constitution regarding the government system, Turkey's parliamentary government system was not implemented. Moreover, the fact that the parliamentary government system in Turkey has changed has been expressed by the President himself in a speech he made on 14 August 2015. A practical example of this situation is seen in the press with an incident named 'May 4th Palace Coup'. Prime Minister Ahmet Davutoğlu's announcement that he would withdraw as Prime Minister following his meeting with the President on the 4 May 2016 is a good indication that the Prime Minister in Turkey is no longer responsible to Parliament as stipulated by the Constitution, but instead is responsible to the President.

Secondly, Article 26 of the 1968 Constitution states that 'everyone has the right to express and disseminate their thoughts and opinions individually or collectively by speech, writing, painting or other means'. However, Minister of Justice Bekir Bozdağ stated in a speech he made at the General Assembly of the Turkish Grand National Assembly on 1 March 2016 that the Ministry of Justice was given permission to prosecute in 1,845 cases of insulting the President.

If this is the case, it is necessary to ask whether Articles 99, 104, 105, 109, 110, 111, 112 of the Constitution regarding the government system, and Article 26 are still in effect. Undoubtedly, these articles are in force. Because some articles that are a part of the Constitution are still in force, the whole Constitution with all its articles must apply. The reason for ongoing discussions is that these constitutional rules that are in place are not enforced.

4 FINAL COMMENTS

There have been different legal systems in the lands of the Turks. Legal systems and implementations have been different: (1) before the adoption of Islam, and (2) after Islam was accepted in Turkey. The Turks founded a state in 220 BC and developed a unique and independent legal system structure. Turks, who maintained their existence on the stage of history with various social structures such as principality, khanate, state and empire, had often been in a position of regional or world power. They applied the system of Customary Law called the Turkish Customs that originated from their social structures before accepting Islam.

The turning point in the Turkish Legal System was when the Turkish nation accepted Islam as its religion, which paved the way for the incorporation of Islamic values and norms in the legal system.[46] Following the adoption of Islam, the transition from a customary legal system to Islamic law was not realised within a short time with a war or revolution, but gradually, over a period of time, as a result of the process of Islamisation. In the Ottoman Empire, customary law and Islamic law were implemented together. However, these two systems could not respond fairly and quickly to the legal, political, military and social needs of the Ottoman Empire that emerged as a result of the growth in all areas.

The economic, technological and cultural developments that emerged towards the end of the feudal system in Western Europe exerted tremendous influence on the Ottoman Empire. When the second half of the nineteenth century arrived, they paved the way for radical changes in the Ottoman system of governance. Legal innovations were used as a means of adapting to new internal and external conditions. It is possible to classify the legal reforms made after the Tanzimat as codification activities and resorting to innovations in judicial institutions.

---

[46] Murat Şen, "The Historical Development Of Turkish Law," *Hufs Global Law Review,* no. 2 (2014): 65-76.

Codification activities had emerged as a means of converting Ottoman legal rules into laws and law transposition from the West, especially France.

Significant among the reforms to the Ottoman Legal System were the establishment of secular courts and the adaptation of the Western European legal system. The Tanzimat reforms ended the hegemony of Islamic law and replaced it with a new approach based on the co-existence of two totally different law systems – European and Islamic. This dualistic structure has caused trouble from time to time. It was attempted to implement reforms made in the Tanzimat and afterwards in accordance with the spirit of the Tanzimat and Islahat Edicts. Most of the laws, which were implemented in the nearly eighty years from the Tanzimat Period to the Republic Period, largely preserved the traditional line of Ottoman law.[47]

When the Ottoman Empire started declining and later collapsed, the Turkish nation began adopting European legal norms and rules. As a result, Turkey's inevitable step was to establish a new legal system and turn towards laws from western nations. Subsequently, the Ottoman-Turkish modernisation process went one step further with the establishment of the Republic in 1923.[48] Many laws adopted from the West after the establishment of the Turkish Republic were amended according to the needs of the people. Unlike the reforms of the Ottoman period, the old legal system was completely removed, and a brand new legal order was established in its place, with steps taken to create a secular and contemporary legal system in the Atatürk period. However, over the last few decades, the Republic has seen its fair share of tumultuous history that permeates into its legal system.

---

[47] Ercimet Sarıay, "Tanzimat Sonrasi Kanunlaştirma Çalişmalarinin Kaynaklari Ve Metodolojisi," *Bayterek Uluslararası Akademik Araştırmalar Dergisi,* no. 1 (2019): 9-35.
[48] Manley O. Hudson, "Law Reform in Turkey," *American Bar Association Journal,* no. 1 (1927): 5-8.

BIBLIOGRAPHY

Secondary Sources

Journal Articles

o   Akif Tögel, "Ottoman Human Rights Practice: A Model of Legal Pluralism," Yıldırım Beyazıt Hukuk Dergisi no. 2 (2016): 201-220.

o   Aydın Yetkin "Osmanli Devleti'nde Hukuk Devletinin Gelişim Süreci," Uluslararası Sosyal Araştırmalar Dergisi, no. 24 (2013): 380-413.

o   Aylin Özman, "Law, Ideology and Modernization in Turkey: Kemalist Legal Reforms in Perspective," Social & Legal Studies, no. 1 (2010): 67-84.

o   Avi Rubin "Legal Borrowing and its Impact on Ottoman Legal Culture In The Late Nineteenth Century," Continuity And Change, no. 2 (2007): 279-303.

o   Bilal Tunç, "Türk Anayasa Tarihinde 1961 Anayasası'Nın Yeri Ve Önemi," Karadeniz Araştırmaları, no. 67 (2020): 657-692.

o   Ercimet Sarıay, "Tanzimat Sonrasi Kanunlaştirma Çalişmalarinin Kaynaklari Ve Metodolojisi," Bayterek Uluslararası Akademik Araştırmalar Dergisi, no. 1 (2019): 9-35.

o   Hakan Özdemir and Ahmet Çiftlikçi, "Conversion of Constitutional State In Membership Process of Turkey To European Union (EU): About Arrangements Performed In Domestic Law From Helsinki Summit Until Today", Fırat University Journal Of Social Science, no. 1 (2015): 123-144.

o   Hıfzi Timur, "The Place Of Islamic Law In Turkish Law Reform", Annales De La Faculté De Droit D'Istanbul no. 6 (2011): 63-74.

o   Hrfzi Veldet Velidedeoğlu, "The Reception of the Swiss Civil Code in Turkey", International Social Science Bulletin, no. 1 (1957): 60-65.

o   Hürol Erbay, "Eski Hukuk Sisteminden Yeni Sisteme Geçiş Ve Turk Hukuk Devrimi," Sinop Üniversitesi Sosyal Bilimler Dergisi no. 2 (2018): 211-238.

o   İbrahim Durhan, "Osmanlı Hukukunun Yapısı Üzerine Bir Etüt," Erzincan Binali Yıldırım Üniversitesi Hukuk Fakültesi Dergisi 3 no. 1 (1999): 215-232.

o   İbrahim Durhan, "Tanzimat Döneminde Osmanlı Yargı Teşkilatındaki Gelişmeler," Erzincan Binali Yıldırım Üniversitesi Hukuk Fakültesi Dergisi no. 3 (2008): 55-111.

o   İbrahim Ülker, "Hukukun Genel İlkeleri Bağlamında Kanun-I Esasi'Deki Yargılamaya İlişkin Hükümlerin Değerlendirilmesi," Selçuk Üniversitesi Hukuk Fakültesi Dergisi, no. 2 (2013): 101-124.

o   İhsan Yilmaz, "Secular Law and the Emergence of Unofficial Turkish Islamic Law," Middle East Journal, no. 1 (2002): 113-131.

o   İhsan Yılmaz and Hüseyin Gündoğdu, "Secular Law in Islamic Polity: The Ottoman Case," European Journal of Economic and Political Studies, no. 2 (2013): 57-81.

o   Manley O. Hudson, "Law Reform in Turkey," American Bar Association Journal, no. 1 (1927): 5-8.

o   Mehmet Akif ÖZER "Avrupa Birliği'Ne Tam Üyeliğin Eşiğinde Türkiye," Yönetim Ve Ekonomi Dergisi, no. 1 (2009): 89-105.

o   Seda Unsar, "A Path-Dependent Analsis of the Ottoman Empire and Its Influence On The Foundation Of The Turkish Republic," The Turkish Yearbook Of International Relations no. 33 (2002):77-121.

o   Temuçin Ertan, "Atatürk, Cumhuriyet ve Hukuk Sistemi," *Cumhuriyet Özel Sayısı* no. 33 (1999): 743-757.

o   Timur Kuran and Scott Lustig "Judicial Biases in Ottoman Istanbul: Islamic Justice And Its Compatibility With Modern Economic Life," Journal Of Law And Economics no. 3 (2012): 631-666.

o   Umut Özsu, "Receiving' The Swiss Civil Code: Translating Authority In Early Republican Turkey," International Journal Of Law In Context, no. 1 (2010): 63-89.

Chapters of an Edited book
o   Macit Akman, "The Closure Of The Sharia Courts" in *Social, Educational, Political, Economic And Other Developments Occurred In Turkey Between The Years Of 1923-193,* ed. Özkan Akman And Mustafa Murat Çay And Fatih Bozbayindir (Turkey: ISRES Publishing, 2018).

Dissertations
o   Mehmet Gayretli"Tanzimat Sonrasından Cumhuriyet'e Kadar Olan Dönemde Kanunlaştırma Çalışmaları," *Ph.D diss.*, (Marmara University, 2008).

o   Ali Sezdi, "Osmanli'nin Son Döneminden Cumhuriyet'in Kuruluşuna Hukukta Modernleşme Sürecinde Millileşme Tartişmalari Ve İslam Medeniyet Tarihindeki Yeri," *Master*, (Ankara Üniversitesi, 2020).

Websites
o   Halim Alperen Çıtak "A Brief History Of Turkish Constitutionalism," Lm-Dp.Org., 2021, http://lm-dp.org/a-brief-history-of-turkish-constitutionalism/, accessed on 20 June, 2021.

o   Serap Yazıcı "UPDATE: A Guide to Turkish Public Law and Legal Research – Globalex," Nyulawglobal.Org, 2017, https://www.nyulawglobal.org/globalex/Turkey1.htm, accessed on 5 July, 2021.

CHAPTER 9
THE CONTRIBUTION OF ISLAMIC LAW AND OTHER HISTORICAL CUSTOMARY LAWS TO LEGAL DEVELOPMENT IN INDONESIA

Attorney Yuliannova Lestari

1 INTRODUCTION

The application of Islamic law in Indonesia is closely related to the early entry of Islam to Indonesia. Since Islam was introduced, Islamic law has been implemented and followed by the adherents of Islam in this archipelago. The prevalence of Islamic law among the natives of Indonesia was later recognized by the colonial Dutch. Early in their tenure, the Dutch government realized that Islamic law was one of the pillars of strength that could threaten Dutch political policies. Accordingly, the Dutch changed their policy by stipulating that Islamic law applied if it had been adopted as the customary law of the natives of Indonesia. The struggle of Indonesian Islamic law scholars in their attempts at having such policies amended has resulted in the new norm in Indonesia, in that any customary law that is not in accordance with Islamic law will not be applied or will be rejected by Muslims.

Following the independence of Indonesia in 1949, the impact of Islamic law progressed steadily within its legal system. This is marked by the enactment of legal statutes by the government and has become the dominant law in Indonesia. This paper describes the existence of Islamic law in Indonesia as outlined through legal outcomes in the form of legislation, showing the nuances of the transformation of the formal and material format of Islamic law through persuasive and authoritative sources. This Chapter will also reveal efforts to reform existing Islamic law in Indonesia.

2 HISTORY OF INDONESIA

The name Indonesia itself was used for the first time at the Second Youth Congress on 28 October 1928. Long before that, the area now called Indonesia was better known as *Nusantara*. Until the 12th century, various kingdoms had ruled in the archipelago, initially kingdoms that were predominantly influenced by Hindu and Buddhist philosophies. Examples of such kingdoms are Sumatra that was ruled by the famous Srivijaya, and Java that was ruled by equally famous Sailendra. In fact, *Borobudur*, the largest Buddhist monument in the world or *Candi Prambanan*, a large Hindu temple in Central Java is testament to prevalence of Hindu and Budhhist philosophies in Indonesia. By the 15th century, another famous ruler, Majapahit, ruled a Hindu kingdom that was located in East Java. Alongside this kingdom, around the same time, Malacca was a powerful region on the West Coast of the Malay Peninsula, later established as a significant Islamic trading place. Thereafter, decades later, it marked the deepening effect of Islam in the Indonesian archipelago.

The archipelago, for the most part, failed to escape the colonization of foreign nations. Inevitably, the abundant natural resources of Indonesia were the target. In 1509, the Portuguese succeeded in controlling the territory of Malacca, Ternate and Madura.[1] There was resistance – Fatahillah from Demak succeeded in seizing Sunda Kelapa from the Portuguese in 1602. After the Portuguese, the Dutch then went to the Banten region under the leadership of Cornelis de Houtman. At that time, the Dutch wanted to form the *Vereenigde Oostindische Compagnie* (VOC) and control trade in the very profitable Indonesian spices.

In forming the VOC, there were several agreements that the Dutch had to obey, such as the *Bongaya* agreement[2] to the *Giyanti* agreement.[3] After the VOC was dissolved, the Dutch finally appointed Herman William Daendels as governor general of the Dutch East Indies. During his time, he forced people on the island of Java to work to build the *Anyer-Panarukan* route, which stretches from East to West of Java Island.[4]

The Dutch controlled Indonesia for approximately 350 years, until the arrival of the Japanese during the Second World War. The Dutch surrendered unconditionally to the Japanese on 8 March 1942. Japanese rule ended after just three and a half years of occupation of Indoneisa, when the Allied forces won World War II. Knowing that Japan had lost, the *Dokuritsu Junbi Cosakai* was formed, chaired by Dr. Radjiman Widyodiningrat. After hearing about Japan's defeat on 14 August 1945, after two Japanese cities, Hiroshima and Nagasaki, were bombed by the

---

[1] It is important for the readers to appreciate that for centuries, present day Malaysia and Indonesia were part of same kingdoms such as Srivijaya, Majapahit and so forth. The current division between Malaysia and Indonesia can be linked to *Anglo–Dutch Treaty* of 1814 and 1824.

[2] This treaty was signed on 18 November 1667 between Sultan Hasanudin of Gowa and the Dutch East India Company (VOC).

[3] This treaty was signed and ratified on 13 February 1755 between Prince Mangkubumi, the Dutch East India Company, and Sunan Pakubuwono III along with his allies. The accord officially divided the Sultanate of Mataram between Mangkubumi and Pakubuwono.

[4] This road was built during the reign of Herman Willem Daendels (1808-1811), governor-general of the Dutch East Indies and historians suggest that it was built using unpaid forced labor that also led to loss of thousands of lives.

allied forces, the young group urged the old group to quickly proclaim independence.[5]

During Indonesia's independence process, the *Rengasdengklok* incident occurred, namely the kidnapping of independence leaders Soekarno and Hatta by young group of people to accelerate the implementation of the proclamation of independence. After their release and subsequent return to Jakarta, Soekarno and Hatta began compiling the text of the proclamation at the house of Admiral Maeda, assisted by Achmad Soebardjo and witnessed by Soekarno, B.M, Diah, Sudiro and Sayuti Melik. The text of the proclamation was finally read out on 17 August, 1945. Once independence was declared, the Constitution (UUD), which eventually became known to the public as the 1945 Constitution, was ratified and established as the basis of the Republic of Indonesia,

3 EVOLUTION OF LAW IN INDONESIA

The concept of Islamic law only became known in Indonesia following the spread of Islam throughout the country. There are conflicting views amongst historians as to the exact timings of the arrival of Islam in Indonesia, and accordingly dates differ from the 1st century *Hijri* (Islamic lunar calendar), or the 7th century CE, to the 7th century *Hijri,* or the 13th century CE. Although historians differ regarding the initial entry of Islam into Indonesia, it can be said that once Islam entered Indonesia, Islamic law was implemented and followed by the adherents of Islam in this archipelago. This can be seen from the seminal works of many Indonesian Islamic jurists. A few examples of such works are – *Miratul Thullab, Sirathal Mustaqim, Sabilal Muhtadin, Kutaragama, Sajinatul Law*, and others.[6]

---

[5] Old guards represented leaders such as Soekarno and Hatta, where young groups also had similar aim for independence of Indonesia, but were willing to take drastic actions to achieve independence of Indonesia.

[6] Muhammad Daud Ali, *Asas-Asas Hukum Islam (Hukum Islam I): Pengantar Ilmu Hukum Dan Tata Hukum Islam Di Indonesia* (Jakarta: Rajawali, 1990), 24.

During the period of Dutch colonial rule, the indigenous peoples, apart from having their own customary customs, also began to interact with outside civilizations, one of which was the Islamic jurisprudence. This resulted in Islamic law, which was also integrated with the local customary culture (*'adat'*) becoming the better known rule of law. In effect, these two cultures (Islam and *adat*) can go hand in hand, intertwined into rules that guard the norms of indigenous peoples. In a state of law, power will be exercised by the government based on the rule of law or what we call the rule of law, which aims to carry out a legal order. Indonesia has gone through several phases in order to evolve its own legal system.

The *first phase* in the evolution of Indonesian law was the period commonly known as the Pre-Colonial Phase. This covered the period lasting many centuries before colonialism, during which Indonesia had adopted a royal system; for example the Maja Bitter kingdom, Sriwijaya kingdom, Mataram kingdom and so on. At that time, these kingdoms would customarily still be applying the system of law that was prevalent within each individual kingdom's territory, influenced by Hindu or Buddhist jurisprudence as the case may be. However, to be precise, there were actually two royal eras during this period, namely the Hindu-Buddhist kingdoms, and a few centuries later, the era of kingdoms influenced by Islamic jurisprudence.

The *second phase* for the evolution of law that needs discussion was the commonly referred to Colonial Phase. After the Dutch colonized Indonesia, there were many changes, especially in the legal system in Indonesia. When the VOC period commenced in the seventeenth century, the legal order was qualified as a repressive legal order in *optima forma*. The legal order in force at that time benefited the Dutch and disadvantaged the natives of the Indonesian archipelago, especially economically. The tolerance for the application of Islamic law at that time materialised, because the *Vereenigde Oostindische Compagnie* (VOC) was busy with the expeditionary tasks of taking agricultural commodities from the colonies to Europe;[7]

---

[7] Djoko Prakoso, *Azas-Azas Hukum Perkawinan Di Indonesia* (Jakarta: Bina Aksara, 1987), 12.

The onset of Japanese colonialism, in March 1942, when they began to occupy the entire area of the Dutch East Indies, occurred at a time when Japan wanted to control the Indonesian archipelago and thus have the power that the Dutch had previously enjoyed in this area. To implement governance in Indonesia, the government of the Japanese army was guided by the law called "*Gunseirei*". During the Japanese occupation, not many legal reforms were planned or implemented; in fact, all laws and regulations that did not conflict with Japanese military regulations remained in full force, however they eliminated the privileges of the Dutch and other Europeans in Indonesia.

The *third phase* for the evolution of law was the Independence Phase. This phase can be sub-divided into 3 periods, namely the old order period, the new order period and the reformation period. In the *Old Order Period*, the Indonesian legal system was a system established by the Indonesian nation itself, or more precisely by the Indonesian State. The Old Order was led by President Soekarno and Vice president Moh. Hatta. From 18 August 1945, the positive legal system in Indonesia became a legal system composed of customary law subsystems, Islamic law subsystems, and Western legal subsystems. Political dynamics at this time experienced ups and downs.

During the *New Order era*, after the G.30.S/PKI S/PKI Coup was thwarted on 1 October 1965, and following the issuance of the 11 March 1966 order, which is often known as "*Supersemar*" a new chapter in the history of the Indonesian nation began, which later referred to itself as the New Order government. The development and dynamics of the law and judicial system under the New Order began with the elimination of laws in the political and governmental processes.[8] Among some of the laws that were eliminated were the main Agrarian Laws, which coincided with the enactments of law to develop economy of Indonesia such as the Foreign Investment Law, the Forestry Law, and the Mining Law.

---

[8] Jimly Asshiddiqie, *Pengantar Ilmu Hukum Tata Negara* (Jakarta: Sekretariat Jendral dan Kepaniteraan, 2006), 40.

The New Order also ensured that legal institutions were subdued, and were placed under the executive branch that already controlled the education system and, to some extent, restricted critical thinking in public discourse. Accordingly, there was no new major development or evolution of laws in Indonesia. The Administration of the New Order government abused the provisions of legislation for the sake of power. The downturn in the condition of the state administration system that was built during the New Order era reached its nadir when it was accompanied by the emergence of an economic crisis that hit the world economy and also affected the Indonesian nation and other Asian countries.[9]

Then, the *Reformation Period* began, with Vice President B.J. Habibie replacing President Suharto. During his tenure, there were four amendments made to the Indonesian Constitution. Since the 2002 MPR Annual Session, the composition of the 1945 *Constitution* has the following structure: 1) the 1945 Constitution, the original text; 2) the first amendment to the 1945 Constitution; 3) the second amendment to the 1945 Constitution; 4) the third amendment to the 1945 Constitution; and 5) the Fourth Amendment to the 1945 Constitution.[10]

3.1 IMPACT OF ISLAMIC LAW IN INDONESIA

Since Islam entered the archipelago, Muslims have had an obligation to obey Islamic law, sociologically and culturally. In fact, its influence never fades away and has always been present in the lives of Muslims regardless of the political system, through both the colonialism and independence periods, and extending into the current reform era. The prevalent view according to the law as seen from the Islamic perspective is that it can always underlie and direct societal change because Islamic law has two dimensions. In the first dimension, Islamic law in

---

[9] H. Mustaghfirin, "Sistem Hukum Barat, Sistem Hukum Adat, Dan Sistem Hukum Islam Menuju Sebagai Sistem Hukum Nasional Sebuah Ide Yang Harmoni," *Jurnal Dinamika Hukum* no. 11 (2011): 92.
[10] M. Solly Lubis, *Asas-Asas Hukum Tata Negara* (Bandung: Alumni, 2021), 22.

relation to sharia contains *na,* which *qaṭ'i* will apply universally. The second dimension of Islamic law is rooted in *naṣ yang anni,* which is the area of ijtihad, whose output is called *fiqhi.*[11]

In this second dimension, Islamic law provides the possibility of legal application, whereby each area inhabited by Muslims can apply Islamic law differently, taking into account regional variations. The differences influence these variations in the political system that has been adopted locally. They are also due to historical, sociological, and cultural factors of the *Mujtahids* (persons accepted as original authorities on Islamic law). Islamic law is a term that developed in Indonesia as a translation of *AL-FIQH, AL-ISLAM, OR AL-SYARÎ'AH AL-ISLAMIYAH.*

In legal sciences in Indonesia, the term Islamic law is understood as a combination of two words, law and Islam, and the word law is based on the word Islam. The significance of these words is felt when we read the formulation of the definitions of jurisprudents, including Amir Syarifuddin, who stated that Islamic law is a regulation formulated based on Allah's revelation and the Sunnah of the Prophet regarding the behavior of the *mukallaf* which is recognized and believed to apply to all adherents of Islam.[12] On the other hand, Ahmad Rofiq defines Islamic law as regulations taken from revelation and formulated in the four products of legal thought (*fiqh, fatwas,* court decisions, and laws) that are guided and enforced by Muslims in Indonesia.[13]

Accordingly, legal institutions in Indonesia gradually opened up to opportunities for Islamic law to contribute to the Indonesian legal system. Bear in mind, that in Indonesia the legal awareness of the community, especially the Muslim community, was once divided due to the political engineering of the Dutch colonial government, which had developed policies pertaining to Dutch law and customary

---

[11] Amrullah Achmad and Busthanul Arifin, *Dimensi Hukum Islam Dalam Sistem Hukum Nasional* (Jakarta: Gema Insani Press, 1996), 32.

[12] Mahatir bin Mohamad and Dasuki bin Haji Ahmad, *Pembaharuan Pemikiran Islam Tun Dr. Mahathir Mohamad* (Kuala Lumpur: RD Network, 2004), 23.

[13] Ahmad Rofiq, *Pembaharuan Hukum Islam Di Indonesia* (Yogyakarta: Gama Media, 2001), 12.

law with the aim of hindering the development of Islamic law. However, soon after Indonesia achieved independence, Islamic law, as part of the Islamic religion, attempted to return to occupy a proper place in the legal system in force in Indonesia.

3.2 CONTINENTAL LEGAL SYSTEM, ISLAMIC LAW AND CUSTOMARY (ADAT) LAW IN INDONESIA

During the period of VOC (1602-1800), the study of customary law actually started, but the term "customary law" (*adatrecht*) was first used in 1900 by Hurgronje, to designate customary forms that could have legal consequences. [14] The development of the study of customary law during the Dutch colonial period can be divided into three periods.

In the *First period*, that is the period from 1602 to 1800, studies on customary law conducted during the VOC were, relatively speaking, very few, except for some works by scholars such as Marooned (1754-1836), a Colonial employee who collected a lot of materials about customs in Sumatra, Raffles (1781-1826), Governor of Central Java during the period of British rule from 1811 to 1816, Crawford (1783-1868), namely Raffles, and Muntinghe (1773-1827), a Dutchman who became an employee in Java for East India Company.

The *Second period* spanned from 1800 to 1865. This period was referred to by Van Vollenhoven as the period of "Western exploration" (*Wertern reconnoitering*). At this time, not many works of customary laws were produced. The *Third period* lasted from post-1865 until the independence of Indonesia in 1945. During this time, various circumstances prompted the Dutch to care more about customary law, for example, the issue concerning agrarian law prompted the government to investigate customary laws in detail. The three main scholars, who focused on

---

[14] Supomo Djokosutono and Pieter Gills, *Sejarah Politik Hukum Adat* (Jakarta: Pradnya Paramita, 1982), 15.

customary law in detail during this period were G.A Wilken, Liefrinck, and Cristian Snouck Hurgronje. These three people, in fact, built a foundation of customary law that could be easily recognised in Indonesia.

Historically, the Indonesian legal system is a legacy of the Dutch who had ruled Indonesia for more than 350 years, so the Dutch (Continental European/civil law) legal system was also applied in Indonesia based on the principle of concordance.[15]

 According to Andi Hamzah, the influence of the Dutch legal system also affects the judge's decision, when the judges in Indonesia are examining, adjudicating, and deciding a case, including the issue of legal discovery. Accordingly, all aspects are influenced by the civil law system.[16] The main characteristic of civil law has always been the codification or bookkeeping of laws or laws in a book (*code*).[17]

Indonesia has, since the post-Independence era, adopted a civil law system, so the main principle is to make the law definitive in the form of written rules or set forth in the form of laws. As a result, unwritten laws are not recognized as law, and this concept is further extended to regulations that are recognised to be out of the state system. Accordingly, such regulations are considered as community morals. However, in practice, the civil law system has many weaknesses because of its written nature, making it inflexible in following the development of society, as it tends to be rigid and static.

---

[15] Ansori Z Ahmad, *Sejarah Dan Kedudukan BW Di Indonesia* (Jakarta: Rajawali, 1986), 23.

[16] Lukman Hakim, *Asas-Asas Hukum Pidana* (Sleman: Budi Utama, 2020), 16.

[17] Wirjono R Prodjodikoro, *Tindak-Tindak Pidana Tertentu Di Indonesia* (Jakarta: Refika Aditama, 2010), 20.

4 ISLAMIC LAW & ITS POSITION IN THE CURRENT INDONESIAN LEGAL SYSTEM

Since the entry of Islam into the Indonesian archipelago, it can be said that empirically Islamic law is the living law of current Indonesian society. In a note from J.C. Van Leur, the possible entry of Islam into Indonesia, which at that time was still referred to as the "archipelago", began in the 7th century CE.[18] It demonstrates that acceptance of Islamic law by the community within Indonesia occurred in the early phase of the birth of Islam in the Arabian Peninsula and lasted until the entry of the Dutch colonial reign in the archipelago. However, it is also a fact that the acceptance of Islamic law as a living law in society has been challenged since the start of Dutch rule in Indonesia.

During the VOC governance, a rule was imposed that all areas under VOC rule had to use Dutch law. However, since people preferred to use Islamic law, the VOC government allowed people to use Islamic law in resolving various kinds of disputes in society. Then in 1760, the VOC government through D.W. Freijer created the "Compedium Freijer", which was used as a legal reference to solve legal problems of Islamic society in areas controlled by the VOC.[19]

After the VOC administration, further challenge to Islamic Law came from the coercive efforts to reduce the importance of Islamic law normatively by the Dutch East Indies government through *Staatsblad* 1937 Number 116. According to Yahya Harahap, this regulation was the result of Ter Haar's recommendations which contained, among other things: (1) recognition that Islamic inheritance law had not been fully accepted by the community; (2) to revoke the authority of the Religious Courts (*Raad Agama*) for inheritance cases and transfer them to *Landraat*; (3) put the Religious Courts (*Raad Agama*) under the supervision of

---

[18] Rofiq Ahmad, *Pembaharuan Hukum Islam Di Indonesia* (Yogyakarta: Gama Media, 2001), 33.
[19] M. Husnu Abadi, *Pemikiran Kodifikasi Hukum Administrasi Negara Indonesia* (Pekanbaru: UIR Press, 2004), 12.

Landraat; and (4) that the decision of the Religious Courts cannot be implemented without an *executoir verklaring* from the chairman of *Landraat*.[20]

Long before *Staatsblad 1937 Number 116*, Islamic law had actually been implemented and developed by the community in religious courts. Formal religious courts had existed since the days of the sultanates and Islamic kingdoms in Indonesia; for example, the Penghulu court in Java, the Syari'ah court in the Islamic Sultanate in Sumatra, and the Qadli Court in the Sultanate of Banjar and Pontianak. In 1937, *Staatsblad* 1937 Numbers 638 and 639 were issued, which regulated the Qadli Density and the Grand Qadli Density for the South Kalimantan region. The Qadli Density and the Grand Qadli Density had the same authority as the Religious Courts in Java and Madura. Based on Staatsblad 1937 Number 116, these religious Courts' powers were limited to – (1) resolving disputes between husbands and wives who were Muslims; (2) cases regarding marriage, reconciliation, and divorce for people who were Muslims and required an intermediary for Muslim judges; (3) giving a decision on divorce; (4) declaring that the conditions for the fall of the suspended divorce (*taklik talak*) are no longer presented; (5) dealing with the issue of dowry; (7) dealing with problems about the needs of wives that were to be provided for by their husbands.

Normative and authoritative acceptance of Islamic law began to take shape from the time of the enactment of the *Constitution 1945*. According to Ismail Sunny, the enactment of the Constitution 1945 and Pancasila as the basis of the state, even though it did not contain the seven words of the *Jakarta Charter*,[21] had the effect of making invalid the *receptie* theory (conflict theory) that was developed by Snouck Hurgronje, as it had lost its legal basis. On the other hand, Islamic law was increasingly recognized constitutionally in Article 29 of the 1945 Constitution. At that time, Islamic law was accepted as a persuasive source.[22] Acceptance of

---

[20] Hasan Bisri, *Dimensi-Dimensi Kompilasi Hukum Islam* (Bandung: Ulul Albab Press, 1998), 22.

[21] Ismail Sunny, *Kompilasi Hukum Islam Ditinjau dari Sudut Pertumbuhan Teori Hukum di Indonesia.* (Jakarta: Direktorat Pembinaan Badan Peradilan Agama Islam, 1991), 22-23.

[22] M. Yahya Harahap, *Beberapa Tinjauan Permasalahan Hukum Buku Kesatu* (Bandung: Citra Aditya Bakti, 1997), 36.

Islamic law was gaining prominence after the enactment of regional autonomy, where various regions of Indonesia started to compete for the right to regulate their own regional affairs.

Local governments took this opportunity to give shape to regional regulations based on regional characteristics. Many communities living within these regions had a desire for regional regulations with Islamic nuances based on Sharia principles, in accordance with the sociological conditions of their people. One of the regions that wanted Sharia nuanced regulation was Aceh Province, with a regional regulation called *Qanun*.

Through *Law Number 11 (2006)* concerning the Government of Aceh, the government gave authority to the Government of Aceh, which included: (1) the implementation of religious life in the form of the implementation of Islamic law for its adherents in Aceh, while maintaining the harmony of life among religious believers; (2) organizing traditional life based on Islam; providing quality education and adding local content in accordance with Islamic law; (3) defining the role of *Ulema* in setting Aceh policies; and (4) the organization and management of pilgrimage in accordance with statutory regulations.

In addition to the Qanun in Aceh Province, several State Institutions and other institutions with an Islamic spirit evolved, for example the Indonesian Ulema Council, followed by the establishment of other bodies such as the National Amil Zakat Agency and the Indonesian Waqf Board. The first Indonesian Ulema Council that evolved in 1958 was known as the West Java Ulema Council. The Central Ulama Council was established in 1962, which was then followed by various Ulama Councils at a provincial level. In 1975, a new Ulema Council was formed as the Indonesian Ulema Council (MUI).[23] In fact, the Indonesian Ulema Council plays an important role in ensuring the realization of religious harmony

---

[23] Ahmad Sukardja, *Piagam Madinan Dan Undang-Undang Dasar Republik Indonesia* (Jakarta: Sinar Grafika, 2012), 38.

through various *fatwas* (ruling on a point of Islamic Law) that are issued by this Council.

One of the articles of legislation that clearly accommodates religious values is *Law Number 1 (1974)* concerning Marriage. Article 2 within *Law Number 1 (1974)* places religion as a determinant of the validity of a marriage, so that marriages in Indonesia adhere to the law of religious marriage. The formulation of Article 2 of the Marriage Law has a logical consequence that all Indonesian citizens who are adherents of Islam must fulfil the provisions of Islamic law first, so that their marriage can be said to be religiously valid. This seems to demonstrate that the existence of Islamic law is very influential in the life of the nation and state in Indonesia.

The regulation on *zakat* is another proof of the existence of Islamic law in the life of the nation and state in Indonesia. The first regulation regarding zakat (a payment made annually under Islamic law on certain kinds of property and used for charitable and religious purposes - one of the Five Pillars of Islam) was promulgated through the *Circular Letter of the Ministry of Religion Number A/VII/17367* (1951). This circular continued the provisions of the Dutch ordinance, which stated that the state would only supervise, and would not interfere in the collection and distribution of zakat.

In 1991, the government issued a *Joint Decree of the Minister of Home Affairs and the Minister of Religion of the Republic of Indonesia Numbers 29 and 47* of 1991 concerning the Development of the *Amil Zakat, Infaq,* and *Shadaqah* Agency. Currently, the management of zakat is regulated by *Law no. 23* (2011), which is the result of a Revision of *Law No. 38* (1999) on Zakat Management. In addition to marriage and zakat, *Law Number 13* (2008), concerning the Implementation of the *Hajj* (Islamic pilgrimage), also demonstrates the existence of Islamic law in Indonesia. Article 8 paragraph (2) of *Law Number 13* (2008) explains that policies and implementation in organizing the pilgrimage are a national duty and a responsibility of the government.

Law No. 41 (2004) concerning Waqf is one form of application of Islamic law in the national legal system which contains several new and quite important matters, including the issue of *nazhir, maiquf bi*h (waqf property), *mauquf 'alaih* (allocation of property as waqf).and also the need to establish an Indonesian Waqf Board. In Article 28 paragraph (2) of *Law Number 41 of 2004* concerning *Waqf*, it is stated that the Indonesian *Waqf Board* can cooperate with government agencies both at the Central and Regional levels, community organizations, experts, international agencies, and other parties if necessary.

Interestingly, there is also bookkeeping (codification) of the rules of Islamic law in the Compilation of Islamic Law ('KHI'). KHI regulates various matters relating to Islamic law, for example the issue of inheritance, which is regulated in the Second Book of the Compilation Of Islamic Law, itself based on the science of *Faraidl* - namely the knowledge of the provisions on the distribution of inheritance in Islam. KHI consists of 3 (three) books, namely Book I on Marriage, Book II on Inheritance, and Book III on *Waqf.*

5 STATUS OF HISTORICAL CUSTOMARY LAW IN THE INDONESIAN LEGAL SYSTEM

Peter Burns in his writing *"The Leiden Legacy: Concepts of Law in Indonesia"*, argued that the existence of customary law as the living law of the Indonesian nation is increasingly marginalized.[24] Customary law, which was originally a living and developing law and able to provide solutions to various problems in the lives of the Indonesian people was, in his view, increasingly disappearing. Currently, if you look at empirical facts in society, you can find various complexities of

---

[24] Peter Burns, *The Leiden Legacy*, 1st ed. (Leiden: KITLV Press, 2004), 183-205.

problems faced by indigenous peoples in Indonesia, especially when the customary law is dealing with definitive written law. For example, complexities arise when the traditional rights of the community are confronted with the interests of investors (domestic and International) as a result of applicable state law on those issues.[25] The development of the Indonesian legal system, which tends to prefer the civil legal system model from western countries, and Indonesian legal politics, which leads to the codification and unification of law, has accelerated the disappearance of the existence of customary law and its institutions.

The loss of the existence of customary law as a source of law in Indonesia is caused by the assumption that customary law is very traditional, vestigial, and antiquated, so it cannot match the development of law in modern times. The implications of Indonesian legal politics can be seen from the fact that while solving problems in society, politics tend to override customary law and prioritize state law, even though the former is actually more relevant than using state law. For example, the number of horizontal conflicts between indigenous peoples in one area should be resolved through the customary community settlement institutions.[26] The critical problems that arise in daily life do so due to the difference in perception between community land tenure that is based on customary rights, and the public interest, which is the burden and obligation of the state. Another example of acceptance of customary law is the idea that the basis for a criminal act should be extended to the realm of customary law values.[27]

In fact, if you look at historical legality, the enactment of law in Indonesia actually notes that many legal experts, especially from Western countries, were overwhelmingly interested in studying the customary law of Indonesia as a law that has shaped Indonesian society for thousands of years. This customary law

---

[25] Syamsudin, "Beban Masyarakat Menghadapi Hukum Negara," *Jurnal Hukum Ius Quia Iustum* 15, no. 3 (2008): 345.

[26] Jacoba Sahalessy, "Peran Latupati Sebagai Lembaga Hukum Adat Dalam Penyelesaian Konflik Antar Negeri Di Kecamatan Leihitu Propinsi Maluku," *SASI* 17, no. 3 (2011): 45.

[27] Handrawan, "Sanksi Adat Delik Perzinahan (Umoapi) Dalam Perspektif Hukum Pidana Adat Tolaki," *Perspektif* 21, no. 3 (2016): 199.

was itself influenced by much jurisprudence based on various religions and dynasties that ruled Indonesian regions over the centuries. Snouck Hurgronje, for example, the first expert to study Indonesian law, wrote a book entitled "De Atjehers", mentioning the term customary law as *adat-recht*, to give a name to the social control system that lives in Indonesian society. Furthermore, Snouck Hurgronje's theory was developed by Cornelis van Vollenhoven, who later became known as an expert on Customary Law in the Dutch East Indies.

Considering that customary law is a law that reflects the personality and soul of the nation, it is believed that some customary law institutions are still relevant in shaping the Indonesian legal system.[28] Customary law that can no longer be defended will become extinct over time, in accordance with its flexible and dynamic nature (i.e. not static). According to Von Savigny, as quoted by Soepomo, it is emphasized that customary law is a living law, because it is the embodiment of the real legal feelings of the people. According to its own nature, customary law continues to grow and develop like life itself.[29] In the opinion of Savigny, van Vollenhoven said that customary law was, in the past, somewhat different in content, and had shown evidence of development. Furthermore, Vollenhoven emphasized that customary law develops and continues, as customary decisions give rise to customary law.

If the enactment of a law is contrary to the values and legal norms that live and apply in the community, of course it will be rejected. In the Indonesian context, the living law of the Indonesian people is the customary law. Customary law can also be used as a source of law by judges if the law so orders.[30] Customary Law is a law that is not codified for Indonesians and foreigners living in Indonesia (among others Chinese and Arabs).

---

[28] Ratna Winahyu Lestari, "Peranan Hukum Adat Dalam Pembangunan Dan Pembangunan Hukum Pidana Nasional," *Perspektif* 10, no. 3 (2005): 265.

[29] Herlambang P. Wiratrama, "Perkembangan Politik Hukum Peradilan Adat," *Mimbar Hukum-Fakultas Hukum Universitas Gadjah Mada* 30, no. 3 (2018): 488.

[30] Hazar Kusmayanti, Sherly Ayuna Putri, and Linda Rahmainy, "Praktik Penyelesaian Sengketa Di Pengadilan Agama Melalui Sidang Keliling Dikaitkan Dengan Prinsip Dan Asas Hukum Acara Perdata," *ADHAPER: Jurnal Hukum Acara Perdata* 4, no. 2 (2019): 145.

To analyze the position of customary law in the legal system, it is necessary to be congnisant of one of the natural streams of legal science, namely, Sociological Jurisprudence presented by Eugen Ehrlich. The basic concept of Ehrlich's thinking about law is living law. A good and effective positive law is a law that is in accordance with the living law of the community, and reflects the values that live within it. Ehrlich's message to legislators is that in making laws one should pay attention to the populace that lives in that society.[31]

It is a fact, and cannot be denied, that the customary law which applies in Indonesia in general, and Aceh Province in particular, is a law that is in accordance with the values of the populace living in those regions as part of society. Therefore, in order for customary law to be effectively applied in that society, the people's representatives who sit in the legislative body must be able to explore and accommodate legal awareness of the populace living in the region as part of society. Only then can the legislative body assist in the formation of laws and *Qanun* in Aceh (currently a province of Indonesia). The legal awareness of the community that has been formalized in both law, and the *qanun* will then be used as a basis for maintaining order and harmony in community life in the regions.

The Dutch colonial government officially recognized customary law as the original Indonesian law and found that it was in line with European law through Article 131 paragraphs (6) of the *Indische Staatsregeling*, which stated "*Indonesian law is a positive law for the Indonesian nation.*" The definition of Indonesian law in the article alluded to the customary law of Indonesia. Article 131, paragraph (6) is a legal umbrella for the recognition by the Dutch East Indies Government of customary law. More importantly, at the same time it demonstrates recognition of customary law as a living positive law for the Indonesian people.

---

[31] Eugen Ehrlich and Lewis Moll Walter, *Fundamental Principles of the Sociology of Law*, 5th ed. (Cambridge: Harvard University, 2002), 26.

Post-Independence, the recognition of unwritten customary law is only explained or included in the General Elucidation of the *Constitution number I (1945)* which states *"... the Constitution is the written basic law, while in addition to the Basic Law the unwritten basic law also applies [which]... are the basic rules that arise and are maintained in the practice of state administration even though they are not written."* Furthermore, in Article 18B, paragraph (2) of the *Constitution of the Republic of Indonesia* (1945), it is stated, *"The State recognizes and respects customary law community units and their traditional rights, as long as they are still alive and in accordance with community development and the principles of the Unitary State of the Republic of Indonesia, which are regulated in law."* According to this article, the customary law that can be recognized is the customary law that is still alive in Indonesian society, with clear relevance and scope for indigenous peoples.

The provisions of Article 18B paragraph (2) above can also be understood in that the *Constitution 1945* still consider the relevance of the customary law of Indonesia. This means that the recognition of customary law that is still alive in the community in an area must be carried out in accordance with statutory regulations (written law) and in line with the principles of the Unitary State of the Republic of Indonesia. This was confirmed by the Constitutional Court through its *Decision Number 31/PUU-V/2007 concerning the Review of Law No. 31 of 2007,* concerning the Establishment of Tual City in Maluku Province. In the decision, the Constitutional Court determined four constitutional requirements for the unity of indigenous peoples in Article 18B paragraph (2) of the Constitution 1945, among others that the customary laws must: (1) still be current; (2) be in accordance with the development of society; (3) be in accordance with the principles of the Unitary State of the Republic of Indonesia; and (4) be regulated by law. In fact, if these conditions for the customary law are not met in any case, then the indigenous peoples cannot become litigants in the Constitutional Court as then, they will be considered to have no legal standing.[32]

In the consideration of *Decision Number 31/PUU-V/2007*, the Constitutional Court further emphasized that "*...the recognition of the existence of indigenous peoples as rights holders or as a legal subject is a fundamental right*". The important and fundamental thing is that the customary law community is constitutionally recognized and respected as a person with rights, which of course can also be burdened by law in a society that has become a state. The decision was given in the context of allocating the resources necessary for life. The provisions of Article 18B paragraph (2) of the Constitution 1945 and Decision Number 31/PUU-V/2007 normatively provide recognition of the existence of customary law, but on the other hand, it also provides restrictions on indigenous peoples and on which customary laws can be recognized by law in the country.

Customary law also has a strategic role in the formation of legal jurisprudence by judges in court. Apart from being a court decision that has become permanent in the field of customary law, jurisprudence based on customary law also means that customary law is recognised in society. The development of customary law through jurisprudence indicates a subtle shift and growth of customary law in Indonesia. The role of customary law in the formation of jurisprudence can be seen through several examples from court judgments given in the following paragraphs.

Customary law, among others, relies on the principles of harmony and appropriateness. This was confirmed in the jurisprudence of the *Supreme Court of the Republic of Indonesia Number: 3328/Pdt/1984* dated 29 April 1986. In the *Supreme Court Decision - RI Number 2898 K/Pdt/1989* dated 19 November 1989, based on the customary dispute that arose at the *Kefamenanu* Court, East Nusa Tenggara, the Supreme Court emphasized the importance of applying customary

---

[32] Julian Rivers, "The Question Of Freedom Of Religion Or Belief And Defamation," *Religion & Human Rights* 2, no. 3 (2007): 115.

law, namely *"The violation of customary law and affirmation of customary sanctions. If, in the trial, the plaintiff can prove the argument of his lawsuit, then the judges must apply customary law regarding the article which is still valid in the area concerned, after hearing the local traditional elders."* The next legal rule: *"The settlement of violations of customary law"*, apart from the civil lawsuits mentioned above, can also be pursued through criminal charges in article 5 (3) b of *Law no. 1 Drt/1951"*.

In general, indigenous peoples in Indonesia consisted of patrilineal, matrilineal, and parental/bilateral groups.[33] It was observed, in the development of customary law, that these various kinds of family system were becoming more recognised within the legal jurisprudence. Furthermore, it was recognised that there was a shift in the family system in patrilineal and matrilineal indigenous peoples towards a parental/bilateral system. Jurisprudence dated 17 *January, 1959 Number 320K/Sip/1958* states that:

> (1) the wife can inherit the property of her husband who dies; (2) minor children are cared for and under the care of the mother; (3) because the child is in the custody of the mother, the assets of the child are controlled and managed by the mother; (4) there is an emphasis on equal status of men and women.

Legal pluralism that exists in Indonesia, even though it is an unwritten law, is actually able to become a unifying factor for the masses, and even provide various solutions to problems. It has created peace in the social life of the community. Legal pluralism in Indonesia dynamically follows the development of its society while still relying on the characteristics of indigenous peoples, and a *participerend coschmish* mindset is attractive enough to attract experts from all over the world for research into this unique aspect. In fact, currently, customary law is used

---

[33] *Patrilineal* kinship system, wherein the lineage is drawn from the lineage of the male relatives or fathers pursuant to which the standing of sons is prioritized over daughters. *Matrilineal* kinship system, wherein the lineage is drawn from the lineage of female relatives or mothers, pursuant to which the standing of daughters is prioritized over sons. *Paternal* or *bilateral* kinship system, wherein lineage is drawn according to the lineage of both father and mother pursuant to which the position of sons and daughters is not differentiated.

extensively in resolving both civil and criminal disputes with the development of methods or approaches that are known as restorative approaches,[34] similar to the *participerend coschmish* approach adopted by the indigenous peoples of Indonesia. Implementation of a *participerend coschmish* mindset to restore the state of balance manifested into several ceremonies, taboos or rites (rites de passage).[35]

The above discussion demonstrates that the legal conceptions and mindsets that live within society are not only still relevant, but also become the inspiration for other countries to develop laws to fulfil the community's sense of justice. Indigenous people have the same concept of laws that are needed to resolve conflicts in the community, in particular the controls required in the community, and a need for imposing sanctions in cases where customary laws are violated, so that recovery within society remains effective.[36] As another example, the University of Utrecht seeks to encourage the use of deliberations and consensus models of the Malay indigenous peoples in solving problems that occur within society.

In indigenous and Islamic societies, dispute resolution through deliberation is a living law and is known in almost every legal circle (*rechtskring*). Dispute resolution through this deliberation always involves the head of the people (customary leader), both in preventing violations of the law (*preventieve rechtszorg*) and in restoring the law (*rechtsherstel*).[37] On the other hand, Indonesia enacted *Law No. 30 of 1999* concerning Arbitration and Alternative Dispute Resolution as an option involving out of court settlements. It is suggested that this was clearly inspired by the development of dispute resolution in countries with a common law system.

---

[34] Romli Atmasasmita, *Globalisasi Dan Kejahatan Bisnis* (Jakarta: Kencana, 2010), 20.

[35] Muhammad Busar, *Asas-Asas Hukum Adat : Suatu Pengantar* (Jakarta: Pradnya Paramita, 1976), 23.

[36] I Putu Agus Arya Dauh, I Ketut Sukadana, and I Made Minggu Widyantara, "Peran Pranata Adat Dalam Pencegahan Konflik Antara Kelompok Masyarakat Adat," *Jurnal Preferensi Hukum* 1, no. 1 (2020): 134.

[37] R. Soepomo, *Bab-Bab Tentang Hukum Adat* (Jakarta: Pradnya Paramita, 2003), 29.

In recognising the importance of customary law, including Islamic law, in bringing order to people's lives, it is necessary to make an effort to involve customary law and Islamic law as part of the source of the formation of national law. In Mochtar Kusumaatmadja's view, the law must be sensitive to the development of society and capable of being flexible and able to adapt to circumstances within society.[38] In progressive legal theory, it is emphasized that the process of forming laws and regulations must absolutely pay attention to the values and legal norms that live and apply within society (living law).

The romanticism of the application of customary law, Islamic law and state law (civil law) can be seen from the mutual harmony of the three legal systems. As previously explained, the rigid and static application of civil law has created a legal gap in society. This legal problem can be overcome by using an unwritten legal system that is flexible and always follows the times, namely through the norms and values of customary law and Islamic law. Von Savigny in his masterpiece entitled "Von Beruf Unserer Zeit fur Gesetzgebung und Rechtswisseschaft", said that law was not made, but grew and developed with society (*Das Recht wird nicht gemacht, est ist und wird mit dem volke*).[39] Customary law and Islamic law grew and developed in society long before the enactment of civil law. In fact, the current development of Indonesian law cannot be separated from the values contained in customary law and Islamic law.

Civil law system adopted by Indonesia, whose main principle is to ensure that law positively is in the form of written codes or set forth in the form of law. It theoretically does not recognize any unwritten law. However, in practice, this civil law system has many weaknesses because of its written nature in that it becomes

---

[38] Munnie Yasmin, "Analysis Of The Legal Thought Of Postmodern Era Of The Development Legal Theory By Mochtar Kusumaatmadja And Progressive Legal Theory By Satjipto Rahardjo For Legal Development Of Indonesia In The Perspective Of Ontological, Epistemological And Axiological," *IOSR Journal Of Humanities And Social Science*, vol. 21, no. 09, (2016): 66-75.

[39] Friedrich Karl von Savigny and Abraham Hayward, *Of the Vocation of Our Age For Legislation And Jurisprudence*, 1st ed., (United States: Lawbook Exchange Ltd., 2011): 50-51.

inflexible in following community developments, and tends to be rigid and static. Rigidity in the form of written rules can be said to be a form of limitation when considering abstracts or in the context of material and dynamics in the dimension of time. Therefore, limiting bringing the value of consciousness of society into law will logically lead to a lag in the substance of law. The totality of mandating the application of written civil law also ultimately creates a legal gap in society. Such a legal gap can only be overcome by using an unwritten legal system, namely customary law or Islamic law.

Customary law as the original law of Indonesia has experienced a period of being allocated secondary status, resulting in its loss as one of the sources of law in Indonesia. The main reason for such a state is the perception of the nature of customary law, which is considered as primitive, superflous, and antiquated. Implications arising from Indonesian legal politics result in the fact that in solving problems in society, there is a general tendency to override customary law and prioritize state law, even though customary law may be more relevant to the issues as compared to state law.

There are many horizontal conflicts between indigenous peoples that are ideally suited to resolution by utilising customary law and customary community settlement institutions. Indeed, in the post–Independence era, the need for customary law has become increasingly important, considering that the Indonesian civil law system has experienced many problems due to its rigid and static nature. In fact, it is submitted that customary law has a strategic role in the formation of legal jurisprudence by judges in court.

6 FINAL COMMENTS

In any state, power is exercised by government based on the rule of law, or what we call the rule of law, which aims to carry out a legal order. Historically, this meant the state applied the system of law that existed between each kingdom's territories. In Indonesia, there were two royal eras, namely the Hindu-Buddhist kingdom era and the Islamic kingdom era.

Since Independence, there has been a tug of war between State laws and customary laws stemming from the two eras. State laws can be considered in periods – the *Older Order*, the *New order* and the *Reformation period*. The Old Order was led by President Soekarno and Vice President Moh. From 18 August 1945, the legal system in Indonesia was composed entirely of customary law subsystems, Islamic law subsystems, and Western legal subsystems.

During the New Order era, after the G.30.S/PKI S/PKI Coup was thwarted, and thereafter from the time of issuance of the *11 March 1966 order,* often known as "*Supersemar,*" a new chapter in the history of the Indonesian nation began.[40] This was later referred to as the Order of the government. Thereafter, this new Order subdued the existing legal institutions and placed them under the executive branch, controlled the education system, restricted public critical thinking and stunted the growth of national law and jurisprudence. The downturn observed in every aspect during this New Order era reached its nadir, and coincided with the emergence of an economic crisis that seriously impacted the economy of the Indonesian nation and Asian countries. Following this difficult time, the Reformation period brought some stability.

However, the issue of state laws combining with Islamic laws and customary laws has not faded from the landscape of Indonesia. The need for customary law to resolve disputes and provide legal solutions to problems in the form of Islamic law and other customary laws will only increase in the future in Indonesian society.

---

[40] Indonesian President Sukarno reluctantly signed a decree that gave army commander General Suharto a full authority to restore order, to protect Sukarno, and safeguard the Indonesian revolution. This decree, which would become the start of a brand new chapter in Indonesian history (*the New Order*) as it marked the transfer of executive power from Sukarno to Suharto, became known as *Supersemar* (*Surat Perintah Sebelas Maret*, or the Decree of 11 March).

BIBLIOGRAPHY

o Amrullah Achmad, and Busthanul Arifin, *Dimensi Hukum Islam Dalam Sistem Huku Nasional* (Jakarta: Gema Insani Press, 1996).

o Ansori Z Ahmad, *Sejarah Dan Kedudukan BW Di Indonesia* (Jakarta: Rajawali, 1986).

o Arya Dauh I Putu Agus, Sukadana I Ketut, and I Made Minggu Widyantara, "Peran Pranata Adat Dalam Pencegahan Konflik Antara Kelompok Masyarakat Adat". *Jurnal Preferensi Hukum* 1, no. 1 (2020).

o Bisri Hasan, *Dimensi-Dimensi Kompilasi Hukum Islam* (Bandung: Ulul Albab Press, 1998).

o Ehrlich, Eugen, and Walter Lewis Moll, *Fundamental Principles of the Sociology of Law*, 5th ed. (Cambridge: Harvard University, 2002).

o Friedrich Karl von Savigny and Abraham Hayward, *Of the Vocation of Our Age for Legislation and Jurisprudence*, 1st ed. (United States: Lawbook Exchange Ltd., 2011).

o H. Mustaghfirin, "Sistem Hukum Barat, Sistem Hukum Adat, Dan Sistem Hukum Islam Menuju Sebagai Sistem Hukum Nasional Sebuah Ide Yang Harmoni," *Jurnal Dinamika Hukum* no. 11 (2011): 90-95.

o Handrawan, "Sanksi Adat Delik Perzinahan (Umoapi) Dalam Perspektif Hukum Pidana Adat Tolaki," *Perspektif* 21, no. 3 (2016): 199-210.

o Jimly Asshiddiqie, *Pengantar Ilmu Hukum Tata Negara* (Jakarta: Sekretariat Jendral dan Kepaniteraan, 2006).

o Julian Rivers, "The Question of Freedom of Religion or Belief and Defamation," *Religion & Human Rights* 2, no. 3 (2007): 115-131.

o Kusmayanti Hazar, Sherly Ayuna Putri, and Linda Rahmainy, "Praktik Penyelesaian Sengketa Di Pengadilan Agama Melalui Sidang Keliling Dikaitkan Dengan Prinsip Dan Asas Hukum Acara Perdata," *ADHAPER: Jurnal Hukum Acara Perdata* 4, no. 2 (2019): 145-161.

o Lukman Hakim, *Asas-Asas Hukum Pidana* (Sleman: Budi Utama, 2020).

o M. Husnu Abadi, *Pemikiran Kodifikasi Hukum Administrasi Negara Indonesia* (Pekanbaru: UIR Press, 2004).

o M. Solly Lubis, *Asas-Asas Hukum Tata Negara* (Bandung: Alumni, 2021).

o M. Yahya Harahap, *Beberapa Tinjauan Permasalahan Hukum Buku Kesatu* (Bandung: Citra Aditya Bakti, 1997).

o Mahatir bin Mohamad and Dasuki bin Haji Ahmad, *Pembaharuan Pemikiran Islam Tun Dr. Mahathir Mohamad* (Kuala Lumpur: RD Network, 2004).

o Muhammad Busar, *Asas-Asas Hukum Adat: Suatu Pengantar* (Jakarta: Pradnya Paramita, 1976).

o Muhammad Daud Ali, *Asas-Asas Hukum Islam (Hukum Islam I): Pengantar Ilmu Hukum Dan Tata Hukum Islam Di Indonesia* (Jakarta: Rajawali, 1990).

o Oktavianto Arto, "Eksistensi Hak Ulayat Masyarakat Hukum Adat Ngata Toro," *Jurisprudentie: Jurusan Ilmu Hukum Fakultas Syariah Dan Hukum* 7, no. 2 (2020): 228-239.

o Prakoso Djoko, *Azas-Azas Hukum Perkawinan Di Indonesia* (Jakarta: Bina Aksara, 1987).

o R. Soepomo, *Bab-Bab Tentang Hukum Adat* (Jakarta: Pradnya Paramita, 2003).

o Ratna Winahyu Lestari Dewi, "Peranan Hukum Adat Dalam Pembangunan Dan Pembangunan Hukum Pidana Nasional," *Perspektif* 10, no. 3 (2005): 265-273.

o Rofiq Ahmad, *Pembaharuan Hukum Islam Di Indonesia* (Yogyakarta: Gama Media, 2001).

o Romli Atmasasmita, *Globalisasi Dan Kejahatan Bisnis* (Jakarta: Kencana, 2010).

o Sahalessy Jacoba, "Peran Latupati Sebagai Lembaga Hukum Adat Dalam Penyelesaian Konflik Antar Negeri Di Kecamatan Leihitu Propinsi Maluku," *SASI* 17, no. 3 (2011): 45-52.

o Sukardja Ahmad, *Piagam Madinan Dan Undang-Undang Dasar Republik Indonesia* (Jakarta: Sinar Grafika, 2012).

o Supomo Djokosutono and Pieter Gills, *Sejarah Politik Hukum Adat* (Jakarta: Pradnya Paramita, 1982).

o Syamsudin, "Beban Masyarakat Menghadapi Hukum Negara," *Jurnal Hukum Ius Quia Iustum* 15, no. 3 (2008): 338-351.

o Wiratrama Perdana Herlambang, "Perkembangan Politik Hukum Peradilan Adat," *Mimbar Hukum-Fakultas Hukum Universitas Gadjah Mada* 30, no. 3 (2018): 491-505.

o Wirjono R Prodjodikoro, *Tindak-Tindak Pidana Tertentu Di Indonesia* (Jakarta: Refika Aditama, 2010).

o Munnie Yasmin, "Analysis Of The Legal Thought Of Postmodern Era of the Development Legal Theory by Mochtar Kusumaatmadja and Progressive Legal Theory by Satjipto Rahardjo for Legal Development Of Indonesia In The Perspective Of Ontological, Epistemological And Axiological," *IOSR Journal of Humanities and Social Science*, vol. 21, no. 09 (2016): 66-75.

CHAPTER 10

THE IMPACT OF HISTORY, COLONISATION, SLAVERY, RELIGION, IMMIGRATION & EXTERNAL LAW ON THE EVOLUTION OF BRAZILIAN LAW

Attorney Flavio Bermudes Damaceno

1. INTRODUCTION

In its current form, Brazilian law can trace its jurisprudence back through the impact/influence of various internal and external laws and philosophies – (1) laws of the original natives, (2) Portuguese laws during colonisation, (3) religion, (3) the influence of immigration from different countries, and (4) the external influence of other countries such as the United States. In order to trace these effects, scholars also need to analyse the interaction of such factors over time.

The objective of this chapter is to provide an overview of this evolution, without going into detail on dates, the background to the events, or resulting legal

345

concepts. The chapter starts with the history of Brazilian law, providing an insight, in particular, into the phases of the *Colonial Period* and the *Imperial Period* in Brazilian history. Later in the chapter, the influence of the *United States Constitution* on the development and evolution of law during the *Republic Period* is discussed. In addition, the issues of immigration over the centuries and the demographic characteristics of Brazil are presented, including the influence of the various religions practiced by these peoples.

Finally, an attempt has been made to demonstrate the impact/influence of all the above factors in evolution of Brazilian law. The chapter concludes by revealing the impact of the evolution of Brazilian law on rulings by the Supreme Court that affect Brazilians' daily life, trade and commerce.

2. HISTORY OF BRAZILIAN LAW

Before the "discovery" of Brazil, the area was populated by **Indigenous peoples**, and historians believe that the number of individuals living in territory could have been as high as 6.8 million.

According to historians, the Indigenous peoples' way of living was rudimentary, relying on hunting, fishing and pursuing basic agriculture. They also domesticated wild pigs and capybaras. Among the Indigenous peoples, there was no social class and accordingly everyone enjoyed the same rights. Therefore, there was no notion of private property existing in the region. The land belonged to all inhabitants of the tribe, and the same applied to the proceeds of hunting or agriculture.

Two individuals were key to the Indigenous peoples within society. The first was the shaman or *"pajé"*. This individual was like a priest, who would be in charge of effecting connections between the gods and the people. He also exercised the role of a doctor or healing person, and ensured knowledge accumulated over the centuries was passed on to the next generations. The other was the tribe's chief or "*cacique*". He would oversee the social organisation of the Indigenous peoples and provide guidance and resolve conflicts within the tribe.

As the Indigenous peoples had a modest way of life and did not have a complex society, they lived in small tribes and did not seem to influence the initial formation of Brazilian law. Their biggest legacy to Brazilian (and maybe global) society and laws could be in the field of environment and forest preservation. By adopting a simple way of life, it meant that the environment was in essence untouched by them over the years, as they extracted from nature only what was needed for basic life.[1]

Present day Brazil was "discovered" by the Portuguese around the year 1500 CE,[2] and remained a Portuguese colony until the country´s independence on 7 September 1822. Therefore, Brazilian law has its roots in Portuguese law. In turn, Portuguese law evolved from elements of Roman law, Germanic law and Canon law and therefore, as a logical consequence, these laws also impacted and have had a role in the evolution of Brazilian law.

Given that Brazil was a colony, Portuguese law required a level of adaptation within society. With this in mind, Portuguese legislation was split in two, one applicable to Portugal and the other to Brazil. The Brazilian portion was named *special legislation*.[3]

---

[1] Over the last few years and especially the last decade, the extraction of minerals from indigenous land has become a controversial topic in Brazil. As a result, it has brought attention from politicians, NGOs and international media. National Geographic Magazine has recently published an article in Portuguese available at: <https://www.nationalgeographicbrasil.com/meio-ambiente/2019/11/entenda-polemica-em-torno-da-mineracao-em-terras-indigenas>, accessed 27 August 2021.

[2] The date Brazil was discovered is a controversial topic. In his book entitled *De Situ Orbis*, Duarte Pacheco Pereira claims the country of Brazil was founded in 1498 at the order of the Portuguese King Manuel I.

[3] See, Paulo Dourado de Gusmão, *Introdução ao Estudo do Direito* (Rio de Janeiro: Forense, 1995), *337.*

Brazilian law is a codified system, and the primary source of rights is the law. The main areas of law have their own codes, such as the *Commercial Code dated 1850.* In this chapter, the author will address the evolution of legislation, in particular, in three periods – (1) the Colonial Period, (2) the Imperial Period and (3) the Brazilian Republic.

2.1 COLONIAL PERIOD (1500-1822)

Law is a reflection of social organisation over time within a certain location. Hence, whilst the Portuguese wished to apply their laws to Brazil, the local reality that existed in the region was different to that which existed within Portugal. Accordingly, there was naturally a need to adapt Portuguese law to the needs of the colony of Brazil. The Portuguese laws that were applicable to the colonies were enunciated in the *Royal Ordinations.* These ordinations were – the *Afonsinas Ordinations*, the *Manueline Ordinations* and the *Philippine Ordinations.*

The *Afonsinas Ordinations* date from the 15th century CE and were finished during the reign of Afonso V.[4] The purpose of these Ordinations was to consolidate and standardise the applicability of law in the region. The Portuguese colonial government saw a need for uniformity, due to laws being applied turgidly by the authorities on behalf of the King. The laws being applied during this period in Portugal were basically grounded in Cannon and Roman law. The application of the Ordinations resulted in five books on – (1) criminal rights, (2) civil rights, (3) commercial rights, (4) judiciary organisation & jurisdiction, and the church relations with the State, and (5) civil and commercial procedures. The Afonsinas Ordinations mark the transition between the middle ages and the modern age of Brazil.

---

[4] It is said that *The* Afonsinas Ordinations were finally completed around 1446 CE, though amendments were made later on.

After the Afonsinas Ordinations, the Portuguese King Manuel I ordered new ordinations named after him, that is, the *Manueline Ordinations* between 1512-13 CE-1521 CE. These ordinations comprised of compiled a large number of laws and acts that modified previous laws. The Manueline Ordinations were also the first printed legislation in Brazil, as the Afonsinas Ordinations were handwritten.

In 1581 CE, when Spain also reigned Portugal (known as the Iberian Union), the King of Spain, Felipe I, ordered a new ordination known as the *Philippine Ordinations* which was finally completed during the reign of Felipe II. In contrast to what one might expect, the Spanish recognised the validity of Portuguese law, which was applicable both in Portugal and Brazil. In fact, these ordinations gave even more importance to Roman law and Common law. As none of the ordinations could address the specific local needs of Brazil, special legislation was enacted, for example that dealt with maritime exchange and insurance.

The importance of Roman law was highlighted with the enactment of the *"Lei da Boa Razão"* or "Good Reason law" in 1769 CE. This law established that Roman law was to apply in the case of a legal gap, provided there was "good reason".

At the end of 1807 CE, the destiny of Brazil changed. Napoleon Bonaparte, a French military leader and emperor invaded Portugal, and D. João VI, the King of Portugal, had no choice but to escape from Portugal. With the help of the British Navy, the Portuguese Court fled to Brazil, with the result that, in 1815 CE, D. João VI enacted the *"Carta-de-Lei"*, the result of which was that Brazil was no longer a Portuguese colony. Brazil became part of the Portuguese Kingdom, and the city of Rio de Janeiro became the political centre.

During his stay in Brazil, D. João VI tried his best to address local needs. Accordingly, various laws were promulgated to deal with the social, political and economic requirements of the country. However, in 1821 CE, he returned to

Portugal. Upon his return, he left his son, D. Pedro I to continue the progress he had made with legislations in Brazil.

As Brazil did not have a constitution at that time, the Portuguese Court issued a decree in 1821 CE imposing the *Spanish Constitution 1812*. This Constitution was only intended to last until a new constitution was drafted in Portugal. However, it did not sit well with the Brazilian aristocracy, who were now used to having their own laws, and were fomenting the idea of becoming independent of Portugal.

The result was that, on the day after a decree which imposed the Spanish Constitution was rejected by the populace, efforts began to draft a Brazilian Constitution based on the *Portuguese Constitution 1821*. Again, this did not meet the expectations of the local people in Brazil and, as a result, in 1822 a decree was issued aimed at calling a constituent assembly. The Portuguese Court reacted by trying to resume the colony regime, and this was just what the locals needed to achieve independence. On 7 September 1822, D. Pedro I declared an independent Brazil.

2.2. IMPERIAL PERIOD (1822-1889)

During the Imperial Period, legislative activity kicked in, and it is during this time that Brazilian legislations were enacted and substituted Portuguese laws.

The first task of D. Pedro I was to make sure his empire had a constitution. It was not long before this was delivered, and the First *Constitution of Brazil 1824* was finally drafted. The Constitution provided for a centralised, or unitary, government, a hereditary monarchy, and the power of the state to be divided among three branches (legislative, judiciary and executive). The caveat here was the moderator power exercised by the emperor. This power was designed to bring balance between the various powers.

The next step forward was to substitute the Royal Ordinations. In 1830, the *Criminal Code* became law and replaced Book V of the Philippine Ordinations. The Criminal Code had four parts – crimes and penalties, public crimes, private crimes and police crimes. No one could be punished due to an offence before this act was foreseen as a crime by law. In other words, punishment could not be applied to an offence that occurred before the law was enacted. The biggest breakthrough, as compared to the previous regime, was in the types of punishments handed out. In Portuguese legislation, punishments such as quartering, amputation and whipping were common. However, these penalties were subsequently replaced primarily with imprisonment. Punishment was now being understood as an educational and corrective tool rather than as revenge.

In 1850,[5] the *Brazilian Commercial Code 1850* was promulgated during the reign of D. Pedro II. This Code was based on Spanish, French and Portuguese Commercial Codes. It replaced the Philipines Ordination and the "*Lei da Boa Razão*" or "Good Reason law". The Code was important to Brazil, as it provided a much needed update to the prevailing circumstances. Accordingly, laws were adapted, and impacted previous legislation in areas of commerce, the stock market, markets and warehousing in general, banking, transportation, and maritime law, to name but a few fields of law. One of the main goals of the Code was to protect the interests of commerce and merchants. It regulated trade and merchants, and clarified prerogatives and obligations of the various parties.

Before the Commercial Code was promulgated, various attempts were made by the authorities to put together a Civil Code, but it was never successfully completed. Given the difficulties at the time, it was decided to first consolidate existing civil laws. This work of collating existing civil law was successfully performed in 1857 by Teixeira de Freitas. This enabled a formulation of the *Civil*

---

[5] Most of the Commercial Code has now been replaced by newer legislation. e.g. the *new Civil Code dated 2002*, leaving only the Maritime law provisions. Therefore, Maritime law remains one of the oldest legislations in Brazil.

Code in later years. However, the Civil Code for Brazil was never fully drafted until the next period - that is, the Republican period.

2.2.1. Influence of the United States Constitution

The independence of the 13 American colonies in 1786 influenced events in Brazil. Similar to what had happened in the US, Brazil experienced growing dissatisfaction with the then-existing governance and the people demanded participation. Even though Brazil had already gained independence from Portugal in 1822, the Brazilians were not being represented in corridors of power.

The *United States of America Constitution 1787* was a modern Constitution and influenced the thought process in Brazil. The principles of federalism as a methodology for state organisation, and presidentialism as a government system were copied by Brazil from the American Constitution.

The American Constitution is rigid in that its' provisions cannot be easily altered. In order to make a constitutional amendment, it is necessary for all states to participate and this result in a slow and complex process. This process partly explains the limited number of amendments introduced over the years - only 27 in total. However, the primary explanation for the restricted number of amendments is that interpretation of the constitution by the Supreme Court provides a degree of flexibility. Therefore, the American Constitution may be considered rigid and the flexible at the same time. The concise wording of just seven articles, which laid down concepts and principles, allows the Supreme Court to adapt their interpretation over time, to respond to the needs of American society.

The various versions of the *Brazilian Constitution,*[6] the first of which was in 1824, have also been rigid, but the amendment process is not as complex as in the USA.

---

[6] Brazil had 7 constitutions in total, and here a comparison is made to the last constitution dated 1988. The First Constitution was the *Imperial Constitution of 1824*. Thereafter, it was followed by the

In the current *Brazilian Constitution 1988*, all which is required in Brazil is to have the amendment proposal voted and approved by 3/5ths of the representatives in each house of Congress. This, relatively easier, process explains the need for 111 amendments to the *Brazilian Constitution 1988* in just 33 years. The number of amendments is explained by the fact that the Brazilian version is very long - over 250 articles originally - and has an analytical text which requires constant change over time.

The decentralised organisation of states in the United States was replicated in Brazil. All Brazilian states have their own constitution and specific laws. However, the American federal system provides much more freedom locally. For example, in Brazil, most taxes are levied by the Federal Government, and it is then distributed to the states and cities. This is known as upside-down federalism and is a remnant of Portuguese colonialism.

2.3. BRAZILIAN REPUBLIC (1889-PRESENT)

During the Imperial period, which lasted almost 70 years, the cities expanded, and an urban aristocracy formed in the region. These people were businessman, liberal professionals (such as lawyers, doctors and so forth), leaders of the state forces and farmers, especially the coffee farm owners or "barões" from Rio de Janeiro and São Paulo states. The aristocracy had no voice before the emperor, D. Pedro II (son of D. Pedro I),[7] and thus had no influence on the decisions that were taken. Therefore, the only option for such aristocracy to achieve political representation was to overthrow the imperial regime.

In addition to the lack of political representation, another point of dissatisfaction was the abolishment of slavery. In 1889, whilst D. Pedro II was travelling in

---

Old Republic Constitution 1891, the *Third Constitution 1934*, the *"Estado Novo" Constitution 1937*, the *Fifth Constitution 1946*, the *Sixth Constitution 1967*, and the *Citizen's Constitution 1988* until present.
[7] D. Pedro I left Brazil in 1831 for Portugal and abdicated his throne in favour of his son, D. Pedro II.

Europe, his daughter, Princess Isabel, approved the *"Áurea"* law freeing all slaves in the country. However, this law created a problem in that it did not foresee the call for an indemnity by the slave owners who lost their "property".

The overthrow process was not a popular movement, in the sense that this movement did not represent the bulk of the population. The process of overthrowing the monarchy was led by Marshal Deodoro da Fonseca on 15 November 1889, with the support of the military barracks. After the king was overthrown, all the politicians in favour of the monarchy were imprisoned. Thereafter, the Royal Family received an order to leave Brazil immediately, and Marshall Fonseca became the first President of the Republic of Brazil.

The new Republic of Brazil was federal in nature, and centralised power was substituted by a decentralised political-administrative structure in its provinces, similar to what had occurred in the United States of America in the 18th and 19th centuries.

In 1891, the *first Republican constitution* 1891 was promulgated. It had the following main characteristics – (1) presidentialism, (2) federalism, (3) separation of the three powers (the moderator's power was suppressed), and (4) the autonomy of the States.

Now that Brazil was a republic, it accordingly had a Criminal Code, a Commercial Code and a new Constitution; the next step was to have a Civil Code. Work began on this in 1899, and four projects were gradually accomplished. The version that gained traction was the one created by Clóvis Beviláqua. His Civil Code was inspired by the French, Austrian and German Civil Codes. The Italian doctrine was also taken into consideration, in addition to these doctrines. After intense debate and extreme care with literary and juridical precision, *the Civil Code 1916* was approved by Congress in 1916.

The *Civil Code 1916* was divided into two parts – (1) general, and (2) special. The *general* part laid down rules in relation to people, property, legal facts and legal acts, discussed the nullity theory and gave rules for time bars. On the other hand, the *special* part laid down rules for – (1) family law, that included rules for marriage, protection for minors and so forth, (2) property rights, making necessary distinctions between possessory rights and property rights, (3) laws of obligation, for example, type of contracts, unilateral will declarations and illicit acts, and (4) rules for succession rights and testaments.

There are legal scholars who have pointed to the fact that the Civil Code was born old, as a result of the influence of conservative members of society - that is, politicians, lawyers, property owners and so forth.[8] One criticism of the Civil Code was that property rights were made absolute. In this regard, the Code excessively focused on individual rights, as it failed to give importance to the fact that property has a social role in Brazil.

Another criticism was the distinction made between children born within marriage (considered as legitimate in law) and children born out of wedlock (considered as illegitimate in law). This Code took the same approach as other similar legislations that had been promulgated in foreign countries, adopting the concept of the constitution of a family by marriage. Modern law has abandoned this concept, replacing it with the principle that a family is formed by social-affective ties.

However, all in all, *Civil Code 1916* was an important accomplishment of the Republic.

---

[8] C. Pereira, *Instituições de direito civil, vol I*, 19th ed. (Rio de Janeiro: Grupo Gen - Editora Forense, 2000), 58.

3. IMPACT ON BRAZILIAN LAWS DUE TO IMMIGRATION INTO BRAZIL

The formation of the current composition of the Brazilian population began with the immigration of Indigenous people. The Indigenous peoples are thought to have been living in the area for thousands of years. It is believed that they migrated from Asia during the ice age, around twelve thousand years ago, using the Bering Strait to cross to the Americas. When the Portuguese arrived in Brazil, the number of Indigenous people living in Brazil was estimated between 1 million and 6.8 million, spread across the region.[9]

With the arrival of Portuguese explorers, a new immigration phase began in the region. In particular, in the first few decades following their arrival in the 15th and 16th centuries CE, very few Portuguese people settled in Brazil. Those who were willing to migrate from Portugal were mainly criminals, renegades or shipwrecked sailors, who did not leave much behind, and thus had nothing to lose by settling in the new land. These few immigrants started to integrate with the Indigenous population, and a process of inter-mixing started.

Over time, with the development of sugar cane farms in the region, Portuguese immigration increased. However, as Portugal had a small population and other colonies to explore, immigration to Brazil from Portugal remained relatively low. During the period 1500 CE to 1700 CE, only a few thousand Portuguese immigrated to Brazil annually. The biggest pull for Portuguese immigration into Brazil pertained to sugar production. However, the production of sugar required high investment, was labour intensive and there were harsh working conditions on the sugar farms.

---

[9] Brasil Official Publication, *500 anos de povoamento* (Rio de Janeiro: Ministério do Planejamento, Orçamento e Gestão, 2007), 39.

As Portuguese migration was low and there was a labour shortage on the sugar cane farms, the issue was resolved by bringing in slaves from Africa.[10] In fact, prior to the 15th Century and the discovery of Brazil, the Portuguese were already cultivating sugar cane on Madeira Island, São Tomé and Cabo Verde (all islands on the west coast of the African continent). Around 4 million African slaves, men, women and children, were brought to Brazil from sub-Saharan Africa.

Although Africans were initially brought in after the year 1500 CE to work on the sugar cane farms, over the period of more than 300 years of the slavery trade they were being used in every sector of the economy. In rural areas, slaves from Africa worked on farms cultivating sugar, coffee, cotton and so forth. They also worked in the mining industry. In cities, they performed domestic work, sold food, and worked in mechanical shops.

Prior to independence, the Portuguese would attack and destroy European ships, burning any vessel that approached Brazilian ports. However, after the independence of Brazil in 1822 CE, the dynamics of immigration changed completely. The prior fierce Portuguese approach of not allowing other European nationals to settle in Brazil eased. This change of policy encouraged the immigration of Germans, Italians and Spanish nationals; however, Portuguese nationals remained in the majority in Brazil.

After 1877 CE, Italians made up almost half of all nationals immigrating to Brazil. They were attracted by the incentives provided by Rio Grande do Sul State (South Brazil) and a policy to replace African slaves on the coffee farms of São Paulo State. The Italian immigrants' integration into the country was facilitated by the fact that they all spoke a neo-Latin language. The same applied to Spanish nationals, who also spoke a neo-Latin language.

---

[10] Portuguese initially coerced indigenous people to work on the farms initially, before they began to rely on slaves from Africa.

Japanese immigrants started to arrive in 1908 CE, encouraged by incentives from their government to emigrate, following a period of population growth in Japan which had resulted in a lack of available land to farm and high debt levels among rural workers. Their settlement in the country went well, despite the harsh realities of the new land. Brazil now boasts the biggest Japanese community outside Japan - about 1.5 million people.

After the First World War, the country attracted immigrants of many other nationalities, such as Polish, Russian and Romanian, most likely due to the political situation in their countries, along with Syrians and Lebanese. The immigration influx into Brazil continued, especially during the Second World War which had resulted in widespread violence and famine in Europe.

All the above immigration into Brazil definitely swayed legislation in Brazil, as these immigrants began to influence society and brought their own cultural norms.

4. IMPACT ON BRAZILIAN LAWS DUE TO THE PRACTICES OF VARIOUS RELIGIONS

A direct consequence of the immigration of so many nationalities into Brazil was the introduction of multiple religions into Brazilian society. According to IBGE (Brazilian Statistics Institute),[11] in the year 2010,[12] there were 25 religions in the country. This included non-religious, non-determined/multiple religions and people who "did not know" at the census. If sub-religions were to be added, then there were over 40 religions. Examples of sub-religions are Presbyterian and Lutheran, which form part of the Evangelical Religion.

---

[11] See <https://cidades.ibge.gov.br/brasil/pesquisa/23/22107>, accessed 21 March 2021.

[12] The last census was taken in 2010 and it is supposed to be repeated every 10 years. The census helps the government in Brazil to allocate appropriate assets (such as for schooling, health care and so forth) across the country. Due to the pandemic, the 2020 census has been postponed.

The most practised religion in Brazil is *Roman Catholic Apostolic*, followed by around 123 million people, about half the country's population. This is explained by the fact that the Portuguese colonists brought Jesuit priests to Brazil to catechise the local population and Indigenous peoples. The catechisation meant that the Indigenous peoples had to learn the Portuguese language in order to be able to read the *Bible*. Over the centuries, in addition to the native population, the slaves brought from Africa also became Catholic.

As the roots of the country are Roman Catholic Apostolic, many people end up stating on the census that they are Catholic, however, in practice this does not mean that the majority attend religious mass regularly.

In the last few decades, the Protestant values are increasing in the society.[13] As a result of which, the second most practised religion in Brazil is the *Evangelical* religion followed by around 42 million people. This is also a consequence of Portuguese colonisation, which introduced Christianity to the country.

The third most practised religion that is not related to Christianity is *Spiritism*, followed by almost 4 million people. This is linked to the fact that the Christianity believes in the concept of life after death and accordingly, the faith of Spiritism may have been able to pick up followers who were not entirely satisfied with the Catholic and Evangelical religions.

The other relevant religions in Brazil, although with fewer followers, are *Umbanda* and *Candomblé* followed by about 1 million people each. These religions developed when the Portuguese imposed mandatory conversion into Catholicism on the slaves. Therefore, to preserve their own beliefs, the slaves related their African spirits to the Catholic saints. It is believed that the number of people who follow these religions could be higher than 1 million; however, Candomblé was forbidden under Portuguese rule.

---

[13] See <https://www.coha.org/evangelicals-in-brazil/>, accessed on 15 November 2021.

The last religion that it is important to note is *Buddhism*. This is practiced by almost 250,000 people, and was brought to Brazil by the Japanese during their immigration in the 20th century.

There is a large part of the population who do not practice any religion. About 15 million people stated that they simply do not follow any religion. It is necessary to understand that this does not mean that people do not believe in God as, out of this group, only around 600,000 people stated they were atheist.

The introduction of so many religions into the social fabric of Brazil resulted in new concepts and new perspectives being added to the ethos of Brazil. It is submitted that this influenced laws in Brazil to some extent through religious jurisprudence and beliefs.

5. EVOLUTION OF BRAZILIAN LAW

Over the five centuries of Brazil's existence, the law has evolved considerably. The death for crime punishment it is long gone, following adoption of the concept that a penalty is an educational tool rather than revenge, as defended by Cesare Beccaria.[14] The concept of power has also shifted, from emanating from one person - the King (Monarchy) - to the people (Republic), by electing its representatives.

One area of law impacted largely by religion was family law. It was only in 1977 that divorce was finally allowed in Brazil. From the time the first bill was presented in 1893, it took 80 years of debate for divorce to be legalised in Brazil. The Catholic Church was against divorce and, along with conservative sections of

---

[14] Cesare Beccaria was Italian, a jurist, philosopher, politician, and lawyer. In 1764 CE, he wrote a treatise entitled *Crimes and Punishment* or *Dei Delitti e Delle Pene* which was against torture and the death penalty. He is considered the father of modern criminal law and criminal justice. *Crimes and Punishment* is a must read for any law or philosophy enthusiast.

society, blocked any attempt in parliament to present a bill foreseeing this possibility. The absence of divorce meant that unhappy couples could split and divide assets by dissolution of the marital society, but they remained bound by matrimonial ties. Therefore, parties in unhappy marriages could not remarry.

Couples unable to remarry lacked legal rights and were often in relationships that did not have the sanctity of law. This resulted in such parties suffering intense discrimination from society. Another problem was that if children were born outside marriage, these children were considered illegitimate in the eyes of the law.

It was not easy to implement divorce in the country, not only because of the Catholic Church's strong opposition to the idea of divorce, but also due to the legislative process required to bring in such a radical change in social norms. To bring in the concept of divorce, a constitutional amendment was required.[15] Finally, *amendment number 9, and a law, 6.515*, regulating the subject of divorce was sanctioned in Brazilian Congress on 26 December 1977.

The culmination of the evolution of Brazilian law is marked by the *Brazilian Constitution 1988*. In 1988, after more than two decades of military dictatorship, Brazil gained its 7th Constitution,[16] commonly referred to as the Civic Constitution. The citizens of Brazil participated intensively in the drafting process by submitting 112 "popular amendments".[17]

The *Brazil Constitution 1988* is quite different from the *United States' Constitution*. The Brazil Constitution 1988 is relatively long and has over 200 articles. It consolidates social rights in its article 6 that provides, *"Social rights are education,*

---

[15] Refer to the discussion on the issue of amendment to Constitution in §2.2.1 of this Chapter.

[16] As this is a concise chapter, detailed discussion on other constitutions was intentionally omitted.

[17] "Popular amendments" or "*emendas populares*" were an instrument created to allow the population to submit amendment requests to the *draft constitution*. There were formal requirements for these submissions, one of which was the necessity for thirty thousand citizen signatures. Over 12 million people in Brazil participated in this process, highlighting its popularity.

health, food, work, housing, transport, leisure, safety, social security, protection of maternity and childhood, assistance to the unaided, in the form of this Constitution". This jurisprudence in the Constitution was in sharp contrast with the elitist earlier Constitution during the colonization of Brazil, when the country was divided into provinces and land titles were given to friends of the King.

The mode through which the people elect their representatives changed pursuant to the Brazil Constitution 1988. Voting rights became universal (everyone is now allowed to vote), and representatives are elected directly. *Art. 14 of the Brazil Constitution 1988* provide, *"Popular sovereignty will be exercised by universal suffrage and by a direct and secret vote, with equal value for all, and under the terms of the law...."* For many years, before the advent of new Constitution, voting rights in Brazil had been restricted to certain sectors of the population, and representatives were chosen indirectly.

The importance of African immigration is recognized by the Constitution, as well as that of other nationals who immigrated to Brazil, and accordingly it protects their cultures. The Indigenous peoples are also mentioned in the Brazilian *Constitution 1988, Art. 215*, which provides:

> The State will guarantee everyone the full exercise of cultural rights and access to the sources of national culture and will support and encourage the appreciation and dissemination of cultural manifestations.
>
> § 1 The State will protect the manifestations of popular, indigenous and Afro-Brazilian cultures, and those of other groups participating in the national civilizing process.

The Indigenous peoples were finally given rights to the lands they occupy, and this was considered a significant achievement - after all, they were in Brazil before everyone else. *Art. 231 of Brazil Constitution* provide:

> The Indians are recognized for their social organization, customs, languages, beliefs and traditions, and their original rights over the lands they traditionally

occupy, and the Union is responsible for demarcating, protecting and enforcing all their assets.

Other gains brought by the *Constitution 1988* that are worth mentioning are freedom of the press and protection of the environment.

The evolution of law is also marked by the emphasis on movement to decode the existing codes due to a need for specialised codes for various topics. Whilst during the Imperial period and part of the Republican period it was important for Brazil to have Criminal, Commercial and Civil Codes, the increasingly complex society and economy in modern Brazil demanded specific and specialised laws.

Drafting any code is usually a long process and encompasses many topics. Reforms to a drafted code are usually difficult to carry out in any country. For example, the *Civil Code 1916* needed an update after half a century. Update works began in 1969, but it was only in 2002 that the code reforms became law in Brazil as *Civil Code 2002*. Therefore, the decoding movement leads to the rise of specialised laws.

Law no. 4.591 1964 is one example of a specialised law in Brazil, which regulated urban condominiums and real state incorporations and came into effect in 1964. Another is *decree law 227 1967*, which regulated the mining industry. With an increasing number of specialised laws, conflicts between provisions on Codes and on specific laws became more common. However, these conflicts were addressed by the precedence of specialised laws over general laws through a concept called as *lex specialis derogat legi generali*.

The most recent evolution of Brazilian law is the new *migration law 13.445 2017*. This statute demonstrates how a country founded on immigration can translate the importance of immigration into a friendly approach toward immigrants at a policy level. Whilst richer developed countries such as the USA and some European nations have embarked upon a stringent and seemingly very harsh approach to immigrants, Brazil, on the other hand, has amplified immigrants' rights by facilitating access to documentation, public services such as social benefits, education, and dedicated social schemes.

One significant change introduced by the new *migration law 13.445 2017 was* that immigrants are no longer subject to imprisonment for being "illegal aliens" in the country. Art 3° of new *migration law 13.445 2017* provides that:

> Brazilian immigration policy is governed by the following principles and guidelines: III - non-criminalization of migration.

Another important change brought by the new *migration law 13.445 2017* was to leave open the type of travel document that can be accepted by Brazilian authorities. Art. 5° *migration law 13.445 2017* provides that:

> Travel documents are: IX - others that may be recognized by the Brazilian State in regulation.

6. FINAL COMMENTS

Brazilian courts are primarily organised into Federal and State courts. The Federal courts' jurisdiction is linked to disputes relating to the Union´s interests. [18] Therefore, if a company has a tax dispute with the Union, a claim is filed before the Federal courts. On the other hand, the State courts deal with daily disputes between private parties. If someone crashes their car and destroys another person's property, the indemnity claim will be heard before the State courts. In addition to the Federal and State courts, there are Special courts. These courts

---

[18] Union here is referred as Federal Government. In Brazil, there are three levels of government – Federal or Union, State and Municipal (cities).

are the Labour courts, Military courts,[19] and Electoral courts. The top court in the hierarchy is the Superior Court of Justice ('STJ'). One of the mandates of the STJ is to provide standardisation in the interpretation of laws. Their mandate excludes interpretation of the Constitution; this is performed by the Supreme Federal Court ('STF').

The STF recently ruled on a case, on 28 October 2021, that illustrates the impact of religion and immigration in interpreting laws in Brazil - in this case, the Constitution.[20] The case before Ministers referred to a crime of racial injury attributed to a citizen who addressed a petrol station clerk as an "ignorant, audacious, little Nigger".[21] The question the Court had to rule upon was whether the crime of racial injury could be considered as racism and thus not be subject to a limitation period. Before continuing with the details of the case, it is important for readers to know that there are exceptions under Brazilian law for legal actions that are not subject to a time bar.

In general, legal actions must be initiated within a period determined by law. As an example, the time limit to commence an action under the Consumer Code ('CDC') is five years. *Article 27 of the CDC* provides, *"The claim for compensation for damages caused by the product or service provided for in Section II of this Chapter shall be time barred in five years, starting the counting of the term from the knowledge of the damage and its authorship."*

It is believed that the statute of limitations aims to bring certainty to legal relations by imposing nullity for claims filed after the deadline. According to Brazilian law, nullity can be invoked by a respondent to a lawsuit, as it is recognised by the court. The reasoning behind the concept of a time limit is that an individual or legal entity

---

[19] There are ongoing discussions amongst the Brazilian judiciary as to how broad a military jurisdiction should be, i.e. during peace time. The point of debate is – should these courts hear disputes between citizens and the military or should it hear cases only during times of war, or cases relating only to soldiers?

[20] The case concluded on 28th October 2021, and was decided on the lawsuit *"HC 154248"*.

[21] The STF judges are referred to as Ministers.

may no longer have memory of the facts and/or documentary evidence of what happened after a certain period.

Going back to the aforementioned case, the lawyers acting for the citizen claimed that the case was time barred. The Court decided that the crime of racial injury features elements related to race, skin colour, ethnicity, religion or origin, intended to offend or insult someone and, therefore, is racism and not subject to a time limit.

Reporting Minister Edson Fachin stated:

> Racial injury consummates the concrete objective of the circulation of racial stereotypes and stigmas by reaching a specific recipient, the racialized individual, which would not be possible without their belonging to a social group also demarcated by race. Here, the argument that racism is directed against a social group, while insult affects the individual singularly, is rejected. Distinction is an impossible operation; a subject is only conceived as a victim of racial injury if he conforms to the stereotypes and stigmas forged against the group to which he belongs.

He went further by stating:

> The attribution of negative value to the individual, in relation to his race, creates the ideological and cultural conditions for the institution and maintenance of subordination, which is so necessary to block the accesses that build structural racism. They also increase the burden of this manifest civilizing backwardness and make even more difficult for the already Herculean task of healing the wounds opened by slavery in order to build a country that truly lives up to the constitutional project in this regard.

This decision is important, as it affirms the Brazilian State's mission to integrate people of all religions and philosophies by creating the tools necessary to punish those who try to create disharmony in society. This mandate is clear in the *Brazilian Constitution 1988,* where it states that racism is not subject to a time limit in its Art. 5, XLII:

All are equal before the law, without distinction of any kind, guaranteeing Brazilians and foreigners residing in the country the inviolability of the right to life, liberty, equality, security and property, in the following terms:

XLII - the practice of racism constitutes a non-bailable and imprescriptible crime, subject to the penalty of imprisonment, under the terms of the law.

Similarly, the Indigenous peoples' legacy pertaining to the preservation of forests may have been translated into another recent ruling of the Supreme Court. In April 2020, the STF concluded an analysis of the issue of whether a time limit is applicable to the Public Civil Action for issues of repair and damages caused to the Environment. In the case,[22] an indemnity claim was brought by the Federal Public Prosecutor against a few citizens and a company, aiming to secure repair material, moral and environmental damages resulting from the invasion of indigenous lands between 1981 and 1987, with the intention of illegally extracting logs from those lands.

The defendants' counsel claimed they could not be punished on the basis that the suit was time-barred. By a majority, the STF disagreed with the defendants and established the precedent that a claim for civil reparation for environmental damage is not subject to a time limit. The reporting Minister Alexandre de Morais stated:[23]

…illegal and disorderly deforestation brings severe consequences such as the destruction of biodiversity, impoverishment of soil, rising temperatures, among other ills. Thus, although the indigenous community is directly affected, the environmental impact is directed to the whole society. And, many times, its effects will only be noticed years later.

This ruling not only impacts citizens and companies, but also liability insurers who may be on the hook for a foreseeable long term.

---

[22] See *RE 654833 / AC.*
[23] Ibid. See *RE 654833 / AC*, page 16.

Another ruling that it is worth considering to observe the impact of history, religion and immigration is a case where the issue concerns abortion.[24] This case was decided by the STF in 2012. It was brought by the National Confederation of Health Workers who argued that, pursuant to *Criminal Code 1940, articles 124, 126 and 128, lines I and II* criminalise abortion, and accordingly these articles are against the Constitution on this issue.

The claim was filed using a writ foreseen in the Constitution called "*Arguição de Descumprimento de Preceito Fundamental*", or Claim to Argue Non-Compliance of a Fundamental Precept.

The main discussion point of the case was whether said criminal provisions were against the Constitution when the foetus is *anencephalic* (foetus having the cerebral hemispheres and a large part of the skull congenitally absent; exhibiting anencephaly) and therefore, those provisions criminalising abortion should not be applied under this specific circumstance. The case drew immense public interest, and the National Conference of Brazilian Bishops made an application to intervene in the proceedings as an "*amicus curiae*", or friend of the court, but this request was rejected by the reporting Minister.

The case was the subject of intense debate, and the final decision ran to over 400 pages.[25] The first page of the judgement stated that the State is Secular and should be completely neutral in relation to religion.

The reporting Minister Marco Aurélio stated in his reasoning that, up to the year of 2005, the lower instance courts had issued an estimated three thousand authorisations for abortion because of the incompatibility of a foetus extrauterine life,[26] and therefore he was of the view that this fact alone demonstrated a need to the STF to clarify the subject. However, the Minister was very careful in

---

[24] See *ADPF 54 /DF.*
[25] See *ADPF 54 /DF.*
[26] See *ADPF 54 / DF,* page 32.

applying his decision to the specific points raised and accordingly did not give a blank right of abortion within Brazil. He stated:

> ...the question put on trial is single: whether the criminal classification of termination of pregnancy in a foetus anencephalic is consistent with the Constitution, notably with the precepts that guarantee the secular state, the dignity of the human person, the right to life and the protection of autonomy, liberty, privacy and health. For me, Mr. President, the answer is hopelessly no.

The reference to "Mr. President" refers to the president of the STF. The judgment was not unanimous, as two ministers dissented from the view of the reporting Minister. This decision helps to illustrate that despite about half the Brazilian population claiming to be Catholic, the courts apply the law without being subject to external factors. [27]

It is finally submitted that laws are still evolving in Brazil; however, the impact and influence of history, Indigenous peoples, the immigration of various nationalities into Brazil, various religions and the Portuguese heritage of the majority of the people will also be there waiting in the shadows.

BIBLIOGRAPHY

o   C. Beccaria, *Dei delitti e delle pene* (Milano, 1764).

o   Brazil Government Publication, *Brasil, 500 anos de povoamento* (Rio de Janeiro: Ministério do Planejamento, Orçamento e Gestão, 2007).

o   C.Fiuza, *Direito civil*, 8th ed. (Belo Horizonte: Del Rey, 2004).

o   C. Gonçalves, *Direito civil brasileiro*, 1st ed. (São Paulo: Saraiva, 2005).

---

[27] Brazil became a secular country in 1890 when the *decree law 119-A* broke the link between the Brazilian State and the Catholic Church. Prior to 1890, all other religions were forbidden in the country.

- C. Pereira, *Instituições de direito civil, vol. I.*, 19th ed. (Rio de Janeiro: Grupo Gen - Editora Forense, 2000).

- D. Pacheco Pereira, Esmeraldo De Situ Orbis (Lisbon: Imprensa Nacional, 1892).

- IBGE, (2021), [online] Cidades.ibge.gov.br. Available at: <https://cidades.ibge.gov.br/brasil/pesquisa/23/22107>, accessed on 21 March, 2021.

- Mapa.an.gov.br. 2021, *Código Criminal do Império*, [online] Available at: <http://mapa.an.gov.br/index.php/menu-de-categorias-2/281-codigo-criminal>, accessed 23 August 2021.

- Mundo Educação, *Brasileiros descendentes que migram para o Japão - Mundo Educação* (2021), [online] Available at: <https://mundoeducacao.uol.com.br/japao/brasileiros-descendentes-que-migram-para-japao.htm>, accessed 31 October, 2021.

- National Geographic, 2021 *National Geographic - Homepage* [online] Available at: <https://www.nationalgeographicbrasil.com/meio-ambiente/2019/11/entenda-polemica-em-torno-da-mineracao-em-terras-indigenas>, accessed 27 August, 2021.

- P. Gusmão, *Introdução à ciência do direito*, 17th ed. (Rio de Janeiro: Forense, 1995).

- Pt.wikipedia.org 2021, *Imigração no Brasil – Wikipédia, a enciclopédia livre.* [online] Available at: <https://pt.wikipedia.org/wiki/Imigra%C3%A7%C3%A3o_no_Brasil#cite_note-4>, accessed 18 September 2021.

- Só História 2021, *Os índios no Brasil*, [online] Available at: <https://www.sohistoria.com.br/ef2/indios/>, accessed 27 May, 2021.

CHAPTER 11

THE IMPACT OF INDIGENOUS LAW ON LAWS IN NIGERIA

Dr. Olugbenga Oke-Samuel

1. INTRODUCTION

Nigerian law is sometimes referred to as law that is plural in nature. This plural nature is due to a mixture of different sources of law.

For a long time, from 1800 to 1960, the territory now known as Nigeria was under British rule (the colonial period), which explains the important and dominant role of English law as a source of law in the country. Prior to the *Declaration of Independence 1960* in Nigeria, many *indigenous groups* in the country lived according to their *own customs and traditions*. In fact, these are indigenous laws that are peculiar to specific communities. Similarly, several peoples are still subject to indigenous customary law including Islamic law and practices even after independence.

A few of the important milestones in the legal history of Nigeria include – (1) the independence of 1960, (2) military interventions at different times, and (3) the return to civilian rule in 1979 and 1999 respectively. The *1960 Constitution* in the aftermath of Independence in 1960 marked the end of colonialism in the country, while both the *Constitution of 1979* and *Constitution of 1999* established new dispensations that ended military regimes in the country. Both dispensations provide for the establishment of modern democracy, rule of law and application of human rights in Nigeria. This chapter examines the extent of the impact of the indigenous laws of the people of Nigeria, despite the overwhelming influence of important sources of law like the Constitution, common law and statutes.

1.1 HISTORY OF NIGERIA AS AN ENTITY

By 1900, the introduction of a British imperialist government (colonial period) was already in full swing in areas designated as the colony of Lagos, the northern part of the country (Northern protectorate)[1] and the Southern protectorate (formerly Oil rivers protectorate in the southern part of Nigeria). By that year, various pacts between the different local communities and British merchants had been used as the basis for British control over those communities and the appointment of

---

[1] Created after the *Berlin Conference* of 1884 and 1885. Consequently, the resultant area comprised of territories from Sokoto Caliphate to Bornu Empire.

different British officials to oversee the territories. In 1914, the Northern protectorates and the Southern protectorates were amalgamated by Lord Fredrick Lugard to give birth to what is now known as Nigeria. It is therefore not unreasonable to assert that the present political structure or outlook of Nigeria was a creation of the British government. The amalgamation of territories prepared the ground for the present state of the country as a potpourri of people, cultures, and law.

In pre-colonial Nigeria, in terms of state formation, most empires or regimes emerged from independent settlements being brought together through the ability of warriors or powerful individuals to integrate different societies as an entity.[2] Prior to 1900, there had been interaction, particularly on an economic front, between the different elements that later formed the Northern and Southern protectorates of Nigeria, despite their disparity. It is recorded that in pre-colonial Nigeria people exchanged goods and services and, in some cases, demonstrated common religion beliefs.[3] For instance, Ehiabi, a historian, recounts that the brass beads and bronze cultural practices in places like Ife, Benin were associated with what was obtainable in places around the Niger-Benue axis.[4]

While some major groups appeared to dominate in Nigeria, it is useful to state that many of the groupings or territories that made up what is known today as Igbo land, Hausa land and Yoruba land were not necessarily united, nor to be considered as homogenous entities. These territories existed prior to the arrival of the British and were independent territories.

---

[2] For instance at a particular time, the Yoruba nation under the leadership of Alafin of Oyo was said to consist of 1060 kings and princes who were heads of different clans. See G.N. Uzoigwe, "The Warrior and the State in Precolonial Africa: Comparative Perspectives," *Journal of African and Asian Studies* XII, 25.

[3] O. S. Ehiabhi, Simon Odion, "A History of Precolonial Nigeria" in *Nigerian Peoples and Cultures – A Reading,*" eds. I. E. Alumona and C. C. Ezeogidi (Nigeria, Rhyce Kerex, 2015), 107.

[4] I. Saa'ba Jimada, "The Foundations of Nupe, Benin and Ife Relations," in *Aspects of Niger State History Essays in Honour of Professor Ibrahim Adamu eds. Kolo* Wuam T and M.L Salahu (Niger State: Ibrahim Badamasi Babangida University, 2014), 44.

Prior to colonialism in Nigeria, some territories were quite large with many villages and towns under centralised authorities. Each village or community was under a local leader or chief who was subject to the next line of hierarchy leadership, under the overlordship of the central leader or king. Examples of such states were – Oyo Kingdom, Kanem Bornu Empire, Igala, Nupe and Ebira (Land).[5] These structures evolved over a long period at different times in each territory. The vassal states paid tributaries to the central "government". In these centralised states, a central leadership existed that was headed up by individuals who were mostly warriors with coercive power and a strong military, to compel compliance by lesser settlements and leaders.

Despite the prominence of centralised territories, some territories existed on their own without being part of any 'commonwealth of states' or centralised territories. In these settlements governance and decision making were vested only in a co-ordinating group of individuals.[6] These societies were found in areas that are not easily accessible, such as forested, rocky and mountainous environments[7]. The terrain made the areas less vulnerable to being conquered in inter-tribal wars or dominated by bigger empires in the past. Examples in the pre-colonial era are the Igbos, Tiv, Idoma, Ebira, Ijaw, Ibibio, Anang, Oron and others. In these states, there was no single political authority; societies were run by social institutions that were based on cultural beliefs and religion. These states were divided into smaller units or clans that were constituted based on the age or wealth of individuals.

According to Ehiabhi,[8] politically,[9] the structures were established in order of hierarchy. In such a structure the pre-colonial centralised states were headed up

---

[5] Don Steve, Centralised states, available at www.studynotes.com.ng/2021/06/13/centralized, accessed 01 February, 2021.
[6] Don Steve, Centralized states, available at www.studynotes.com.ng/2021/06/13/centralized, accessed 01 February, 2021.
[7] Don Steve, Centralised States available at www.studynotes.com.ng/2021/06/13/centralized, accessed 01 February, 2021.
[8] O.S Ehiabhi, Simon Odion (2015), "A History of Precolonial Nigeria" in *Nigerian Peoples and Cultures – A Reading*, eds. I.E Alumona and C.C Ezeogidi (Nigeria, Rhyce Kerex, 2015), 107.
[9] Don Steve Non Centralisd States available at www.studynotes-sattes/.com.ng/2021/06/13/non-centralised-states-in-pre-colonised-nigeria/, accessed 01 February, 2021.

by a leader who extended his influence, together with other local leaders, from a small state to other states, forming a much bigger entity. In this arrangement, leaders of relatively small entities would allow the leader of a larger central entity to take charge and in turn reported to that central leader. This arrangement was also quickly endorsed by the British as a basis for the introduction of indirect rule. However, it should be noted that Nigeria did not exist as a country prior to 1914. It is therefore not out of place to state that Nigeria was a creation of British colonial rule.

2. LEGAL HISTORY OF NIGERIA

Before the introduction of British rule[10] and the subsequent amalgamation of territories in 1914 within the combined entity then called Nigeria, different independent territories with separate cultures and political formations were in existence. Within these independent territories, there was an element of social, religious and economic contact between the peoples living in the different settlements.

In his magnum opus, *"Politics"*, Aristotle wrote that only a beast or a god could live outside a political community, without the protective shelter of government for *"man is by nature a political animal"*.[11] Prior to the introduction of colonial rule, the different nationalities in Nigeria had their respective and peculiar indigenous political structures with local, usages, practices and customs as rules to regulate conducts and relationships in each nation.

---

[10] Lagos colony in 1863, Northern and Southern Protectorates in 1900.
[11] Aristotle *politics* (translated by Benjamin Joewett) (New York: Random House, 1943), 54.

In pre-colonial Nigeria, the Yoruba, the Hausa, the Kanuri, the Edo, the Jukun and the people and societies influenced and/or conquered by these entities had centralised forms of state.[12]

2.1 THE YORUBA PRE-COLONIAL LEGAL ADMINISTRATION (1500 -1800)

Yoruba land covers present-day Lagos, Ondo, Ogun, Oyo, Osun, Ekiti, together with some parts of Kwara, Kogi and Edo States. In the period before colonisation, settlements in Yorubaland had three tiers of government, which included a structured judicial system. One important feature of the judiciary is the Palace Courts, which outlived the pre-colonial period. Nevertheless, these seemingly informal courts served their purpose very well. According to Onadeko, each family unit and extended kin were recognised judicial units and were important channels for legal and political control in Yorubaland.[13]

The idea of the separation of political powers was never strange to Yorubaland. In the era before colonisation, there existed three arms of political governance – the executive, legislature, and judiciary branches.[14] Each of these arms of political governance was invested with separate powers within the political structure.

In any Yoruba settlement the King, known as the Oba, was highly revered; accordingly, he sat as head of the political structure and his authority was unquestionable. He was known as the Igbakeji Orisa (second in command to God). He was aided in governance by the council of chiefs or Igbimo.

---

[12] Atanda Joseph Adebowale, "Government of Yorubaland in the pre-colonial period," *Periodical: Tarikh*, vol. 4, no. 2 (1971): 1-12.

[13] Onadeko Tunde, "Yoruba Traditional Adjudicatory Systems," *African Study Monographs*, 29 (1) (March 2008): 15-28, 15.

[14] Peter Cutt Lloyd, *The Political Development of Yoruba Kingdoms in the 18th and 19th Centuries* (London: Royal Anthropological Institute of Great Britain and Ireland, 1971).

In the old Oyo kingdom, the Alaafin was considered the ultimate leader. There were provinces led by subservient chiefs that were also called *Obas*.[15] In Idanre in Ondo State, the Oba known as *Owa* would rule with a cabinet or council of chiefs known as *Ugha* (inner circle) which was composed of 'high chiefs'. These were members of the executive arm of government, and they worked with the Obas on tasks related to dispute resolution and the formulation of policies. The composition of the Igbimo was usually made up of titled or high chiefs and chiefs that represented sections of the community.

Chiefs in Yorubaland were expected to swear an oath of allegiance before a deity for absolute loyalty to the Oba (king), this was called *"Umale awe"* in Idanre kingdom in Ondo State. The oath imposed obligations on the chiefs to ensure the enforcement and implementation of decisions reached under the leadership of the Owa of Idanre (the Oba) and also to defend Obas' positions on any issue in their jurisdictions.

During British colonial rule (1800 -1960), the Obas, or Palace Courts, also known as native courts were very popular and were encouraged to thrive by the colonial government to address personal issues under indigenous or customary laws.

While the power of the king to adjudicate over a matter was unfettered, the Ogboni sect, a socio-religious group in Yorubaland equally had the responsibility of serving as a tribunal and sometimes would act as lawmakers together with the Oba.

While chiefs had obligations to enforce laws and pronouncements by the *Oba*, there existed a belief within the population that offenders and transgressors of taboos or rules in the land would also be punished by divine visitations and sanctions. For instance, it was believed that the god of thunder *Sango* and the god of iron *Ogun* were responsible for the punishment for certain offences. In

---

[15] Max Siollun, *A Short History of Conquest and Rule: What Britain Did to Nigeria* (London: Hurst Publishers, 2021), 33.

places such as the Ikale area of Ondo State, persons accused of witchcraft or stealing were taken before the Ayelala shrine and, if found culpable by the deity, were often left to die at the shrine unless the deity was appeased by certain rituals.[16] In Ile-Ife, the *Olomode Ife* (youths) had the responsibility of enforcing rules, and in fact, were in charge of detention facilities called Gbere, where criminals awaiting trial or convicted criminals were kept.[17]

2.2 The Igbo Pre-Colonial Legal Administration (before 1860)

The Igbo people of Nigeria can be found in today's Anambra, Enugu, Abia, Ebonyi, Imo and some parts of Delta and Rivers states. The Igbo society had decentralised social organisations. Administration of justice under indigenous or customary laws in Igbo lands pre-dated the British colonial period. Checks and balances were inbuilt within the system that regulated interpersonal relations and order matters related to society, for its progressive transformation. These mechanisms of checks and balances formed the structure of Igbo indigenous law. The Igbo pre-colonial political system was known to be acephalous, that is without an arrow head,[18] in other words, there was no paramount ruler in Igbo traditional society, except in some communities such as Onitsha and Agbor, which shared boundaries with towns having a system of monarchy, such as the Kingdom of Benin.[19]

According to Okafor, the legislative process in Igboland was rooted in the principle of 'Ohacracy'[20]; meaning that in order for rules to be acceptable by the populace, they must be created by a general assembly of the people. As a result, it became

---

[16] See Daniel G. Offiong, *Witchcraft, Sorcery, Magic and Social Order among the Ibibio of Nigeria* (Lagos: Fourth Dimension, 1991), 325-325.
[17] WilliamsBascom, *The Yoruba of Southwestern Nigeria* (New York: Holt, Rinehart and Winston, 1965).
[18] Omipidan Teslim *Igbo Pre-Colonial Political System/Administration*, available online <https://oldnaija.com/2019/12/20/igbo-pre-colonial-system/>, accessed 21 January, 2022.
[19] Max Siollun, *A Short History of Conquest and Rule: What Britain Did to Nigeria* (London: Hurst Publishers), 33
[20] Coined by Okafor and see, F.U. Okafor, *Igbo Philosophy of Law* (Enugu: Fourth Dimension Publishing Co. Ltd, 1992), 57.

futile for anyone to conceive the idea of making sectional or bias laws.[21] Laws made under this principle were mostly in the interests of society, with a special impetus on the protection of the vulnerable in the community.[22]

Law making was the business of everyone in Igboland, [23] this was done through membership of different groups like the Umunna (people with common ancestry and family); age grading (people born within a particular period in a village, who regulated the conduct of their age-peers); Umuada (married women); Umuokpu (the elderly); Umudibia (medicine men, in charge of divination and cures for ailments); Ndi nze (titled and well respected men in every community); deities/gods (with dedicated shrines, priests and priestesses); Oha (the general assembly, and the supreme group in law making); Mmanwu (the guild of masquerades, the voice of the ancestors).[24]

At the centre of Igbo justice administration were the principles – (1) restorative justice, (2) equality, and (3) access to justice for everyone. According to Elechi, the justice system was process-oriented, victim-centred and humane.[25] Some of the lawmaking institutions identified above equally acted as quasi-judicial institutions. Recourse could also be made to the oracle through oath taking and swearing at shrines, with the expectation of divine wrath like sudden death or affliction by strange diseases on wrong-doers.

2.3 THE HAUSA/FULANI PRE-COLONIAL LEGAL ADMINISTRATION

The Hausa/Fulani pre-colonial political system in the northern part of the country was preceded by the Holy Jihad fought by Uthman Danfodio in 1804. The Jihad

---

[21] F. U. Okafor, *Igbo Philosophy of Law* (Enugu: Fourth Dimension Publishing Co. Ltd, 1992), 57.

[22] F. U. Okafor, *Igbo Philosophy of Law* (Enugu: Fourth Dimension Publishing Co. Ltd, 1992), 57.

[23] Bonachristus Umeogu, "Igbo African Legal and Justice System: A Philosophical Analysis," *Open Journal of Philosophy*, vol. 2, no. 2, (2012): 116 -122, available at 02. 10.4236/ojpp.2012.22018.

[24] F. U. Okafor, *Igbo Philosophy of Law* (Enugu: Fourth Dimension Publishing Co. Ltd, 1992), 57.

[25] Elechi, O. Oko, et al. (2008) "*The Igbo Indigenous Justice System,*" *Colonial Systems of Control: Criminal Justice in Nigeria,* University of Ottawa Press, (2008) 395–416, <https://doi.org/10.2307/j.ctt1ckph37.26>.

was fought against the existing Hausa states that were accused of idolatry and contaminating Islam with animist rituals by Dan Fodio, who was hired by the Sarki of the Hausa state of Gobir as a mallam to the royal house.[26] After Jihad, Islamic law was introduced to many communities in the region. Major areas in the northern region include states like Katsina, Zamfara, Bauchi, Borno, Kano, Yobe, Kaduna, Adamawa, and others.

Before the advent of colonial rule in Nigeria, the system of government in Northern Nigeria was based on the Emirate system. Hausa/Fulani pre-colonial administration was highly centralised and hierarchical in natur.[27] Political authority was vested in the Emir, who was an absolute ruler. However, he governed along with certain office holders, who had specific functions. The Emirates were divided into districts. Each village was administered by a village head. Tax collectors (including village heads) retained a certain proportion of the tax collected for themselves.

Muslim laws known as *Sharia* were used in the Emirates and they were held to be the Supreme laws of God. The Emir had the power to make laws outside Sharia, provided these laws were not contrary to it. He delegated authority and set the laws aside when he considered them inappropriate.

Accordingly, the Emir was the chief executive of the Emirate, being both the political and religious head of the people. He equally acted as both the chief executive and chief law maker and was assisted in the discharge of these functions by a council of ministers. The council members included – (1) the Galadima (Minister for the Capital Territory, who was in charge of the administration of the capital city); The Waziri (Head of Service), (2) the Madawaki

---

[26] Max Siollun, *A Short History of Conquest and Rule: What Britain Did to Nigeria*, (London: Hurst Publishers, 2021), 31.
[27] Boypa O. Egbe, Ibiang Obono Okoi, "Colonialism and Origin of Boundary Crisis in Nigeria," *LWATI: A Journal of Contemporary Research* vol. 14, no. 4, (2017): 95-110.

(Commander-in-chief of the Cavalry), (3) the Sarkin Fada (the Chief Palace Officer), (4) the Magaji (Minister for Finance, in charge of revenues).[28]

The Emir was also Head of the Judiciary, as the final court of appeal. The lowest judge in the Emirate judicial system was the village head who settled minor cases and would punish offenders. Emir's court dealt with serious crimes, settled land disputes and even had the authority to punish offenders. Even death sentences could be pronounced on offenders, but the final power was vested only in the Emir.

Offences were divided into minor and serious offences. Justice in legal issues like marriage and divorce, the custody of children, inheritance, debt, slander and so forth were administered by the Alkali, a trained Judge who administered *Sharia law*. Serious offences such as murder, theft, homicide, witchcraft and so forth were tried in the Emir's Court. The Emir had the final say in judicial matters. Village heads could also settle minor disputes and breaches of the Emir's order.

3 CURRENT NIGERIA LEGAL SYSTEM

The Nigerian legal system is a combination and coalescence of several sources and origins, a form of amalgamation of different rules governing various aspects of life and human interactions. In its infancy, the components of this new nation were several small tribal societies. These diverse societies were capable of maintaining socio-economic interactions informally and smoothly.

The origins of the current Nigerian legal system can be traced to the latter part of the 19th century. It consists of the laws, courts, and personnel associated with – (a) law and order, and (b) the administration of the justice system.[29] As a former

---

[28] Chigozie Ifekwe Okonkwo, Richard Amechi Onuigbo and Okechukwu Eme, "Innocent & Ekekwe, Ezinwanne, *Traditional Rulers and Community Security in Nigeria: Challenges and Prospects,*" *International Journal of Innovative Social Sciences & Humanities Research* 7 (2) (2019):145-159.
[29] Ese Malemi, *Outline of Nigerian Legal System* (Lagos: Grace Publishers Inc., 1999).

British colony, Nigerian law drew heavily on its colonial history, which aided the introduction of the English common law tradition in the fast-evolving legal system in the country. It also ensured continuity in the application of existing customary laws of the local people from different groups/clans/societies that were amalgamated into the new nation of Nigeria. While English laws form a substantial part of Nigerian law,[30] it must be emphasised that the existing customary laws of the people continue to exist side by side with other sources of law, particularly in addressing the multifarious issues facing the most populous country on the African continent that is Nigeria.

3.1 SOURCES OF NIGERIAN LAW

The sources of Nigerian law can be subdivided into two: (1) The Nigerian Constitution and (2) Primary Sources.

3.1.1 History of Constitutions in Nigeria

The *Constitution of the Federal Republic of Nigeria 1999 (as amended)* (Nigerian Constitution) was written and contained in a single document. The constitution pronounced its supremacy as the ground norm in the country. As a result, all other sources of law must trace their validity to the constitution to remain applicable or enforceable within the country.[31] Section 1(3) of the *Constitution of the Federal Republic of Nigeria*, clearly provides that "*If any law is inconsistent with the provisions of this constitution, this constitution shall prevail, and that other law shall to the extent of the inconsistency be void*". As a legal document with varying standards, the Constitution provides the ultimate principles, rules and doctrines by which the legitimacy and hierarchy of all other legal norms in Nigeria are validated.

---

[30] Obilade, Akintunde. O., *The Nigerian Legal System* (London: Sweet & Maxwell, 1979), 69-81, 100-110.
[31] See Section 1(1) of the *Constitution of the Federal Republic of Nigeria 1999*.

The *Constitution 1999* is the organic law or ground norm which not only provides for the machinery of government, but also gives rights and imposes obligations on the people.[32] Therefore, any law of the land that is inconsistent with the provisions of the constitution is void. This position was asserted in the case of *Obasanjo v Yusuf,* [33] where the courts emphasised that the constitution is not subject to electoral laws but rather, the reverse is the case. In the words of Augie Justice of Supreme Court, *"the constitution is only subject to itself."*[34]

The Nigerian Constitution is fashioned after the American presidential system of government at a provincial and central level, with important features such as the separation of powers, independence of the judiciary, and rule of law. It also recognises the diverse nature of the Nigerian people by providing for a federal structure.[35]

However, the current *Constitution 1999* should be seen through the prism of earlier constitutions. As a result of political instabilities in the past, the drafting of a constitution was a torturous exercise in Nigeria. Between 1922 and 1960, the period before independence, there were four different types of constitution: *the Clifford Constitution of 1922, the Richard Constitution of 1946, the Macpherson Constitution of 1951, and the Lyttleton Constitution of 1954.* Each of the above constitutions had special features, some of which are retained under the present *Constitution 1999.*

3.1.1.1 Clifford Constitution of 1922

The main feature of the constitution was the attempt to allow Nigerians to participate in their own affairs "though in a circumscribed manner over limited

---

[32] *The Supreme court in the case of Peoples Democratic Party v I.N.E.C* [2001] 1 W.R.N. 1.
[33] (2005) 20 WRN 1 S.C.
[34] Oke-Samuel, Olugbenga, *An outline of Nigerian legal system: student edition* (Nigeria: O.G.I publishers, 2008).
[35] Section 2(2) *Constitution of the Federal Republic of Nigeria,* 1999.

subjects."[36] Essentially, the constitution introduced the following – (1) the first electoral system in the country, (2) a legislative council, and (3) the executive council. Although most of the positions were occupied by colonial officials, four Nigerians were elected under the constitution into the legislative council.

3.1.1.2 The Richards Constitution of 1946

The Richards Constitution 1946[37] was enacted as an improvement upon the *Clifford Constitution 1922*. Its main aim was to promote unity of Nigerians and give room for greater participation by Nigerians in the administration of the country.

Some of the features included – (1) bicameral legislatures, (2) regionalism (Western, Eastern and Northern regions), (3) elective principles with limited franchise, and (4) regional parliaments. Importantly, for the first time the constitution brought the two components of present-day Nigeria - the northern and southern territories - together in the same parliament.[38]

3.1.1.3 The Macpherson Constitution 1951

After wide consultation across the country, *the Macpherson Constitution* was enacted in 1951.[39]

It provided for – (1) a Federal House of Representatives, (2) a central executive council (Council of Ministers), (3) regional legislatures and executive councils, and (4) direct and indirect primaries. There were bi-camera legislatures in the Northern and Western Regions (the house of Assembly and House of Chiefs), but the Eastern Region had only the House of Assembly. The Macpherson

---

[36] Malachy Ugwummadu, *"Nigeria Needs New Constitution, Not Amendment,"* (2021), <https://www.thisdaylive.com/index.php/2021/06/03/nigeria-needs-new-constitution-not-amendment/>, accessed 10 January, 2022.
[37] *Nigerian Constitution Order – in -Council 1922.*
[38] *Nigerian Constitution Order – in – Council 1946.*
[39] *Nigerian Constitution Order – in -Council 1951.*

Constitution can be considered important for deepening federalism in the country, as it provided for power sharing between the central government and the regions.

3.1.1.4 The Lyttleton Constitution 1954

Between 1953 and 1954 there were two major conferences in London and Lagos, where the *Macpherson Constitution 1951* was reviewed. As a result, *the Lyttleton Constitution 1954*[40] was drafted, which included important features such as full blown federalism with the Northern Region, Eastern Region, and Western Region/Southern Cameroon as federal units. A Supreme Court was established to replace the West African Court of Appeal ('WACA') as the final court for the federation.

3.1.1.5 The Independence Constitution 1960

The *Independence Constitution 1960*[41] maintained some of the provisions of previous constitutions in addition to pronouncing Nigeria as an independent state, though without full sovereignty since the Queen of England retained her position as Head of State. Notable provisions included – (1) the supremacy of the constitution, (2) a procedure for amendment of the constitution, (3) a parliamentary system of government, (4) legislative lists and (5) the sharing of legislative responsibilities between central and regional governments.

3.1.1.6 The Republican Constitution 1963

After the constitutional conference held in Lagos on July 25 and 26 1963, *the Republican Constitution 1963* was passed into law by the Federal House of Representatives on September 19, 1963, and came into force on 1st October

---

[40] *Nigerian Constitution Order - in - Council 1954.*
[41] *Nigerian Constitution Order – in – Council 1960.*

1963. In this constitution, issues in relation to the sovereignty of Nigeria were resolved. Features of the new constitution included – (1) the republican status of the country was confirmed, signaling an end to the Queen's reign as the head of the Nigerian state, and (2) the role of the Supreme Court as the highest court of appeal, replacing the Privy Council of the British House of Lords. Due to political crises in the country, the republican constitution did not last long in the country. On January 15 1966, there was a coup d'etat which removed the elected politicians. This brought about military rule which lasted until October 1979.

3.1.1.7 The Presidential Constitution of 1979

The *Presidential Constitution of 1979*[42] jettisoned the parliamentary system of government and replaced it with a presidential system fashioned after the American system of government. Under the constitution, the president was both Head of State, Head of Government and Commander in Chief of the Armed forces. The president was elected by the electorate in a general election. There was also an executive governor for each state.

The legislature, known as the National Assembly, was bicameral, consisting of the Senate and the House of Representatives. The Senate had 95 members, while the House of Representatives had 450 members. The states, on the other hand, had a unicameral legislature. According to the constitution, the legislature had the power to impeach the president. Similarly, the provincials' Houses of Assembly had the power to impeach the governor.

The Judicial Service Commission was re-introduced in Nigeria. It had the power to recommend judges for appointment, subject to assent by the president and screening by the legislature. The judiciary was also given the power to interpret the constitution and authority to declare laws/orders as null and void that were contrary to the constitution.

---

[42] *Constitution of the Federal Republic of Nigeria* 1979.

3.1.2 Primary Sources of Law

3.1.2.1 Legislation (Ordinances, Acts, Laws, Decrees, Edicts and Bye-laws)

Nigerian legislation comprises of statutes, primary and subsidiary legislation. The National Assembly (consisting of the Senate and the House of Representatives) and the States Houses of Assembly are vested with the power to make laws under the provisions of *the Nigerian Constitution 1999.*[43] The subsequent enacted laws are usually in a written form or code.

Nigerian statutes are identified with different titles, determined by the authority making said law;

   i. Ordinances refer to laws made under the colonial regime.

   ii. Laws made by the National Assembly are known as acts - that is, Acts of Parliament - and State Houses of Assembly make what are known as 'laws'.

   iii. Decrees were made by military regimes and edicts are laws made by military administrators at the state level. However, governments can choose to legally convert decrees and edicts into acts or laws respectively. Also, decrees and edicts not repealed by the constitution are automatically converted to Acts and Laws when civil law is instituted.

   iv. Bye-laws are legislations passed by Local Government Councils. Local Government Councils across the country have the power to create and institute bye-laws in their constituencies, with respect to matters on which they have the authority of the constitution to make law, as provided under the functions of a Local Government Council in the constitution[44]

---

[43] *Constitution of the Federal Republic of Nigeria 1999*, s. 4(2) and (7).
[44] *Fourth Schedule of the Constitution 1999*; See also, *Akingbade v Lagos Town Council* (1955) 21 NLR 90.

3.1.2.2 Judicial precedents

Nigeria has imbibed the tradition of *stare decisis* (let the decision stand) from *English common law* principles, which enjoins that those earlier decisions should be binding authorities for subsequent cases. The court in which the decision is given may depart from it only in special cases, while that precedent strictly binds the lower Courts even where they are inclined by good reasons to go against the earlier decision. This practice of obeying precedents has been justified on the grounds that it enhances certainty and predictability in the law and minimises the influence of personal bias against settled principles of law. Judicial precedents are also case law, which has been referred to as that body of principles and rules which, over the years, have been formulated or pronounced upon by the courts as governing specific legal situations.[45] Case law is formed from the legal principles of a case.[46]

3.1.2.3 Indigenous or Customary law

Indigenous law is known under the Nigerian legal system as *customary law*. Custom refers to the established or common usage of a particular people.[47] The *Evidence Act*[48] defines custom as a rule which in a particular district has, from long usage, obtained a force of law within the legal system. For a custom to be considered as a customary law, it must be both custom and be law.

Customary law has been defined by the court as the *"organic or living law of the indigenous peoples of Nigeria, regulating their lives and transactions"*. It was the law of the people of Nigeria before other systems of law, English or otherwise, were brought into the country to displace or modify customary law.[49] According to

---

[45] John Ohireime, *Introduction to Nigerian Legal System* (Lagos, Ababa Press Ltd, 2005), 73
[46] *Clement v Iwuanyanwu* (1989)3 NWLR Pt 107, p.39 at 53 SC; See also, *Agbai v Okogbue* (1991)7 NWLR Pt 207, p.391 SC.
[47] Osita Nnamani, Ogbu, *Modern Nigerian Legal System* (Enugu: Snaap Press NIG. Ltd., 2013)
[48] *Laws of the Federation of Nigeria 2011.*
[49] *Princess Bilewu Oyewunmi & Anr. V Amos Owoade Ogunesan* (1990) 3 NWLR (pt. 137) 137.

Justice Obaseki,[50] "*it* [customary law] *is regulatory in that it controls the lives and transactions of the community subject to it*". Niki Tobi, Judge of the Court of Appeal, outlines the nature of a customary law to include the following:[51] (1) it must be in existence at the time it is being invoked, (2) it must be custom as well as law, (3) it must be acceptable, (4) it is largely unwritten, (4) it is flexible, and (5) it should be universally applicable within the area of its acceptability.[52]

It is noteworthy that before the amalgamation of its individual parts and ethnic groups, the territory that is now Nigeria consisted of a host of different settlements. Among these settlements were some 350 ethnic groups and 500 dialects. Each had its own language(s), cultures and customs. Each of the ethnic-linguistic groups therefore had its own concept of law, judicial process and customary laws, without which human society could not exist. From ancient times, these laws played a prominent role in the regulation of the affairs of members of the group. They varied with the circumstances space, character and level of socio-economic development and represented challenges which faced the various settlements over time.

Customary or indigenous law is an important constituent of Nigerian law governing many aspects of people's lives, for instance marriage according to native law and custom, divorce, succession or inheritance, land tenure and chieftaincy matters. As such, customary law is law which evolved or crystallized from the numerous customs of the various groups of people in Nigeria.

Customary law is recognized by the Nigerian constitution. The importance of the customary laws of the indigenous peoples of Nigeria can be found in the pronouncement of the Supreme court of Nigeria in the case of *Zaidan v Mohosen,*[53] where the court held that *"customary law is not enacted by any*

---

[50] *Princess Bilewu Oyewunmi & Anr. V Amos Owoade Ogunesan* (1990) 3 NWLR (pt. 137) 137.
[51] *Ojisua v Aiyebelehin* (2001) 11NWLR (pt. 723)44.
[52] Osita Nnamani, Ogbu, *Modern Nigerian Legal System* (Enugu: Snaap Press NIG. Ltd., 2013)
[53] 1973 11 F.S.C. 1.

competent legislature in Nigeria and yet it is one that is enforceable and binding within Nigeria between parties subject to its ways". The legal and constitutional basis of Customary law is section 315(3)–(4)(b) and (c) of the Constitution of the Federal Republic of Nigeria,1999. The constitution also provides for a Customary Court of Appeal at the Federal Capital Territory and other states of the federation. States are further empowered to establish a customary court system within their territories.

There is no doubt that indigenous or customary laws differ from one community to another, particularly where there is no common root or ancestral ties, but their character and nature are same. Some of the features of customary law include that they– (1) are largely unwritten, (2) must be in existence at the material time, (3) must be accepted as a binding custom, (5) must be flexible or elastic, and (6) must enjoy general application among the people.

3.1.2.3.1 Validity Test for Customs

In order for a custom to be applied as a customary law in Nigeria, the custom must satisfy or pass the validity test, which is a prerequisite for its application[54]. The tests are as follows:

(i) *the law in question is not repugnant to natural justice, equity and good conscience.*

The above validity test has been the opinion of the court in the following cases:

(a) *Edet vs Essien,*[55] where a man who had been jilted by his bride-to be later claimed the two children she had with another husband, on the grounds that his partly paid dowry was not refunded. The court ruled that a custom

---

[54] S. 14(3) of *Evidence Act 2004* and *Agbai v Okogbure* (1991) 7 NWLR Pt 512, p. 283 CA.
[55] (1932) 11 N.L.R. 4.

which permitted that claim by the jilted man was unreasonable, and repugnant to natural justice, equity and good conscience.

(b) *Re Effiong Atta*[56]

In this case, the head of a family attempted to rely on a custom in order to deprive a woman (who had been a slave before the abolition) of issuance of a letter of administration in respect of the estate of her deceased sister, on the grounds that the deceased sister, also a former slave, had continued to live on the family property after emancipation. The claim was rejected by the court. Said custom was held by the court to be contrary to natural justice.

(c) *Mariyama v. Sadiku Ejo*[57]

In the case, the court held that a child born within ten calendar months after a divorce belonged to the former husband of a woman. It stated that it would be contrary to natural justice, equity and good conscience to give such a child to the new husband.

(ii) *it must not be incompatible either directly or by implication with any law for the time being in force,* as found by the court in the following cases:

(a) *Taiwo Aoko v. Fagbemi*[58]

The court held that the conviction of the appellant by a customary court for adultery was wrongful and illegal, as adultery was not known to be an offence under any law in the Southern part of Nigeria.

---

[56] (1930) 1 N. L. R. 41

[57] (1961) N.R.N.L. R 81.

[58] (1961) 1 ANLR. 400.

(c) *Adesubokan v. Yinusa*[59]

An earlier decision of a High Court declaring a will void for non-conformity with Islamic law because the testator was a Muslim in his lifetime was quashed by the Supreme Court. The Supreme Court held that, in making a will under the *Wills Act 1837*, a testator is not encumbered by any requirement of native law and custom.

(iii) it must not be contrary to public policy, as held by the court in the following case:

(a) *Cole V. Akinyele*[60]

The court held that the fact a deceased person acknowledged children born outside wedlock in his lifetime did not confer legitimacy on the children, since the man was married in his lifetime.

3.1.2.4 Islamic law

Islamic law was brought into Nigeria by the arrival of Arabs in the northern part of Nigeria during the Fulani Jihad of 1804. As a general rule, where Islamic law is the law applicable in a transaction, Islamic law will apply between Muslims.[61]

Islamic law regulates the rights, obligations and duties of a Muslim devotee or believer. In Nigeria, Islamic laws are applicable in matters before the Area Court, Upper Area Court, Sharia Courts of Appeal,[62] High Court,[63] Court of Appeal,[64] and the Supreme Court.[65]

---

[59] (1971) 1 LRLR Vol. 1 321.
[60] (1960) 15 WACA 20.
[61] *Tapa v Kuka* (1945)18 NLR 5. *Usman v Umaru* (1992)7 NWLR Pt 254, p. 377 SC.
[62] *Constitution of the Federal Republic of Nigeria 1999* (as amended) s. 272.
[63] *Constitution of the Federal Republic of Nigeria 1999* (as amended), ss. 244 (1) & (2),
[64] *Constitution of the Federal Republic of Nigeria 1999* (as amended), ss.244 (1) & (2), 262 (2).
[65] Cap. 550 LFN 1990 (as amended)

In Nigeria, the *Maliki school of Islam* is mostly applied in areas governed by Islamic law, with some local variations. The difference between Islamic law and customary law was judiciary acknowledged by the Supreme Court in *Usam v Umaru*[66]. In this case, Bello JSC defined Customary law as *"the rule of conduct which governs legal relationship as established by custom and usage and not forming part of the common law of England nor formally enacted ..."* Accordingly, by implication, Islamic law in Nigeria does not come under custom and usage.

The above viewpoint of the Supreme Court of Nigeria is in line with a previous decision in the case of *D.W Lewis v V. Bankole*[67] where it was said, *"unwritten customary law, recognized as law by the members of an ethnic group and it is a mirror of accepted usage"*. On the other hand, Islamic law jurisprudence is taken from various books, such as the Holy Koran and other books written by prophets and clerics over time.

Some scholars in Nigeria have contended that customary law in Nigeria includes Islamic law; for instance, it is the view of Obilade[68] that customary law in Nigeria may be divided in terms of nature into two classes - namely, ethnic or non-Islamic customary law and Islamic law. Asein, however, has disputed this as he is of the view that *"Muslim customary law, unlike the indigenous customary law, is based on the Islamic faith, largely written, relatively more rigid and uniform"*.[69]

This nature of Islamic law does not conform to the meaning and nature of indigenous customary law as ascribed and defined by the various writers and courts above. It is therefore safe to state that indigenous customary laws are different from Islamic laws. As such, generally, going by the nature and

---

[66] (1992) 7 NWLR (Pt. 254), 277.

[67] (1901) 1 NLR 82.

[68] A. O. Obilade, *Nigeria Legal System* (London: Sweet and Maxwell, 1979), 83; See also, G. Ezejiofor, "Source of Nigerian Law" in Okonkwo, (ed) *Introduction to Nigeria Law* (London: Sweet & Maxwell, 1980), 14. There Obilade had said, *"it is relevant to recall that Moslem Law is customary because the Native Courts Law Provides that "native law and custom include Moslem Law"*.

[69] J. O. Asein, *Introduction to Nigerian Legal System* (Lagos: Ababa Press Ltd, 2005), 113.

characteristics of customary law, Islamic law is not customary law; both sources of law are very important, but distinct and independent of one another.

The fact remains, however, that in several parts of Northern Nigeria, the Islamic way of life has supplanted local customs. In these areas, Islamic law should not be seen as the customary law of the area, but as the equivalent of customary law, which has been suppressed by dominant jurisprudence.

In Islamic communities, the Holy Qu'ran is the supreme law, and final authority. Accordingly, it prevails in all issues to which Islamic law applies. It applies over all persons who are its adherents. For instance, Islamic law will apply – (1) to Muslims, and (2) to transactions where Islamic law or statute so declares.

Islamic Law applies if it is the personal law of the parties or the predominant law. For example, where Islamic law is the law prevailing in the area but a different law binds the parties, (for example, where two Ibos are parties in a Muslim court in an area where Muslim law prevails) the Native Court will, in the interest of justice, be reluctant to administer the law prevailing in the area. If it tries the case at all, it will, in the interest of justice, choose to administer the law, which is binding between parties.

The author submits, however, that although Islamic law has become integrated into the lives of several million Nigerians, it is essential that a distinction is established between customary and Islamic law, the latter being an off-shoot or arising from religious jurisprudence.

3.1.2.5 Courts applying indigenous laws in Nigeria

As discussed earlier, indigenous or customary law is an important source of Nigerian law, among others. A custom is a rule which, in a particular district, has from long usage obtained the force of law.[70] It is basically unwritten, can be proven by evidence of its existence,[71] and depends on what the appropriate authority believes or is persuaded to believe by evidence as customary law. Customary law varies from place to place, except where the particular custom has gained notoriety to the extent that the courts would take judicial notice of it. Where there is arbitration under customary law, the court or the arbitral body will only apply customary law and not the principles of common law.[72]

Different statutes provide for the application of customary or indigenous law Nigeria. For instance, in Ondo State, South West Nigeria, *High Court Law*[73] provides conditions for the observance and enforcement of the observance of all applicable customary laws in a cause. This is, however, subject to certain conditions as follows:[74]

i.   It is not repugnant to natural justice, equity and good conscience

ii.   It is not incompatible either directly or indirectly or by implications with any written law for the time being in force, and

iii. No law should deprive any person of the benefit of any such customary law.

The above conditions form part of what is known as the tests of validity of customary law in the Nigerian legal system. Similar provisions are found in the high court laws of different states in the Nigerian Federation.

The courts have also upheld the application of indigenous laws in the following areas. The following are instances:

---

[70] See section 258 of the *Evidence Act 2011*.
[71] See the case of *Omaye v Omagu* (2008)7 NWLR (Pt 1087) 447.
[72] The Supreme Court of Nigeria in *Pius Umeadi & Ors v Victor Chibunze & Or* (2020) 10 NWLR 405.
[73] CAP. 62, *The Laws of Ondo State 2006*, Vol.2
[74] See section 13 of *High Court Law of Ondo State*, CAP. 62, The Laws of Ondo State, Vol.2

i) *Land transactions*

The court in Nigeria has, in different cases, accepted and upheld customary laws in respect of ownership and transactions of land. On the issue of title to land, the position of the court is that there are customs where mere verbal declaration in the presence of witnesses can confer title. The court has also held in the case of *R.I.C Maneke v Osita Ngwu Maneke*[75] that verbal conveyances can be valid when done at a family meeting in the presence of witnesses.

ii) *Tenancy*

The Court of Appeal in *Idowu Adeagbo Ajao & Ors v Arasi Obele & Or,*[76] on the right of customary tenancy, held that under Yoruba customary law, a tenant is allowed to remain on the land in perpetuity, subject to good behaviour.

iii) *Determination of customary tenancy*

The position of the court is that a customary tenancy is determined by forfeiture. Where a tenant under customary tenancy is found guilty of misconduct or misbehaviour, this will render the tenancy liable to forfeiture. The misbehaviour in this case may be by "alienation of a part of the land, or a claim of ownership, or refusal to pay the tribute due or direct denial of overlords title by setting up a rival title in the customary tenant himself".[77]

iv) *Succession / Inheritance*

The court in the case of *Mojekwu v Mojekwu*[78] invoked the constitutional right to equality and freedom from discrimination under the Nigerian constitution in invalidating a customary law of the Igbo people, wherein the property of a man that dies intestate without a male child but with a female child would have the property inherited by his brother to the exclusion of his widow or daughter.

---

[75] (2020)13 NWLR 311.
[76] (2004) LCN/1621(CA)
[77] Court of Appeal in *Idowu Adeagbo Ajao & Ors v Arasi Obele & Or. (2020)13 NWLR 311.*
[78] (1997) 7 NWLR Pt 512 p. 283

v) Freedom of Association

The court upheld the constitutional right to freedom of Association in the case of *Agbai v Okagbue.*[79] In the case, an attempt to confiscate the properties of the appellant and compel him to be part of the activities of a village cultural association was declared by the court to amount to a violation of his right to Freedom of Association.

3.1.2.6 English law (in force in England on 1 January 1900)

English law is the common law legal system of England and Wales, comprising mainly criminal law and civil law, each branch having its own courts and procedures.[80] As discussed earlier, being a former British colony it is no surprise that several elements of English law have had a major influence on the Nigerian legal system. English law is made up of rules of common law, doctrines of equity and statutes of general application. The use of English law in Nigeria is supported by the following authorities:

- *Interpretation Act S 45(1):*[81] This act provides that the common law of England, the doctrines of equity and statutes of general application that were in force on 1st January 1900, will be in force.

- *Supreme Court ordinance 1914*, section (14): Subject to the terms of this or any other ordinance, the rules of common law, doctrines of equity and statutes of general application. It is in force from 1 January 1900 in the jurisdiction of this court.

- *Ordinance No. 3 1863* which introduced English Law into Lagos Colony.

---

[79] (1991) 7 NWLR, Pt. 204 p.391
[80] <https://en.m.wikipedia.org/wiki/English_law&ved=2ahUKEwi75MeiifvkAhVLQUEAHS9pCJcQmhM wAnoECA4QAg&usg=AOvVaw0YaO1UjEI0FS8-Yw-SXAZQ>, accessed 3rd January 2021.
[81] CAP 1. 23, 2004, s.32.

- *Court of Appeal Act*[82] and *Federal High Court Act.*[83]

- *The High Court Laws*[84] of the different states in Southern Nigeria.

3 FINAL COMMENTS

The purpose of law is to keep a check on the tendency of humans to become involved in deviant behaviours that are in excess of reasonable conduct expected of them in a particular society, and to curtail absolute freedom. As a result, the main goal of a legal system is to maintain order and harmony in any given society.

Prior to the advent of British colonialism in the territories now known as Nigeria, each society/clan/group of people in Nigeria had its own way of controlling the social behaviour of its group members in order to reach its desired goals. The importance of a legal framework in this regard cannot be dispensed with. It is an indisputable fact that indigenous or customary law played this role effectively before and after the advent of both Islamic and English law. As stated earlier, the invading imperialists found the structure of customary law and its acceptance by the local people a great asset. As a result, even under the British colonial justice system, the application of customary law was adopted in the indirect rule system and remains applicable to the people of those territories, which are now amalgamated into a single entity known as Nigeria.

Indigenous law is one of the significant sources of the Nigerian legal system. While indigenous law is largely unwritten, its status as a source of law is not diminished, though there have been serious misconceptions about that status. This unique source of law is written on the minds of the people who are subject to

---

[82] CAP. C37, *Laws of the Federation of Nigeria 2004* (as amended in 1993, 2005, and 2013).
[83] *Federal High Court (amendment) Act 2005.*
[84] For example, *High Court of Lagos State Law*, CAP H. 3, *2003* ss. 19(2), 13 and 15.

it and can be applied anywhere the people subject to it reside. The existence of customary law does not interfere with the existence of other sources of law.

In the Nigerian state, the judicial system is multiple; courts and tribunals exist based on secular, religious and traditional jurisprudence. This complex system of law explains the heterogenous nature of society and the cultural divergence among the people of the country. While custom is said to be a mirror of the culture of the people, the position has been canvassed that indigenous law goes further than that and actually impacts justice relevant to the lives of those who are exposed to it.[85] The application of indigenous law is, however, subject to certain principles, particularly the provisions of the *Constitution of the Federal Republic of Nigeria 1999,* in order to safeguard the rights of the people.

In Nigerian society, indigenous laws have their own uniqueness and peculiarities, particularly as a medium of adjudication. Each group of people has its own unique indigenous laws based on their cultural practices, against the universal nature of modern law. They are found to be less technical, and thus time saving and economical.

While modern law is focused on individual rights, indigenous or customary law promotes communal rights, duties and interests. The uniqueness of indigenous law and its startling qualities have been applauded by Umeogu,[86] and a few of these qualities include – (1) speedy trials and hearings that are free of adjournments, (2) less expensive trials, (3) the regulation of personal issues such as marriage performance and others, and (4) strong control and crisis free titles in land and ownership of land without the need for paper work.

In terms of governance, some communities have solutions to rancorous problems that are associated with modern day electioneering. For example, in Ibadan city in

---

[85] Court in the case of *Oyewunmi v Ogunesan* [1990] 3 NWLR (pt. 137) 20.
[86] Umeogu Bonachristus Igbo, "African Legal System: A Philosophical Analysis," *Open Journal of Philosophy* vol. 2, no. 2, (2012): 116 -122.

south west Nigeria, succession to the position of the paramount traditional ruler is clearly settled under the customary law that the next in line to the throne is known before the demise of the incumbent.

BIBLIOGRAPHY

Books

- O. Obilade, *Nigeria Legal System* (London: Sweet and Maxwell, 1979).

- Daniel G. Offiong, *Witchcraft, Sorcery, Magic and Social Order among the Ibibio of Nigeria* (Lagos: Fourth Dimension, 1991).

- Ese Malemi, *Outline of Nigerian Legal System* (Lagos: Grace Publishers Inc., 1999).

- J. O. Asein, *Introduction to Nigerian Legal System* (Lagos, Ababa Press Ltd, 2005).

- Max Siollun, *A Short History of Conquest and Rule: What Britain Did to Nigeria* (London: Hurst Publishers, 2021).

- Olugbenga Oke-Samuel, *An outline of Nigerian legal system*, student edition (Nigeria: O.G.I publishers, 2008).

- Osita Nnamani, Ogbu, *Modern Nigerian Legal System* (Enugu: SNAAP Press Nig. Ltd 2013).

- Peter Cutt Lloyd, *The Political Development of Yoruba Kingdoms in the 18th and 19th Centuries (*London: Royal Anthropological Institute of Great Britain and Ireland, 1971).

- William Bascom, *The Yoruba of Southwestern Nigeria* (New York: Holt, Rinehart and Winston, 1965).

Chapters

- G. Ezejiofor, "Source of Nigerian Law" in Okonkwo, (ed) *Introduction to Nigeria Law* (London: Sweet & Maxwell, 1980).

- Saa'ba Jimada, "The Foundations of Nupe, Benin and Ife Relations," in *Aspects of Niger State History Essays in Honour of Professor Ibrahim Adamu eds. Kolo*

Wuam T and M.L Salahu (Niger State: Ibrahim Badamasi Babangida University, 2014).

- o Simon Odion Ehiabhi, "A History of Precolonial Nigeria" in *Nigerian Peoples and Cultures – A Reading*, eds. I.E Alumona and C.C Ezeogidi (Nigeria: Rhyce Kerex, 2015).

Journals

- o Atanda Joseph Adebowale, "Government of Yorubaland in the pre-colonial period," *Periodical: Tarikh*, vol. 4, no. 2 (1971): 1-12.

- o Bonachristus Umeogu, "Igbo African Legal and Justice System: A Philosophical Analysis," *Open Journal of Philosophy*, vol. 2, no. 2, (2012): 116 -122, available at 02. 10.4236/ojpp.2012.22018.

- o Boypa O. Egbe, Ibiang Obono Okoi, "Colonialism and Origin of Boundary Crisis in Nigeria," *LWATI: A Journal of Contemporary Research* vol. 14, no. 4, (2017): 95-110.

- o Chigozie Ifekwe Okonkwo, Richard Amechi Onuigbo and Okechukwu Eme, "Innocent & Ekekwe, Ezinwanne, *Traditional Rulers and Community Security in Nigeria: Challenges and Prospects*," International Journal of Innovative Social Sciences & Humanities Research 7 (2) (2019):145-159.

- o Malachy Ugwummadu, "*Nigeria Needs New Constitution, Not Amendment*," (2021), available online @ <https://www.thisdaylive.com/index.php/2021/06/03/nigeria-needs-new-constitution-not-amendment/>.

- o Onadeko Tunde, "Yoruba Traditional Adjudicatory Systems," *African Study Monographs*, 29 (1) (March 2008): 15-28, 15.

INDEX

A

ahimsa, 30, 157, 160, 161, 187, 188, 190, 192, 194, 197, 203, 204

anekantvada, 30, 161

Anthropology, *39, 42, 48, 50*

Arabic, **see, languages, Arabic**

B

Brazil

Afonsinas Ordinations, *348, 349*

Afonso V, *348*

African immigration, 362

african slaves, *357*

Áurea, 354

Bering Strait, *37*

Bible, 359

Brazilian Commercial Code 1850, *351*

Brazilian Constitution 1988, *353, 362*

Brazilian Republic, *353*

cacique, *347*

Canon law, *347*

Carta-de-Lei, 349

Catholic Church, *361, 369*

Civil Code 1916, *355, 363*

colonial Period, *348*

Criminal Code 1830, *351*

Criminal Code 1940, *368*

D. Pedro I, *350*

D. Pedro II, *353*

Deodoro da Fonseca, *354*

ethnicity, *366*

evangelical, *358*

evolution of Brazilian law, *360*

First Republican Constitution 1891, *354*

First World War, *358*

Freitas, *351*

Germanic law, *347*

history of Brazil law, *346*

Iberian Union, *349*

immigration, *356, 357*

imperial Period, *350*

indigenous peoples, *346*

influence of the United States Constitution, *352*

Italian immigration, *357*

Japanese immigratuion, *358*

Lebanese immigration, *358*

Lei da Boa Razão, *349*

Manueline Ordinations, *348, 349*

migration law 2017, 363

Napoleon Bonaparte, *349*

overthrow of monarchy, *354*

pajé, 346

Philippine Ordinations, *348*

Polish immigration, *358*

Portuguese, *37, 345, 347, 348, 349, 356, 357, 359*

Princess Isabel, *354*

racism, *366*

rapid development, *37*

religions, *358*

Roman Catholic Apostolic, *359*

Roman law, *349*

Russian immigration, *358*

skin colour, 366

slavery, *354*

Spanish Constitution 1812, *350*

Christian Jurisprudence, **see,** *Jurisprudence, Christian jurisprudence*

colonisation, see, History, colonisation

common law system, *see,* Legal Systems, *common law system*

Comparative law, **see,** Laws, *Comparative laws*

Constitution, *7, 9, 27, 29, 32, 35, 37, 38, 80, 83, 86, 87, 88, 90, 93, 112, 115, 139, 144, 146, 147, 148, 149, 157, 183, 184, 194, 195, 210, 211, 217, 220, 229, 230, 231, 232, 234, 237, 238, 240, 242, 253, 254, 263, 268, 277, 284, 301, 302, 306, 307, 308, 311, 312, 313, 321, 324, 329, 336, 337, 345, 346, 350, 352, 353, 354, 361, 362, 363, 365, 366, 368, 369*

Community Law, **see,** Laws, *community law*

Confucianism, **see,** *Jurisprudence, Confucianism*

customary law, *see, Laws, custormary law*
   see also, Laws, customs
   see also, Laws, norms
   see also, Laws, culture
   see also, Laws, unwritten laws

D

demography, *1, 2, 3, 40, 80, 96*

dharma, 32, 33, 161, 170, 174, 175, 182, 210, 214, 215, 216, 222, 227

E

emigration, see *History, emigration*

Empires, see, *History, Empires*

European Union/Europe, **see,** History, *membership with a bigger group*

Ethnologist, *50*

G

Gandhi, *30, 157, 160, 180, 185, 186, 187, 207, 208, 222, 227, 242*

GDP, *16, 17, 18, 20, 32, 48, 159*
   2050 forecast, *20*
   PPP, *16, 17, 18, 20, 48*

H

Hebrew, **see,** *Languages, Hebrew*

Hinduism, **see,** *Religions, Hinduism*

Hindu Juirisprudence, **see,** *Jurisprudence, Hindu Jurisprudence*

Hinduism & India
   Ajurveda, 218
   Arthasastra, 32, 210, 215
   Atharvaveda, 218
   Bhagavad Gita, 222
   British colonial rule, 213
   British Empire, *32, 38, 217*
   dharma, **see,** *dharma*
   Dharmasatras, 213
   evolution and source of Hindu Law, *212*
   foreign Hindu empires, *32*

405

racism, 366

revolutions, **see,** Revolutions

slavery, *2, 4, 5, 7, 16, 32, 37, 38, 43, 189,
345, 354, 357, 366*

  slavery outlawed, *38*

human rights, *42, 47, 75, 83, 146, 148, 152,
205, 259, 275, 309, 310*

I

Indigenous peoples, *7, 8, 12, 13, 38, 337,
346, 357, 372, 389, 390*

Influence of external laws, *see,* Laws,
external law

Immigration, see, *History, immigration*

Invasion, see, *History, invasion*

Indonesia

  Aceh, *330*

  adat, 326

  adatrecht, 326

  adat-recht, 334

  Amir Syarifuddin, *325*

  Anyer-Panarukan route, *320*

  B.J. Habibie, *324*

  Civil law system, *340*

  Compedium Freijer, 328

  Constitution 1945, *329*

  Continental Legal System, *326*

  customary law, *326, 332, 334, 337*

  De Atjehers, *334*

  Dokuritsu Junbi Cosakai, *320*

  Dr. Radjiman Widyodiningrat, *320*

  Dutch colonial rule, *322*

  Dutch East Indies, *335*

  Dutch government, *318*

  evolution of law, *321*

  family system, *338*

  Fatahillah, 320

  fiqhi, 325

  first phase of evolution of law, *322*

  Gajah Mada, *36*

  Gunseirei, *323*

  Hatta, *321, 323*

  Herman William Daendels, *320*

  Hindu and Buddhist, *319*

  Hindu-Buddhist kingdom era, *342*

  Hurgronj, *334*

  independence of Indonesia, *319*

  indigenous people, *322, 337*

  Indonesian Waqf Board, *330*

  Islamic jurists, *321*

  Islamic law, *318, 32, 326, 33, 342*

  Japanese colonialism, *323*

  Joint Decree 1991, *331*

  Law No. 41 (2004), *332*

  legal pluralism, *338*

  Majapahit, *319*

  Mataram kingdom, *322*

  Mujtahids, 325

  National Amil Zakat Agency, *330*

  New Order era, *323*

  Nusantara, 36, 319

  Old Order Period, *323*

  participerend coschmish, *338*

  Portuguese, *2, 12, 36, 44, 320, 347, 348,
350, 351, 353, 356, 357, 359, 369*

  Qanun, 335

  rechtskring, *339*

  Reformation Period, *324*

  Sailendra, *319*

  second phase for the evolution of law, *322*

  Second World War, *320*

Hart, *6, 8, 9, 41, 47, 48, 49, 215, 241*

Hayden, *136*

Jefferson, *9*

João VI, *349*

Konrad Zweigert, *23, 25, 40, 41, 49*

Kotz, *5, 23, 25, 40, 41, 48, 49*

Lambert, *15, 49*

Ma, *9, 50*

MacCormack, *43, 48*

Menski, *171*

Moore, *3*

Nobles, *9, 50*

Obilade, *393*

Onishchenko, *133, 135*

Palmer, *24, 50*

Peter Burns, *332*

Piagnet, *10, 11, 49*

Rabinovych, *135*

Rable, 5

Raz, *6, 49*

Reimann, *39, 40, 41, 47, 50*

Sachs, *8, 45, 50*

Savigny, *334*

Schiff, 9, 47, 50

Snouck Hurgronje, *334*

Swanson, 39, 48

Teixeira de Freitas, *351*

Umeogu, *399*

Varner, *13, 49*

Weir, *23, 25, 40, 41, 49*

Zeng, *9, 50, 126*

L

law-making, *2, 3, 37, 47, 150, 229*

liberal jurisprudence, **see,** *Jurisprudence,*
liberal jurisprudence

languages, *24, 25, 44, 74, 87, 163, 167, 180,*
250, 253, 258, 261, 268, 273, 311, 363
  Arabic, *245, 250, 257-59, 268, 273, 279*
  Cuman, *141*
  Hebrew, *250, 252, 258, 279*
  Iranian, *105*
  Latin, 53, 191, 357
  Portuguese, 359
  Prakrit, *163, 16*
  Sanskrit, *15, 16, 31, 94, 214, 216, 219, 222,*
  224, 227
  Turkish, *304*

Laws

  Byzantine Law, *see below, Graeco-Roman*
    law

  Canon law, *347, 348*

  case law, *45, 55, 57, 92, 153, 170, 299,*
    388

    judicial precedents, *138, 149, 150, 154,*
      371, 388

  common law, *4, 29, 33, 38, 44, 57, 62, 65,*
    68, 96, 106, 115, 118, 132, 137, 138,
    149, 150, 151, 339, 349, 372, 382, 388,
    393, 395, 397, 398

  Community law, *27, 37, 56, 57, 62, 63, 76*

  Comparative Law, *5, 23, 24, 25, 39, 40, 41,*
    45, 47, 48, 49, 50, 151, 155

  culture, *3, 9, 12, 13, 24, 30, 32, 39, 41, 44,*
    52, 58, 67, 97, 99, 100, 101, 102, 107,
    108, 133, 135, 136, 137, 142, 162, 164,
    167, 179, 180, 189, 206, 211, 214, 216,
    224, 234, 252, 253, 261, 265, 266, 322,
    362

  customary law, *2,4, 6, 8, 13, 32, 38, 35, 36,*
    38, 41, 42, 46, 281, 286, 287, 288, 289,
    314, 318, 319, 323, 326, 327, 332, 333,
    334, 335, 336, 337, 338, 229, 340, 341,
    342, 389

    customs, *2, 3, 6, 7, 8, 9, 10, 11, 12, 13,*
    27, 30, 32, 35, 38, 39, 41, 42, 44, 46, 55,
    56, 58, 61, 63, 65, 68, 70, 87, 92, 111,
    137, 158, 168, 171, 210, 211, 213, 216,

220, 222, 230, 231, 232, 234, 235, 236,
237, 240, 283, 288, 292, 322, 326, 363

norms, 2, 3, 7, 8, 9, 10, 11, 12, 13, 39,
40, 41, 42, 44, 47, 110, 133, 134, 135,
136, 146, 148, 152, 170, 211, 214, 222,
228, 236, 283, 314, 315, 322, 334, 340,
358, 361

Historical customary law, 332

unofficial law, 6, 9, 14, 171

unwritten laws, 340, 341, 393

non-official law, 6

divine law, 9

Dutch law, 36, 44, 326, 328

etiquettes, 11, 28

English law, 29, 85, 132, 138, 150, 153,
154, 371, 372, 382, 388, 397

external laws, 4, 5, 7, 8, 16, 29, 33, 40, 44
345

family law, 5, 7, 56, 59, 63, 68, 89, 270,
274, 355, 360

Germanic law, 347

Graeco-Roman (Byzantine) law, 56, 58,
141, 142

historical laws, 2, 8

indigenous law, 6, 38, 388, 389, 395, 390,
394, 395, 396, 398, 399

influences of foreign laws, 4, 5

transplanted law, 6

external laws, **see,** Laws, external laws
Islamic law, 380, 392, 394

Sharia law, 38, 64, 287, 298, 380, 381

Law and Religion, 9, 10, 11, 12, 48, 50,
208

legal postulates, 6

legal rules, 6, 45, 103, 104, 106, 143, 151,
315

nuances in languages, 44

official law, 6

Roman law, 141, 347, 348, 349

social function, 3

state centred law, 3

substantive law, 5, 45, 150

Torah Law, 270

traditional Chinese Law, 9, 43, 48, 50

legal ethnology, 40, 41

legal Ethnologist, 12

Merry, 12, 50

legal pluralism, 3, 5, 6,12,47, 49, 297, 316,
338

plurality of sources, 2, 36

legal sociology, 40, 41

Legal Systems

Civil law system, 340

Continental legal system 109, 318, 326,
327

Roman Dutch, 138, 154

Roman law family, 85, 119

Romano -Germanic, 137

common law system, 4, 29, 33, 38, 44, 57,
62, 65, 68, 96, 106, 115, 118, 132, 137,
138, 149, 150, 151, 339, 349, 372, 382,
388, 393, 395, 397, 398

legal system, 4, 7, 12, 13, 28, 32, 35, 36,
39, 40, 45, 82, 85, 93, 102, 103, 104,
105, 106, 107, 109, 115, 117, 119, 120,
132, 133, 134, 135, 136, 137, 138, 139,
141, 144, 145, 146, 149, 150, 151, 152,
153, 154, 155, 159, 170, 171, 187, 191,
192, 203, 205, 210, 211, 213, 214, 216,
217, 219, 221, 233, 234, 235, 239, 240,
247, 254, 257, 260, 263, 265, 267, 270,
271, 273, 280, 281, 282, 283, 285, 286,
287, 289, 291, 293, 299, 302, 303, 304,